The Serpent Column

Onassis Series in Hellenic Culture

The Age of Titans: The Rise and Fall of the Great Hellenistic Navies
    William M. Murray

Sophocles and the Language of Tragedy
    Simon Goldhill

Nectar and Illusion: Nature in Byzantine Art and Literature
    Henry Maguire

Adventures with Iphigenia at Tauris: A Cultural History of Euripides' Black Sea Tragedy
    Edith Hall

Beauty: The Fortunes of an Ancient Greek Idea
    David Konstan

Euripides and the Gods
    Mary Lefkowitz

Brother-Making in Late Antiquity and Byzantium: Monks, Laymen, and Christian Ritual
    Claudia Rapp

The Treasures of Alexander the Great: How One Man's Wealth Shaped the World
    Frank L. Holt

The Serpent Column: A Cultural Biography
    Paul Stephenson

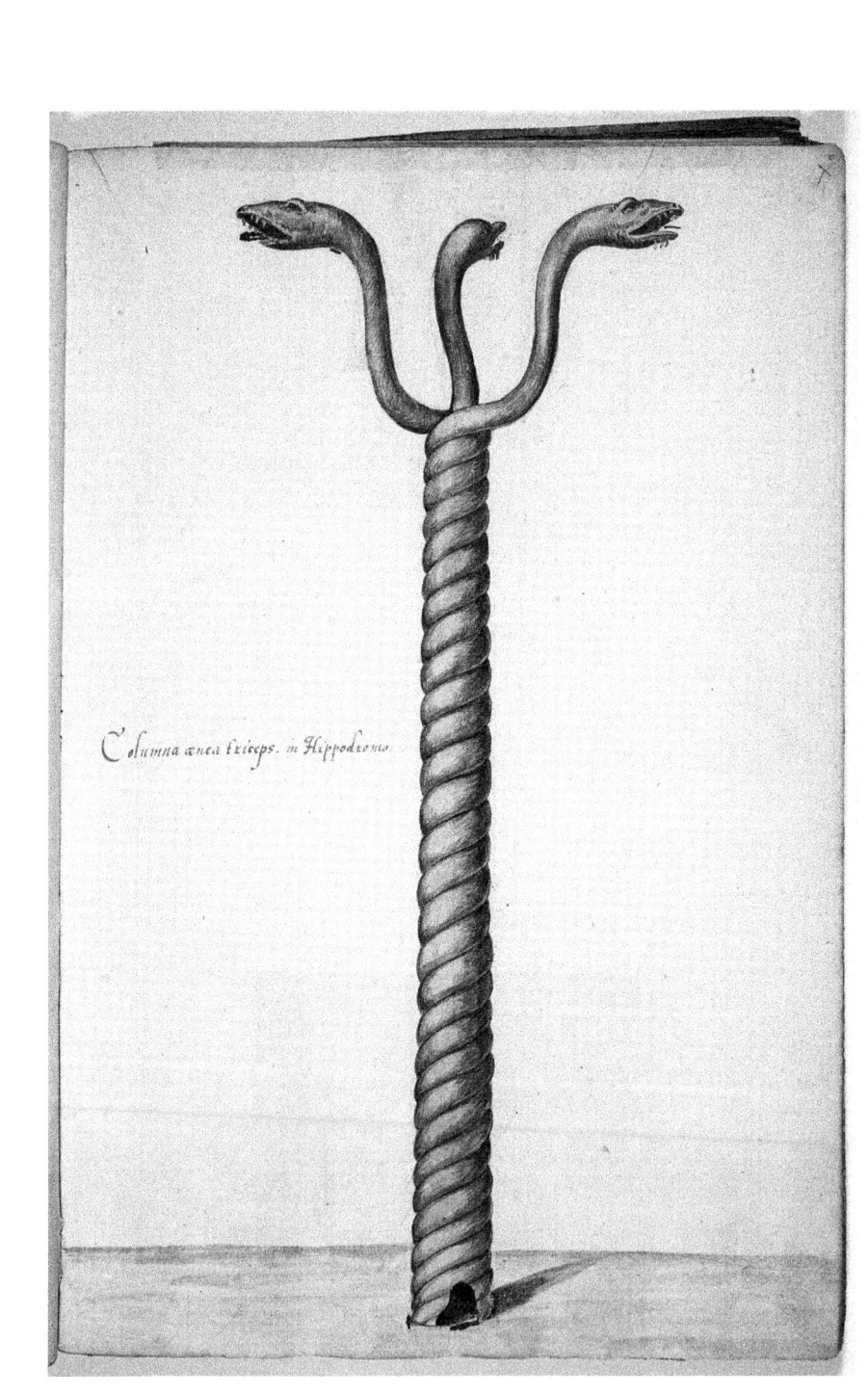

Columna ænea triceps. in Hippodromo

The Serpent Column
A CULTURAL BIOGRAPHY

Paul Stephenson

UNIVERSITY PRESS

Oxford University Press is a department of the University of Oxford. It furthers
the University's objective of excellence in research, scholarship, and education
by publishing worldwide. Oxford is a registered trade mark of Oxford University
Press in the UK and certain other countries.

Published in the United States of America by Oxford University Press
198 Madison Avenue, New York, NY 10016, United States of America.

© Stephenson 2016

All rights reserved. No part of this publication may be reproduced, stored in
a retrieval system, or transmitted, in any form or by any means, without the
prior permission in writing of Oxford University Press, or as expressly permitted
by law, by license, or under terms agreed with the appropriate reproduction
rights organization. Inquiries concerning reproduction outside the scope of the
above should be sent to the Rights Department, Oxford University Press, at the
address above.

You must not circulate this work in any other form
and you must impose this same condition on any acquirer.

Library of Congress Cataloging-in-Publication Data
Names: Stephenson, Paul.
Title: The Serpent Column : a cultural biography / Paul Stephenson.
Description: New York, NY : Oxford University Press, 2016. |
Series: Onassis series in Hellenic culture | Includes bibliographical references and index.
Identifiers: LCCN 2015043340 (print) | LCCN 2016021717 (ebook) |
ISBN 9780190209063 (hardback) | ISBN 9780190209070 (ebook)
Subjects: LCSH: Serpent Column (Istanbul, Turkey) |
Bronze sculpture—Turkey—Istanbul. | Istanbul (Turkey)—Antiquities. |
Delphi (Extinct city)—Buildings, structures, etc. |
Istanbul (Turkey)—Buildings, structures, etc. | Istanbul (Turkey)—Social life
and customs. | BISAC: HISTORY / Ancient / Greece. |
ART / History / Ancient & Classical.
Classification: LCC DR739.S47 S74 2016 (print) | LCC DR739.S47 (ebook) |
DDC 938/.3—dc23
LC record available at https://lccn.loc.gov/2015043340

9 8 7 6 5 4 3 2 1
Printed by Sheridan Books, Inc., United States of America

For Caroline and Samuel

When *we* concentrate on a material object, whatever its situation, the very act of attention may lead to our involuntarily sinking into the history of that object. Novices must learn to skim over matter if they want matter to stay at the exact level of the moment. Transparent things, through which the past shines!

                                  Vladimir Nabokov, *Transparent Things* (1972)

CONTENTS

Preface xi
Acknowledgements xv
List of Illustrations xvii

1. Studying the Plataian Tripod 1
2. Plataia 29
3. Delphi 67
4. Constantinople in Late Antiquity 97
5. Constantinople in the Middle Ages 127
6. Fountain 151
7. Talisman 183
8. Istanbul 205

   Conclusion 241

   Bibliography 243
   Index 263

PREFACE

Experimental psychologists and cognitive neuroscientists have demonstrated that fear of serpents is shared by primates and humans. It is an evolutionary relic that is hard to unlearn, although genetic variability and learned behaviour determine that not all humans fear snakes. However, and conversely, it has been demonstrated that fear of snakes is as easy to learn as fear of knives and guns, which today pose a far greater threat to most participants in psychological studies. We have evolved to fear snakes when we see them. Furthermore, it has been argued recently that the need to spot and identify serpents conditioned the evolutionary development of vision. Humans are able to spot and avoid stepping on snakes before they have realised what is about to happen. Young children, for whom it is not a taught behaviour, when shown multiple images on a computer screen, immediately spot snakes. Moreover, because the same structures in the visual cortex which process sight also produce mental imagery to complete complex images or images partially seen, we might also see a snake when none exists, conjuring it from a coiled hose, for example. Just as we have evolved to fear snakes when we see them, so we have evolved to see snakes because we fear them. To put that another way: when a human sees a snake, he or she sees a threat. Consequently, and conversely, where a human sees a threat, he or she might imagine a snake.

The same experimental psychologists and cognitive neuroscientists subject living brains to functional magnetic resonance imaging (fMRI) and other tests to ascertain which areas are activated when snakes are seen or imagined. Such experiments cannot be conducted on Greeks, Romans, Byzantines, or Ottomans, although we might conclude that their responses, like our own, would be both natural (by which I mean evolutionary) and cultural (by which I mean learned). The latter are our concern in the following chapters, because, while the fear of serpents is universal, responses to serpents vary greatly from culture to culture—as indeed it does among the eleven primate groups that show fear-related responses, including alarm calls, avoidance, mobbing, etc. Which part of a historical brain might have been recorded as active during fMRI is far less interesting to us than what the owner of the brain consequently thinks, writes, paints, and sculpts. Observing how people think about snakes is a wonderful entry point into cultural history. And at the center of this series of reflections stands the Serpent Column, a spiralling bronze pillar forged 2,500 years ago, which has provoked responses from observers of diverse backgrounds since then.

To explain my approach to writing the cultural biography—I shall return to this terminology shortly—of a monumental bronze forged in classical southern Europe, I shall invoke the northern European maypole, a wooden pillar with prehistoric origins and shifting symbolism, in its modern English derivation. The tall wooden maypole is erected with ribbons attached firmly to its top. Dancers holding the lower ends of the ribbons prance back and forth, in and out, braiding their ribbons firmly around the pole. Dancing around the pole long predates the nineteenth century, when the ribbons were introduced in part due to efforts led by John Ruskin to revitalize lapsed traditions in English villages. However, it is the ribbons in which we are interested, for in my analogy these are the strands of meaning and interpretation, of biography, that I shall seek to unwind from the serpentine column. Every strand is attached somewhere on the pole, but not all equally firmly, and many may appear to be bound too loosely or to unravel too quickly, while others clearly are attached, but not to the top of the pole, covering only part of it. Some readers might have preferred to observe a single ribbon, firmly attached to the top, unwound clearly and cleanly in a straightforward narrative (more like a Roman historiated column than a maypole). The evidence does not allow for this approach, nor is it a helpful way to present the many receptions of a polyvalent object. Chapters often proceed by inference and suggestion, by the accumulation and conjoining of discrete elements, rather than the systematic manufacture of a singular and convincing argument. However, as a matter of style as well as method I have sought to avoid presenting every part of the book as contingent or conjectural. The reader must also think with the evidence and accept or reject what she or he finds compelling or invalid. Some suggestions will be easier to accept than others, and experts in many fields will know far more than I do about the contexts in which the Serpent Column is placed.

A word on the subtitle of this book, chosen only when a full first draft was complete, seems necessary, since it suggests this is a work not of cultural history nor of reception history—it is certainly both, and the subtitle could easily have been "a cultural and reception history"—but of cultural "biography." As the author, so far, of two historical works that have been classified by the Library of Congress as biography—in itself, this is an interesting facet of reception history—my choice may appear obtuse or obscurantist. But I believe, to the contrary, it is accurate and helpful, based on my reading of the late Igor Kopytoff's seminal, and now rather famous, study "The Cultural Biography of Things." As Kopytoff wrote,

> Biographies of things make salient what might otherwise remain obscure. For example ... they can show what anthropologists have so often stressed: that what is significant about the adoption of alien objects—as of alien ideas—is

not the fact that they are adopted, but the way they are culturally redefined and put to use.[1]

This captures my approach to the Serpent Column perfectly, since through its life history, its biography, the manner in which it has been received has been dependent on cultural redefinition, whether by its being moved or by its observers moving through space and time. The book seeks to make salient what has hitherto remained obscure by focusing on a singular object—Kopytoff distinguishes between the singular and the common—that has in the course of its life history been both sacralized and commoditized (another distinction important to Kopytoff's analysis) and imbued with a range of concomitant values and meanings. Kopytoff illustrates his argument by sketching the multiple lives of "useful" objects, for example a car, which has various biographical strands: the technical (its service records provide the bare bones), the economic (how much it cost, and how its resale value plummeted the moment it was driven off the dealer's lot), the sociopolitical (what its value said about its owners, their relative wealth and their values, whether it is a Bentley Continental or Toyota Prius, or indeed a Toyota Camry), and the personal (the memories formed around it from road trips and vacations, drives to hospitals to collect new babies or visit sick parents, dangerous encounters with wild animals and taxis). Cars are bought and sold frequently, and many are imported and exported, multiplying their biographies. The list is not exhaustive, but together these biographical strands—the ribbons of my metaphorical maypole—when braided together, offer insights into the culture, or cultures, where a car was owned and valued.

Ostensibly more pertinent to this book are Kopytoff's brief comments on the aborted plan to erect a statue of "Rocky" (the fictional boxer Rocky Balboa) on the Parkway in front of Philadelphia's Art Museum. Koyptoff suggests that to a "working-class sector of Philadelphia," the planned statue "was a singular object of ethnic, class, and regional pride—in brief, a worthy public monument."[2] "Monument" does not appear in the subtitle of this book, although clearly the Serpent Column is a monument in a particular sense, since it was conceived as a votive offering to a god, in Greek an *agalma*, to commemorate a great victory and those who fought to achieve it. If monuments appear to be less "useful" than cars, like cars (and people) they have life cycles that include damage (illness), restoration (healing), and eventually destruction (death). Monuments, like cars, cannot think or feel, but people think and feel about them. Although they may not move around as much as people (especially people in cars)—in fact the Serpent Column moved quite some distance—people

---

[1] Kopytoff 1986: 67.
[2] Kopytoff 1986: 81.

come to them, to observe them or confront them, to pray before them or swear at them, to strike or deface them, to excavate, restore, and photograph them. Although memories adhere to many objects, monuments are explicitly created to be sites or environments of memory.[3] This much is clear from the word we use, derived in English as well as the Romance languages from Latin *monumentum*, whose Greek equivalent is *mnemeion*. That monuments are good to think with is self-evident: they are designed to provoke thought, as is manifest in the German term, *Denkmal*. We tend to think, in English, of monuments erected to heroic deeds and memorials dedicated to the lost, hence the distinction one might care to draw between the intents of the Washington Monument and the Lincoln Memorial. This distinction is less clearly drawn by those who visit monuments and memorials and even those who write about them than by those who conceived of them.[4] To say this is to make no more than the most obvious point in reception history that the intended meaning of an object is not always, or even frequently, the meaning ascribed to an object by an observer. Responses are subjective, culturally conditioned, and fluid. How observers responded to the Serpent Column through 2,500 years and what it tells us about their cultures is as much the subject of this book as its creation, relocation, and mutilation.

---

[3] Nelson 2003: 74. I shall not invoke here the seminal, and now ubiquitous, works of Pierre Nora, since they have not explicitly informed my approach in this book, which does not treat the Serpent Column extensively as a site of memory.

[4] See for example Marcuse 2010: 53, n. 3: "I do not distinguish rigidly between 'monuments' and 'memorials,' although the choice of terms can be used to reflect objects that may be more heroic versus those that are more contemplative." One might observe, to the contrary, that all monuments, including those called memorials, are contemplative.

ACKNOWLEDGEMENTS

In research and writing this book I have incurred many debts. My employers while the book was in progress offered generous periods of research leave and other support. In Durham, I am grateful to Giles Gasper, with whom I organized a small international colloquium on Water and Scripture: Reflections on Antiquity and the Middle Ages, at which my first thoughts on Christian interpretations of the Serpent Column were presented to a learned audience. In Nijmegen, I have benefited from the help and consideration of many in organizing talks and workshops related to the project, principally Sible de Blaauw and Mariëtte Verhoeven. More than this, I am beholden to Gerda de Kleijn for correcting an important mistake in my interpretation of the Serpent Column's plumbing. In Lincoln, I thank Matthew Cragoe for allowing me time at the start of a new job to complete this task, and Joy Knight and Krista Cowman for making that job much easier.

I am especially grateful to two institutions at which I spent extended periods devoted largely to research. First, the University of California, San Diego, where as Alkiviadis Vassiliadis Visiting Professor in Byzantine History I spoke on several occasions about the project to colleagues and talented, interested graduate students. I offer my profound thanks to Thomas W. Gallant and to the Greek community of San Diego for providing that enriching opportunity. I am deeply grateful to the principal, Björn Wittrock, the staff and the 2010–11 fellows of the Swedish Collegium for Advanced Study (SCAS), Uppsala, where many of the key ideas presented in the book were first formulated. I owe a great intellectual debt to David Pankenier, who is responsible for my introduction to archaeoastronomy and for producing the images of the night sky that illustrate my findings. Ingela Nilsson, Professor of Greek at Uppsala University, invited me to deliver the 2010 Lennart Rydén memorial lecture, which appeared in the *Bysantinska sällskapet Bulletin* 28 (2010) and is reproduced here in an edited form. Ingela was also my co-organizer for a conference devoted to the Fountains of Byzantion—Constantinople—Istanbul, staged at the Swedish and Dutch research institutes in Istanbul in June 2012, funded by the Swedish National Bank's Cultural Foundation. My reflections on the Serpent Column as a fountain, which appear here in one form and in another in an edited conference volume, were honed for that occasion. Additionally, I am grateful to listeners who offered interesting and useful observations when I delivered developing ideas at the department of history, Duke University; the Army Museum, Stockholm; SALT, Uppsala University; CAARI, Nicosia; Studium

Generale, Leiden University; Byzantine and Modern Greek Studies, University of Amsterdam; and SUNY Stony Brook.

At an early stage in the project, the British Academy awarded me a research grant in support of research trips to Athens, Washington, DC, and Istanbul. In Athens, I was offered accommodation by the National Hellenic Research Foundation (EIE), and am grateful, as with prior projects, for the generosity and vision of Paschalis Kitromilides. In Washington, I received a postdoctoral stipend from Dumbarton Oaks, which allowed me to spend a month at that incomparable library. In Istanbul, I was hosted by the Swedish Research Institute and the Netherlands Institute in Turkey, and offer my thanks to their directors at that time, Birgit Schylter and Fokke Gerritsen. Immediately prior to the completion of the project I was offered the valuable opportunity to present papers at the University of Pennsylvania and the Ohio State University. I thank Robert Ousterhout at Penn and Anthony Kaldellis at OSU for hosting me, and Maria Sereti at the Onassis Foundation, New York, for arranging these visits so effectively.

I am immensely grateful to the staff at Oxford University Press in New York. Stefan Vranka saw the merits of the project and steered it from first draft to its current form, ensuring it was considered for the prestigious series in which it appears. To that end, I am indebted to the Alexander S. Onassis Foundation for awarding me a senior visiting scholarship and for offering a generous subvention that has allowed the volume to be so richly illustrated. Steve Dodson, a polyglot copy editor, greatly improved the text.

I owe photographs and permissions, as well as specific insights and observations, to many institutions and to friends and colleagues whose names appear in notes and the list of illustrations. I acknowledge the generosity of all, but notably that of the Master and Fellows of Trinity College, Cambridge, who provided freely the illustrations from the Freshfield and Dryden Albums, including that which graces this book's jacket. The two anonymous readers appointed by the press made many valuable observations. While I was based in the United States in 2012, my good friend, the historian Graham Stewart, conducted essential research on my behalf at the British Museum and British Library, establishing that no original papers relating to C. T. Newton's excavation in the hippodrome were preserved there. Francesca Dell'Acqua of the University of Salerno generously shared her ideas on the Serpent Column with me at an early stage and much later read a full second draft of the book. She offered valuable comments that improved the work in significant ways. My wife and colleague Brooke Shilling supplied countless insights necessary to a historian venturing into the realm of art history. Brooke is also coauthor of a paper which informed my reflections on triple tempters, and offered me her translations of texts and thoughts on images related to the Virgin, prepared for her own projects, to use here. The book is dedicated to our daughter and our son, Caroline and Samuel.

LIST OF ILLUSTRATIONS

Maps

1. Greece and the Aegean the time of the Persian Wars   31
2. The Site of the Battle of Plataia   36
3. The Near East in the Age of Gudea of Lagash   59
4. The Greek World in the Archaic and Classical Periods   69
5. Byzantine Constantinople   99
6. The Hippodrome in Constantinople   115

Table

1. Transcription and translation of the inscription on the base of the Serpent Column   10

Figures

Frontispiece: Freshfield Album, Wren Library, Trinity College, Cambridge, MS 0117.2, fol. 6. Master and Fellows of Trinity College Cambridge.

1.1 General view of the twisted bronze column in Istanbul   3
1.2 Detail showing scratches and deeper cuts in the surface of the bronze.   5
1.3 Large opening in the base of the column, a hole cut in the bronze to allow water to exit. A channel is carved in the marble base for the same purpose.   5
1.4 Large hole in the bronze column, upper coils.   6
1.5 Large hole in the bronze column, lower coils.   6
1.6 Smaller hole in the bronze column, lower coils.   7
1.7 Cracks in the bronze column.   8
1.8 Photograph of the inscription on coils 3, 4, and 5 (9, 10, and 11) taken by Anne Jeffery in July 1949. L. H. Jeffery Archive, Centre for the Study of Ancient Documents, Oxford University.   13

1.9 Photograph of the inscription on coils 6 and 7 (7 and 8) taken by Anne Jeffery in July 1949. L. H. Jeffery Archive, Centre for the Study of Ancient Documents, Oxford University.   14
1.10 Bronze upper jaw of a serpent, now in Istanbul Archaeological Museums.   16
1.11 Upper surface of a bronze upper jaw of a serpent, showing cut marks towards the break.   17
1.12 Atlas 408, excavated at Delphi in the 1890s, once held to be the composite limestone base of the Plataian Tripod.   19
1.13 Marble base of the Serpent Column, Istanbul.   20
1.14 Base of the Masonry Obelisk, showing a carved channel through which water would exit.   22
2.1 The night sky above Plataia at sunset on the evening of 1 September 479 B.C.   41
2.2 The night sky above Plataia at sunrise on the morning of 2 September 479 B.C.   41
2.3 A silk tomb banner from Gaochang (Turfan), dated ca. A.D. 500, showing Fu Xi and Nu Wa.   46
2.4 Corinthian *alabastron* showing Typhon, seventh century B.C., Erlenmeyer Painter.   53
2.5 Chalcidian black-figured hydria, a large water vessel painted in around 550 B.C., showing Zeus battling Typhon.   54
2.6 Bluebeard, a triple-bodied demon (*trisomatos daimonas*) that adorned the Hekatompedon, a temple erected on the Athenian acropolis in ca. 560 B.C.   55
2.7 The night sky above Plataia at sunset of 29 August 479 B.C.   61
2.8 Libation vase of Gudea, dedicated to Ninĝišzida. Neo-Sumerian. Lagash (Tello), ca. 2150 B.C. Green Steatite, Musée du Louvre, Paris.   63
2.9 Elamite cylinder seal of the judge Ishme-karab ilu, ca. 1600 B.C.   65
3.1 Helmet discovered at Afrati, Crete, with winged youths controlling entwined serpents, seventh century B.C.   72
3.2 Running Gorgon clutching snakes. Bronze handle ornament, probably Lakonian, ca. 540 B.C.   73
3.3 Gorgon with two serpentine legs. Bronze volute krater handle, sixth century B.C.   77
3.4 A Lakonian cup dated to ca. 550–40 B.C., attributed to the Rider Painter, or Painter of Horsemen, in the Musée de Louvre, Paris.   79
3.5 Griffin protome, sixth century B.C., Lakonia.   83
3.6 Serpent protome, bronze, possibly from a candle-holder, fifth century B.C., Delphi, Museum inv. 9420.   95
4.1 The night sky above Byzantion at sunset before the Battle of Chrysopolis, 17 October A.D. 324.   98

4.2	The night sky above Byzantion at sunrise before the Battle of Chrysopolis, 18 October A.D. 324.	98
4.3	Skylla, terracotta from Melos, fifth century B.C., now in the British Museum.	107
4.4	Ivory casket, carved in the late fourth century, showing the *ketos* as the beast that swallowed Jonah.	108
4.5	Small bronze coins Constantine minted exclusively at Constantinople in 327–8 A.D. showing a serpent pierced by a military standard.	109
4.6	Northeastern face of the lower marble base of the Theodosian Obelisk, also known as the Egyptian Obelisk, a granite monolith carved for Pharaoh Thutmose III (r. 1479–25 B.C.).	116
4.7	Southeastern face of the bases of the Theodosian Obelisk.	117
4.8	Theodosian Obelisk standing on two marble bases carved for its erection in Constantinople in ca. 390.	117
4.9	Drawing of the Theodosian Obelisk as it appeared in 1574.	118
4.10	Detail of carving of the *euripos* on the southeastern face of the lower marble base of the Theodosian Obelisk.	119
4.11	Ivory diptych of the Lampadius family, Constantinople, fifth century A.D. Museo di Santa Giulia, Brescia.	120
4.12	Kugelspiel, carved game of chance showing hippodrome scenes, sixth century A.D.	121
4.13	Two extant statue bases of Porphyrios, both excavated from the Topkapı Palace, now in Istanbul Archaeological Museums.	122
5.1	Ivory plaque depicting Adam in the pose of an exhausted Herakles, Walters Art Museum, Baltimore, Byzantine, tenth century.	128
5.2	Detail of Eros between entwined serpents. Silver inkpot showing stylized entwined serpents amid mythological figures. Byzantine, tenth century.	130
5.3	Detail of Ares between entwined serpents. Silver inkpot showing stylized entwined serpents amid mythological figures. Byzantine, tenth century.	130
5.4	Detail of Apollo between entwined serpents. Silver inkpot showing stylized entwined serpents amid mythological figures. Byzantine, tenth century.	131
5.5	Detail of a river god between entwined serpents. Silver inkpot showing stylized entwined serpents amid mythological figures. Byzantine, tenth century.	131
5.6	Detail from a scene of the Last Judgment, Cathedral of St. Lazare, Autun, France, twelfth century.	137
5.7	Princeton, Univ. Library Garrett MS 16, fol. 194r.; includes the earliest extant depiction of a dragon at the foot of the Heavenly Ladder.	140

5.8 Ivory plaque depicting the Last Judgement, now in London's Victoria and Albert Museum, possibly Constantinople, eleventh century. 145

6.1 Red breccia basin, with carved serpent snaking around the rim, Hellenistic (reused). Now in the outer narthex of Hagia Sophia, Istanbul. 152

6.2 Bronze *strobilion*, the only Byzantine fountain finial currently known to have survived, Great Lavra Monastery, Mt. Athos, Greece. 153

6.3 Gregory of Nazianzos' homilies, Paris, BN Cod. gr. 550, fol. 59v., Constantinople, twelfth century. 155

6.4 Gregory of Nazianzos' homilies, Paris, BN Cod. gr. 550, fol. 166v, Constantinople, twelfth century. 156

6.5 The Larnaka Tympanum, Victoria and Albert Museum, London. 160

6.6 Detail from the Larnaka Tympanum, Victoria and Albert Museum, London. 161

6.7 Entwined serpent fountain in a depiction of the Annunciation, Church of the Panagia, Moutoullas, Cyprus. 162

6.8 Great Canterbury Psalter, Paris BN Lat. 8846, fol. 43v. 163

6.9 A Lion fountain, apparently terminating an aqueduct, discharges into a basin. 165

6.10 Annunciation to St. Anne in the garden, mosaic at Daphni, near Athens, Byzantine, eleventh century. 168

6.11 Annunciation to St Anne in the garden, homilies of James, monk of Kokkinobaphos, Vat. gr. 1162, fol. 16v., Constantinople, twelfth century. 169

6.12 Annunciation to St. Anne in the garden, homilies of James, monk of Kokkinobaphos, Paris BN gr. 1208, fol. 21v., Constantinople, twelfth century. 170

6.13 Christ militant, preserved in a sixth-century mosaic at Ravenna's Archbishop's Chapel. 175

6.14 A late-fifth-century stucco relief in the Orthodox Baptistery of Neon depicts a militant Christ militant trampling the serpent and lion. 176

6.15 Clay icon of St. Theodore, discovered at Vinica, possibly sixth–seventh century. 180

6.16 Saints George and Theodore killing a polycephalous (three-headed?) serpent at Yusuf Koç church, Göreme, Cappadocia. 181

6.17 St. George slays a polycephalous (three-headed?) serpent at Kırkdamaltı church, Ihlara, Cappadocia, thirteenth century. 181

7.1 *Hünername*, Topkapı Palace Museum Library H.1523, fol. 162v., Mehmed II throws his mace at the Serpent Column in the At meydanı. Topkapı Palace Museum Library. 184

7.2 Hartmann Schedel, *Liber Chronicarum* (1493), woodcut showing the column and equestrian statue of Justinian. 187

7.3 Eagle and snake motif, mosaic floor of the Great Palace of Constantinople, Byzantine, sixth century. 190

7.4 An apotropaic knot, formed from entwined acanthus leaves, repeated along the marble band which forms part of the entabulature in the gallery at Hagia Sophia, Istanbul. 192

7.5 Silver statue of Mercury holding a serpentine caduceus, where the snakes are attached to the staff by forming a reef knot, A.D. 175–225. Discovered in 1830 at Berthouville, France. 193

7.6 Christ crucified, his cross piercing a serpent. Ninth-century ivory, Frankish, now in the Walters Art Museum, Baltimore. 197

7.7 Enamel plaque showing the baptism of Christ in the River Jordan, incorporated into the Pala d'Oro, St Mark's, Venice, Byzantine, twelfth century. 199

7.8 Ivory carving of the goddess Hygieia, "health," daughter of Asklepios, among the Liverpool ivories, where her serpent is entwined around a tripod with two smaller serpents above. 202

7.9 Carved plaque with cryptographic inscription, showing Constantine between the Theodosian Obelisk and a headless Serpent Column, now in the Benaki Museum, Athens, originally from Siphnos, nineteenth century. 203

8.1 Bronze portrait medallion, John VIII Palaiologos by Pisanello, ca. 1438–43. 209

8.2 Bronze portrait medallion, Mehmed II by Costanzo de Ferrara, 1481. 209

8.3 "El Gran Turco" (Hazine 2153, 2160), etching contained in the Fatih Album, ca. 1470. 210

8.4 "El Gran Turco" on a majolica storage jar manufactured in Florence, ca. 1470. 211

8.5 An illustration, perhaps by Felice Feliciano, ca. 1471–2, depicting a dragon, a rooster perched on its rump, and a writhing serpent bound around the neck and front leg of a griffin. 212

8.6 A huge capital in the grounds of the Topkapı Palace which once supported a statue, perhaps the equestrian statue of Justinian that stood in the Augusteion. 215

8.7 Pieter Coecke van Aelst's woodcut, *Les moeurs et fachons des faires des Turcs*. The Serpent Column can be seen clearly in its correct location, between the obelisks to the right of the picture, immediately above the rump of the sultan's horse. 218

8.8 Hagia Sophia and monuments of the hippodrome as they appeared in 1574. 219
8.9 Drawing of the Serpent Coilumn as it appeared in 1574. 221
8.10 Fantastic sketch of the Serpent Column. 222
8.11 *Hünername*, Topkapı Palace Museum Library H.1523, fol.158b–159a, offers tiny representations of the defining monuments of the At meydanı, namely the two obelisks and, between them, the Serpent Column. 224
8.12 Palace of Grand Vizier Ibrahim Pasha, built 1524, under renovation, opposite the Serpent Column in Istanbul. 227
8.13 *Surname-i hümayun*, Topkapı Palace Museum Library H. 1344, fol. 327a, bird-sellers. Topkapı Palace Museum Library. 230
8.14 *Surname-i hümayun*, Topkapı Palace Museum Library H. 1344, fol. fol. 103b–104a, snake charmers. Topkapı Palace Museum Library. 231
8.15 William Hogarth, A Procession through the Hippodrome, plate 15 in A. de La Mottraye, *Travels through Europe, Asia, and into Part of Africa*, 2 vols. (London 1723). 234
8.16 Photograph from 1850, taken by James D. Robertson, showing the Serpent Column, of which only the top fourteen coils are visible above the surface. 236

The Serpent Column

1}

Studying the Plataian Tripod

*Golden Cauldron – Bronze Column – Inscription – An Upper
Jaw of a Serpent's Head – Original Base, Delphi – Marble Base
and Foundation, Water Pipes, Constantinople – Stamped Lead
Fistula – Reconstructions*

The Serpent Column as it appeared in the later sixteenth century was sketched twice, and faithfully, by an artist whose drawings have been preserved in the Freshfield Album, Trinity College, Cambridge (frontispiece and figs. 6.11, 6.12). Shortly before this, Pierre Gilles had described the Serpent Column, and his report, which was known to the Freshfield artist, is among the earliest to employ classical scholarship to elucidate the object's history.[1]

> In the range of obelisks there stands another column of bronze (*columna aenea*), which is not fluted but formed from the winding around of three serpents in the manner we see in great ropes ending in the triple head of the three snakes which rise very high above the shaft of the column. There are many fabulous and trifling reports among the Constantinopolitans about the erection of this column which are occasioned by their ignorance of their ancestral history. Zosimus, among other historians, writes that Constantine the Great placed in the hippodrome the tripod of Delphic Apollo and which had on it the image of that god. Sozomen of Salamis adds that Constantine did not only place the Delphic tripods in the hippodrome, but also that celebrated tripod which Pausanias the Spartan and the Greek cities consecrated to Delphic Apollo after the Persian War. Eusebius is more clear on this occasion and says that Constantine in some part of Constantinople erected the Sminthian Apollo, in the hippodrome he set up the Pythian tripod around which a serpent was coiled in a spiral, from which it appears evident that a tripod once stood on this bronze tricephalic column, which was from Delphi.

---

[1] Gilles: II. 13, in my own translation from the Latin text. The translation at Ball 1729: 111–12, is rather too free to be useful.

As Gilles knew, the bronze spiral he saw was only one part of a composite monument created and erected more than two millennia earlier at Delphi. Classical authors relate that when it was first dedicated the monument included a golden tripod, a cauldron on three legs. Gilles continues by recording accurately a story from Herodotos that the golden tripod was made from a tithe of the Persian spoils following the battle of Plataia, although "it is a mistake of those who imagine the column was once overlaid with gold but was plundered of it by the Turks, since it was stripped of its gold many centuries before the Turks, according to Pausanias."[2] At Delphi the bronze column and golden tripod together stood on a limestone base, until first the cauldron and later the column were removed, and subsequently the base was destroyed. The bronze column alone then stood on a new marble base following its transfer to Constantinople, until 1700 with its serpent necks and heads intact. It stands there still but headless, a bronze stump in a paved hole surrounded by railings. The production and peregrinations, adaptations, mutilations and receptions of this remarkable monument will be explored in following chapters, after an introduction to the object, its constituent parts, and scholarship devoted to them.

Golden Cauldron

Little can be said about the golden, or gilded, cauldron that once was the uppermost part of the composite monument other than that, according to Pausanias (10.13.9), it was removed from the column by the Phokians, the local population of Delphi, during the Third Sacred War, which began in 356 B.C.[3] It was on the cauldron and not the column or its base that an epigram in praise of Pausanias, commander of the Spartans, was once engraved. Sir James Frazer, in his remarkable commentary on Pausanias, proposed that only the bowl was of pure gold, whereas the tripod legs which supported it would have been of gilded bronze. His further suggestion, that the bowl was taken by the Phokians but the tripod legs were left behind, resting on the heads of the bronze serpents, has not been taken up in later scholarship.[4]

Bronze Column

The hollow bronze pillar takes the form of three entwined serpents (fig. 1.1). It was once held to have been cast in two halves, joined along an invisible

---

[2] Gilles II. 13; trans. Ball 1729: 112.
[3] Frazer 1898: V, 300–1.
[4] Frazer 1898: V, 307, suggesting that his preferred solution "would harmonise both with the language of Pausanias, who perhaps implies that more than the mere serpent-column survived to his day, and with the language of the Byzantine writers, who certainly speak as if the tripod, and not merely

FIGURE 1.1 General view of the twisted bronze column in Istanbul. Photo: L. H. Jeffery Archive, Centre for the Study of Ancient Documents, Oxford University, with permission.

seam.[5] However, a detailed examination by Kurt Kluge determined that it was cast in one piece. This would make the spiral pillar among the earliest and largest bronze sculptures produced as a single piece by a hollow lost-wax casting technique.[6] There is no reason to surmise, however, that the necks and heads were also cast as a single piece with the twisted column, and it would follow established practice for them to have been cast separately and attached with flow welds using molten bronze.[7] Since the necks and heads were separated from the column in 1700, no trace of the original joins have survived, but it is

---

the serpent-column, had been transferred by Constantine to Constantinople." We shall return to these issues below at chapter three.

[5] Newton 1865: II, 34: "The entire mass of bronze appears to have been cast. Dr. Dethier with the most minute examination could not detect any join in the metal; yet it is not likely that so great a length should have been cast in one piece."

[6] Published two years later as Kluge 1929: 3. Frazer 1898: V, 302 is among the earliest to suggest a single piece was cast. Hemingway 2004: 3–13 summarizes Greek techniques for casting, joining, and finishing bronze sculpture from the fifth century B.C.

[7] Hemingway 2004: 6: "While it is technically possible to cast an entire statue as a unit, there is no evidence that this was done in antiquity."

probable that these welds eventually failed, having supported the weight of the projecting snake protomes and their overhanging necks for nearly 2,200 years.

Today, headless and neckless, the spiral column is 535 cm tall, and stands on a marble base of another 60 cm. The hollow bronze shaft comprises a spiral of twenty-nine coils that taper in diameter as they increase in thickness from base to top. The lowest coil has a diameter of 63 cm. The thickness of the bronze is uneven, but is generally thicker (1.7–2.0 cm) toward the bottom and thinner (1.1-1.3cm) toward the top.[8] The surface of the bronze is greatly scratched and in places marked by deep cuts, probably made by weapons and tools (fig. 1.2). There is a large opening at the base of the column (fig. 1.3), which was deliberately cut, and two larger holes (figs. 1.4, 1.5,) and two smaller holes (fig. 1.6) are visible higher up, the largest of which is oval and seems also to have been cut or trimmed (fig. 1.4). Two long deep cracks run vertically up the uppermost coils (figs. 1.7).

Until 1855, for at least two centuries and possibly for longer, the lower fifteen coils of the column were buried beneath a layer of earth. The level of the ground on which it stands was raised substantially with the construction of the Sultan Ahmed ("Blue") mosque, in 1609–10. Thereafter, only fourteen coils were visible until an excavation was conducted by the British classicist C. T. Newton and "twelve lusty Croats."[9] Newton, later Sir Charles, was unconvinced that this was the original bronze pillar of the Plataian Tripod, which may explain his willingness to depart before excavations were complete. A decade later he would write:

> I must confess . . . in the general treatment of the surface in the Hippodrome bronze, [I could not] recognize that force in the indication of structure, those refined gradations in the modelling which characterize Greek art even at so early a period as the Delphic dedication; and it was this want of *style* which led me, on first examining the serpent, to consider it a Byzantine restoration from the original,—an opinion which has been strongly maintained by Professor Curtius, but which has been condemned by the general voice of German archaeologists.[10]

When Newton left Constantinople prematurely, those German archaeologists took over, clambering into the hole Newton had dug to expose an inscription (see below). Lord Napier was then authorized to continue excavation, in April 1856, which by the efforts of forty British soldiers ("a company of sappers") exposed also the bases of the Masonry Obelisk and Theodosian Obelisk.[11] Inspired by the discovery of the inscription, which proved that the bronze

---

[8] Gauer 1968: 78.
[9] Newton 1865: II, 27; Frick 1859: 491; Bourquelot 1865: 27.
[10] Newton 1865: II, 34. For his judgment on the serpent head see Newton 1865: I, 44, and below.
[11] A note in *Revue archéologique* 13, 1856: 316. See Frick 1857–60: 490; Newton 1865: II, 36.

FIGURE 1.2 Detail showing scratches and deeper cuts in the surface of the bronze. Photo: L. H. Jeffery Archive, Centre for the Study of Ancient Documents, Oxford University, with permission.

FIGURE 1.3 Large opening in the base of the column, a hole cut in the bronze to allow water to exit. A channel is carved in the marble base for the same purpose. Photo: author.

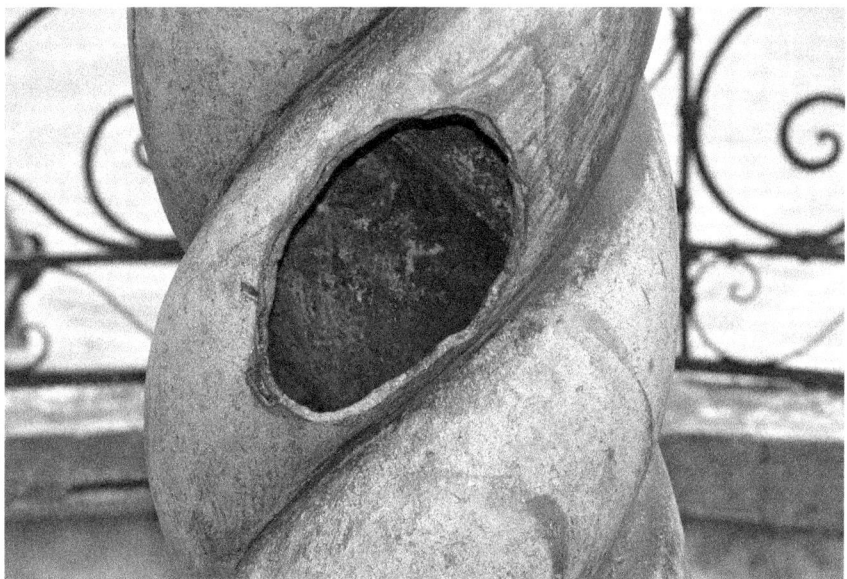

FIGURE 1.4 Large hole in the bronze column, upper coils. Photo: author.

FIGURE 1.5 Large hole in the bronze column, lower coils. Photo: author.

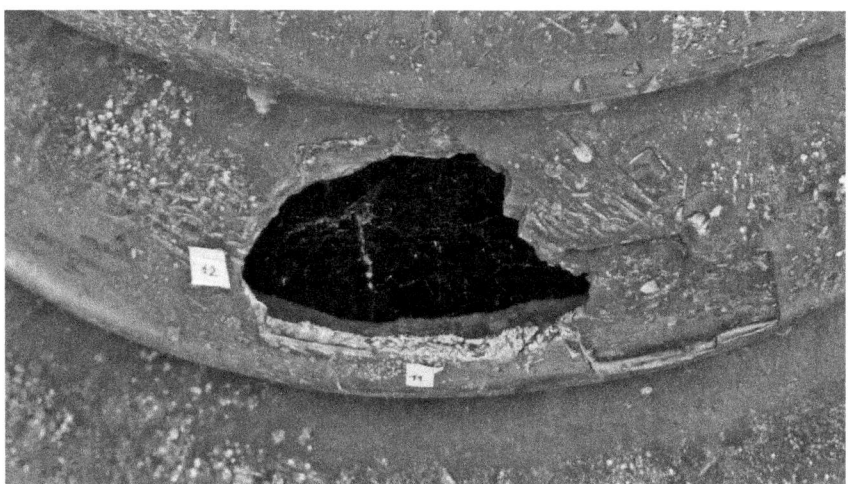

FIGURE 1.6 Smaller hole in the bronze column, lower coils. Photo: author.

column was indeed part of the Plataian Tripod, scholars published short notes and longer studies, although many added little to what had been established by Pierre Gilles three centuries earlier.[12] French excavations at Delphi provided further opportunity for reflection. A long note by Frazer, in his commentary on Pausanias, stands out for its thoroughness and inventive use of all evidence available in 1898.[13]

The exact height of the original bronze column, and therefore the number of coils it comprised, has been disputed. It has been suggested that the column may have lost six coils at its base, forming a wider, flatter base, like a rope coiled on the floor, of around 150 cm in diameter and adding another 38 cm in height.[14] By this account, which posits a final upper coil resolving in the necks, the column originally had thirty-six coils. Alternatively, but with less conviction, it has been suggested that the monument may have had three tails projecting out from the base of the column, although no source records this, and it would appear to be contradicted by the fact that both Herodotos and Pausanias described the column as comprised of a single snake with three heads.[15] Hypotheses relating to the bottom of the bronze column were based in part on the determination that it was broken higher than the base for transportation to Constantinople. This appeared to be confirmed by markings on a composite limestone base discovered at Delphi, which was believed to be the column's original plinth. More

---

[12] For example, Bock 1857: 48, a short note citing Zosimos (sixth century) and the destruction of Ibrahim Pasha's classical statue in Constantinople's hippodrome (sixteenth century).

[13] Frazer 1898: V, 299–307.

[14] See Gauer 1968: 78–9, 82–3, who follows Studniczka 1929, and is in turn followed by Ridgway 1977: 374, n. 1.

[15] Frick 1857–60: 491–2; Gauer 1968: 79.

FIGURE 1.7 Cracks in the bronze column. Photo: author.

recently, as we shall see shortly, an alternative base has been identified, with markings that correlate well with the diameter of the lowest coil of the bronze column as it is today. Didier Laroche examined the bottom of the column in December 1987, determining that the bronze at the base of the lowest coil is turned up and inwards, creating a base, rather than fractured.[16] If there were no tails and no wider, flatter coil at the base of the original monument, then the column originally comprised thirty coils, which number corresponds with the number of poleis that participated in the battles commemorated by the monument (omitting the Tenians). Their names were inscribed at its base somewhat later than its manufacture and erection at Delphi.

Inscription

The greatest attention was lavished not on the bronze stump, which had failed to excite Newton and Curtius, but on the inscription discovered on its lower coils. Newton himself, although an avid epigrapher, failed to reveal the inscription, and it required the application to the column's base by O. Frick and P. A.

---

[16] Laroche 1989: 187.

Dethier of a liberal splash of acid to remove accretions.[17] They knew to look for a list of Greek poleis, participants in the battles at Salamis and Plataia, and like other early interpreters came armed with copies of Herodotos and Pausanias. The former supplied a muster list for Plataia,[18] and the latter a list of twenty-seven cities engraved on a complementary votive to Zeus dedicated at Olympia.[19]

> First the Spartans, after them the Athenians, third the Corinthians, fourth the Sicyonians, fifth the Aeginetans; after the Aeginetans, the Megarians and Epidaurians, of the Arcadians the people of Tegea and Orchomenos, after them the dwellers in Phlios, Troizen and Hermion, the Tirynthians from the Argolid, the Plataians alone of the Boiotians, the Argives of Mykene, the islanders of Keos and Melos, Ambrakiotes of the Thesprotian mainland, the Tenians and the Lepreans, who were the only people from Triphylia, but from the Aegean and the Cyclades there came not only the Tenians but also the Naxians and Kythnians, Styrians too from Euboia, after them Eleans, Potideians, Anaktorians, and lastly the Chalcidians on the Euripos.[20]

The inscription on the Serpent Column is a similar, but not identical, list of Greek poleis, in fact a list of peoples.[21] It appears on the lower coils of the entwined serpents, with two names inscribed on the third coil from the bottom (called by some coil 11) as one faces the inscription, four names on the fourth coil, and three further names inscribed on each coil from the fifth to twelfth coils except for the seventh, which also has four names. There are, therefore, thirty-one names, corresponding with the observation by Plutarch (*Themistokles* 20.3) that "only thirty-one cities had taken part in the war, and that the most of these were altogether small." However, it has been established that the name of the Tenians was inscribed later than the others, at the bottom of the seventh coil, and therefore that the original list may have comprised thirty peoples.[22] This corresponds with the total number of coils, which may, therefore, be of some significance, particularly since the inscription was added to the votive only after it was erected at Delphi.[23] This hypothesis is less convincing if one accepts that the Siphnians were also inserted later, as the fourth name on the fourth coil from the bottom (or coil 10), unless their omission was by mistake not rather than design. The thirteenth coil from the bottom of

---

[17] Newton 1865: II, 29.
[18] Herodotos 9.28.
[19] See below, chapter two.
[20] Pausanias 5.23.1–2. As Frazer 1898: V, 306, observes, "When and by whom the list was placed on the Olympic trophy, we do not know. [Therefore] . . . we are not in a position to explain the discrepancies between that list and the list on the Delphic trophy."
[21] Excellent high-resolution photographs can be viewed at the Oxford University Centre for the Study of Ancient Documents: http://www.csad.ox.ac.uk/LSAG/ESEGW.17.html.
[22] According to Herodotos 8.82, a Tenian warship, deserting the Persians at Salamis, persuaded the Peloponnesians of the new situation, and "for this service the name of the Tenians was afterwards inscribed on the tripod at Delphi amongst the other states who helped to defeat the invader."
[23] See below, chapter three

the column, the topmost inscribed coil (hence referred to by many as coil 1, and now illegible), introduces the list with three words, which Ernst Fabricius was the first to identify as ΤΟΙΔΕ ΤΟΝ ΠΟΛΕΜΟΝ ΕΠΟΛΕΜΕΟΝ, "By these the war was fought."[24] Alternatively, τὸν Μήδον πόλεμον ἐπολέμεον, has been suggested, thus identifying the enemy.[25] To name the Persians in this context, however, seems unnecessary. The established list of names is as follows.[26]

TABLE 1. } Transcription and translation of the inscription on the base of the Serpent Column.

Coil	Transcription	Translation	Polis (city-state)	
13 (1)	το[ίδε τὸν] πόλεμον [ἐ-] πολ[έ]μεον	Those who fought the war		
12 (2)	Λακεδ[αιμόνιοι] Ἀθαναῖο[ι] Κορίνθοι	Lakedaimonians Athenians Corinthians	Sparta Athens Corinth	1 2 3
11 (3)	Τεγεᾶ[ται] Σικυόν[ιο]ι Αἰγινᾶται	Tegeans Sikyonians Aiginetans	Tegea Sikyon Aigina	4 5 6
10 (4)	Μεγαρὲς Ἐπιδαύπριοι Ἐρχομένιοι	Megarians Epidaurians Orchomenans	Megara Epidauros Orchomenos	7 8 9
9 (5)	Φλειάσιοι Τροζάνιοι Ἑρμιονὲς	Phleiasians Troizanians Hermionians	Phleious Troizen Hermione	10 11 12
8 (6)	Τιρύνθιοι Πλαταιὲς Θεσπιὲς	Tirynthians Plataians Thespians	Tiryns Plataia Thespeia	13 14 15
7 (7)	Μυκανὲς Κεῖοι Μάλιοι Τένιοι	Mykaneans Keians Melans Tenians	Mykene Keos Melos Tenos	16 17 18 19
6 (8)	Νάξιοι Ἐρετριὲς Χαλκιδὲς	Naxians Eretrians Chalkidans	Naxos Eretria Chalkis	20 21 22
5 (9)	Στυρὲς Ϝαλεῖοι Ποτειδαιᾶται	Styrians Elians Potideians	Styra Elis Potideia	23 24 25
4 (10)	Λευκάδιοι Ϝανακτοριὲς Κύθνιοι Σίφνιοι	Leukadians Anaktorians Kythnians Siphnians	Leukas Anaktorion Kythnos Siphnos	26 27 28 29
3 (11)	Ἀμπρακιῶται Λεπρεᾶται	Amprakiotans Lepreans	Amprakia Lepreon	30 31

[24] Fabricius 1886: 179. According to Newton 1865: II, 29, this uppermost coil was not buried and its inscription was exposed, leading to its more rapid deterioration.
[25] Meister 1957.
[26] Meiggs and Lewis 1969: 57–60, no. 27; Steinhardt 1997: 51–69. See also Jeffery 1961: 104, no. 15, which can now be viewed at Oxford University's database *POINIKASTAS: Epigraphic Sources for Ancient Greek Writing*: http://poinikastas.csad.ox.ac.uk/

It took decades for this list of poleis to be established and widely accepted by scholars, although attempts to decipher the inscription began immediately upon its exposure. Frick rushed a report on the excavation and his first attempt to decipher the inscription back to Germany to be read on his behalf on 24 February 1856 at the Berlin Academy of Sciences by Ernst Curtius. In this earliest report, Frick did not refer to a version of the inscription by the esteemed epigrapher Kyriakos Pittakis published in the Athenian *Éphémeride archéologique*, and he ignored Newton's role in uncovering the inscription, instead attributing the excavations of the three bases in the hippodrome entirely to "the English military authority, under the leadership of the secretary to the ambassador, Mr. Napier."[27] The report was published as read by Curtius on Frick's behalf in the monthly bulletin of the academy dated 13 March 1856, but with comments by Curtius appended which undermined Frick's case, suggesting that the sculpture was of "ungriechische Form" and that the shoddy inscription and letter forms were hardly as one would expect to find on such an important monument. Curtius concluded that it must be a copy.[28]

In an article published in the third supplementary volume to the *Jahrbücher für classische Philologie*, dated 1857–1860, Frick established that this was indeed the original inscribed monument, listing several works by scholars who had already attempted to reconstruct and publish the inscription in addition to his own first attempts, notably Pittakis. Additionally, accounts of the discovery had been reported in popular venues, including two by Dethier in the *Presse d'Orient* (19 June 1856) and *Journal de Constantinople* (10 July), following a short note in *l'Athenaeum français: Revue universelle* (1 March).[29] The first report to appear under Frick's own name was in the *Archäologischer Anzeiger* of June 1856, published as a gazetteer appended to the *Archäologische Zeitung*, journal of the Deutsches archäologisches Institut.[30]

The very first report on the discovery of the inscription appears to have been a letter from Dr. Otto Blau published in the *Journal de Constantinople* on 24 January 1856, just days after the discovery. Blau must have descended into the hole after dark to scoop Frick and Dethier, providing his own first reading of the inscription. As Frick pointed out, Blau had failed in his enthusiasm to record all the visible names, and in his report via Curtius he, Frick, offered for the first time "the complete inscription, that is 28 names" on the third to twelfth coils.[31] These were, from bottom (third coil) to top (twelfth): Lepreatai,

---

[27] Frick 1856: 217. Napier supervised continued excavations once Newton had departed. See Bourquelot 1865: 30–1, for Pittakis' alternative readings.
[28] Curtius 1856: 179–80. See also Newton 1865: II, 32.
[29] See Frick 1857–60: 488–9, n. 8, 9; Bourquelot 1856: 29–30. It is worth reiterating that the note was in the *Revue universelle* (dated 1 March 1856, no. 9, p. 175), and not the *Bulletin archéologique de l'Athenaeum français*.
[30] Frick 1856: 217–24.
[31] Curtius 1856: 163.

Amprakiotai, Sifnioi, Kythnioi, Fanaktorieis, Leukadioi, Potedeiatai, Faleioi, Styries, Chalkides, Eretries, Naxioi, Tenioi, Malioi, Keioi, Mykanes, Thespies, Plataies, Tirynthioi, Ermiones, Troizani[oi], Flieiasi[o]i, Erchomenioi, Epidaurioi, Megares, Aiginatai, Sikyon[ioi], Korinthioi, [. . .], [. . .]. The final places, being the uppermost, were identified as lacunae where the Athanaioi and Lakedaimonioi, Athenians and Spartans, would have appeared. The forms of the names were identified as Doric.[32]

In June 1856, Frick revised his reading to identify thirty-one names on thirteen coils, positing a phantom Mantines on the ninth coil,[33] and inserting Athanaioi on the thirteenth coil. Additionally, Frick signaled his most important update to be the discovery of a hitherto unnoted dedicatory element, comprising the first two lines on the thirteenth coil, which he deciphered as ΑΠΟΛΟΝΙ Θ[Ε]Ο ΑΝΑΘΕΜΑ[Τ]Ο[Ν], "Dedicated to the god Apollo."[34] In November 1857, Frick presented a series of photographs and two sketches by Dethier to a gathering of the Berlin Academy to support his readings.[35] These were incorporated into Frick's fuller 1857–60 article, where he explained the difficulties involved in discerning and deciphering individual letters of the inscription. Dethier, who had uncovered the inscription with Frick and supplied drawings for his 1857–60 article, in 1862 provided his own interpretation in a fuller context, within his edition with A. D. Mordtmann of *Epigraphik von Byzantion und Constantinopolis*.[36] However, Fabricius was unsatisfied and determined that a new edition of the inscription was necessary, observing that Dethier and Mordtmann had published letters that they explained were unclear or subject to dispute, and had not sufficiently presented the form of the letters. Moreover, the plaster casts that most scholars had consulted, for example the one in Berlin, only adequately communicated the forms of the best-preserved names.[37] In September 1885, Fabricius took the opportunity to study the column in person and to make a new plaster cast of the inscription, from which Paul Graef produced an illustration.

Subsequent authors incorporated Fabricius' interpretation into their collations or syntheses. Whereas Hermann Roehl's *Inscriptiones Graecae antiquissimae* of 1882 had recorded Dethier's and Mordtmann's reading and sketch under *tituli laconici*,[38] in a companion volume of images of inscriptions

---

[32] Curtius 1856: 165. See also Bourquelot 1865: 32.

[33] The Mantineans had fought at Thermopylai, but withdrew before the final battle, and arrived late for Plataia. This has been used to explain their omission from both votives at Delphi and Olympia. See Herodotos 7.202, 222; 9.77. However, the Eleans were also late but feature in the lists. See Flower and Marincola 2002: 243.

[34] Frick 1856: 219. This reading is incorporated into early general accounts, for example Bourquelot 1865: 29.

[35] Frick 1857: 98.

[36] Frick 1862; Dethier and Mordtmann 1862.

[37] Fabricius 1886: 177.

[38] Roehl 1882: 28.

FIGURE 1.8 Photograph of the inscription on coils 3, 4, and 5 (9, 10, and 11) taken by Anne Jeffery in July 1949. L. H. Jeffery Archive, Centre for the Study of Ancient Documents, Oxford University.

produced for teaching, which appeared in 1894, Roehl included instead a sketch of the column and inscription following Fabricius.[39] Similarly, in his 1924 entry for the Pauly-Wissowa *Realencyclopädie* synthesizing decades of personal research on Delphi, Pomtow reproduced Fabricius' reading of the inscription.[40] The inscription ceased to be controversial until, in her 1951 Oxford dissertation and subsequent publication devoted to the *Local Scripts of Archaic Greece*, L. H. Jeffery demonstrated that the letters employed on the column were Phokian.[41] Jeffery made a close study of the column and its inscription, taking many excellent photographs (figs. 1.8, 1.9). The script and dialect employed in the inscription had not hitherto been disputed, since early commentators concurred that it was Doric or, more specifically, Lakonian. This appeared to correlate with the narrative accounts that credited Pausanias, commander of the Spartans, with the monument's erection. However, Jeffery's

---

[39] Roehl 1894: 28, no. 15, which becomes by the third edition of 1907: 101 no. 16.
[40] Pomtow 1924: col. 1405–6.
[41] Jeffery 1961; 1991: 99–104. The suggestion that the Spartans drew their knowledge of writing from Delphi is made by Carpenter 1945: 455–6, stating that the inscription on the Serpent Column "is actually an excellent example of early fifth-century Delphic."

FIGURE 1.9 Photograph of the inscription on coils 6 and 7 (7 and 8) taken by Anne Jeffery in July 1949. L. H. Jeffery Archive, Centre for the Study of Ancient Documents, Oxford University.

suggestion made greater sense, because the column was inscribed not for Pausanias, but only after it had been erected at Delphi, where Phokian was the local dialect.[42] The quality of the inscription is poor, as Curtius had pointed out soon after its discovery. This was now read as confirmation that it was an afterthought rather than an element of the design of the bronze sculpture. One might posit that, had it been part of the original plan for the votive, a single name would have been inscribed on each coil, or as a list winding around the column, rather than in unequal groups stopping halfway up the column. A more splendid and extensive inscription would have been achieved more easily before the tall pillar was erected, or might even have been made part of the casting process.

One wonders whether subsequently the inscription served a liturgical function, whereby the names of the peoples were intoned during a ritual performance commemorating the battle. This would require that all who mustered for the war always be present and correct, hence the later additions of the Tenians

---

[42] Gauer 1968: 94, to the contrary, maintained that the script and dialect were Lakonian. Opinions were fully reviewed by Steinhart 1997: 53–9.

and Siphnians, whose fallen and fortunes would otherwise be neglected by Apollo. For the same reason, other poleis erected their own monuments.[43]

An Upper Jaw of a Serpent's Head

An upper jaw of a serpent's head, now in the Istanbul Archaeological Museums (founded in 1891), was discovered during the Fossati excavations and restoration work at Hagia Sophia, which took place between 1845 and 1847 (fig. 1.10). Newton records having seen the head in 1852, in a small ad hoc museum then set up in St. Irene, in the grounds of the Topkapı Palace. He found it to be "rather coarsely executed and deficient in style."[44] Frick reported seeing the *Drachenkopf* in the weapons collection at the "Irenenkirche" in 1856, and said that the space between the eyes was sufficiently wide that the foot of a large tripod could have been placed there.[45] It would later be misreported that the head was discovered in 1848, although it had already been recorded in a publication of 1847.[46] The column lost its heads one night in 1700, and quite how a single upper jaw came to be buried hundreds of meters away, to be discovered a century and a half later, cannot be ascertained. However, this jaw is held to have been part of the Serpent Column, and on 1 December 1887, at a meeting in London of the Society of Antiquaries, H. A. Grueber, a fellow of the society, exhibited a plaster cast of it "obtained by Mr. Stanley Lane Poole during a recent visit" to the Seraglio Museum at Istanbul. In a short lecture delivered to the assembled fellowship, Grueber commended Dethier's and Mordtmann's *Epigraphik von Byzantion und Constantinopolis* and Charles Newton's travelogue, from which he had taken all his material.[47] Other plaster casts had been made of the jaw, one of which was displayed in Berlin's Neues Museum from 1868. Dethier, who had examined the whole column in detail, obtained a cast for his private collection and is shown holding it on his lap surrounded by other monuments of Greek art in a photograph taken in ca. 1863.[48]

---

[43] As Meiggs and Lewis 1969: 59–60 note, besides the tardy Mantineans, "Of the states mentioned by Herodotus as participating in the war, Kroton (viii. 47), Pale in Kephallenia (ix. 28, 31), Seriphos (viii.46, 48) and the Opuntian Lokrians (vii. 203, 207; viii. 1–2) are unaccountably absent." Kroton erected a very similar votive column shortly afterwards, so its absence from a liturgical inscription added later can be understood.

[44] Newton 1865: I, 44.

[45] Curtius 1856: 179–80.

[46] As noted by Stichel 1997: 346, attributing the error to Frick 1857–60: 493. The error was repeated by others, including Fabricius 1886: 177; Devambez 1937: 10; and Gauer 1968: 79. Stichel 1997: 347, draws attention to the testimony of Anton Korfiz von Ulfeld, in 1739, that two heads had been transferred to the sultan's palace.

[47] Grueber 1887.

[48] Eldem 2012–13: 500, fig. 1, 513–15.

FIGURE 1.10 Bronze upper jaw of a serpent, now in Istanbul Archaeological Museums. Photo: author.

Shortly after the foundation in 1891 of the Istanbul Archaeological Museums, the serpent jaw was removed to their collections. In his 1927 examination of the upper jaw, Kurt Kluge identified a remnant of hard solder on its upper surface.[49] The location suggests that this may best be understood as part of a repair, or perhaps as related to a tripod and cauldron which once stood upon it. In 1937, the serpent jaw was published by Pierre Devambez in the catalogue of bronzes in the Istanbul Archaeological Museums, as "Tête du serpent de Delphes."[50] In fact, Devambez did not seek to establish a connection between the jaw and the column, but took this as his predicate to offer another partial history of the Serpent Column. Devambez described the upper surface of the jaw as having been thinned by its exposure over centuries to precipitation to a thickness of as little as 1 mm, whereas the left and right sides are up to 12 mm and 15 mm respectively. The preserved part of the jaw is 33.8 cm in length, has a width of 16.7 cm at the fracture diminishing to 3.5 cm at the nose, and has a height of 11.6 cm at the break and 6.4 cm at the nose. The eye sockets have a diameter of 33 mm and a depth of up to 27 mm. Devambez, in contrast to earlier judgments, felt that the artist had imbued his work with both softness and brutality, so that the jaw, even in its fragmented state, evinced a sense of ferocity, as if the serpent were poised to strike at its prey.

Damage to the serpent head, in the form of cut marks near the break (fig. 1.11), seems to support the idea that the head was removed deliberately, or

---

[49] Kluge 1929: 27. See also Gauer 1968: 79–80; Mansel 1970; Ridgway 1977.
[50] Devambez 1937: 9–12.

FIGURE 1.11 Upper surface of a bronze upper jaw of a serpent, showing cut marks towards the break. Photo: author.

that once the whole upper part of the column fell, those who witnessed it set to work cutting off the heads or jaws individually. In the absence of metallurgical analysis it remains possible, if unlikely, that this bronze jaw has no connection to the Serpent Column.

Original Base, Delphi

The desire to identify the original base of the famous Plataian Tripod has at least twice provoked scholars into error. That is to say, three bases have been identified as having supported the Plataian Tripod. In 1894, during excavations at Delphi by the French School in Athens under the direction of Théophile Homolle, a large square base, "Atlas 509," was discovered at the highest point of the Sacred Way to the east of the Temple of Apollo. This was announced to be the base of the Plataian Tripod, although it was uncovered some distance from the recorded location of that monument, which was reported by Herodotos (IX.91) to be "near the altar," and implied by Pausanias (10.13.9) to be adjacent to a Tarentine votive statue of horses and footmen. Frazer, who visited Delphi in October 1895, reported its identification in his commentary on Pausanias, first published in 1897–8.[51] In 1898, a campaniform or bell-shaped base, "Atlas 408," was discovered in fragments during excavations at Delphi. A bell shape offered an attractive and functional transition between a square base and the circular bottom of the object it supported, for example a tripod or bronze pillar. This campaniform pedestal formed from some forty separate blocks, rather than the square plinth, had a central depression on its upper surface suited to supporting a column, and additionally three depressions around this that were matched to the feet of a tripod. It was posited that this was

---

[51] Frazer 1898: 299, 310–11.

suitable to have supported the Plataian Tripod.[52] Homolle pronounced without further explanation, in a list of achievements of the French School in 1898, that "le socle du trépied de Platées [avait été] reconnu"[53] Quickly, Homolle's attribution was accepted as proven and the base incorporated into studies of the composite monument. Besides its suiting the posited form of the Plataian Tripod, two arguments were employed in favor of Atlas 408. First, the workmanship has been identified as appropriate to the first half of the fifth century B.C., employing limestone blocks held together with double gamma clamps. Second, the location in which it was discovered was held to correspond with that of the Plataian Tripod, as reported by Herodotos and Pausanias, although, as Pierre Amandry has since observed, there is no record of where the blocks were found, only of where they were placed by Homolle.[54]

In preparation for a celebration in 1903 marking the end of the French School's excavation campaign at Delphi, Atlas 408 was reconstructed in a manner, according to Amandry, that displays all the problems associated with restorations conducted in haste and without sufficient research (fig. 1.12).[55] Rectangular limestone blocks, many with cavities for double gamma clamps, were formed into a square foundation onto which two rows of blocks with curved edges, a row of six and a row of three, were placed in a circular arrangement. Both curved and rectangular blocks with cavities for gamma clamps, twenty-five in total, derived from the same original base. However, the reconstructed base mistakenly also included fourteen blocks that derived from neighboring monuments (seven), or were of the wrong stone (seven).[56] In 1906, the base was taken apart for several hours by H. Pomtow, but it was reconstructed exactly as before.[57]

Other campaniform bases have been uncovered at Delphi—so far the total is seven bases, whole or partial—and the identity of the base of the Plataian Tripod has been reconsidered by Amandry and Didier Laroche.[58] Atlas 408 has been deconstructed and extraneous parts removed. In its newly reconstructed form, it has been identified as the base for the Tripod of Kroton, which was manufactured to resemble the Plataian Tripod and was placed beside it at Delphi.[59] Laroche has, meanwhile, identified a fragment of grey limestone as part of the original base of the Plataian Tripod. This fragment—no. 416, also

---

[52] Drawings and photos at Amandry 1987: 104–5, show thirty-nine blocks with diverse provenances and space for a fortieth block, at the northeast corner of the lowest register, filled with rubble and mortar.

[53] Homolle 1898: 565; Laroche 1989: 185.

[54] Amandry 1987: 103–6, n. 49.

[55] Amandry 1987: 102.

[56] Amandry 1987: 103–6.

[57] Pomtow 1924: col. 1406–7; Amandry 1987: 103, n. 48.

[58] Amandry 1987; Laroche 1989.

[59] Jacquemin and Laroche 1990; Luce, Laroche, Déroche, and Petridis 1993: 631–41. See below, chapter three.

FIGURE 1.12 Atlas 408, excavated at Delphi in the 1890s, once held to be the composite limestone base of the Plataian Tripod. Photo: Marco Prins, Livius.org, with permission.

called base G, pending the discovery of additional fragments—was excavated below gate C at the peribolos wall, near building 14 (often but mistakenly called the Prytaneion). It is 49.8 cm high and is part of the upper curved element of a campaniform base, with a curved cavity on its upper surface. All campaniform bases found at Delphi other than Atlas 408 are monolithic, so a grey limestone base carved from a single piece of rock is posited, which would have been approximately 90–100 cm high. An examination of the base and interior of the bronze column in Istanbul allowed Laroche to posit that it matched exactly the curved cavity in the upper surface of fragment 416, at least insofar as he was able to calculate the dimensions of the circular cavity in base G from the single fragment. Laroche's observations mean it is no longer feasible to believe that the bronze pillar once had a flatter, wider base, resembling a rope coiling on the floor, nor is it possible that serpent tails once projected out from the pillar. Laroche's identification of the base at Delphi, if it is correct, demonstrates that the bronze spiral column would have stood on a grey limestone base exactly as it does on its current marble base.

Marble Base and Foundation, Water Pipes, Constantinople

The base on which the bronze pillar stands today in Istanbul appears to be an upturned, trimmed capital of white marble (fig. 1.13). It is around 60 cm high and 150 cm across its upper surface, and more on the lower, since its sides taper

FIGURE 1.13 Marble base of the Serpent Column, Istanbul. Photo: author.

outwards. Laroche's examination in December 1987 confirmed that the bronze pillar rests not directly in a shallow circular depression carved into the stone, but upon cast lead footings that connect bronze to marble. In gaps between the lead footings, Laroche was able to slip his hand between the marble and bronze. Additionally, four blobs of metal, apparently also lead, were identified within the lower spirals, probably serving to anchor the bronze better to the lead footing.[60] The ends of two lead footings can be seen clearly as a material with an irregular pocked surface between the bronze spiral—marked 1 and 8 in blue ink on white tabs which had been attached to the monument in spring 2012—and white stone (see fig. 1.3). Green staining can also be seen clearly on the marble, where water has long passed across the bronze from within the column. The reasons for this were elucidated in the excavations conducted in 1855 and 1927–8.

According to Newton's account of his 1855 excavation:

> After digging to the depth of rather more than 6 feet, I came to the base of the serpent, a rough-hewn stone plinth, evidently of the Byzantine period. A few feet from this plinth, at the depth of 8 feet below the surface, was an ancient aqueduct formed by cylindrical earthen pipes jointed one into the other, and laid continuously with an oblong block of marble 16 inches long, through which an earthen pipe passed lengthways ... Close to this aqueduct was a foundation of tiles bound in strong mortar, which appeared to be the remains of a small square tank. Within three-quarters of a yard of the serpent was a marble archway, like that of a *cloaca*, and near it a drain large enough to admit a man's body. The serpent ... being placed in the centre of the tank, has probably been used at some period as a fountain.[61]

---

[60] A lead post, which Frick (1857: 550) originally identified as a means to secure the column to its base, was shortly afterwards identified as the lead pipe, explored below.

[61] Newton 1865: II, 27–9. As Newton proceeds to relate, he was rushing off to join a cruise, so did not find time to examine the base properly and did not notice the inscription. His trip led him to his greatest discovery, the Mausoleum of Halikarnassos, which he excavated in 1856–8.

At the base of the coils there is a large hole in the bronze, and below it the marble base has been carved to form a channel reaching almost to the bottom of the 60-cm block at its front. It is clear from close inspection of the large hole in the bronze and the channel in the marble base that the modifications are deliberate. The edges of the channel in the marble are straight and regular, there are tool marks on the bronze, and the water channel in the marble was carved.

Prior to Newton's dig, a water conduit had been discovered in the vicinity of the Serpent Column.[62] This was located several feet from the base of the column and, more significantly, was a foot higher than the marble base on which the column stood, and so cannot have supplied it directly.[63] The conduit supplied the Sultan Ahmed Mosque, and so was found at a level that the surface of the hippodrome did not reach until after construction of the mosque began in 1609.[64] The conduit was cleared very shortly after its discovery, during widening and clearance of the At meydanı, the Turkish name for the hippodrome.[65] In 1927 and 1928, excavations along the axis of the At meydanı, for 48 meters both parallel to and at right angles to the posited line of the median, the *spina* or *euripos*, revealed many water conduits.[66] According to Stanley Casson, the director of excavations for Oxford University and the British Academy, seven water conduits were identified in the vicinity of the Serpent Column.[67] In Casson's words, the "basis of the Serpent Column is of peculiar importance in this connexion, since it proves to be founded not on masonry at all, but upon a water-conduit which runs at right-angles to the axis, and which is itself bedded in the yellow clay," a layer that defines the Byzantine levels of the hippodrome, at that time beneath 4.5 m of black earth. The Serpent Column stood in a tank constructed simply from rubble lined with mortar, from which a larger conduit allowed the water to run off. The marble base on which the

---

[62] Newton 1865: II, 27, relates that as he began to excavate he noticed that around the Serpent Column, "[t]he soil had evidently been disturbed at no very distant period, and contained no ancient remains, except very small fragments of marble."

[63] Gerhard and Curtius 1856; Frick 1857–60: 550–1; Bourquelot 1865: 33–4. See also Crow, Bardill, and Bayliss 2008: Appendix 1, 227 (CIG 8611), and 142: "Over 150 lead fistulae, many with stamps, survive from ancient Rome, evidence for the widespread distribution and supply from public reservoirs to private households and baths. By contrast, only one stamped fistula is known at Constantinople—intended to supply a water fountain close to or inside the Serpent Column in the Hippodrome."

[64] Casson 1928: 9; Tanman and Çobanoğlu 2010: 32–50. The discovery may have been made two decades earlier, in May 1834, when the famous Kugelspiel was discovered during digging at the edge of the hippodrome. It was published by Texier 1845, who mistook it for a fountain, due to the survival of pipes within it. Bourquelot 1865: 33, appears to suggest that it was found "with the remains of pipes [avec les restes de tuyaux]," but this is his own interpretation of Texier's explanation (p. 146) that the interior of the block had traces of pipes.

[65] Frick 1857–60: 550.

[66] Casson 1928; 1929. Subsequent hippodrome excavations by Rustem Duyuran in 1950–1 did not approach the Serpent Column. Some excellent photos from this later dig are published in Pitarakis 2010: I, 348–57.

[67] Casson 1928: 25–6. These had nothing to do with the seven water basins identified in the hippodrome in the tenth century, on which see Mango 1949.

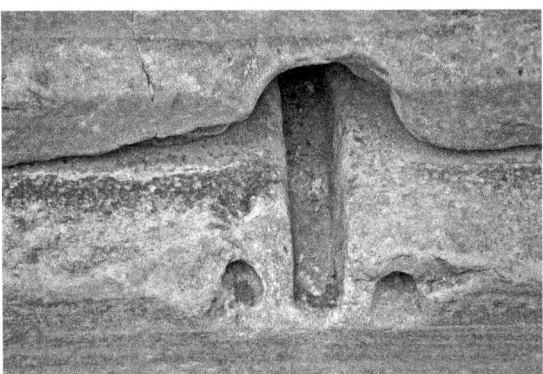

FIGURE 1.14 Base of the Masonry Obelisk, showing a carved channel through which water would exit. Photo: author.

column stood Casson determined to be "an old column capital trimmed and reused." A hole had been bored in this, "through which is it possible to look up from the conduit inside and through the column itself."[68] This hole can still be seen when looking into the column at its base (fig. 1.3).

If water entered the column from the conduit below through a pipe inserted in the bored hole in the manner described by Casson, one must imagine that at least some of it exited through the hole in the bronze column's lowest spirals and associated channel in the marble base, cascading gently into the pool below. The base of the Masonry Obelisk was also plumbed and served by the same water conduits, so that today one can still see the channels on all sides through which water would have exited (fig. 1.14). The hole at the base of the Serpent Column is not unlike the lowest spout of a multipart fountain depicted in the Annunciation mosaic at Daphni, Greece (eleventh century, see fig. 7.13 below), and the carved marble channel closely resembles that in the Annunciation mosaic in the Chora Church, now the Kariye Mosque (fourteenth century). Water may also have exited the column higher up if it entered under pressure, for example from a pipe emerging through an oval hole (fig. 1.4).[69]

Stamped Lead Fistula

When looking at the hole drilled though the marble base on which the Serpent Column stands, Stanley Casson conjectured that a lead pipe would have been inserted into it to connect it to the water supply lines that ran beneath the

---

[68] Casson 1928: 12–13. Curtius had already hinted at this in reporting the findings by Lord Napier's dig (Gerhard and Curtius 1856: 287).

[69] For a fuller consideration of the Serpent Column fountain, see chapter six.

hippodrome floor. According to Newton, "Subsequently to my excavation, a piece of leaden pipe was discovered inside the serpent, on which was part of an inscription in Byzantine Greek, relating to someone who was praefect, ἔπαρχος, of Constantinople."[70] A single fistula about a meter long, which happens to be the only Byzantine stamped lead pipe ever discovered during excavations in Constantinople, was identified by Frick and Dethier during their investigation of the column early in 1856. At first, it appeared to them that a lead post was inserted into the column to support it and secure it to its marble base. However, a closer inspection led to their identification inside the column of a "heavy leaden pipe, similar to a gutter but closed, some three feet long, mangled at both ends, badly bent and covered in bumps."[71] The pipe bore an inscription in letters "about one inch high." According to the transcription made at the time of discovery, the visible letters were recorded and deciphered as [. . . . . .]AP[O HY]PATWN PATRIKIOU K[AI] EPARCHOU ROM[H THS NEAS], "[name missing] proconsul, patrician and prefect of [the New] Rome." Although no name was discerned, the inscription, and therefore the original installation of the pipe, was attributed to Proklos,[72] the eparch of New Rome under Theodosios I, who was responsible for raising the Theodosian Obelisk.[73] This reading supported a contention, advanced by Dethier, that the Serpent Column became a fountain in the reign of Theodosios, modifying Frick's suggestion that it followed swiftly on the completion of the Aqueduct of Valens in the 370s.[74] Another reading of the inscription might be *Apo hypaton patrikiou kai eparchou Rom[anos, or Romulianos]*, or "Romanos/Romulianos, proconsul and eparch." A Romulianos was eparch of the city of Constantinople from 1 February to 11 July 398.[75] The name Romanos is far more common, and many were *patrikioi*, although no one by that name is reported to have been eparch of the city in its earliest centuries.[76] The 390s would be a suitable time for the hippodrome to be plumbed, as part of Theodosios' grand redevelopment of the city. Moreover, the arrival of "the necessary water" was still recent enough that one might anticipate that existing monuments would be modified to incorporate the display of water. That is to say, a second, higher water line had entered the city in 373, during the reign of Valens.

Flowing from Thrace, the water passed through channels and aqueducts that crossed the countryside circuitously, with channels totaling some 268

---

[70] Newton 1865: II, 35.

[71] Gerhard and Curtius 1856: 286–7.

[72] PLRE II, xxxix (Proclus); cf. I, 749 (Proculus).

[73] Kirchoff (= CIG 8611), cited by Frick 1857–60: 551; Dethier and Mordtmann 1864: 20–8; Newton 1865: II, 35.

[74] Frick 1856: 223–4; Frick 1857–60, 551.

[75] PLRE: II, 949, 1255.

[76] PLRE: II, 943–8. Frick 1856: 223–4, preferred the name Romanos, and drew attention to a certain Romanos who was *magister equitum* under Valens, which supported his preferred date for the pipe.

kilometers. It terminated in the famous viaduct of the Aqueduct of Valens, today's Bozdoğan Kemeri, which surmounts the valley between the city's fourth and third hills. The waters flowed thence into a new Great Nymphaeum (*nymphaeum maius, hydreion megiston*) at the Forum Tauri, where the Forum of Theodosios would shortly afterwards be built.[77] The completion of the high water line, able to supply locations at an elevation of ca. 56 meters or lower, was reported succinctly by Jerome: "Klearchos, eparch of the city of Constantinople, is well known, by whom the necessary water which was daily awaited with vows is brought to the community."[78] Themistios praised the undertaking more lavishly, alluding to the arrival of water nymphs, whose "names are Thracian and manly, but the beauty and the splendour are exceedingly delicate."[79] Eventually this high line comprised almost 500 kilometers of channels, with expansions at the supply end and an extension, certainly before A.D. 450, from the Forum of Theodosios to the Forum of Constantine.

Although it is an appealing conclusion, it is not certain that the lead pipe was placed within the Serpent Column during the reign of Theodosios I. Seals show powerful and wealthy men holding the title *apo hypaton* acting as important functionaries in Constantinople and the provinces from the fourth century until ca. 700, largely in positions related to trade and provisioning (controlling various state monopolies).[80] There are a number of seals with the title *apo hypaton* in the Dumbarton Oaks and Fogg Collections, most dating to the seventh century.[81] Only one of those so far published pairs *apo hypaton* with *patrikios*, the seal of "Stephanos *apo hypaton, patrikios, stratiotikos logothetes*, and general *kommerkiarios* of the *apotheke* of Paphlagonia."[82] Two silver ewers discovered in Syria, in the collection of the Abegg-Stiftung in Bern, are inscribed "For the salvation of Megalos, glorious *apo hypaton* and *patrikios*, curator of

---

[77] Crow, Bardill, and Bayliss 2008, 127.

[78] Jerome, *Chronicle* s.a. 373, quoted in translation at Crow, Bardill, and Bayliss 2008, 225. Also cited at Dagron 1984, 248–9, who refers to a rather later reference written in Rome by Cassiodorus, *Chronicle*, ed. Mommsen, *Chron. min.* II, 153.

[79] Themistios, *Oratio* 11.151c, quoted in translation from Crow, Bardill, and Bayliss 2008, 224.

[80] See Oikonomides 1986: 26, 28, 30–1, 35, 37, for firmly dated examples, all from the seventh century.

[81] *DOS* 1, 23, 194; *DOS* 2, 167, 170–1; *DOS* 3, 41–2, 76, 105, 149–50; *DOS* 4, 164–5. These general dates are not altered by examples among the seals sold at auction 1991–2001, listed in *SBS* 6 and 8. Notable examples from Constantinople are published at *DOS* 5: 52–3, where 23.10 is the seal of "Kosmas *apo hypaton* and general *kommerkiarios* of the *apotheke* of Constantinople," dated to 685–95; 23.8 is the seal of John, also an *apo hypaton* in 692/3; 23.6 is the seal of "George *apo hypaton. Apotheke* of Constantinople [and] ..." A number of George's seals are among those listed in other volumes and at Oikonomides 1986: 37. See also *DOS* 5, 45–8 no. 22.1–8, for seals of those who held the office "*eparch* of the city," most from the ninth and tenth centuries, and at the rank of *protospatharios*. The earliest seal, 22.5, sixth or seventh century, of one Markellos has no rank; one of the eighth century, Sergios, is *hypatos* and *spatharios*.

[82] *DOS* 4: 33, no. 11.20. Stephen is in charge of provisioning the army in the province of Paphlagonia, and to that end has control of trade and the imperial entrepôts and storehouses. However, see Laurent 1962: 85–7.

our most pious sovereign, and for the peace of the soul of Peter, son of Pelagia, and of Nonnous." These are dated securely by silver stamps to early in the reign of Maurikios (A.D. 582–602).[83] After ca. A.D. 700, just when those men who held it seem to be at the height of their powers and numbers, the rank of *apo hypaton* disappeared. By the time the *Kleterologion*, a precedence list recording bureaucratic and imperial hierarchies, was compiled in 899, *hypatos* was the rank below *spatharios*, and therefore considerably less elevated than *patrikios* and *anthypatos*, the new equivalent to the late Roman rank of proconsul.[84] If the honorific "former consul" or "proconsul" (*apo hypaton*) was held with the rank of *patrikios* only between the fourth and eighth centuries, then the lead pipe could have been stamped at any point between ca. 350 and ca. 700. It may, however, have been reused at any time after that.

Reconstructions

Based on surviving material, textual and visual evidence, scholars have attempted to recreate the original composite monument, the Plataian Tripod. Alternative reconstructions were proposed by Dethier and Mordtmann and by Fabricius.[85] Most later impressions are variants of these.[86] The single significant difference between them is the shape and size of the golden tripod, of which no physical trace has survived. In the first reconstruction, the tripod and cauldron are smaller, with feet resting on the serpent heads. In the second reconstruction, a far larger tripod surmounts the entire bronze sculpture, its feet resting on the same stone base as the column. Newton was in no doubt: "The tripod, of course, rested on the heads."[87] In other words, he favored Dethier and Mordtmann's "imaginary recreation." The most recent recreation, by A. Tayfun Öner, replicates this form digitally.[88] A modification of this form by Ridgway imagines the cauldron resting within the circle formed by the serpent protomes, resting on their necks. Frazer concurred with Newton, but suggested additionally that, since the Byzantines called the object the Delphic Tripod, the heads still supported gilded bronze legs for the golden cauldron, which alone had been stolen by the Phokians.[89]

---

[83] Dodd 1968, ewers A and B. Brooke Shilling provided this reference.
[84] *Kleterologion*, ed. Oikonomides 1972. ODB, s.v. *Hypatos*, provides a useful summary of the changing status of the title, office, and rank. The equivalent rank in 899 would have been *anthypatos*, proconsul.
[85] Fabricius 1886: 177,
[86] Fabricius 1886; Ridgway 1977; Steinhart 1997: 35–45 for analysis.
[87] Newton 1865: II, 33.
[88] See: http://www.byzantium1200.com/tripod.html
[89] Frazer 1898: 306–7.

Scholars who favored the larger tripod found support for this contention in the identification of Atlas 408 as the Plataian Tripod's original base. Atlas 408 has a central depression, where a column would have rested, and in addition three depressions around it where tripod feet would have rested.[90] Those who could not imagine a tripod of such dimensions, at least seven meters tall and of gold or gilded, suggested that the three serpent tails may have rested in the depressions. However, Laroche's identification of Base G has dispensed with this discussion, lending support to the reconstruction that features a smaller tripod, each of its three feet resting on a serpent head. Kluge's identification of a trace of hard solder in the depression on top of the serpent head in Istanbul Archaeological Museums would appear to support this solution also. However, it may have been the case that something else later was placed atop the serpent's head, or this marked a later repair.

The principal objection to the second reconstruction has been that such a huge tripod is too large sensibly to have been made. It was not, however, beyond the ability of archaic Greek metalworkers to fashion a very large cauldron, at least if we believe Herodotos' accounts of three great bowls. First (1.70.1–2), he reports on a huge bronze mixing bowl with figures around the rim, created in Lakonia to seal the alliance between the Spartans and Lydians in around 550 B.C., which held 300 amphorae. Second (4.81.4), he records a cauldron in Scythia that held 600 amphorae and was six fingers thick, "which [and here he refers to a third bowl] was six times greater than the cauldron dedicated by Pausanias son of Kleombrotos at the entrance of the Pontos." This Pausanias was the very man, the Spartan general, who dedicated the cauldron of the Plataian Tripod. The size of the bowls in each case depends upon the size of the amphorae with whose capacity they are compared. If one estimates that an amphora might hold between 34 and 40 liters (9–11 gallons), then Herodotos has in mind bowls holding more than 11,500 liters (3,000 gallons). In 1886, Fabricius estimated that the golden cauldron of his recreation would have been not quite 300 cm in diameter.[91] A circular tank with a diameter of 300 cm would need to be 165 cm deep to hold 11,500 liters. To account for its tapering sides, a cauldron holding that much liquid would require a depth at its center of closer to 200 cm, which is not out of line with Fabricius' schematic drawing.

External evidence can be advanced in support of both reconstructions. The first type appears to draw on the form of *perirrhanteria*, marble basins supported by female figures (frequently holding leashed lions), all of which date from the seventh century B.C. *Perirrhanteria* found in Greece are all from sanctuaries, including Delphi, Olympia, Isthmia, and five from Lakonia.[92] John Boardman has suggested a Lakonian origin for these marble basins, drawing

---

[90] Kluge 1929: 27.
[91] Fabricius 1886: 189.
[92] See Ducat 1964; Boardman 1978: 25–6.

on established eastern influence. The second type is known from smaller model sculptures of tripods discovered at Olympia, where a central statue supports a cauldron, which also rests on the three legs of a tripod. This type appears to correspond to a description by Pausanias of sculptural tripods he saw at the Amyklaion, the principal Spartan temple to Apollo. Pausanias appears to imply that statues of Aphrodite, Artemis, and Kore were placed entirely beneath tripods, which were larger than others he had seen. However, Pausanias' language is sufficiently ambiguous that one cannot say certainly whether the tripods he described rested upon the heads of statues:

> Under the first tripod stood an image of Aphrodite, and under the second an Artemis. The two tripods themselves and the reliefs are the work of Gitiadas. The third was made by Kallon of Aigina, and under it stands an image of Kore, daughter of Demeter . . . These tripods are larger than the others, and were dedicated from the spoils of the victory at Aigospotamoi. [93]

---

[93] See below, chapter three. Pausanias 3.18.8: ὑπὸ μὲν δὴ τῷ πρώτῳ τρίποδι Ἀφροδίτης ἄγαλμα ἑστήκει, Ἄρτεμις δὲ ὑπὸ τῷ δευτέρῳ, Γιτιάδα καὶ αὐτοὶ τέχνη καὶ τὰ ἐπειργασμένα, ὁ τρίτος δέ ἐστιν Αἰγινήτου Κάλλωνος· ὑπὸ τούτῳ δὲ ἄγαλμα Κόρης τῆς Δήμητρος ἕστηκεν . . . οὗτοι δὲ οἱ τρίποδες μεγέθει τε ὑπὲρ τοὺς ἄλλους εἰσὶ καὶ ἀπὸ τῆς νίκης τῆς ἐν Αἰγὸς ποταμοῖς ἀνετέθησαν.

2 }

Plataia

Herodotos on the Battle of Plataia – The Night Sky over Plataia, Summer 479 B.C. – Greeks, Gods and the Night Sky – Zeus and Typhon, Apollo and Python – Chaos Contained – Ninĝišzida and the God on the Serpent Throne

The Serpent Column was forged as the central bronze pillar of the Plataian tripod, a votive offering to Apollo dedicated at the sanctuary at Delphi.[1] In Greek it was an *agalma*, a work of art or craft that evoked wonder. It was placed on the eastern terrace of the temple of Apollo following the battle of Plataia, where a federation of Greek poleis, independent cities and their associated territories, defeated an invading Persian army. The land battle at Plataia was a second major Greek victory, coming a year after a sea battle at Salamis. Together, those encounters ended the Persian invasions of the Greek mainland. The story is familiar, told in detail and with great creativity by Herodotos, whose narrative must be the foundation for any reconstruction.[2]

Herodotos on the Battle of Plataia

According to Herodotos (6.48), Darius, the Persian King of Kings, in preparation for an invasion of the Greek mainland, sent messengers to the various Greek poleis demanding tribute in the form of earth and water, acknowledgement of

---

[1] Frick 1857–60 offered a comprehensive account of the pertinent classical sources, with excerpts. Many commentators on the Serpent Column have done the same since. Today, pertinent quotations and translations can easily be located at *Perseus Digital Library*, http://www.perseus.tufts.edu/hopper/; and the *Thesaurus Linguae Graecae*, http://www.tlg.uci.edu/.

[2] This chapter, the first written in full draft, was completed early in 2011. I was then seated in an office at the Swedish Collegium for Advanced Study, Uppsala, next door to David Pankenier, whose influence on its composition was profound. Since this chapter was written, Pankenier 2013 has been published, as have three entirely new accounts, all slim and aimed at distinct readerships, of the Battle of Plataia: Corvisier 2011; Shepherd 2012; and Cartledge 2013. Cartledge's observation (p. 101) that "we shall never be able with total confidence to recapture 'what actually happened' in the critical months of August–September 479" is unimpeachable. Another important approach to the battle, focused on its commemoration and afterlife, including reflection on the Serpent Column, is Jung 2006.

his dominion over their land and sea. In 492 B.C., a preliminary campaign led by Mardonius, Darius' son in law, had confirmed Persian dominion in Thrace and subjugated Macedonia. When Mardonius' fleet was wrecked off the Athos peninsula in northern Greece, new commanders were selected and dispatched at the head of an army to Kilikia, to be joined by the naval contingent and horse transports requisitioned from tributaries.[3] The fleet sailed for Naxos, then Delos and other islands, pressing troops into service and taking children as hostages, punishing those who resisted. At Eretria on Euboia, "the Persians entered, and stripped the temples bare and burnt them in revenge for the burnt temples of Sardis and, in accordance with Darius' orders, carried off all the inhabitants as slaves."[4] Fresh from victory at Eretria, the Persian fleet set sail for Attica, intent on inflicting the same punishment on Athens, and made for Marathon, where there was excellent ground for cavalry operations. There, the Athenians under Miltiades were victorious in a drawn-out battle, losing only 192 men, far fewer than the 6,400 fallen Persians.[5] According to Herodotos, Darius nursed a desire for vengeance, but was prevented from returning to Greece by unrest in Egypt, for which he was preparing to depart when he died in 486.[6] The throne passed to his son Xerxes, who crushed the Egyptian revolt and, at the urging of Mardonius, turned again to Greece, mustering his forces in 481.

Xerxes' mighty army crossed Asia Minor, and in spring 480 at Sardis the King of Kings renewed Darius' demand for earth and water from the Greek poleis, sending messengers "to every place in Greece except Athens and Sparta."[7] When the army proceeded to the Hellespont, a bridge was constructed to link Europe and Asia. After a storm destroyed the bridge, Xerxes ordered that the Hellespont receive three hundred lashes and a pair of fetters be thrown into it before the bridge was reconstructed, a pontoon formed from hundreds of ships.[8] Having sought to humble the sea, rites were performed, perhaps in expiation, prior to the crossing into Europe, which took seven days and nights. Herodotos dwelt on the size and diversity of the huge army, listing the peoples and detailing their exotic costumes.[9]

From the Hellespont, the Persians and their allies advanced without hindrance by land and sea. The fleet sailed towards Artemision, passing through a canal dug across the Athos peninsula, an extravagant response to the storm that had wrecked Mardonius' fleet more than a decade earlier. The land forces

---

[3] Herodotos 6. 95.
[4] Herodotos 6. 101.
[5] Herodotos 6. 117.
[6] Herodotos 7.1.
[7] Herodotos 7.32. Those two cities were exempted because they had mistreated Darius' envoys (7.133).
[8] Herodotos 7.35.
[9] Herodotos 7.60–100.

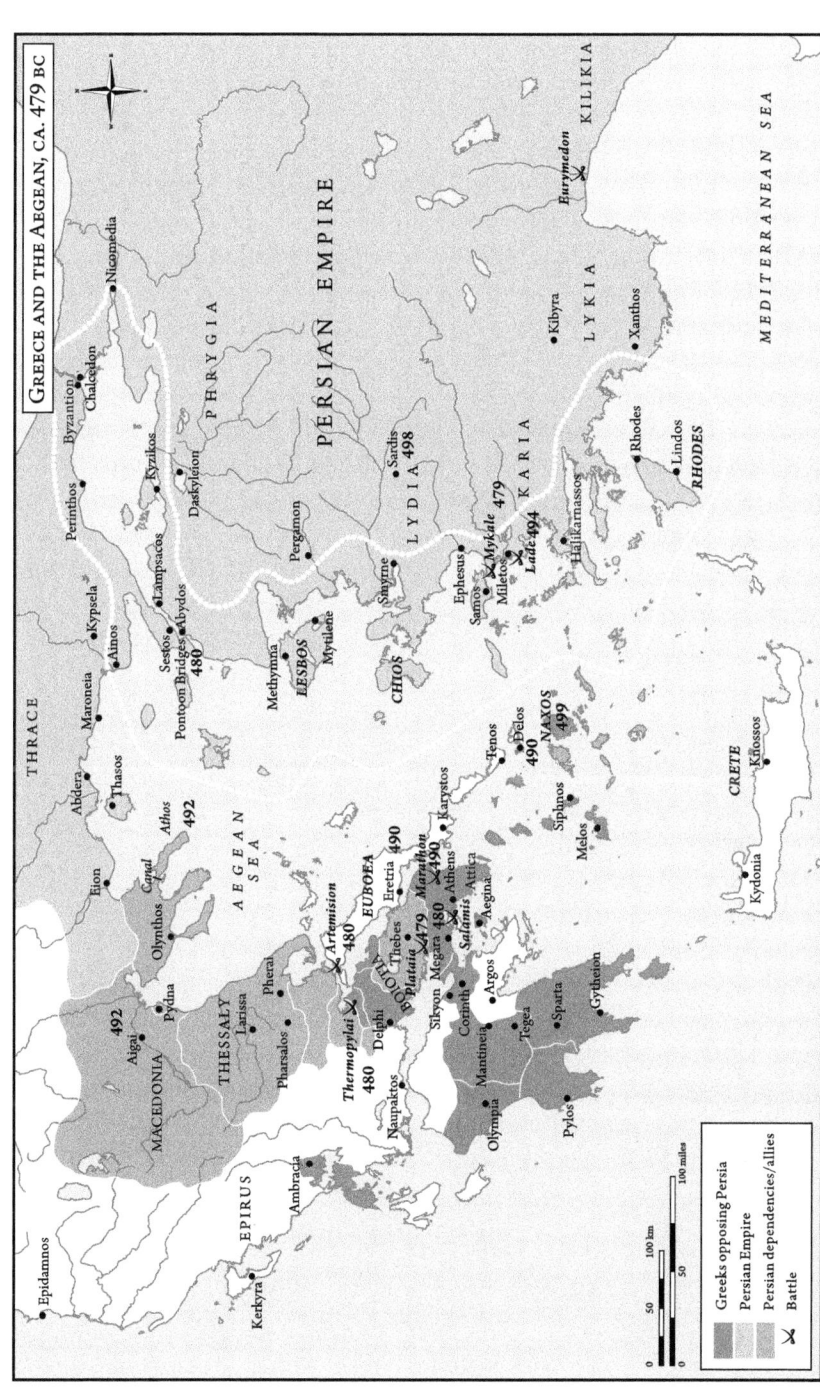

MAP 1 Greece and the Aegean at the time of the Persian Wars.

marched as far as Thermopylai, gathering conscripts and tokens of submission from tributary Greek poleis. While the Greeks who would oppose the Persian advance rebuilt an ancient wall across the pass at Thermopylai and gathered their fleet safely within the straits at Artemision, word was sent from Delphi to "Pray to the winds . . . for they will be good allies to Greece."[10] Subsequently, a storm of such force and duration raged that the Persians, anchored in the open sea, lost 400 war ships and countless merchant vessels until, by Herodotos' account (7.191), magi were able to quell it with their sacrificial offerings and spells. The Greeks, in turn, poured libations to Poseidon the savior.

A defector brought news of the Persian disaster to the Greeks at Artemision, as well as the information that a contingent of 200 ships had been dispatched to sail around Euboia while the rest entered the straits to anchor off Aphetai. Therefore, a Greek squadron was sent to test the mettle of their opponents; despite being greatly outnumbered, it captured thirty Persian ships. Meanwhile, the detachment sailing around Euboia was caught in another squall and driven against rocks at "the Hollows." Fearing worse to come if they waited longer, the Persian captains put to sea in full force to engage the Greek fleet. Both sides lost many men and ships at the Battle of Artemision, which Herodotos claims took place on the same day as the Battle of Thermopylai.[11]

The Greeks mustered at Thermopylai were commanded by Leonidas, a Spartan king reputed to be descended from Herakles, who had hand-picked 300 hoplites, all fathers of living sons. The Spartans were joined by 700 Thespeians, 400 Thebans—according to Herodotos, these were selected because the loyalty of Thebes was doubted[12]—and several thousand others. On the first day of battle, the Greeks took advantage of the confined space to withstand an assault first by a contingent of Medes and Kissioi, and then an elite Persian division, "the King's Immortals." The second day saw a similar result, with far fewer Greek losses than Persian, until a track across the mountain was revealed to Xerxes, allowing him to send men to assault the Greeks from the rear. News of the attack reached the Spartans before a third day of battle commenced, and so Leonidas, fearing his allies had no heart for the battle, dismissed all but the Thebans, whom he detained as hostages, and the Thespeians who had refused to leave. His rump force fanned out across a wider section of the pass to meet the attack, fighting valiantly until Leonidas fell, when they withdrew to the wall and there awaited their own deaths from a renewed Persian advance and by missile assault from above.[13] By his death, Leonidas was held to have saved

---

[10] Herodotos 7. 178.

[11] Herodotos 8.15. A quite different account of the Battle of Thermopylai is given by Diodoros Sikeliotes 11.8–11, who draws on a lost account by Ephoros written in the fourth century B.C., which details a night attack by Leonidas on Xerxes' camp. See Flower 1998, who posits that Ephoros drew upon a narrative elegy, a long choral song by Simonides of Keios, to whose epigrams we shall turn later.

[12] Diodoros Sikeliotes 11.4.7, gives a different account, stating that the Thebans were divided, and some were opposed to the Persians. See Flowers 1998: 371.

[13] Herodotos 7.210–28.

Sparta, for a hexametric oracle from Delphi had foretold that either the city would fall, or it would "mourn the death of a king of the house of Herakles."[14]

After Thermopylai no resistance was found in Attica. The Athenians, like the Spartans, had sought direction from the Delphic oracle, and learned that "only the wooden wall shall not fall," and to "await not the host of horse and foot coming from Asia."

> Nor be still but turn your back and withdraw from the foe.
> Truly a day will come when you will meet him face to face.
> Divine Salamis, you will bring death to women's sons
> When the corn is scattered, or the harvest gathered in.[15]

Themistokles, who had recently come to prominence in Athens by arguing that silver from the new mines at Laurion should be used for the construction of 200 ships, understood that these were the "wooden walls" that would bring death at "divine Salamis." He had commanded the fleet at Artemision, and now withdrew to the island of Salamis, in the Saronic Gulf, a nautical mile from the Athenian harbor at Peiraeus. The citizens of Athens and its surroundings were evacuated, and it seemed even the goddess Athena had abandoned the city when honey-cake left for the giant snake held to guard the Aropolis was found for the first time to be uneaten.[16]

The Persian army advanced through the lands of the Phokians, guided and aided by Thessalians, "and everywhere they went there was devastation by fire and sword, and towns and temples were burned."[17] The oracle and temple of Apollo at Abai was plundered and set ablaze. However, the god is reported to have saved his oracle at Delphi by a series of miracles: moving his sacred weapons outside the temple, throwing boulders down upon the Persians, and unleashing two colossal hoplites, local heroes, to cut them down as they fled.[18] This did not prevent the advance through Boiotia, where the cities of Thespeia and Plataia were sacked, and into Attica, where Athens fell. Only a few holdouts had remained, barricading themselves on the Akropolis behind their own "wooden wall," at which the Persians fired flaming missiles from the Areopagus. Taking the summit, the Persians left no one alive, stripped the temple of its treasures, and burnt it to the ground.[19]

---

[14] Herodotos 7.220.

[15] Herodotos 7.141; trans. Godley, and reproduced by De Selincourt and Marincola.

[16] Herodotos 8. 41.

[17] Herodotos 8.32.

[18] Herodotos 8.36–9. In fact, a Persian attack on Delphi seems very unlikely, since the majority of the members of the Delphic Amphiktyonia, the league that controlled the sanctuary, had sided with Xerxes. We must suppose, therefore, that the miracle stories were disseminated afterwards as a means of absolution. Later, Herodotos (9.42) has Mardonius explain that Delphi was spared because of a prophecy that "the Persians will come to Greece, sack the temple at Delphi, then perish to a man. Very well then, knowing that, we shall keep clear of the temple and make no attempt to plunder it, and so we shall avoid destruction."

[19] Herodotos 8.51–5.

Learning of the sack of Athens, the commanders of the allied Greek fleet anchored at Salamis debated the best course of action.[20] The Peloponnesians determined to leave, to defend their own lands. They were briefly persuaded to stay by the arguments advanced by Themistokles that they might do this better from the narrows at Salamis rather than in the open sea, where the Persians' greater numbers and swifter ships would have the advantage. Themistokles' ruse, not his words, forced them to fight: he sent a secret envoy to reveal to the Persians that the Peloponnesians were set to sail away and to pretend that the Athenians would then change sides, so that the enemy fleet was drawn forward into the straits, blocking both exit routes. A Tenian warship, deserting the Persians, persuaded the Peloponnesians of the new situation, and "for this service the name of the Tenians was afterwards inscribed on the tripod at Delphi among the other states that helped to defeat the invader."[21] Xerxes had also taken counsel, and was advised by all but a woman, Artemisia of Halikarnassos, to attack the Greek fleet. And so he did, watching the engagement from Mt Aigaleos.[22]

According to Herodotos, the thirty ships of the Aiginetans were the most successful of the allies, followed closely by the Athenians, whose 180 ships had comprised half the Greek fleet. The Persian fleet was perhaps twice as large, but lost momentum early, its front line being pushed back by the Greeks. Ships on both sides were rammed and sank, and while Greeks swam to safety, the majority of Persians could not swim and were drowned. Persian ships that were not rammed turned and sailed into their own second line, while those who made it through were ambushed in the narrows by the Aiginetans. Xerxes recognized his defeat and feared that the Greeks might sail from there to the Hellespont and cut his bridges. The King of Kings prepared to return home forthwith, sending his fleet ahead of the army, which marched north along the same route that it had taken south.[23] The Aiginetans, to mark their leading role in the great naval victory, erected a votive to Apollo at Delphi, which took the form of three golden stars raised up on a bronze mast.[24]

As Xerxes returned to Susa, he left an army under Mardonius to winter in Thessalia, to renew the assault on the Greeks the following year. Mardonius sent Alexander of Makedonia as an envoy to the Athenian, to offer favorable terms were they to accept Persian suzerainty. The Athenian reply was delivered in the presence of Spartan ambassadors: they would never relinquish freedom

---

[20] Hammond 1956, offers a compelling reconstruction of the Battle of Salamis, combining the information supplied by ancient authorities with the observations of modern sailors.

[21] Herodotos 8. 82.

[22] Broodbank 2013: 610, envisages Xerxes "enthroned above the battle, look[ing] down on the melee of metal, wood and humanity ... staring unknowingly through the defeat of a day, and deep into the Mediterranean's past."

[23] Herodotos 8. 84–100.

[24] Herodotos 8.122. See also Cook 1914–25: I, 761, and below at chapter three, for astral connotations.

for Persian gold.²⁵ The war was renewed, but by the time Mardonius reached Athens the city had once again been abandoned by its citizens, who fled to Salamis.²⁶ Messengers were sent to the Spartans, who were then celebrating the Hyakinthia, an annual festival held at the Temple of Apollo Amyklaios.²⁷ After a delay of ten days, although the Hyakinthia lasted only three, the Spartans "dispatched a force of 5,000 Spartiates, each man attended by seven helots, under the command of Pausanias, son of Kleombrotos."²⁸ The Athenian envoys returned north accompanied by another 5,000 men from outlying Lakedaimonian or Lakonian towns and villages. Mardonius received news of the mobilization from an Argive runner, provoking him to put Athens to the torch and abandon Attica for Thebes, a friendly polis with good ground for cavalry operations.

The Persian forces arrived to the north of the River Asopos, where they encamped and constructed a wooden stockade. The Peloponnesian forces, having also arrived in Boiotia, encamped on the lower slopes of Mt Kithairon.²⁹ They were drawn up to the east of the modern village of Kriekouki, where at a temple to Demeter the diviner Teisamenos predicted success if the Greeks fought a defensive action.³⁰ An initial skirmish between a Persian cavalry squadron and Megarians, relieved by a troop of Athenians, led to the death of a leading Persian, Masistios.³¹ Sensing an advantage, and seeking a supply of water, the Greeks descended a little towards the river, drawing up on the Asopos ridge, between the Persians and the Gargaphia spring.

> Presently the whole Greek army was arrayed as I will show, both the later and the earliest comers. On the right wing were 10,000 Lakedaimonians; 5,000 of these, who were Spartiates, had a guard of 35,000 light-armed helots, seven appointed for each man. The Spartans chose the Tegeans for their neighbors

---

²⁵ Herodotos 8.143–4.

²⁶ Cf. Diodoros Sikeliotes 11.28: "And Mardonius was so angry with them [the Athenians] that he ravaged the entire countryside, razed the city to the ground, and utterly destroyed the temples that were still standing."

²⁷ Herodotos 9.7; Flower and Marincola 2002: 110.

²⁸ Herodotos 9.10; Flower and Marincola 2002: 117–18.

²⁹ The topography of the battlefield and the relative dispositions of troops have long fascinated scholars. See Grundy 1894; Pritchett 1957; Pritchett 1979; Barron 1988: 599; Shepherd 2012. Most believe Herodotos had visited the site of the battlefield, so detailed and accurate are his topographical descriptions, in contrast, for example, to his descriptions of the Battle of Marathon. Cartledge 2013: 115 is skeptical that the we can identify the exact location of the battle, although even he supplies a rather specific "Sketch Map of the Plataea Battle, Middle Phase," after Shepherd 2012.

³⁰ Herodotos 9.36. Remarkably, a partial inscription, apparently attesting to the presence of a certain Teisamenos, a name otherwise unattested in Boiotia, was discovered at Kriekouki, the site of the temple to Demeter, and hence confirmed as the second Spartan encampment. See Pritchett 1979; and Boedeker 1995: 219–20, for Simonides' account of Teisamenos. Flower and Marincola 2002: 322 offer the "tantalising suggestion" that the inscription may also have named Aimnestos, the slayer of Mardonius.

³¹ Herodotos 9.20–5. The struggle over Masistius' body echoes that over Leonidas' at Thermopylai, and both in turn evoke the Homeric struggle for the body of Patroklos at Troy. See Flower 1998: 376; Flower and Marincola 2002: 139–45.

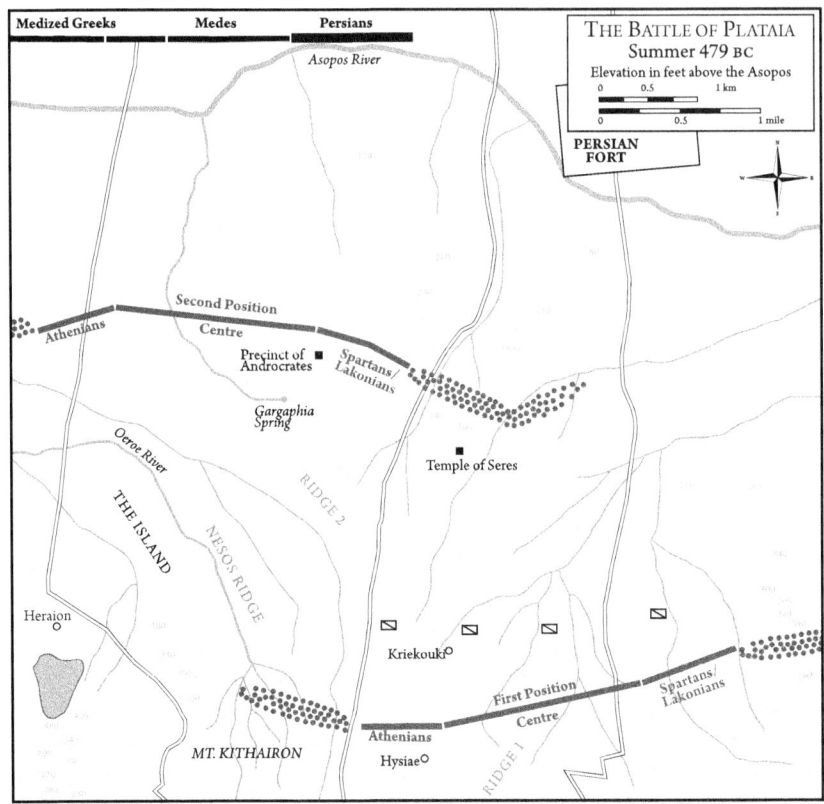

MAP 2 The Site of the Battle of Plataia.

in the battle, both to do them honor and for their valor; there were of these 1,500 men-at-arms. Next to these in the line were 5,000 Corinthians, at whose desire Pausanias permitted the 300 Potidaians from Pallene then present to stand by them. Next to these were 600 Arkadians from Orchomenos, and after them 3,000 men of Sikyon. By these 1,000 Troizenians were posted, and after them 200 men of Lepreon, then 400 from Mykene and Tiryns, and next to them 1,000 from Phlios. By these stood 300 men of Hermione. Next to the men of Hermione were 600 Eretrians and Styrians; next to them, 400 Chalkidians; next again, 500 Amprakiotes. After these stood 800 Leukadians and Anaktorians, and next to them 200 from Pale in Kephallenia; after them in the array, 500 Aiginetans; by them stood 3,000 men of Megara, and next to these 600 Plataians. At the end, and first in the line, were the Athenians who held the left wing. They were 8,000 in number, and their general was Aristides son of Lysimachos.[32]

---

[32] Herodotos 9.28. The English translation given here is adapted from Godley 1920.

To this list, which Herodotos calculates as 38,700 men-at-arms, excluding the helots, he adds 34,500 auxiliaries, many from Lakonia, and 1,800 Thespeians, whose survivors following Thermopylai were not fully armed, for a total force of 110,000.[33] Herodotos' muster list of those assembled at Plataia can be compared to the list of peoples inscribed on the Serpent Column, which also includes those who fought at Salamis and elsewhere against the Persians (see above, table 1, and figs. 1.8 and 1.9).

Both sides drew up their forces for battle. The Spartiates and their helots,[34] plus other Lakonians, including the Tegeans, took the left wing, the place of honor, facing the Persians. The Athenians claimed the right wing through reference to past victories, notably at Marathon but also against the Thebans, whom they now faced alongside other "Medizing" Boiotians and Thessalians. The Plataians and Megarians were to fight alongside the Athenians. Between them and the Lakonians, the citizens of other Greek poleis were arrayed, including the Corinthians, Sikyonians, Arkadians, and Potidaians, who faced the Medes.[35] The Greeks delayed the engagement for eight days, since their forces were growing daily, until Mardonius attempted to block the Kithairon passes. Two days of skirmishing followed, before Mardonius consulted his commanders and issued an order to prepare for battle at dawn. News of this was passed to the Greeks by Alexander of Makedonia, ostensibly a Persian ally, with the further information that Mardonius was short of supplies and his sacrifices had failed to secure good omens.

As dawn approached, the two sides engaged in troop realignments, deciding at short notice to place contingents opposite those against whom they had experienced greatest success in the past. The Spartans and Athenians swapped wings, but when the Persians and Boiotians responded in kind, they changed back, as did their opponents. Mardonius sent a messenger to challenge Pausanias to commit his Spartans to engage the Persians, but before he received a reply sent his cavalry to harry the front line, firing their bows from the saddle and throwing javelins. The Greeks too were running short of food—those bringing supplies from Peloponnesos had been stopped in the Kithairon passes—and were now denied access to water from the nearby spring. It was agreed that a general withdrawal would take place, to secure the water supply, but as night fell after a day of harrying by the Persian cavalry, the greater part of the Greek army determined to retire to Plataia. Only the Athenians and Spartans, and their immediate allies, held their ground. When they found themselves alone as dawn approached, having failed to agree to secure agreement for a Spartan withdrawal, Pausanias ordered the retreat. The Spartans and their

---

[33] Herodotos 9.30. See Flower and Marincola 2002: 158–64, 326, for commentary on the numbers and organization of troops.

[34] Hunt 1997, demonstrates that the helots fought as part of the Spartan phalanx and were not merely present in a supporting role.

[35] Herodotos 9.31.

Tegean allies took a path across Kithairon to avoid the Persian cavalry, but in plain sight, while the Athenians withdrew across lower ground, hidden by the low hills. Observing the Spartans, Mardonius sent his Persian contingent in pursuit, running and losing formation towards an enemy perceived to be fleeing. The Athenians, turning back to relieve the Spartans, were engaged by the Greek forces allied with the Persians. And so the Spartans and Tegeans spun around to engage the Persians alone,[36] drawing on the Persian infantry, whose armor and training were inadequate to challenge the Peloponnesian hoplites. When Mardonius, mounted on a white charger and surrounded by his thousand-man retinue, fell, the Persian ranks broke and fled.[37] Chasing down the fleeing Persians, who escaped inside a wooden palisade, the Spartans and Tegeans were joined by the Athenians, who broke down the walls and shared in the slaughter and ultimate victory.[38]

"Thus," Herodotos concludes, "the prophecy of the oracle was fulfilled, and Mardonius rendered satisfaction to the Spartans for the killing of Leonidas; and thus too, Pausanias, son of Kleombrotos and grandson of Anaxandrides, won the most glorious victory of all those we know."[39]

The Night Sky over Plataia, Summer 479 B.C.

Historians have for centuries looked to Herodotos to reconstruct the battle of Plataia. Many have visited the battlefield itself for additional clues. But until now none has seen what the Greeks and Persians saw on that occasion. It is possible to do this, at least in reconstruction, if we wish to see today what they saw when looking up to the night sky. For twelve nights in late summer 479 B.C., Greek and Persian armies faced each other across the River Asopos south of Plataia. Herodotos does not provide a date for the battle of Plataia, and it is centuries later that Plutarch (*Aristeides* 19) reports that it took place on the fourth day of Boedromion in the Attic calendar, which corresponded to the twenty-seventh day of Panemos in the Boiotian calendar. Elsewhere, Plutarch gives 3 Boedromion as the date of the battle.[40] That became the date on which the Hellenic council would later meet at Plataia to commemorate the victory, and so it is to be preferred. Diodoros Sikeliotes (11.29) reports similarly that a festival of liberation was held on that date every fourth year at Plataia.[41] It

---

[36] Simonides, in his fragmentary elegy on Plataia (FF 15–16), assigns a prominent role to the Corinthians in the battle. See Flower and Marincola 2002: 318–19.
[37] Herodotos 9.33–63.
[38] Herodotos 9.65–70.
[39] Herodotos 9.64.
[40] Plutarch, *Camillus* 19, which lists a number of dates of famous battles; Plutarch, *On the fame of the Athenians* 7. See Greswell 1862: 405–6; Munro 1926: 339.
[41] It is possible that Simonides' elegy was performed on the first such occasion. However, see Boedeker 1995: 222, who cites those who favor this solution, but notes that there is no fifth-century

can be calculated, following Edward Greswell, that the battle took place on 2 September 479 B.C.[42]

According to Herodotos' account, messengers from Athens had arrived at Sparta during the Hyakinthia festival, and ten days later a Spartan detachment marched for Plataia. Unfortunately, there is no agreement on exactly when this festival, the greatest in the Spartan calendar, took place, and estimates range from late spring to midsummer.[43] In his exhaustive study of the ancient Greek calendars, Greswell observed that the Hyakinthia took place on the sixth, seventh, and eighth days of the lunar month Hekatombeion, so in 479 B.C. he reckoned the festival to have started on 30 July. Consequently, he concluded that the Athenian delegation was made to wait until a Spartan detachment was dispatched ten days later, on 9 August. This delay Greswell attributed to the law that prohibited Spartans from marching to war before the full moon. Herodotos (6.106–7) does indeed report, concerning the Battle of Marathon, that the Spartans refused to take the field until the full moon, "not wanting to break the law."[44] We can confirm that the full moon fell on the night of 9 August 479 B.C., which by Greswell's reckoning was the ninth day of the Attic month Metageinion. Greswell calculated that it would have taken the Spartans seven days, marching at a rate of twelve miles a day, to reach the Isthmus, and this is the earliest that the news of their march would have reached Mardonius in Athens. So one must reckon that the Persian destruction of Athens and their withdrawal began on around 16–17 August, and that the Persians arrived at Plataia, a day and a half's march away, on 20 August. According to Herodotos, both sides sacrificed on the second night, which counting inclusively would

---

evidence for the celebration of the Eleutheria, and suggests a formal reburial for the Greeks who died in the battle in new tombs. See also Flower and Marincola 2002: 315–19.

[42] Greswell 1862: I, 405–18; II, 265–72. This is Julian day 1546713, which corresponds in the Babylonian calendar, employed by the Persians, to 9 Ulūlu in the seventh regnal year of Xerxes. Greswell's calculations can be confirmed using the following online calculators:

Attic calendar: http://www.numachi.com/%7eccount/hmepa/
Julian calendar: http://www.fourmilab.ch/documents/calendar/
Babylonian calendar: http://www.staff.science.uu.nl/~gent0113/babylon/babycal.htm

The online Attic calendar appears to assign months to Julian days according to the system introduced by Meton in 432 B.C., and so does not correspond to the calendar of Solon, which was valid at the time of the battle, and which are used by Greswell. Munro 1926: 300, 329, opted for 27 August, which appears to have been adopted by many without further scrutiny or comment, apparently simply by calculating that the ninth month of the year corresponds to Panemos (or Boedromion). This is odd, as Munro was well aware of the dates of full moons in 480 B.C., which he used for dating the Battle of Thermopylai. Still, most of the following observations would apply if the battle had taken place as early as 27 August or later in September. Most recently, Cartledge 2013: 115, states that Boedromion 4/Panemos 27 would be 19 September, but gives no reasons or calculations. He qualifies this by noting that "at most we can say that [the battle] must have happened several weeks after the end of June, when Mardonius had occupied Athens."

[43] Greswell 1862: 409–10. Flower and Marincola 2002: 110, suggest the festival "usually took place in early summer."

[44] Herodotos 6.1–6–7.

have been 22 August, the night before the new moon. The battle took place eleven days later, on Plutarch's given date of 3 Boedromion, which was also 27 Panemos, and therefore on 2 September 479 B.C.[45]

As the armies postponed battle, sacrifices were performed by Greek and Persian diviners, all seeking evidence that heavenly assistance would be forthcoming. Every night all looked across the river to observe the thousands of fires and torches of the enemy, but also up to the night sky over Plataia, still seeking signs from heaven. And in late August and early September 479 B.C., the sky would have offered clues, for those inclined to see them, to the result of the coming battle. As the sun set each evening, Greeks looking north across the river to the Persian stockade saw above it the northern branch of the Milky Way's arc (fig. 2.1). Beside it was the constellation Draco—*drakon*, the dragon—its head high in the night sky.[46] Through the course of the night, for those who lay awake, fearing the day to come, the great serpent would spiral, its head twisting down towards the earth. When those who had slept woke each morning, wondering whether on that day they would face battle and death, the dragon's head plunged down as if to strike at the Persians, before disappearing with the dawn (fig. 2.2).

From the start of August to the end of September, the arc of the Milky Way galaxy from northeast to southwest dominated the sky above Plataia.[47] In the hours after sunset, as the sky darkened, the spiraling tails of the Milky Way, winding around each other as they appeared to descend towards earth, were clearest as one looked southwest. Four of the five planets that can be seen with the naked eye were clearly visible for periods each night. Venus, the evening star, quickly followed the sun down. Mars and Saturn were then seen after sunset. Later, in the pre-dawn hours, when Mars dipped below the horizon, Jupiter and Saturn were both visible. The Greeks knew Saturn as Chronos and Jupiter as Zeus. Mars was Ares, whose role it was to bring war. He was at this time amidst the spiraling tails of the Milky Way (fig. 2.1).

The constellations visible in the same part of the sky as Mars were Scorpius, descending beneath the horizon as the days passed; above this Sagittarius; and Serpens entwined around the body of Ophiuchus, "the serpent-bearer," also identified as Asklepeios, Apollo's son. The relative positions of the armies may also have seemed telling.[48] As each night passed, the Milky Way, Sagittarius,

---

[45] Greswell 1862: I, 417; II, 265–70.

[46] The Greek constellation Ophis was essentially the same as that we today call Draco, although the latter features one additional star in its tail. See Boutsikas 2011: 307.

[47] The night sky on 27 August 479 B.C., Munro's preferred date for the Battle of Plataia, shared many of the same features as that in September, but the Milky Way and Serpens-Ophiuchus were even more prominent. On 19 September, Cartledge's suggested date, the Milky Way was still highly visible, Saturn stood in the middle of the arc it formed, and Mars was in its spiraling tails to the southwest at sunset. At sunrise Jupiter and the Moon were in close proximity to each other and the Milky Way to the southeast.

[48] See Pritchett 1957: 25; Barron 1988: 600, fig. 50, map.

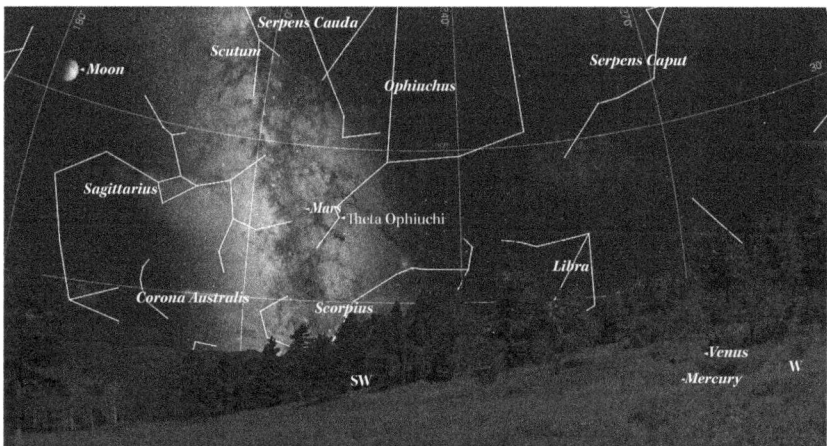

FIGURE 2.1 The night sky above Plataia at sunset on the evening of 1 September 479 B.C. Produced by David Pankenier using Starry Night Pro 6.4.3.

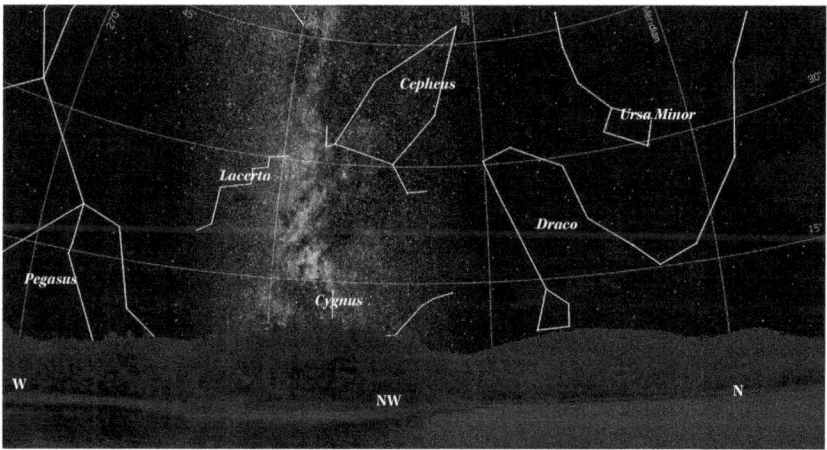

FIGURE 2.2 The night sky above Plataia at sunrise on the morning of 2 September 479 B.C. Produced by David Pankenier using Starry Night Pro 6.4.3.

and the tail of Serpens moved westward and descended in the sky toward the horizon in the hours after sunset. As they disappeared, they will have been immediately above the Greek position as the Persians faced them. The constellation Serpens was known to the Greeks as Ophis, and his coiling form was emphasized in the third century B.C. by Aratos, who reminds us that Ophiuchus' "gleaming shoulders"

> would be clear to mark even at the mid-month moon, but his hands are not at all so bright; for faint runs the gleam of stars along on this side and on that. Yet they too can be seen, for they are not feeble. Both firmly clutch the Serpent,

which encircles the waist of Ophiuchus, but he, steadfast with both his feet well set, tramples a huge monster, even the Scorpion [Scorpius], standing upright on his eye and breast. Now the Serpent is coiled about his two hands—a little above his right hand, but in many folds high above his left. Toward the Crown [Corona Borealis] leans the Serpent's jaw, but beneath his coiling form seek thou for the mighty Claws [Libra]; they are scant of light and nowise brilliant.[49]

Looking to the sky, the Greeks saw a coiling serpent in the grip of its handler, its head reaching above the spiraling Milky Way. They also saw Draco plunging to earth where the Persians were encamped. Were these heavenly signs that the Persian menace would be handled, as the great chthonic beast was defeated, thrown back to the earth whence it came? When the mighty Persian army was indeed defeated and order restored, some may have believed that the outcome was inscribed in the starry sky.

Greeks, Gods, and the Night Sky

Greek observers of the night sky may have seen in the stellar configurations above the battlefield at Plataia an evocation of a cosmic battle in which a serpentine beast was defeated by a tutelary deity and order restored. There is no indication of this conjecture in the written record, but such information is almost never recorded, and therefore absence of testimony is no proof to the contrary. It is possible, however, that a record has been preserved in the form of the Serpent Column, forged after the battle as the spiraling, entwined tails of serpents, and erected on the eastern terrace of the Panhellenic temple to Apollo at Delphi.

Evidence advanced by scholars in the field known as archaeoastronomy— the study of astronomical knowledge and responses to the visible celestial environment in ancient cultures—is only now receiving considered attention from scholars of ancient Greece.[50] That the Greeks took an interest in the movements of the sun and the moon has long been known. More than a century ago, for example, a debate arose over whether Greek temples were oriented east to face the rising sun for cultic reasons. Certain key ideas are well known, for example that sunset was the end of one sacral day and the beginning of another, and that the Olympic games, which lasted for four days, ended on the full moon.

---

[49] Aratos, *Phaenomena* 75–91. This has been interpreted as a poetic rendering of earlier prose descriptions, including those by Eudochos of Knidos, a pupil of Plato. See now Gee 2013: 17: "Aratus is the first author to make the union between astronomy (data) and cosmology (imagination) in a form accessible to many readers."

[50] The most compelling recent treatment is contained in Connelly 2014, a work devoted to the Parthenon, which presents remarkable and pleasing correspondences to arguments worked through in this chapter, all reached independently.

As Greek ritual spaces and landscapes, such as that at Delphi, are reassessed, one anticipates far greater appreciation of the sky and of celestial bodies in ancient cultural history. Many religious festivals or rites had nocturnal aspects, such as the Thesmophoria and the Eleusinian Mysteries, both at Athens, which had associations with blood, death, the underworld, and rebirth.[51] The appearance of the night sky, the heavens, when these annual festivals took place this is an important aspect of the ritual landscape for the experiences of priests, initiates, and other participants. For example, Euripides (*Ion* 1075–80) alludes to the disposition of the stars and moon and how they appear to dance during the Eleusinian Mysteries, referring to the procession of initiates from Athens to Eleusis, which took place on Boedromion 20 (i.e., after sunset on Boedromion 19), therefore generally later in September.[52] A papyrus from Hibeh in Egypt, associated with the temple of Neith at Sais and written ca. 300 B.C., records astronomical observations in relation to festivals for Athena, Prometheus, and Hera.[53] A Hellenistic sundial discovered at Klaros, in Ionia (Asia Minor), suggests that observations were made within a temple to Apollo. While these cannot be taken as proof of such practices two centuries earlier in Greece, the discovery of sundials at two temples, that to Dionysos at Athens and the Amphiareion at Oropos, proves that observations were made in Attica. Moreover, it has been argued that the timing of the great Athenian festival, the Panathenaia, was determined by observation of Ophis/Draco, the constellation most clearly visible from the north porch of the Erechtheion on the Acropolis, where the most important cult offerings took place. According to one ancient account, Draco was created by Athena when during the Gigantomachy she grabbed a huge serpent and thrust it into the sky. Celebrating Athena's role in the Gigantomachy, the battle between the gods and giants, was a central element in the Panathenaia.[54]

There is still more compelling evidence from Lakonia. An ode written in the seventh century B.C., describing a rite that was already then up to three centuries old, proves that astronomical observations were integral to the Spartan festival of Parthenos Orthia, which was timed to take place during the heliacal rising of the Pleiades, at the end of May. A key element of the rite, the "procession of girls," took place in the hour before dawn. Two of the girls are named as the Pleiades, the star cluster that rises just before dawn at the end of May. Agido, one of the named girls, summoned the sun to rise. The altar in the temple of Artemis Orthia at Sparta at the time the ode was composed has been

---

[51] Boutsikas and Ruggles 2011: 56.

[52] Euripides, *Ion* 1075–80: "I am ashamed before the god of many hymns, if he, the sleepless night watcher, shall see the torch procession on the twentieth day, beside the springs with lovely dances, when the starry sky of Zeus also joins in the dance, and the moon dances." See also Cook 1914–25: II.1, 751.

[53] Boutsikas and Ruggles 2011: 56, n. 19.

[54] Boutskias 2011.

excavated. It is oriented on the point at which the Pleiades would have risen above the horizon during this festival.[55]

The appearance of the night sky on the dates set for rites and festivals would change little from year to year, but over centuries the change would be substantial.[56] Moreover, when festivals pertained to more than one city or region, and therefore required the correlation of different calendars, a universally available and acknowledged divine sign might indicate that the time was appropriate for a rite to begin or end. According to Salt and Boutsikas, the heliacal rising—the day on which a star is first visible on the horizon just before dawn—of the constellation Delphinus signaled the return of Apollo to Delphi from his annual sojourn in northern lands, and therefore the time to send queries to the oracle. Since the eastern horizon viewed from Delphi was rather more elevated than at most places in Greece, including Athens and Sparta, Delphinus was visible at the temple about a month later, leaving time for those queries to arrive. This explains why poleis with widely divergent calendars all knew when the oracle would soon be available for consultation, as it was on a single occasion each year.[57]

The heliacal rising of Delphinus at most locations of low elevation in Greece would have occurred in the last week of December each year. It was regular, and even bad weather could not delay its sighting indefinitely. However, ephemeral celestial phenomena were also anticipated and observed. Whether the Athenians sent an annual offering to Apollo at Delphi depended on a divine sign in the heavens. According to Strabo, for three days of three consecutive months, the Pythaistai, priests of Apollo, watched for lightning over Mount Parnes north of Athens. If the sign was seen, then an offering was made.[58] The rite as described is Hellenistic, but its origin appears to predate Apollo's usurpation of Delphi from Zeus, and therefore it retains the lightning bolt, which remained an attribute of the thundering Zeus, but which the archer Apollo also wielded on occasion.

It is a step from these observations to the suggestion that an Archaic Greek artist sought to portray in stylized form a dominant feature of the night sky in bronze. However, it is clear that celestial phenomena appear in Greek art of all periods, becoming ubiquitous in later Greek and Roman art as interest in astrology grew. There are countless representations of Zeus' lightning bolt from the sixth century B.C. and later. Among the most famous was the colossal statue in the council chamber at Olympia, a bolt in each hand, which Pausanias

---

[55] Boutsikas and Ruggles 2011: 60–5.

[56] For example, the altar of the temple of Artemis Orthia was oriented for a declination of the Pleiades of about + 10°, which was roughly accurate to face the rising Pleiades between ca. 1000 and 500 B.C. However, in ca. A.D. 250, when the altar was rebuilt for the final time, the horizon declination of the Pleiades was + 17°, but the altar maintained its original orientation. See Boutsikas and Ruggles 2011: 63.

[57] Salt and Boutsikas 2006.

[58] Cook 1914–25: II.1, 815–16; Boutsikas and Ruggles 2011: 56.

described as standing as late as the second century A.D.⁵⁹ Stellar phenomena may also have appeared early in stylized form. A. B. Cook, in his monumental study of Zeus, long ago suggested that the Temple of Zeus at Olympia, its ceiling "imitating the sky," was probably painted with golden stars.⁶⁰ Cook wrote at length of Zeus as the god of the starry sky and pondered, in typically elegant prose, "What was this 'road of Zeus,' this 'gleaming way' [mentioned in a fragment of Pindar]? If I am not mistaken, it was the broad path of dim and distant splendour that stretches across the abyss of the midnight sky. Our forefathers called it 'Watling Street' or 'London Road." We know it as the 'Milky Way' . . . [and] the world over it has been regarded as a celestial track."⁶¹

To imagine and represent the night sky in such a fashion, as a celestial path or sky river, is indeed ubiquitous. Cultures from Mesopotamia to China to Mesoamerica have imagined and represented the Milky Way in this manner. These same cultures have also seen the path as formed from the twisting tail of a serpentine beast, or as the entwined tails of serpents or dragons, connecting earth to heaven. In Canaanite myth, Anat, the sister or consort of Baal avenges his death by destroying the dragon which "swirled the sea, his double tongue licked the heavens, his twin tails churned up the sea."⁶² No depictions of this survive, to my imperfect knowledge, but the entwined serpentine tails of Fu Xi and Nü Wa, who created heaven and earth, are depicted in numerous media discovered in China, including a silk banner discovered in a tomb at Gaochang (Turfan) (fig. 2.3). As David Pankenier has observed, in this form Fu Xi and Nü Wa each sport one serpentine tail of the sky river, as the Milky Way was known, and "it is precisely from the Northern Cross constellation in Cygnus down through Scorpius that the Milky Way unmistakably bifurcates, like the free ends of the demiurges' tails."⁶³ The silk banner from Turfan dates from ca. A.D. 500, although Pankenier identifies a bicephalic dragon in jade that dates from the Neolithic Hongshan Culture (ca. 4500–2500 B.C.) in northeast China. A similar depiction of the cosmic or plumed serpent in the earliest Mayan murals painted at San Bartolo, El Petén, Guatemala, in c. 100 B.C. Here the serpent is both cosmic monster and road, with footprints depicted on its back. At Chichén Itza, a Mayan fresco shows "a feathered serpent emerging from the elongated body of a sky goddess who may represent the Milky Way."⁶⁴

---

⁵⁹ Pausanias 5. 24, describes a number of statues of Zeus at Olympia, several with bolts, including that in the council chamber. See also Cook 1914–25: II.1, 722–64, especially 731, fig. 663 (our fig. 2.5).

⁶⁰ Cook 1914–25: I, 751–2. The description quoted comes from Propertius, *Elegies*, 3.2.18.

⁶¹ Cook 1914–25: II.1, 37.

⁶² An Ugaritic text, perhaps an incantation to Anat, quoted in translation at Forsyth 1987: 61, with references.

⁶³ Pankenier 2013: 383–403, at 394. He continues: "Their serpentine tails suggest the winding course of the Milky Way, split as it is in places by dark patches of interstellar dust, like islands. The *Sky River*'s gyrations in the sky during the course of the night and through the passing seasons evoke the writhing of a reptilian."

⁶⁴ Milbrath 1999: 275.

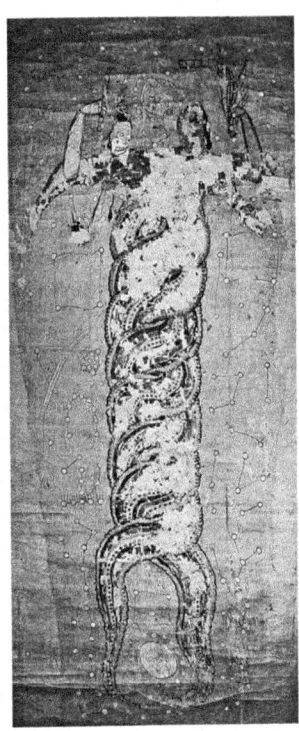

FIGURE 2.3 A silk tomb banner from Gaochang (Turfan), dated ca. A.D. 500, showing Fu Xi and Nü Wa. Photo: Institute of Archaeology, Chinese Academy of Social Sciences.

The Mayan cosmic monster frequently has two serpent heads, for example when represented as a bar held by classic Maya rulers.[65] So close was the association that one of the Mayan names for the Milky Way was *tamacaz*, the fer de lance, a deadly pit viper with a yellow beard native to south and Central America.[66]

It is possible, therefore, that the central bronze pillar of the Plataian tripod was forged as the entwined tails of serpents to portray the Milky Way, which dominated the night sky above Plataia in late summer of 479 B.C. Moreover, there may be a striking and hitherto unnoticed precedent for this brilliant conceit. We have noted that following the battle of Salamis, which took place in the later part of September 480 B.C., the Aiginetans had raised on the eastern terrace at the temple of Delphic Apollo, in the same location as the Plataian tripod would be raised a year later, a votive statue that comprised three golden stars placed high on a bronze mast.[67] The bronze mast appears to evoke an Aiginetan

---

[65] Milbrath 1999: 276–82.
[66] Milbrath 1999: 282–3.
[67] Herodotos 8.122.

ship, and may even have been a mast covered in bronze. However, the golden stars deserve further explanation. Seventy-five years after Salamis, in 405 B.C., the Spartan admiral Lysandros commanded his fleet in its naval victory over the Athenians at Aigospotami, precipitating the end of the Peloponnesian war. According to Plutarch, "There were some who declared that the Dioskouroi appeared as twin stars on either side of Lysandros' ship just as he was sailing out of the harbor against the enemy, and shone out over the rudder-sweeps." In victory, from "the spoils, Lysandros set up at Delphi bronze statues of himself and each of his admirals, as well as golden stars of the Dioskouroi, which disappeared before the battle of Leuktra" (in 371 B.C.).[68] The Dioskouroi, as stars, were installed in the heavens by Zeus as the constellation we call Gemini, and in the erection of his votive at Delphi, Lysandros appears to have emulated quite deliberately the actions of the Aiginetans after the earlier great naval battle at Salamis.[69]

The Dioskouroi are not known to have been worshipped with special devotion at Aigina, so it is important to note that the constellation of Gemini was to be seen in the sky above Salamis throughout the campaign season of 480 B.C., rising to the east around four hours before sunrise and reaching its zenith in late morning. Gemini would not have been visible during daylight hours, but each morning before dawn it was clear to all, between a line of visible planets, including Jupiter, Mars, and Venus. According to Aischylos, who took part in the campaign, the night before the battle of Salamis was especially dark, which played a role in the tactics employed by both sides, and would also have made the appearance of the stars, visible planets, and moon all the more striking.[70] On 23 and 24 September, by most estimates the beginning of the week in which the battle of Salamis took place,[71] the waning gibbous moon passed through Gemini, making it among the brightest areas in the night sky.[72] On 25 September, which has been advanced as the date of the battle, the moon, then entering its last quarter, rose exactly beneath and aligned with the two brightest stars in Gemini, the heads of the brothers, Kastor (Castor)

---

[68] Plutarch, *Lysandros*, 12, 18. This is noted by Cook 1914–25: I, 761–2, who refers also to Cicero, *De divinatione* 1.75.

[69] Cook 1914–25: I, 761–75.

[70] Aischylos, *Persians* 355–70, 425–30. Sacks 1976, calculates the date of the battle as 28 September, when the sky was darker than on preceding nights, since the moon rose much later. This seems to place a little too much weight on Aischylos' verse, which does not state that the night was darker than others, just that it was dark.

[71] The battle took place "a few days" before Xerxes' withdrawal from Attica. Kleombrotos, the Spartan general, failed to give chase because his sacrifice was answered by a solar eclipse, which we know to have occurred on 2 October 480 B.C. See Herodotos 8.113, 9.10, and Sacks 1976: 232. Plutarch, *Camillus* 19, the aforementioned list of famous battles, states that the battle of Salamis took place "around 20 Boedromion," coinciding with the Eleusinian Iacchus procession. In 480 B.C., this occurred on the evening of 22 September and the following morning.

[72] Strauss 2004 proposes 25 September, suggesting that the Persians sailed into the gulf at midnight on 24 September.

and Polydeuces (Pollux), three bright points of light in a dark sky.[73] Since the stars were arrayed vertically, it is possible that they appeared directly behind the mast of an Aiginetan ship as it sailed eastwards towards the Persian fleet. This would explain the form of the votive, if the three "stars" were placed one above the other near the top of the mast in the manner of disks (*phalerae*) placed on later Roman military standards. The votive was intended to represent a heavenly sign of favor offered by the Dioskouroi and a third god, if not the moon then probably, in this context, Apollo himself, who demanded the extra gift as a victor's prize.

Zeus and Typhon, Apollo and Python

The Aiginetans' astral mast and the Plataian tripod were not anthropomorphic statues, in contrast to the other major *agalmata*, wondrous votives, dedicated after the battles of Salamis and Plataia.[74] This in itself suggests a relationship between them, although the form of the Serpent Column differed significantly from the Aiginetans' stellar votive. If its spirals evoked a whole galaxy of stars and planets, our own Milky Way, this serpentine form demands further exploration. The serpentine features of the night sky at Plataia can be read as the cosmic battle of the thundering hero-god Zeus with a chthonic monster, Typhon. As Zeus slew Typhon, following a battle across the sky, so his son Apollo, in a variant of the same myth, slew Typhon's kin, the female dragon Python. These myths were already well known to the Greeks when the battle of Plataia took place, and both are variants of the primordial combat myth.

As Joseph Fontenrose demonstrated in a classic study, variants of the combat myth have been told by diverse peoples for millennia.[75] As Gilgamesh slew Huwawa, guardian monster of the cedar forest, so the Sumerian deity Ninurta, storm god and son of Enlil, slew Asag, a demon who restrained the waters, and Anzu, a lion-bird.[76] The struggle between Ninurta and Asag is echoed in

---

[73] Sacks 1976: 232–3 summarizes the evidence and earlier scholarship relating to the date of the battle, favoring 28 September. On that morning, the waning crescent of the moon was almost extinguished when it rose very late to the east of Salamis in close conjunction with both Mars and Venus, the morning star. These remarkable triplets, however, had no obvious relationship with Gemini, and would not easily be mistaken for "golden stars."

[74] We shall return to this in the following chapter, in exploring archaic bronze-working.

[75] Fontenrose 1959, 1980. Variants can be found to this day. In West Africa, Olokun, god of the sea and waters, is associated in the art of Benin with the mudfish. The Oba, the ruler in Benin, has frequently been represented with twisting mudfish legs, holding entwined mudfish, or wearing a belt with mudfish attachments. An altar tusk in the collection of the Art Institute of Chicago (Gift of Mr. and Mrs. Edwin Hokin, 1976.523) shows several configurations. The ruler, or Oba, like the mudfish that can breathe on land or underwater, rules over both elements, through his connection to Olokun.

[76] Fontenrose 1959, 1980: 146–7; Wakeman 1973: 7–9; Forsyth 1987: 21–66; Lewis 1996; Brown 2000: 56–7, 68–70; Noegel 2007.

the Babylonian creation myth, *Enūma Elish*, where the slayer's role is taken by Marduk, the god of storms and weather.[77] As Ninurta slew Asag and Marduk slew Tiamat, so in two fragments of Old Akkadian cuneiform (CT 13.33-34) Tishpak, chief god of Eshnunna, summoner of storms, slew the lion-serpent Labbu, created by the sea and "offspring of river";[78] so in the Ugaritic *Epic of Baal*, the storm god Baal (Hadad) slew Yam (also *ltn*, "the twisting one," i.e., Leviathan[79]), serpentine god of sea and rivers, and Mot (i.e., Behemoth), the earth-monster;[80] so in Hebrew myth, excised from Genesis but preserved in Psalms, Job, Ezekiel, and Isaiah, Yahweh slew Leviathan (Hebrew: *Liwyatan*, also *Tannin* or *Rahab*, and the Canaanite *Yam*);[81] so in the Hittite (Hattian, Hurrian) New Year (*Puruli*) myth the storm god Tarhun (Taru, Teshub) slew the serpentine Illuyankas.[82] These in turn have correspondences with Egyptian and Indian variants. In the Vedic *Rigveda*, Indra, the god of storms, weather, and war, slew the dragon Vritra, who kept the waters captive;[83] so in the Egyptian *Book of the Dead*, Seth slew Apophis (Apep), the serpent who holds back the sun, Re (Ra).[84]

When the combat myth entered the Greek world, Ninurta and Marduk became Zeus, who slew the serpentine earth monster Typhon, and Apollo, who slew the water dragon Python.[85] The battle between Zeus and Typhon is located by Homer (*Iliad* 2.780–5) in the land of the Arimoi, that is Kilikia, in the vicinity of the Korykian cave. Zeus, "who in his wrath hurled the thunderbolt," in victory cast Typhon into freezing Tartaros, where he dwelt in darkness beneath Mount Etna, occasionally spewing fire. The chthonic creature, dragged from his cave into the heavens, was cast back underground. The battle is referred to by Pindar, in his first *Pythian Ode*, written to celebrate a victory for Hieron of Etna, not simply at the Pythian games staged at Delphi in 474 B.C., but in the battles of Himera and Cumae. There is also an allusion to an eruption of Etna in 476/5 B.C. According to Pindar, the mighty serpentine beast Typhon came from beyond the eastern fringe of Greek lands bordering Persia; he travelled west from Kilikia, where Xerxes had mustered his invasion force in 480 B.C.

---

[77] Fontenrose 1959, 1980: 148–64; Jacobsen 1968; Wakeman 1973: 16–21.

[78] Fontenrose 1959, 1980: 147; Wakeman 1973: 13–14; Wiggermann 1989; Lewis 1996. An online translation, where the text is cited as *CT* 34–5, is included in *Melammu Project: The Intellectual Heritage of Assyria and Babylonia in East and West*: http://www.aakkl.helsinki.fi/melammu/database/gen_html/a0000494.php.

[79] Day 1985: 4–5.

[80] Fontenrose 1959, 1980: 129–38; Wakeman 1973: 37–42; Day 1985: 7–18; Forsyth 1987: 60–1, for variations attributing victory to Anat, Baal's sister/consort.

[81] Wakeman 1973: 56–82.

[82] Fontenrose 1959, 1980: 121–9; Wakeman 1973: 45–7.

[83] Fontenrose 1959, 1980: 194–202; Wakeman 1973: 9–12.

[84] Wakeman 1973: 15–16.

[85] There were many additional variants which Fontenrose examined, including that of Kadmos and Drakon, explored below. See now Ogden 2013, which appeared after this chapter was written.

Typhon floundered in battle with Zeus, to be crushed and cast into the underworld. "Once the famous Kilikian cave nurtured him but now the sea-girt cliffs above Cumae, and Sicily too, lie heavy on his shaggy chest. And the pillar of the sky holds him down, snow-covered Etna, year-round nurse of bitter frost, from whose inmost caves belch forth the purest streams of unapproachable fire."[86] Hieron, who founded a city at Etna and was favored with victory at the Pythian games, had also enjoyed victory in a sea-battle off Cumae (north of Naples, where an entrance to Hades lay[87]). This victory is, in the ode, compared directly with the battles at Salamis and "Kithairon," the mountain backdrop to the Battle of Plataia, "those battles in which the Medes with their curved bows suffered sorely."[88] Apollo was the god of archers, whose wrath one wished not to earn, for, as Teukros had learned (*Iliad* 23.865), it meant defeat or death for bowmen who did not pray for his favor.

The earliest extant account of Apollo slaying Python, which is rather later than the passing reference to Zeus and Typhon in the *Iliad*, is contained in the *Homeric Hymn to Apollo*, generally dated to the sixth century B.C.[89] Here the beast is not named, but her form is revealed: *drakaina*, a she-dragon. The name by which she came to be known is not yet her given name, but we are told that the rotting of her corpse in the hot sun—*pytho*, "to rot"—gave the name to the place, and hence also to the beast.

> With a gasp she breathed out her gory soul, while Phoibos Apollo boasted: "Rot now right here on the man-nourishing earth; you shall not ever again be an evil bane for living men who eat the fruit of the earth that nurtures many, and who will bring hither perfect hecatombs. Against cruel death neither Typhon shall avail you nor ill-famed Chimaira, but here shall the Earth and shining Hyperion make you rot." Thus he spoke boasting, and darkness covered his eyes. And the holy fury of Helios made her rot away; hence the place is now

---

[86] Pindar, *Pythian* 1. See also *Prometheus Bound* (350–74), traditionally attributed to Aischylos, where there is another description of the battle between Zeus and Typhon, and again an allusion to an eruption of Mount Etna in 476/5 B.C.: "Pity moved me, too, at the sight of the earth-born dweller of the Kilikian caves curbed by violence, that destructive monster of a hundred heads, impetuous Typhon. He withstood all the gods, hissing out terror with horrid jaws, while from his eyes lightened a hideous glare, as though he would storm by force the sovereignty of Zeus. But the unsleeping bolt of Zeus came upon him, the swooping lightning brand with breath of flame, which struck him, frightened, from his loud-mouthed boasts; then, stricken to the very heart, he was burnt to ashes and his strength blasted from him by the lightning bolt. And now, a helpless and a sprawling bulk, he lies hard by the narrows of the sea, pressed down beneath the roots of Etna; while on the topmost summit Hephaistos sits and hammers the molten ore. There, one day, shall burst forth rivers of fire with savage jaws devouring the level fields of Sicily, land of fair fruit—such boiling rage shall Typhon, although charred by the blazing lightning of Zeus, send spouting forth with hot jets of appalling, fire-breathing surge."

[87] Depictions of Zeus' battle with Typhon were popular on ceramics produced in southern Italy, and can also be seen in tomb art. See Rupp 2007: 28–32.

[88] Pindar, *Pythian* 1.75–8. This is the same Hieron, ruler of Syracuse, who raised at Delphi both a beautiful statue of a charioteer and a column that emulated the form of the monument to Plataia. See Schoder 1943; Scott 2010: 88–90, 191–2.

[89] *Homeric hymn* 3.355–62. Cf. Ibid., 300–4. See now briefly Graf 2009: 25–32.

called Pytho and men call the lord Apollo by another name, Pythian; because on that spot the power of piercing Helios made the monster rot away.[90]

If not derived from "to rot," the name Python (labial-vowel-dental) requires only a slight transposition of sounds, a metathesis, to derive from Typhon (dental-vowel-labial), the mighty and cruel beast named in the *hymn*.[91] The close relationship between Typhon and the dragoness is only hinted at by Apollo, who boasted that Typhon could not save the she-dragon. Typhon had been entrusted to the *drakaina* by "cow-eyed, mighty Hera," his mother according to the hymn, who had brought him forth having struck the Earth in anger at Zeus, when Zeus gave birth to Athena from his head. Hera, "piling evil upon evil," gave Typhon to the *drakaina* to suckle, which she did in the Korykian cave in Kilikia.[92] In related myths, Typhon was not Hera's child, but the offspring of Earth (Ge); or the dragoness was not only Typhon's nursemaid, but his sibling, or his wife, also called Echidna, meaning Viper. Typhon was the father of Echidna's polycephalous offspring, Orthos, Kerberos, Chimaira, and Hydra.[93]

Typhon's form is discussed more fully than Python's, and both written and visual depictions survive. Typhon is called *drakon*, dragon (the masculine of *drakaina*), and *hemither*, half-beast, half-human. His theriomorphic lower half consisted of one or more serpentine tails, and his human upper half featured still more snakes, projecting either from a hand or his shoulders.[94] Hesiod's description of Typhon is the fullest to predate any known visual representation:

> Strength was with his hands in all that he did and the feet of the strong god were untiring. From his shoulders grew a hundred heads of a snake, a fearful dragon, with dark, flickering tongues, and from under the brows of his eyes in his marvelous heads flashed fire, and fire burned from his heads as he glared. And there were voices in all his dreadful heads, which uttered every kind of sound unspeakable.[95]

Apollodoros (1.6.3) offered a rather different description in the second century B.C.:

> When the gods had overcome the giants, Earth, still more enraged, had intercourse with Tartaros and brought forth Typhon in Kilikia, a hybrid between man and beast. In size and strength he surpassed all the offspring of Earth. As far as the thighs he was of human shape and of such

---

[90] *Homeric hymn* 3.364–74. Cf. Pausanias 10.6.5.
[91] Fontenrose 1959, 1980: 91–2. But see Ogden 2013: 151–3. The name Typhon appears in many forms, including Typhaon, Typhoeus and Typhos, and "Typhon" may not pre-date the first use of "Python."
[92] *Homeric hymn* 3.349–55. Cf. Ibid., 305; Fontenrose 1959, 1980: 72–3.
[93] Fontenrose 1959, 1980: 77–93.
[94] *LIMC*, and *IDD*, s.v. Typhon, identify five phenotypes, two of which feature Typhon alone and three in combat with Zeus.
[95] Hesiod, *Theogony* 8.22–7.

prodigious bulk that he out-topped all the mountains, and his head often brushed the stars. One of his hands reached out to the west and the other to the east, and from them projected a hundred dragons' heads. From the thighs downward he had huge coils of vipers, which when drawn out, reached to his very head and emitted a loud hissing. His body was all winged, unkempt hair streamed on the wind from his head and cheeks, and fire flashed from his eyes. Such and so great was Typhon when, hurling kindled rocks, he made for the very heaven with hissings and shouts, spouting a great jet of fire from his mouth.[96]

The oldest extant visual representations of Typhon do not have the human feet and polyanguid shoulders described by Hesiod, nor do they match Apollodoros' description in all its parts, notably omitting the hundred-headed hands. Several Corinthian *alabastra*—small, perfumed oil containers—of the seventh century B.C. show Typhon with a single human upper body and a single serpentine tail.[97] An example in the collection of the Yale University Art Gallery shows Typhon, painted in red and black, with a single human head facing to the viewer's right; he is bearded, with long, curly black hair emerging from beneath a cap or diadem to cover the nape (fig. 2.4). Typhon's upper body has no serpents emerging from his hands or shoulders, but he has two wings curving gracefully upwards behind his arms. Below Typhon's waist, where his short tunic ends, a single serpentine tail curves out to the right before looping back to the left. In some similar representations, the tail coils upwards around the vessel, passing across the upper body and ending in a snake's head.

On a Chalcidian black-figured *hydria*, a large water vessel painted in around 550 B.C., now in the Staatliche Antikensammlungen in Munich, Zeus is shown in battle with Typhon (fig. 2.5). The god is named, although his identity is clear from the lightning bolt he holds high in his right hand. Typhon sports a mane of long red hair and beard through which a pointed horse ear pokes. His shoulders, reaching to the sky, have wings formed from scales and ending in feathers, all in black and red. Two muscular black arms reach across his chest and abdomen, and below the cinched waist of his yellow chiton project two serpent tails, curled and entwined to form three loops. One tail is striped, while the other has a regular pattern of red keyholes against a black background. Both patterns appear to emulate those on living snakes.

At Athens, Typhon was imagined with three anthropomorphic upper bodies and three entwined serpentine tails. Euripides (*Herakles*, 1271) later called

---

[96] Apollodoros, *Library* 1.6.3.
[97] For example, University of Iowa Museum of Art, 1971.273, which can be seen at: http://digital.lib.uiowa.edu/u/?uima,20968.

It is described by Moon 1980, at Perseus: http://www.perseus.tufts.edu/hopper/text?doc=Perseus%3Atext%3A1999.04.0045%3Aentry%3D10.

A similar example was sold by Christie's in December 2007: http://www.christies.com/LotFinder/lot_details.aspx?intObjectID=5004880.

FIGURE 2.4 Corinthian *alabastron* showing Typhon, seventh century B.C., Erlenmeyer Painter. The Harold A. Strickland, Jr, Collection, 1998.23.2, Yale University Art Gallery.

him *trisomatos*, triple-bodied, and just such a triple-bodied demon (*trisomatos daimon*) appeared in sculptural form on the Hekatompedon, the temple on the Athenian acropolis that was erected in c. 560 B.C. and destroyed by the Persian invaders (fig. 2.6).[98] The resemblance between Typhon of the alabastra and the *trisomatos daimon* is striking. The resemblance between Typhon's entwined tails and the form of the Serpent Column seems equally compelling.

Chaos Contained

The *Homeric Hymn to Apollo*, which first reports Apollo's battle with the *drakaina*, dwells on the Cretans who accompanied the god in finding Delphi,

---

[98] Hurwit 1999: 108–9, for discussion of the "Bluebeard aguiped," and whether he was Typhon. See also Rupp 2007: 30; Spivey 2013: 158–9, following a hypothesis of John Boardman, wonders whether "Bluebeard" is a symbol for the union of the three peoples of Attica, peoples of the shore, hills, and plain, united by Peisistratros (Herodotos 1.59). Connelly 2014: 54–5 presents a compelling argument that complements my own.

FIGURE 2.5 Chalcidian black-figured *hydria*, a large water vessel painted in around 550 B.C., showing Zeus battling Typhon. Staatliche Antikensammlungen und Glyptothek, Munich/Renate Kühling.

following a tour around central Greece.[99] The foundation of a city following the defeat of the dragon is an important variant of the combat myth, which is most captured clearly in the myth of Kadmos and the foundation of Thebes.[100] Although Kadmos had appeared in myths related to the abduction of Europa and the invention of Greek letters,[101] the myth of his foundation of Thebes appears to be no older than that of Delphi's foundation by Apollo, which is first recorded in the same *Homeric Hymn to Apollo*. The first extant version of Kadmos slaying Drakon, the dragon, and founding Thebes is told in Euripides' *Phoenician Women*, which in its details apparently follows the account presented

---

[99] See Graf 2009 on this; on Cretan bronze deposited at Delphi in the eighth century B.C., see Morgan 1990: 142–6, who posits that it came via Corinth, which had established links with Crete.

[100] Fontenrose 1959, 1980: 274–320. See now Ogden 2013: 291–2.

[101] The early Greeks called their alphabet, which is not attested before the eighth century, Phoenician or Kadmean letters, because according to legend Kadmos appeared with his Phoenician followers bringing the alphabet. Kadmos, according to a theory reprised at Morris 1992: 153, means simply eastern, deriving from Semitic QDM. See also Fontenrose 1959, 1980: 307–8, n. 60, refuting those who have denied the eastern connection.

FIGURE 2.6 Bluebeard, a triple-bodied demon (*trisomatos daimon*) that adorned the Hekatompedon, a temple erected on the Athenian acropolis in ca. 560 B.C. Hekatompedon pediment, full view, Acropolis Museum, Athens/Socratis Mavrommatis.

by Hellanikos, a contemporary of Herodotos whose work is preserved only in fragments.[102] Details were far later incorporated into *Ethnika* by Stephanos of Byzantion, in the sixth century A.D., and Hellanikos' account was still available to Photios in the tenth century A.D. in Constantinople, also a city founded twice, and where the Serpent Column then stood.

The Kadmos story that was written down in a form known to us only in the fifth century cannot be shown to predate the myth of Apollo and Python.[103] Nor is the iconography devoted to Kadmos and the dragon much older than that. However, the story of Kadmos was greatly elaborated upon by both Greek and Roman authors, and the story of his dragon-slaying was given greater prominence both in texts and art, notably as told by Apollodoros (3.4) and Nonnos. In Nonnos' account, Kadmos was sent forth to find the cow by the Pythian oracle, which led him first past the very spot where Apollo had slain Python.[104] And when he was locked in battle with Drakon, standing upright, wrapped up in the serpent's coils, Athena appeared to harangue him with a recollection of the slaying of Typhon. By Ovid's telling, Drakon had three tongues, and his sharp teeth formed three rows.[105] His writhing coils were pierced with Kadmos' javelin, which at first he could not shake free, before the hero plunged it once again through his neck, suspending him from a tree. Sowing the dragon's teeth,

---

[102] Euripides, *Phoinissai*, 638–75, 930–44, 1060–5. The Kadmos myths were studied critically, and somewhat controversially, by Vian 1963, who is among those to deny the derivation of Kadmos from QDM. Edwards 1973, focusses on the value of the myths for the study of the Mycenaean age, but offers useful general commentary.

[103] This was stated by Gomme 1913.

[104] Nonnos, *Dionysiaka* 4. 315–19, 356–420. See also Ovid, *Metamorphoses* 3; Pausanias 9.12.

[105] Ovid, *Metamorphoses* 3.34: "tres vibrant linguae, triplici stant ordine dentes." Later (7.150), a triple-tongued dragon guards the golden fleece.

the Spartoi, armed warriors, grew immediately, spear-points first, from the Theban soil and fought each other until only five survived. The five would help Kadmos raise Thebes' mighty walls.[106]

The combat myth remained vital through the Middle Ages, renewed and refreshed by new variants. For Christians, the original battle between Yahweh and Leviathan, the twisting, coiling serpent of the deep, was the true and original version of the combat myth.[107] The tale of Leviathan's defeat in the creation of the cosmos is excised from Genesis 1, but preserved in numerous passages in the Old Testament, notably in Psalms, Job, Ezekiel, and Isaiah.[108] At Isaiah 27:1, we learn: "In that day, the Lord will punish with his sword, his fierce, great and powerful sword, Leviathan the gliding serpent, Leviathan the coiling serpent; he will slay the monster of the sea."[109] At Isaiah 51:9–10, Leviathan is Rahab: "Was it not you [Lord] that hewed Rahab, that pierced the dragon? Was it not you that dried up the sea, the waters of the great deep?" When Leviathan appears at Job 40–1, the beast of the sea is joined by Behemoth, an earth monster: "His tail sways like a cedar; the sinews of his thighs are close-knit. His bones are tubes of bronze, his limbs like rods of iron. He ranks first among the works of God, yet his Maker can approach him with his sword." [110]

Leviathan is later taken as a metaphor for Pharaoh, ruler of Egypt, who enslaved the elect as the beast had enslaved the waters.[111] Thus, at Ezekiel 32, a speech is addressed to Pharaoh:

> "You are like a lion (*kepir*)[112] among the nations; you are like a monster (*tannin*) in the seas thrashing about in your streams, churning the water with your feet and muddying the streams." This is what the Sovereign Lord says: "With a great throng of people I will cast my net over you, and they will haul you up in my net. I will throw you on the land and hurl you on the open field. I will

---

[106] The motif of warriors growing from the sown teeth of a mighty serpent features also in Apollonios, *Argonautika* 3.401–21, 492–501; Ovid, *Metamorphoses* 7.120–58.

[107] Forsyth 1987: 68–71, 87–9, 358–83, illustrates the position of Christian apologists that their scripture gave rise to the pagan myths, which were corruptions and misunderstandings of the truth. See also Eusebios of Caesarea, *Preparatio evangelica*, 1.10. 35–44, who reports on a "Phoenician" text by a certain Sancuniathon, which was translated into Greek by Philo of Byblos (d. ca. A.D. 140).

[108] Wakeman 1973: 56–82, collects all references to "The Sea Monster," Rahab, Leviathan, and Tannin. See, for example, Psalm 74.12–14: "But you, O God, are my king from of old; you bring salvation upon the earth. It was you who split open the sea by your power; you broke the heads of the monster in the waters. It was you who crushed the heads of Leviathan and gave him as food to the creatures of the desert." Psalm 89.10: "You rule over the surging sea; when its waves mount up, you still them. You crushed Rahab like one of the slain; with your strong arm you scattered your enemies."

[109] Isaiah 27.1.

[110] Job 40.15–19. Day 1985: 62–87, rejects the claims that Job here is referring to actual creatures, the crocodile and hippopotamus, exaggerating their natures by association with Leviathan and Behemoth.

[111] Wakeman 1973: 73–5; Day 1985: 88–95, 139–40.

[112] Lewis 1996: 38, n. 70, observes that "The majority of LXX [Septuagint] manuscripts render [Hebrew] *kepir* by [Greek] *leon* and *tannin* by *drakon*. It should be noted that, on two occasions (Job 4:10; 38:39), LXX translators chose *drakon* to translate *kepir*."

let all the birds of the air settle on you and all the beasts of the earth gorge themselves on you. I will spread your flesh on the mountains and fill the valleys with your remains. I will drench the land with your flowing blood all the way to the mountains, and the ravines will be filled with your flesh. When I snuff you out, I will cover the heavens and darken their stars."[113]

As Mary K. Wakeman has observed, "The [primordial combat] myth consists of *all* its versions."[114] Even within each tradition and variant there are variations, of which the most striking is an apparent inconsistency: the beast is destroyed and its power dissipated; but the beast is captured its power contained. This is captured most clearly in the Greek myths in the distinct fates of Python, who is slain and left to rot, and Typhon, who is imprisoned beneath Etna, returned to his chthonic state in captivity. In the Babylonian epic, Tiamat is both killed and captured, her corpse split in two, her power set free but also contained. Similarly, in the *Rig Veda* (1.32) Indra "slew the serpent then discharged the waters … He slew the serpent lying on the mountain." But in the *Shatapatha Brahmana*, Vritra begs, "You are what I was before … only cut me in two, but do not let me be annihilated."[115] Tension is felt, evidently, in containing the chaos beast's power, which is resolved by the champion absorbing that power, sublimating its destructive force into constructing order. But the champion is also now mighty and terrible, the beast within him and its markers about him.[116] Ninurta, having slain his lion-serpent, declares, "I am the lord, I am the lion of the pure heavens, the foremost lion. [Ninurta] with the power of a lion, the overpowering great serpent."[117] Ninurta has become the lion-serpent.

There is a local version of the combat myth that captures this tension and ties it directly to the Greek victories over the Persians at Salamis and Plataia. Diodoros Sikeliotes (4.72.4) records that Salamis, a daughter of the Theban river god Asopos, "was seized by Poseidon and taken to an island which bore her name; there she lay with Poseidon and gave birth to Kychreus, who became king of the island and gained fame by his slaying a huge snake which was killing the inhabitants of the island."[118] According to Pausanias (1.36.1), "It is said that while the Athenians were engaged in the sea-fight with the Medes, a serpent appeared among the ships, and the god announced to the Athenians that this serpent was the hero Kychreus," who had evidently taken on the form

---

[113] Ezekiel 32.2–6. Lewis 1996: 38–9, supplies an alternative translation with notes.
[114] Wakeman 1973: 4.
[115] Wakeman 1973: 9–10, 21–2. They are patronized similarly: Tvashtri is the creator of Vritra and of Indra's weapons; El supports Yam and Mot, but sends Baal against them.
[116] Wakeman 1973: 49–51; Lewis 1996: 42–3.
[117] Lewis 1996: 43.
[118] The story is perhaps as old as Hesiod, although a fragment preserved by Strabo tells a slightly different tale. See Neils 2013 for references.

and characteristics of the creature he slew. It has recently been suggested that Kychreus appears on the famous Pella Hydria, as a man holding a snake and a battle trumpet, an Athenian motif for the victory at Salamis.[119]

By this interpretation, therefore, the Plataian tripod proved that the chaos unleashed by the Persians had been contained by the victory at Plataia. Its bronze core took the form of Typhon, a three-bodied serpentine monster, and it represented also Python, Typhon's female counterpart. The triple-braided twisting form, rising from the earth, evoked the chthonic nature of both creatures, ripped from their subterranean lairs, forced into the sky by thundering hero-gods, Zeus and Apollo, before being cast back upon, or beneath, the earth. These cosmic battles, variants of the same primordial struggle, could be seen in the starry sky above Plataia, in the constellations Ophis/Serpens-Ophiuchus which flanked the spiraling tails of the Milky Way. When the destructive advance of the Persian army was ended at Plataia, the arms and armor of the Persians were subsumed into the bronze column. Apollo's golden tripod sat atop the entwined serpents, his power over the oracle at Delphi derived from his slaying Python, her corpse left to rot but her power contained and wielded by the champion god.

Ninĝišzida and the God on the Serpent Throne

A series of Greek perspectives has to this point been presented to support an interpretation of the form of the Serpent Column. However, it is important to note that the Persian army saw the same night sky at Plataia from a different position. The Persians told variants of the same combat myth, transmitted and adapted in a similar manner to that of the Greeks. As a coda, at the least, in a chapter of cultural biography, these Persian perspectives deserve consideration. Moreover, as will become clear, a remarkable precedent for the form of the Serpent Column exists in Mesopotamian art, although no direct link between this and the column can be demonstrated, despite strong and clear evidence for Near Eastern influence on archaic Greek art.

At the time of the Battle of Plataia, Mesopotamian astronomy-astrology was far more sophisticated than that practiced by the Greeks; indeed, the detailed observational and recording techniques established by the Babylonians, notably those called Chaldeans, were later emulated by the Greeks, certainly by the Hellenistic period.[120] Among the cuneiform astronomical texts, the best known are MUL.APIN, a composite text that begins with a catalogue of stars and

---

[119] Neils 2013. See also Livanos 2011: 130, 138.

[120] Babylonian astronomy-astrology has a large and specialist literature, and not a few controversies. Hunger and Pingree 1999 summarizes the state of the field at that time, including major contributions by those authors, and includes full commentary on the astronomical diaries. Brown 2000, whose book has been described as "startlingly original," argues against Hunger and Pingree that there was

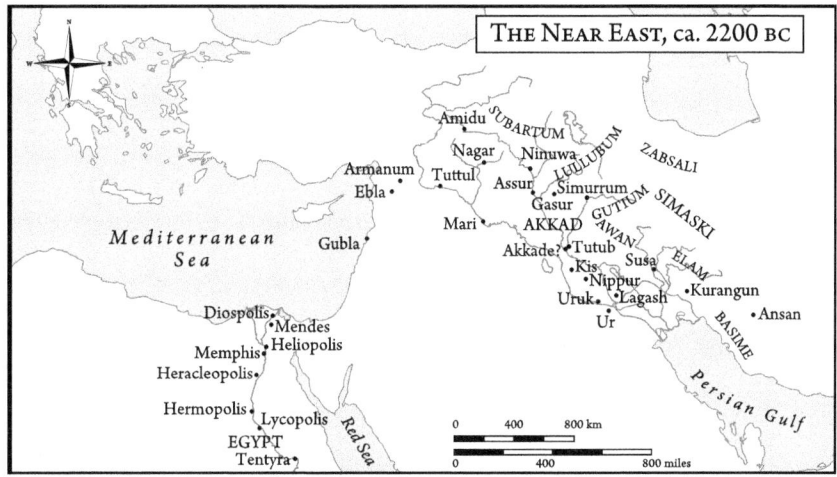

MAP 3 The Near East in the Age of Gudea of Lagash.

ends with a list of omens, and the *Enūma Anu Enlil*, a series of seventy tablets setting out around 7,000 omens in four categories: lunar omens, solar omens, meteorological omens, and omens of stars and planets.[121] Both were produced originally between 2000 and 1000 B.C., but were revised and updated thereafter. In addition, Babylonian astronomical diaries, in the form of cuneiform tablets, were produced certainly in the eighth century B.C., and have survived from the middle of the seventh century—the earliest is dated to −651, according to the astronomical dating convention, which corresponds to 652 B.C.—and although none has yet been dated definitively to the reign of Xerxes, at least three survive from that of his son Artaxerxes (465–424 B.C.).[122] Scribes listed observed astronomical and meteorological data alongside historical events, extrapolating likely connections for future divination.[123]

Herodotos reports that the principal reason the Persians waited for eleven days and twelve nights was their failure to secure good omens for launching

---

no division to be drawn between astronomical and astrological observations, with all empirical recording of observed phenomena intended principally to aid in the prediction of celestial phenomena and divination. The importance of understanding Babylonian astronomical-astrological materials in their own contexts, rather than choosing elements which suit a western history of science, is emphasized by Rochberg 1999. The astronomical diaries have been edited and translated, starting with Sachs and Hunger 1988, which is for the astronomical years −651 to −261 (652–262 B.C.).

[121] See Swerdlow 1998: 2. Mars was also the Plough Star, which appears as the first line of, MUL. APIN. *Enūma Anu Enlil* is named from its incipit, "When the gods Anu and Enlil . . ."

[122] Sachs and Hunger 1988; Rochberg-Halton 1991.

[123] Surely the most famous records are those for months VI and VII of the reign of Darius III, corresponding to 330 B.C., which report a lunar eclipse on 20 September, during which Saturn was visible close to the moon and Jupiter set in the west, and that Darius' army was defeated at the Battle of Arbela (Gaugamela) by Alexander the Great, who proceeded to enter Babylon. See Sachs and Hunger 1988: 176–9; Swerdlow 1998: 21–2.

an attack. Although his account refers to sacrifice rather than to astronomical observation, the two practices were entwined.[124] Herodotos explains much by reference to oracles and omens, but in this case he places greater emphasis on its significance for decision-making, since the Persians were short of supplies and the Greek forces were increasing as they waited. If the principal reason for Mardonius' delay was the Greeks' unwillingness to descend to the plain, still we cannot dismiss explicit testimony that he considered the omens carefully in postponing further provocations and skirmishing.

Omens were signs from the gods, used to advise kings on the best course of action. Consequently, to avert predicted misfortunes, apotropaic (*namburbû*) rituals, magic, might be performed.[125] It was standard for Mesopotamian diviners to compare terrestrial and celestial portents, the scrutiny of entrails (extispicy), in particular the liver (hepatoscopy), and of the heavens (astrology), seeking correspondences and contradictions.[126] We cannot recover the livers of the sacrificed animals, but we can see what the Persian astronomer-astrologers saw. The visibility of planets and the moon, as well as their apparent interactions with stars and constellations, was ominous. If, as we believe, the Battle of Plataia took place on 9 Ulūlu, then there were four planets and the moon visible to the naked eye in the night sky, each interacting with each other and with other celestial bodies. Venus, known as Delebat, presided over Ulūlu. Delebat, the planet, when it appeared as the morning star was female and bore signs and omens from Ishtar, also known as the goddess Inana, but as the evening star was male, bearded, and a god of war.[127] An Old Babylonian prayer of the diviner, the haruspex or *barû*, addresses the evening star as Ninsianna (later Ninana, from which Inana derives), usually female but in the prayer a male stellar deity, asking for favorable signs in his inspection of entrails.[128] Mars was Ṣalbatānu, who conveyed omens from Nergal, the god of war and bringer of pestilence.[129] Mars, the red one (*makrû*), was also called the "enemy" (*nakru*).[130] As darkness fell, Mars-Ṣalbatānu-Nergal was seen to the east of the tails of the Milky Way, and from 28–30 August it was in close proximity to the moon between the constellations Scorpius and Sagittarius (fig. 2.7).[131] The incipit of

---

[124] Herodotos 9.36–7. Earlier, Herodotos 1. 181–2, describes the temple at Babylon, with which the Chaldeans were most closely associated, and where many of the omens of *Enūma Anu Enlil* were composed.

[125] Reiner 1995: 81–96. See also Oppenheim 1974, which is a diviner's manual, and Swerdlow 1998: 2–3.

[126] Reiner 1995: 61–80; Worthington 2004, a review essay, discusses the pertinent recent literature.

[127] Reiner 1995: 6; Kasak 2001: 22.

[128] Reiner 1995: 68–9.

[129] Reiner 1995: 6–7; Kasak 2001: 27–8.

[130] Reiner 1995: 4; Brown 2000: 70–1.

[131] Brown 2000: 105–6: "For example in 8219 an omen concerning the proximity of Mars ... and Scorpius is given. Mars is frequently an ill-boding planet, and Scorpius an ill-boding constellation. The proximity of the two would lead one to suspect the prognosis also to bode ill."

FIGURE 2.7 The night sky above Plataia at sunset of 29 August 479 B.C. Produced by David Pankenier using Starry Night Pro 6.4.3.

an apotropaic ritual begins "if Mars and the moon go side by side," saying that some form of evil will befall, although exactly what is lost. According to a planetary omen in *Enūma Anu Enlil*, "If Mars comes close to Scorpius, the ruler will die from the sting of a scorpion; variant: He will be seized in his palace."[132] In another *namburbû* ritual the evil to be averted is attributed to the conjunction of Mars and Sagittarius.[133]

Immediately above the ridge of Kithairon, where the Greeks would have seen the constellations of Sagittarius and Serpens-Ophiuchus, Persian diviners saw a quite different set of stellar configurations: Mars stood right next to the star Theta Ophiuchi—one of the so-called "normal stars," used to give the position of the moon and planets in Mesopotamian astronomical-astrological texts—which was the arrow tip of Pabilsag, a cognate of Ninurta, who was also known as Ninĝirsu.[134] Other stars of Ophiuchus and of Serpens Cauda were together understood as Zababa, tutelary of Kis and the warrior

---

[132] Similarly, at *Enūma Anu Enlil*, tablets 50: "If Mars approaches Scorpius: there will be a breach in the palace of the prince. If Mars approaches Scorpius: the city will be taken by a breach." See Reiner and Pingree 1981: 40–1. Mars was aligned with Scorpius on 1 August 479 B.C., and had passed into Sagittarius by the middle of September. Swerdlow 1998: 14 lists a series of conjunctions of Mars and their meanings.

[133] Reiner 1995: 93. The second *namburbû* commends offerings to Hendursaga, god of law and justice. Remarkably, a cuneiform tablet now in the Vorderasiatisches Museum, Berlin, reads: "For Hendursaga, his master, Gudea, ruler of Lagash, built his house." We shall turn shortly to Gudea of Lagash. See also the Nanshe Hymn, which mentions both Gudea and Hendursaga, who is Nanshe's herald: Heimpel 1981.

[134] Its Babylonian name was MÚL KUR ša KIR$_4$ šil PA, and its elliptic coordinates in –600 were 225.30/–1.48. See Sachs and Hunger 1988: 18.

god of the Hittites, also a cognate of Ninurta.[135] The visible planet Saturn was Kaiamānu, also understood to bring signs from Ninurta, storm god and son of Enlil, who slew Asag, a demon who restrained the waters.[136] In *Enūma Elish*, Ninurta becomes Marduk, state god of Babylon and lord of armies, who was associated with the visible planet Jupiter.[137] Jupiter had many appearances, but in the month of Ulūlu he appeared as SAG.ME.GAR, the bearer of signs.[138] In *Enūma Elish*, Marduk slew the terrible, serpentine sea goddess Tiamat.[139] At her death, Marduk split Tiamat's body to create heaven and earth from its two halves. He fixed the constellations and the polestar, arranged the calendar, instructed the sun and moon, and then "her tail he bent upwards into the sky to make the Milky Way, and her crotch he used to support the sky."[140]

To the Persian astronomer-astrologers present at Plataia, the constellation Draco was associated with Ningišzida, the serpent, "Lord of the Netherworld."[141] In a local Mesopotamian variant of the combat myth, the horned serpent-demon is Bašmu and the hero-god Ningišzida.[142] In lists of gods, Ningišzida is a subordinate of Ningirsu, the tutelary god of Lagash (and a precursor to Ninurta). But he also is the son of Anu, lord of heaven, associated with the constellation Draco.[143] The earliest extant representation of Ningišzida features on a Sumerian libation vase carved from green steatite

---

[135] Serpens Caput perhaps formed the sitting gods, which may have been expressed as the upper torso of a man with a serpentine tail. Hunger and Pingree 1999: 60, 93, 275, 277 is authoritative, and tentatively locates the sitting gods in Virginis; White 2007: 187–8 offers a more popular interpretation, and locates the sitting gods in Ophichus-Serpens.

[136] Brown 2000: 56–7, 68–70; Fontenrose 1959, 1980: 146–7; Wakeman 1973: 7–9; Lewis 1996.

[137] Brown 2000: 64 quotes the following invocation: "(O Marduk) your name when you are visible (as the planet Jupiter) is ᵈsag.me.gar, the foremost god, the leader of [. . .] who when he shines forth, shows a sign . . ."

[138] Reiner 1995: 4 notes that no translation is conclusive. However, see Brown 2000: 54–5, 65, who states that Sagmegar is the "A-name," or primary name, of Jupiter, never applied to another celestial body. Shortly after 479 B.C., in astronomical diaries for –463, –453 and –440, Jupiter appears for the first time as ᵐᵘˡbabbar = peṣû, "white planet." See Brown 2000: 66.

[139] Fontenrose 1959, 1980: 148–64; Jacobsen 1968; Wakeman 1973: 16–21.

[140] Jacobsen 1976: 179; *Enūma Elish*, 5; trans. Dalley 2009: 255. This might be compared to an Aztec myth, preserved in the *Historia de México*, where the gods Tezcatlipoca and Quetzalcoatl transformed themselves into great serpents and tore apart the earth goddess, so that her lower body rose up to the sky, forming the Milky Way. Elsewhere, the Milky Way is a white celestial road for those same gods, a sky river, or a star-skirted goddess. See Milbrath 1999: 274–5.

[141] Hunger and Pingree 1999: 60, citing MUL.APIN and "astrolabe B." On the former, see Hunger and Pingree 1989: 32, s.v. ii.8: "The snake, Ningizzida, lord of the Netherworld."

[142] *The Melammu project* collects several texts as "1.1.6 Primordial battle and defeat of the Dragon": http://www.aakkl.helsinki.fi/melammu/database/gen_tpl/t01/t0000020.php.

[143] See Van Buren 1934: 62–3, where Ningišzida is assimilated with a Sumerian serpent god; and Hunger and Pingree 1999: 60, for the association of Ningišzida with the constellation Draco in MUL. APIN. In Middle Persian cosmogony, Draco is associated with Gōčihr, a sky dragon, "similar to a snake with the head in Gemini and the tail in Centaurus, so that at all times there are six constellations between its head and tail." See *EI*, s.v. Aždahā: 197.

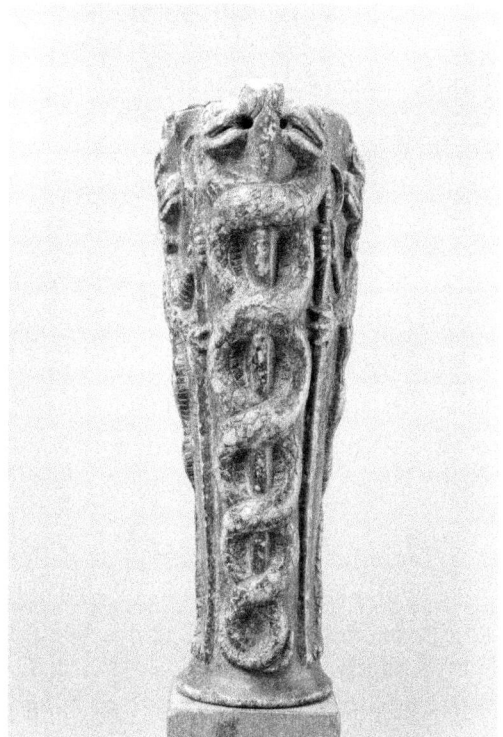

FIGURE 2.8 Libation vase of Gudea, dedicated to Ningišzida. Neo-Sumerian. Lagash (Tello), ca. 2150 B.C. Green Steatite, Musée du Louvre, Paris. Photo: Réunion des Musées Nationaux/Art Resource, NY.

now in the Louvre (fig. 2.8).[144] The vase has an inscription revealing that it was dedicated to the god Ningišzida by Gudea, the priest-king of Lagash (2144–24 B.C.) "for the prolongation of his life." Two serpents are shown, coiling around each other rather than the pillar in front of which they are placed. Their heads are confronted, facing each other with mouths open and sharp teeth visible. Ningišzida has appropriated the destructive force of the serpent demon Bašmu. Standing to each side of the serpent demon, winged creatures holding staffs, perhaps doorposts representing the entry to a temple, look up toward the snakes' heads. These appear to be both lions and birds, with the heads of serpents, wearing horned hats. Both the serpent and the lion-bird are aspects of Ningišzida.[145] Gudea the priest-king understood that his tutelary Ningišzida, "Lord of the Good Tree," had inherited Gilgamesh's power over Huwawa, guardian of the cedar forest, and boasted that he, "Gudea, the great

---

[144] Frothingham 1916: 181–92; Van Buren 1934: 62–5, 78–9.
[145] Van Buren 1934.

en-priest of Ningursu, made a path into the Cedar mountains which nobody had entered before; he cut down its cedars with great axes . . . Like giant snakes, cedars were floating down the river" for the construction of Gudea's temple.[146] Gudea has tamed nature, he has harnessed the destructive force of Ninĝišzida to honor Ninĝirsu.

A Sumerian *balbale*, a prayer poem, to Ninĝišzida describes him as a spreader of confusion, the chaos god.[147]

> Hero, lord of field and meadow, lion of the distant mountains! Ninĝišzida, who brings together giant snakes and dragons! Great wild bull who, in the murderous battle, is a flood that [. . . . . .]! Beloved by his mother, he to whom Ningirida gave birth from her luxurious body, who drank the good milk at her holy breast, who sucked in lion's spittle, who grew up in the *abzu*! . . . Mighty power, whom no one dare stop when he spreads confusion! Mighty Ninĝišzida, whom no one dare stop when he spreads confusion!

Ninĝišzida is represented on the cylinder seals of the same Gudea, priest-king of Lagash. Ninĝišzida wears a helmet with serpents rising from his shoulders, leading the priest-king by the wrist to worship the great god seated on a throne. Behind Gudea is a woman in a horned helmet, and behind her the lion-bird is the last figure in the procession.[148] The worship of Ninĝišzida was a feature of Gudea's reign at Lagash, but elements of the iconography endured and developed.[149] In the Bakhtiari mountains at Kurangun (Fars province, Iran), a carved relief which has been dated to ca. 1600 B.C. features in its central panel a male figure wearing a horned crown, clutching a pair of serpents in his left hand, and seated on a throne formed from a coiled serpent.[150] He faces figures, badly abraded, who approach him, while behind him a female figure sits, also wearing a horned hat, also holding two snakes in her left hand. The figures cannot be identified precisely, since no written information on Elamite mythology has survived, but the male figure is likely to be the "great god" Napirisha or Inshushinak, the tutelary god of Susa (modern Shush, Iran). If this is correct, then the female figure is Kiririsha, the "great goddess."[151]

---

[146] Quoted in translation by Forsyth 1987: 37.

[147] *The Electronic Text Corpus of Sumerian Literature*, Oxford University: http://etcsl.orinst.ox.ac.uk/cgi-bin/etcsl.cgi?text=t.4.19.1#.

[148] Van Buren 1934: 72. A similar presentation scene is posited on a relief plaque discovered at the Temple at Lagash, where an inscription names Gudea. See Hansen 1963: 149–50.

[149] One might note the advice of Boardman 1968: 37: "the properties of an eastern demon could be borrowed for a Greek monster without the iconography being borrowed as well; the corollary of which is that Greek artists might have been led to adopt certain iconographic features of eastern demons into their repertory without taking any notice of the identity of context of the eastern figures."

[150] Seidel 1986; Potts 1999: 182–3; Garrison 2009: 2–3.

[151] Hinz 1965; Garrison 2009. The qualities and deeds of Napirisha/Inshushinak are equivalent to those of Ninurta. The goddess is not Napirisha, a male deity, which is a misreading by Potts 1999: 182.

FIGURE 2.9 Elamite cylinder seal of the judge Ishme-karab ilu, ca. 1600 B.C. Line drawing after Barnett 1987.

The god on a serpent throne features on several cylinder seals from Susa, one of which is remarkable for its congruence with the Serpent Column.[152] An Elamite cylinder seal, which dates from the same century as the Kurangun relief, belonged to the judge Ishme-karab ilu (fig. 2.9).[153] The seal leaves the impression of a column formed from entwined serpents, which terminates in two visible heads, surely two of three protomes, which support a bowl. These, unlike the confronted serpents on the Gudean libation vase, face outwards. Atop the bowl, a figure is seated upon a throne formed from a coiled serpent, the head forming the throne's back. The column and seated figure face a far larger figure, standing on a platform, who is surely a worshipper, perhaps Ishme-karab ilu

---

[152] Barnett 1987; Morris 1992: 290, has posited that the "inspiration for this monument," the form of the Serpent Column, was "Oriental ... Extravagant metal cauldrons with animal heads [had] adorned Greek sanctuaries since the eighth century, and had already been imitated by Greek artists since the seventh. A specific version of the column made of entwined snakes appears on an Elamite seal of the Late Bronze Age, where it supports a seated snake-god before a worshiper. The motif joins those found in Bronze Age glyptic of the Near East that resurface in Greek Iron Age art, but here it contributes to a symbol of Greek triumph over the Near East, perhaps conceived as a deliberately ironic tribute to the East."

[153] Amiet 1973: 37–8, pl. IX; Barnett 1987; Porada 1993.

himself. The god on the serpent throne has harnessed the power of the serpents. He sits on a coiled serpent, grasping serpents in his hands, and is supported on a column formed from serpents. At the base of the column, two bearded figures are kneeling on imbrications, representing a range of high mountains. Just such a mountainous setting is evoked in the Sumerian *balbale* to Ninĝišzida:

> Ninĝišzida, when taking your seat on the throne-dais in an elevated location, lord, god, youth, right arm—clothed in your [...] with the shining scepter grasped in your hands . . . Hero who, after surveying the battle, goes up to the high mountains! Ninĝišzida, who, after surveying the battle, goes up to the high mountains![154]

The relationship of this image, if any, to the Serpent Column cannot be ascertained, but the similarities are striking.[155]

---

[154] *The Electronic Text Corpus of Sumerian Literature*, Oxford University: http://etcsl.orinst.ox.ac.uk/cgi-bin/etcsl.cgi?text=t.4.19.1#.

[155] The broader Neo-Assyrian context for the development of Archaic Greek art, eschewing older notions of transmission between East and West, is presented by Gunter 2009.

3 }

Delphi

Archaic Greek Bronze-working – Lakonian Bronze – Engaging Apollo – Pausanias, Archegos *of the Greeks – Dedications following the Battles of Salamis and Plataia – Seven Centuries at Delphi*

The Plataian tripod was placed on the eastern terrace of the Sanctuary of Apollo at Delphi. It commemorated a Greek victory over the Persians in a form that reflected the profound influence of the Near East upon the Greeks over the preceding centuries.[1] In evoking the Orient directly, it repudiated its influence, and Persian power, over Greeks. The Plataian tripod was fashioned for Apollo from the bronze arms and armor of the defeated Persians. Bronze once forged into breastplates and helmets in the Near East, where Kothar—an Ugaritic metalworking god who created Baal's weapons—once held sway, was recast under the gaze of his Greek cognate Hephaistos. The god of smiths appears in the Greek pantheon several centuries before he achieves his Homeric form, depicted in the *Iliad* finishing the handles of twenty self-propelling tripods on golden wheels.[2] Homer also described Agamemnon's bronze arms and armor and his "richly inlaid, furious shield" from which hung a baldric of silver, "and on it writhed a serpent of cyanus, that had three heads turned in different directions, growing out from one neck."[3]

Technologies, as well as gods and ritual practices, were communicated from the Near East to the western Greek world by sea, through traveling artisans and traders and through gifts exchanged or votives dispatched by the wealthy and powerful.[4] On Bronze Age Cyprus, copper extracted from local mines was exported across the Levant, and metalworking was practiced at sanctuaries, for example at Kition and Enkomi.[5] A shipwreck of the

---

[1] Gauer 1968: 91–2 sees the Plataian tripod as an Orientalizing bronze statue produced at a transitional time in Greek art. For a nuanced reappraisal of Orientalizing art in Greece, leaving room for local and regional meanings, see Gunter 2009.

[2] *Iliad* 18.373–9. For commentary, see Papalexandrou 2005: 30–3.

[3] *Iliad* 11.39–40.

[4] López-Ruiz 2010, argues convincingly for the primary role of Phoenicians as intermediaries in this trade in ideas.

[5] Morris 1992: 88, with references. But see now Gunter 2009: 80–4.

fourteenth century B.C., excavated at Uluburun (near modern Kaş, Turkey), contained both copper and tin ingots, glass ingots, and unworked ivory, as well as manufactured cargo, notably Cypriot pottery.[6] Bronze-workers traveled with their tools and metals across the eastern Mediterranean, as is demonstrated by the smiths' tools discovered with a cargo of bronze and copper ingots in the Cape Gelidonya shipwreck from ca. 1200 B.C. (also near Kaş).[7]

Archaic Greek Bronze-working

According to Linear B tablets, Hephaistos was worshipped in late Bronze Age Crete at Knossos, where *ka-ke-we* (χαλκῆες), bronze-workers, enjoyed a privileged status, just as they had in the temple culture of ancient Ugarit.[8] A bronze bowl from around 1000 B.C. unearthed in a Knossos cemetery bore an inscription in Phoenician letters, suggesting the presence of literate Levantine craftsmen before the Cretans had adopted their own Greek alphabet, the closest to Phoenician.[9] Analysis of the tin and alloy content of bronzes from the ninth to seventh centuries suggests that not only were oriental techniques and motifs emulated but the same craftsmen were at work, settled in Cyprus and Crete.[10] Two large statuettes of Leto and Artemis and a still larger Apollo, discovered at the Temple of Apollo at Dreros in eastern Crete, have been attributed to Near Eastern immigrants and compared to Syrian limestone figures covered with gold and silver foil.[11] Each figurine is formed of a wooden core encased in hammered bronze by the technique known in Greek as *sphyrelaton*. The Dreros Apollo has lost his right hand above the wrist and his left arm above the elbow. It would appear that the raised right arm, level with the chest, once held an object. In contrast to Apollo, who has two legs (both feet are missing), Leto and Artemis resemble chess pieces, having no discernible legs or feet, which are hidden beneath floor-length gowns, and arms pressed close to their sides. On their heads they wear cylindrical crowns or caps.[12]

---

[6] See Bass 1986.

[7] This was found off the coast of modern Turkey between Fethiye and Antalya, and published as Bass 1967.

[8] Morris 1992: 73–100.

[9] Morris 1992: 124–49 cites approvingly S. Frankenstein's definition of Phoenicians as "a category of people involved in certain recognizable activities rather than ... a single ethnic group, e.g., in the Homeric poems all traders are 'Phoenicians.'" See also Snodgrass 1971, 2000: 342–52; Gunter 2009: 91–5; López-Ruiz 2010: 23–6.

[10] Filippakis et al. 1983; Rolley et al. 1986.

[11] Marinatos 1936; Morris 1992: 163–4. On the dangers of distinguishing between a "Greek hand" and "Oriental" influence, see Gunter 2009: 86–91.

[12] Rolley 1994: I, 112–13; Vincent 2003: 38.

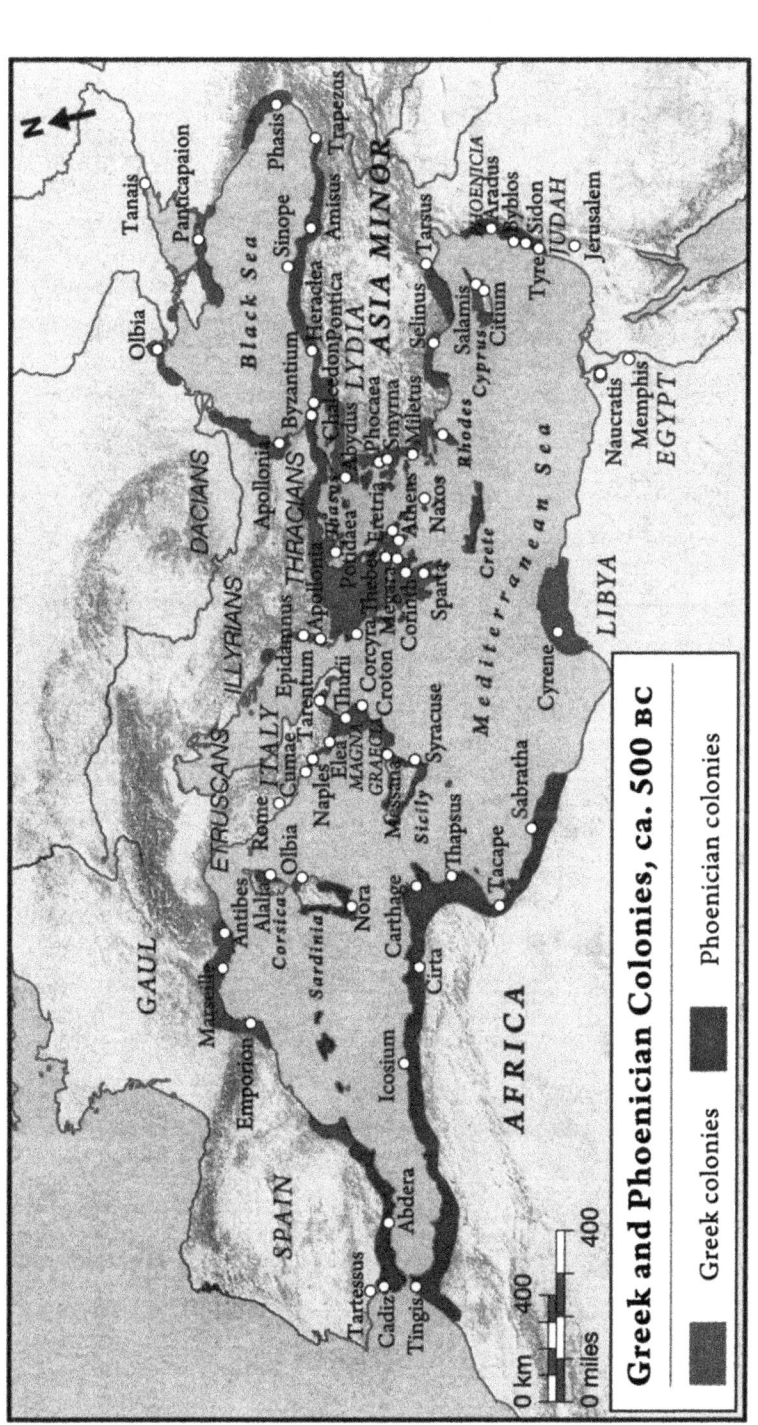

MAP 4 The Mediterranean World, ca. 500 BC.

Oriental motifs and themes define the hammered bronze votive shields discovered in a cult cave at Mount Ida, Crete.[13] These were produced by a community of bronze-workers over a generation or more, gradually integrating local ideas with established oriental themes and motifs. According to Anthony Snodgrass, who dated the first pieces to around 750 B.C., the "most natural explanation of this phenomenon is that a guild of immigrant craftsmen, perhaps from northern Syria, settled in Crete and gradually imbibed more and more elements of Greek art."[14] One shield appeared to early interpreters to present Marduk, god of storms and weather in *Enūma Elish*, who to the Phoenicians was Melqart.[15] He is standing on a bull and holding a lion above his head, flanked by two male figures, both bearded and winged. Later commentators have identified the central figure as Zeus, confirming the synonymy of the two thundering gods.[16] A second shield, 68 cm in diameter but hammered to only 1 mm in thickness, is more badly damaged. Its central figure, missing its head, is a bird perched on a sphinx, its wings stretching beyond the frame of the central panel, their tips reaching into the last of four concentric rings, each of a different width and containing a different motif. Within the central panel, small lions stride above the elbows of both wings, and beneath that to the viewer's left stands a goat, while in the same space to the right is the head of the sphinx. Two serpents rise to the left and right, crossing above the goat and beneath the sphinx's paw, the heads turned inwards and confronted, either side of the bird's tail. The serpents are horned, and their forked tongues hang forwards, almost touching the heads of the small lions beneath their beardless chins. This has been read as an allegory of the confrontation between the Egyptian and Assyrian empires, as imagined by a Phoenician artist.[17]

Orientalizing works in bronze from Crete, including a helmet and votive shields similar to those discovered on Mount Ida, were deposited at Delphi as early as the eighth century B.C., perhaps by Cretans, perhaps by Corinthians or others who had dealings with the islanders.[18] A great deal of Near Eastern

---

[13] Frothingham 1888, summarized then recent Italian publications recording and interpreting the early discoveries and excavations; Kunze 1931 is the authoritative study of the bronze shields; Boardman 1961: 79–88 addresses additional finds from the cave, some in Oxford; Rolley 1983: 67–70 presents synthetic commentary and color photographs; Morris 1992: 152, alludes to more recent discussions and literature.

[14] Snodgrass 1971, 2000: 340–1, in agreement with Boardman 1961: 84, 138–9, who proposed similarly production over a period of a century, starting in the eighth century, and the presence of oriental craftsmen. However, more recently the clear distinction between local and immigrant artisans has been questioned. See Gunter 2009: 92, citing Hoffmann 1997.

[15] Frothingham 1888: 437–40. The same Marduk slew the terrible, serpentine sea goddess Tiamat, as Apollo slew Python. See Fontenrose 1959, 1980: 148–64; Jacobsen 1968; Wakeman 1973: 16–21.

[16] Kunze 1931: no. 74, p. 49.

[17] Frothingham 1888: Plate 16.

[18] See Hoffmann 1972: 31, pl. 18, 46, for illustrations of the Cretan helmet and a Cretan *mitra* deposited at Olympian; Morgan 1990: 142–6 attributes the dedication to Corinthians; Papalexandrou 2005: 191, 210, n. 18 demurs; Rolley 1983: 20 provides an illustration of an eighth-century Cretan shield from Delphi.

material also reached the Archaic Greek mainland. Most has been lost, and much of the bronze was reworked by Greek craftsmen. This is well illustrated by a remarkable find in a well at Olympia of seventy-eight fragments of a north Syrian repoussé bronze frieze, reconstituted into thirteen registers, which represents the largest such find in Greece. It also highlights the fact that more Near Eastern bronzes have been excavated in Greece than in the lands of their manufacture. The motifs and scenes depicted on the surviving parts of the frieze can be compared in many cases with known cylinder seals. In the same Olympian well were found 110 fragments of bronze incised with Orientalizing motifs by Greek artists. Chemical analysis of the bronze demonstrates that it was smelted at the same time as that from which the Near Eastern fragments were made, and therefore represents reworked elements of a far larger frieze.[19]

Entwined confronted serpents feature on a bronze helmet discovered at Afrati, Crete, which attest to a continued tradition of superb bronze-working on the island into the seventh century (fig. 3.1).[20] The decoration is executed in a combination of repoussé and incision. The serpents rise from the floor, on which their tails rest, forming three loops, all raised. The middle loop is perfectly circular and once held a medallion (attached by a silvery solder, traces of which survived), while the uppermost loop is almost closed by the serpents' forked tongues, darting out from the open jaws between rows of five sharp teeth. The serpents' confronted heads are not repoussé work, but incised in double outline. The lower jaw of each serpent is adorned with two beard tufts, and the upper jaw features a snout, a crest above the eye and an ear-like curve, resembling a displaced eye ridge. The tympanum formed by the tails is filled in by two panthers sharing a single head. Outside each snake is a winged youth in a pose suggesting swift forward motion, but looking away from the serpents. They are holding the throats and stepping on the tails of the snakes, taming and controlling them. The youths, like the serpents, are identical but for a few details. They wear checkered kilts fastened at their slim waists, diadems at the brow, and clasps at the neck that divide their hair into two long braids. A small wing sprouts from each heel and a larger one from each armpit.

The winged youths on the Afrati helmet have drooping wings attached across the shoulders, apparently by harnesses. These have few parallels, although a bronze cut-out plaque also from Afrati depicts a similar figure with wings

---

[19] Guralnik 2004. Still more of the same bronze was, in ca. 600 B.C., hammered onto statuettes to form three *sphyrelaton* korai.

[20] See Mitten and Doeringer 1967: 45–7 for a photograph taken before restoration by the Metropolitan Museum of Art. For later photographs and the fullest commentary, see Hoffman 1972: 2–4, 17–18, 29, 30–1, 34–40, pl. 1–5. A further helmet, discovered at Axos, Crete, on which the main design is of Pegasoi, features incised serpents on the brow guard. See Boardman 1961: 142–4; Mitten and Doeringer 1967: 48–9; Hoffmann 1972: 21, 29, pl. 14, 15. Very similar beasts, with serpentine bodies each forming two loops before ending in a whale's tail, are incised above a Gorgoneion on a bronze roundel discovered at Dreros. See Marinatos 1936: 222, 270–4, pl. 29

FIGURE 3.1 Helmet discovered at Afrati, Crete, with winged youths controlling entwined serpents, 7th century B.C. Nobert Schimmel Trust gift, 1989.281.50, The Metropolitan Museum of Art/Art Resource, NY.

attached to his waist and heel.[21] Winged figures, running demons and gorgons clutching or stepping on serpents, are depicted on many Archaic Greek gems.[22] On a unique bronze *hydria* handle, now in Brussels, two winged men are fashioned, each standing on the neck and kneeling on the tail of a snake. The serpents are joined by a fan-shaped palmette, which forms the base of the handle, the top of which is formed from two recumbent lions. In the Yale University Art Gallery there is a fine bronze running Gorgon clutching snakes, which have coiled around her forearms (fig. 3.2).[23] The fronts, rather than the heels, of her boots have small wings. This is also probably from the base of a handle attached to a bronze vessel, perhaps a volute krater. Both bronze handle fixtures have been identified as Lakonian.[24]

---

[21] Boardman 1961: 48, pl. 16, as drawn by Sir Arthur Evans, reproduced with commentary at Hoffmann 1972: 34–6. See also Mitten and Doeringer 1967: 47.

[22] For example, Boardman 1968: 31, no. 38 and pl. 2; 33, no. 44 (both four-winged running Gorgons clutching snakes); 81, nos. 204–5 and pl. 13 (winged demons clutching snakes); Hoffmann 1972: 60, n. 22.

[23] Yale University Art Gallery, 2002.95.2, dated ca. 540 B.C. Stibbe 2000a: 198–201, illustrates a number of similar bronze Gorgons, although none is holding snakes.

[24] Hoffmann 1964: fig. 1.

FIGURE 3.2 Running Gorgon clutching snakes. Bronze handle ornament, probably Lakonian, ca. 540 B.C. Ruth Elizabeth White Fund and gift of Cornelius C. Vermeule in memory of Emily Townsend Vermeule, 2002.95.2, Yale University Art Gallery.

Lakonian Bronze

Spartans certainly produced and dedicated bronze statues and tripods to Apollo at their own temples in Lakonia, and here one can detect clear associations with the Orientalizing style familiar from Crete and points further east.[25] In the late sixth century, a temple was erected to Apollo just south of Sparta. The Amyklaion was constructed around an older colossal cult statue, which dated perhaps to the late seventh century.[26] The god was older still. The worship

---

[25] Stibbe 2000a offers a clear overview of Lakonian bronze-working in the sixth century through a series of papers; Cartledge 2001b places bronze-working in its broader Spartan contexts. There is, in contrast, no strong tradition of marble sculpting in the Peloponnesos at this time, which has never been fully explained, and follows a brief period in the seventh century when the production in marble of *perirrhanteria* flourished, on which see chapter one. The color of Lakonian marble, dark bluish grey, perhaps contrasted poorly with the cream or white marbles from Attika and the Aegean islands, and would take colored paints less well. See Stibbe 2000a: 21–2 for references.

[26] Martin 1976; Morris 1992: 244; Faustoferri 1993; Georgoulaki 1994; Vlizos 2009. A new archaeological campaign has been conducted at modern Amykles since 2005 by the Benaki Museum, and a great deal of information can now be found online at http://amyklaion.gr/.

of Apollo Amyklaios is attested at Gortyn and posited at Kommos, both in Crete.[27] In both cases, Apollo has been identified as a Phoenician import.[28]

Pausanias provides a full description of the Amyklaion, where the Spartans annually celebrated the Hyakinthia, a three-day festival; this is the very festival in which they were engaged late in July 479 B.C., immediately prior to marching to Plataia. On the first day they honored the local hero Hyakinthos, a character with a pre-Greek name reimagined as Apollo's young lover, who was killed accidentally by the god's own hand, and whose body was held to be buried beneath the temple's altar. Thereafter, they honored Apollo. Around the tomb and altar was built an elaborate throne comprised of friezes depicting mythical scenes.[29] Atop the throne stood the colossal cult image of Apollo, believed to be a wooden monument of great antiquity clad in bronze,[30] which was described by Pausanias (3.19) in the following terms:

> I know of nobody who has measured the height of the image, but at a guess one would estimate it to be as much as thirty *pecheis*. It is not the work of Bathykles [who had fashioned the throne and surrounding temple], being old and fashioned without much art; for though it has a face, feet, and hands, the rest resembles a bronze column. On its head it has a helmet, in its hands a spear and a bow.[31]

The Amyklaion was ancient when Pausanias wrote, in the second century A.D., and it had undergone changes over the centuries. However, the cult statue was already venerable at the time the Plataian tripod was fashioned. We might imagine, therefore, that the artist knew the form a colossal statue dedicated to Apollo should take: a column, thirty cubits high, made of bronze. But representations of Apollo Amyklaios have survived on later coins, struck in Lakonia in the reigns of the Roman emperors Commodus and Gallienus, which suggest that at that time the statue was not simply a pillar, nor even a baetyl—a conical form that came to be considered sacred to Apollo—but rather was a column widening from base to shoulder. The god's head bears a crested helmet, a short

---

[27] Shaw 1978: 152–4 suggests that the ancient name for Kommos was Amyklaion. See also Shaw 1989: 173–4.

[28] Morris 1992: 155. For a fuller context, see López-Ruiz 2010: 23–47.

[29] The scenes depicted are described somewhat enigmatically by Pausanias, and reconstructed variously by Martin 1976; Pipili 1987: 81–2; and Faustoferri 1993, summarizing a forthcoming monograph in Italian, 1996, to which we have not had access. Delivorrias 2009, in a brisk summary of his views on the entire complex, suggests that the friezes were painted wooden panels.

[30] As Vincent 2003: 38 observes, although Pausanias refers elsewhere to the oldest statue in a complex as the *xoanon*, and does so frequently of wooden statues, he uses neither term in his description of Apollo Amyklaios. Pausanias refers to the statue as the *agalma* and "bronze pillar" (χαλκῷ κίονι). Nevertheless, the object is referred to frequently as a wooden statue clad in bronze, and as the *xoanon*, in secondary literature. See Georgoulaki 1994: 96.

[31] Pausanias 3.19.2. Bathykles of Magnesia is earlier said to have made the throne (Pausanias 3.18.9). See also Graf 2009: 40–1.

curved bow is gripped in his outstretched left hand, and a spear is held aloft in his right hand. The slim, elongated, anthropomorphic statue finds parallels in the Dreros Apollo, although we cannot be sure that the original form was more than a pillar.[32]

The Plataian tripod's serpentine column was cast in bronze on a grand scale and with consummate skill.[33] It was the work of a master craftsman in an established workshop. Appropriately for a chthonic beast, the bronze serpents would have been cast in a pit dug into the earth, by the lost wax method.[34] Conrad Stibbe has written that "Sparta [was] the capital of bronze working during the archaic period (around 625–525 B.C.)."[35] Stibbe is referring to the quality of pieces more than quantity, although he has produced a comprehensive list of more than one hundred Archaic Lakonian bronzes discovered in Sparta and Lakonia, and suggests that local finds would amount to a small fraction of those exported.[36] Luxury items such as volute kraters, bowls for mixing wine and water, have been found in Italy, France, the Balkans, and Asia Minor. "Sparta's showroom for bronzes" on a monumental scale was Olympia, although a few larger bronzes found elsewhere have also been attributed to Lakonian workshops.[37] However, the only written evidence that monumental bronzes were both produced and displayed at Sparta is provided, once again, by Pausanias, who records that outside the Amyklaion stood bronze tripods supported by statues of goddesses. So far as we can tell, this form of tripod was unknown at Delphi until the dedication of the Plataian tripod. Pausanias also supplies the names of the goddesses, the artists who fashioned the tripods, and the victories for which they were dedicated:

> The older ones are said to be a tithe of the Messenian war. Under the first tripod stood an image of Aphrodite, and under the second an Artemis. The two tripods themselves and the reliefs are the work of Gitiadas. The third was made by Kallon of Aigina, and under it stands an image of Kore, daughter of Demeter. Aristandros of Paros and Polykleitos of Argos have statues here; the former a woman with a lyre, supposed to be Sparta, the latter an Aphrodite called "beside the Amyklaion." These tripods are larger than the others, and were dedicated from the spoils of the victory at Aigospotamoi.[38]

---

[32] For pillar worship, and its relationship to Apollo on Crete, see Shaw 1989.
[33] Rolley 1983: 25–36.
[34] Kluge 1927: 3; Hemingway 2004: 3–13, for casting techniques.
[35] Stibbe 2000a: 159; Stibbe 2009: 148.
[36] Stibbe 2009: 149–52, 153. For example, eight bronze *hydriae* are identified as discovered in Lakonia, whereas around eighty are known from elsewhere.
[37] Stibbe 2000a: 180–1; Stibbe 2009: 148. The awkward fact remains that very few large-scale works of sculpture, either in bronze or marble, can be attributed with certainty to Lakonia.
[38] Pausanias 3.18.7–8. See above, at the end of chapter one.

Gitiadas, named as the sculptor of Artemis and Aphrodite with tripods at the Amyklaion, was also responsible for the temple to Athena Chalkioikos at Sparta itself, with a bronze *agalma* of the eponymous goddess and bronze reliefs attached to the temple's walls.[39] It is notable that next to the altar in the brazen temple to Athena stood two bronze statues of Pausanias the general, who had fled there seeking sanctuary when accused by the Spartans, but alone of those who had sought the protection of the goddess had been denied. The statues of the general were fashioned "in fulfillment of a command from Delphi," within a decade of, and perhaps by the same artist or workshop responsible for, the Plataian tripod.[40] The furnishings of the Chalkioikos and Amyklaion as described by Pausanias may be considered further evidence that the sixth century was a "golden age" for Lakonian bronze sculpting. Gitiadas the Spartan was evidently a leading artist who, together with Kallon of Aigina, is the first known to have devised a tripod formed from a supporting statue and separate cauldron. Gitiadas appears to have been active towards the middle of the sixth century B.C., and Kallon somewhat later. Kallon may still have been active in the first decades of the fifth century, although by most estimates Gitiadas would not.[41] However, it makes little sense to pursue the identity of the artist responsible for the Plataian tripod, since his name is not recorded. Pausanias took a great interest in reporting those names that were recorded on inscriptions or preserved by local legend.

Serpent protomes were a staple of Lakonian bronze-working in the sixth century, notably on the handles of drinking cups and other, larger vessels for holding liquids.[42] Snakes, often elements of Gorgoneia, feature on a number of luxury bronze vessels that may have been manufactured in Lakonia, for example a bronze volute krater handle now in the British Museum (fig. 3.3).[43] Gorgon handles on a volute krater of exquisite quality, and a second that is

---

[39] Pausanias 3.17.2. See also Stibbe 2000a: xiii–xiv, 180.

[40] Pausanias 3.17.7–9; Thucydides 1.134.

[41] Frazer 1898: III, 350–1 summarizes older views. The discussion is still active. Pipili 1987 dates Gitiadas' active years rather later than most, at ca. 530–490. Stibbe 2000b argues that Gitiadas was active from ca. 570 B.C. Kallon is stated, at Pausanias 7.8.10, to be a contemporary of Kanachos the Sikyonian. There were two sculptors from Sikyon named Kanachos, although the younger, according to Pausanias 10.9.10, is said to have made, with Patrokles, statues of two Spartans following the victory at Aigospotamoi, in 405 B.C. Chamoux 1970: 320–2, suggests that Gitiadas and Kallon were of separate generations in the second half of the sixth century, referring to a long-known inscription, dated epigraphically to the end of the sixth century, perhaps found on the Athenian acropolis, which states Κάλων ἐποίησεν Αἰ[γινήτης] (Frazer 1898: II, 282). This may, therefore, be the older Kallon, whose career may have overlapped briefly with that of Gitiadas.

[42] Gauer 1991: 135–6, 153–4; tables 62, 68, 69, 76, 108, for photographic illustrations; and Abb. 1, which provides sketches of twenty-two types of serpent protomes discovered at Olympia. Stibbe 2000a: 143–9 studies a hitherto unpublished bronze *oinochoe* handle with snake protomes, which are of a type not recorded by Gauer. See also Stibbe 2009: 153 for a more recent list.

[43] British Museum bronze 583, considered western Greek (Taras/Taranto). See Pipili 1987: 17–18 and Stibbe 2000a: 149, who notes that the handle has also been attributed to a Corinthian workshop.

FIGURE 3.3 Gorgon with two serpentine legs. Bronze volute krater handle, sixth century B.C. British Museum, bronze 583. Photo: The Trustees of the British Museum.

almost as splendid, were found at Trebeništa in what is now the Republic of Macedonia.[44] There are four stunning serpents entwined with the arms and legs of a Gorgon on the famous volute krater found at Vix, France, and now in the museum at Châtillon-sur-Seine.[45] Werner Gauer regarded the serpent heads as the defining motif of the workshop responsible for the Vix krater.[46] The workshop has been located, variously, in Sparta, Corinth, and southern Italy, but most recently Conrad Stibbe has argued that it was the product of a Lakonian master, perhaps working at Dodona, an oracle and shrine in Epirus.[47]

There are no surviving examples of monumental bronze serpents from Lakonia. However, Pausanias, in describing the Amyklaion, observed that to

---

[44] Stibbe 2000a: 61–3, esp. figs. 37 and 38, where it is considered a Lakonian product; also see 93–8, esp. figs. 58 and 59, for a second, somewhat later, volute krater, which may be Lakonian or Corinthian.

[45] See Stibbe 2000b, 107–8, fig. 53 (= Stibbe 2006: 155), for a detail of stunning bronze serpent heads on the Vix krater.

[46] Gauer 1991: 153–4; Stibbe 2000b: 77, n. 94.

[47] Stibbe 2000a: 159–61; see Stibbe 2000b for a full conspectus of earlier literature. Cartledge 2001b: 181 ruled certain decorative elements of the Vix krater "almost unthinkable as creations of any community other than Sparta."

the left of the throne were placed representations of Echidna and Typhos, also called Python and Typhon.[48] These were either free-standing sculptures placed beside the throne or sculptural elements of the throne, and as such may have been the work of Bathykles of Magnesia. While representations of Typhon were known at this time,[49] the Amyklaion sculpture would be the earliest known depiction of Python, unless she can be identified as the serpent on a Lakonian cup now in the Louvre, dated to ca. 550-40 B.C., and attributed to the Rider Painter, or Painter of Horsemen (fig. 3.4).[50] The interior of the cup is painted with a scene of combat between a serpent and warrior. The serpent rises from the base of a column supporting the portico of a temple. The snake is not coiled around the column, but painted in front of it. The column features a central pillar picked out in the same manner as the serpent itself, black with white zigzags. The serpent's head is disproportionately large, with its mouth wide open, revealing lines of sharp white teeth picked out against the black head, contrasting with a darting forked tongue in red and a long red beard dangling beneath the lower jaw. The serpent is thrusting its head forward, so that the tip of the lower jaw and the beard both just disappear behind the round shield of a kneeling warrior. The shield is a Gorgon's mask, with its own teeth and beard, shown frontally. The warrior wears a helmet with a high, curving crest of Corinthian type, three strands of hair falling from beneath its neck guard. His huge, muscular right arm holds a spear aloft, clearly aimed at the snake's head. Additional creatures ring the combatants. Behind the temple, a second snake is the same beast shown earlier, waiting for the arrival of the warrior. Two birds sit on the roof of the temple, looking down on the fight. Two similar birds fly, the larger behind the warrior's back, the smaller in the background, seen beneath his helmet's crest. These are the same birds, scared into flight by the serpent's lunge. Beneath, in the foreground, a hare runs beneath two palmettes from left to right, indicating both the speed and direction of action and the passage of time.

The Rider Painter produced several other known works, including two depictions of Achilleus' ambush of Troilos at a temple to Apollo outside Troy, which share a great deal with the Louvre cup, and have been dated somewhat earlier, to ca. 560 B.C.[51] A warrior is shown kneeling before a similar temple. He wears a similar crested helmet and holds a circular shield and a spear, although the last is not held aloft in combat, nor is the warrior fully kneeling, to provide grounding for a spear thrust, but is crouched, waiting. Birds are perched on

---

[48] Pausanias 3.18.9. Jacquemin 1999: 176 draws attention to the significance of the Amyklaion and the artists who furnished it to the form of the Serpent Column, and the subsequent tripod of Gelon, fashioned by Bion of Miletos.

[49] In addition to those explored above, several images of Typhon have survived from sixth-century Lakonia, as noted by Pipili 1987: 68–70.

[50] Pipili 1987: 50–1, 99.

[51] Pipili 1987: 27–30, figs. 42 and 43. One cup is in the Villa Giulia, and the second, once on Samos, has been lost, but pictures exist.

FIGURE 3.4 A Lakonian cup dated to ca. 550–540 B.C, attributed to the Rider Painter, or Painter of Horsemen, in the Musée de Louvre, Paris. Réunion des Musées Nationaux/Art Resource, NY.

the temple's roof, and a serpent slithers forward from the column, but it does not rear to strike the warrior, nor does he seem intent on striking it. A second scene, smaller and below, depicts Troilos riding a horse away towards his sister Polyxene while a hare runs in the opposite direction beneath. These cups display similar motifs to the Louvre cup, informed by the artist's past work, but the composition is entirely different. It provokes us to interpret the combat scene on the Louvre cup not as another version of the ambush, but rather as the battle between Apollo and Python. The birds are ravens, birds of prophecy, which like the hare are sacred to Apollo.[52]

Engaging Apollo

Serpents were a prominent motif in the finest Lakonian bronze sculpture of the sixth century. It is tempting, therefore, to propose that the Plataian tripod was the

---

[52] It has also been suggested that the Louvre cup depicts the battle between Kadmos and the Drakon. But depictions of that combat are just as rare before the fifth century, and it seems less likely, given the presence of Apollonian creatures. In this we agree with Pipili 1987: 50–1, 99, n. 496.

product of a Lakonian artist working either near Sparta or at Delphi. This cannot be stated with any degree of certainty, because long before it was cast, artists from Corinth had begun to emulate the Lakonians, and also to work alongside them in workshops located at the sanctuaries.[53] There were also highly skilled bronze-workers from many other places in mainland Hellas, including Athens and Sikyon; the Aegean islands, notably Samos; Asia Minor; and especially southern Italy. Yet there is a strong Lakonian connection in the fact that the individual most clearly associated with the Plataian tripod is Pausanias, the Spartan general who had commanded the forces of Lakonia and Tegea at Plataia. The Plataian tripod appears to be the first monument at Delphi for which a Spartan was principally responsible, in contrast to the many dedications at Olympia.[54]

The Spartans had two kings, one each from the Agiad and Eurypontid royal houses. Pausanias, the son of Kleombrotos, was a nephew of Leonidas, king in the Agiad line. When Pleistarchos, the son of Leonidas, became king upon his father's death at Thermopylai, Pausanias was appointed as his regent until Pleistarchos came of age, and therefore exercised the most important prerogative of a Spartan king, to lead his men in war. It was on campaign that a king's power was least limited by the *gerousia*, a council of freeborn Spartan elders, and the board of five ephors, whose members were elected by the full assembly of Spartiates to monitor the kings and ensure that they obeyed the laws.[55] After victory at Plataia, the Spartans were confirmed as the greatest power in the Greek world, and Pausanias as the leading man of Sparta. Herodotos (9.81) describes the division of spoils after the battle:

> When all the loot had been collected, a tenth was set apart for the god at Delphi, and from this was made the gold tripod which stands next to the altar on the three-headed bronze snake ... How much was set apart and given to those who had fought best at Plataia, no man says. I think that they also received gifts, but tenfold of every kind, women, horses, talents, camels, and all other things also, was set apart and given to Pausanias.[56]

Quite another Pausanias (10.13.9), writing in the second century AD, follows Herodotos, but omits any mention of his own namesake: "The Greeks in common dedicated from the spoils taken at the battle of Plataia a gold tripod set on a bronze serpent."[57] According to Thucydides (1.132), Pausanias is said "to have inscribed on the tripod at Delphi, which was dedicated by the Greeks from

---

[53] Stibbe 2000a: 63–4, 159–62.

[54] Jacquemin 1999: 53–7, 336, 338; Scott 2010: 146–52 notes that this is in contrast to Olympia, where Spartan dedications from the late seventh century have been found.

[55] Cartledge 2001a offers a succinct overview of the Spartan "constitution," defending an expansive view of kingship. Earlier scholarship had posited "antagonism between the kingship and the ephorate ... [as] the key to the practical working of the whole Spartan system of governance."

[56] Herodotos 9.81.

[57] Pausanias 10.13.9.

the booty of the Medes [Persians], this elegiac couplet: 'Leader of the Greeks, having destroyed the army of the Medes/Pausanias raised this as a memorial to Phoibos [Apollo].'"[58] Demosthenes (59.97), in his speech *Against Neaira*, replicates Thucydides' story and his rendering of the inscription on the votive tripod, emphasizing that the monument was to celebrate an allied Greek enterprise.[59] Diodoros Sikeliotes (11.33.2) describes quite another inscription: "The Greeks, taking a tenth part of the spoils, made a gold tripod, and set it up in Delphi as a thank-offering to the god, inscribing on it the following couplet: 'This is the gift the saviors of far-flung Hellas upraised here/Having delivered their states from loathsome slavery's bonds'."[60] The epigram, which he attributes to Simonides of Keios, must have been on the golden tripod itself, for the bronze column is not mentioned.[61] This would suggest that Pausanias' dedication was also on the golden bowl, that it was excised and replaced by "Simonides'" couplet, and that additionally a list of cities was inscribed on the bronze column at the same time.[62]

The placement of a dedication to a god high on the monument was appropriate, since Apollo would glance down upon it. More than this, he was understood to descend from the heavens and appear upon the tripod, perched on high in the position assumed by the Pythia when she consulted his oracle.[63] Euripides would later observe to Apollo, "you sit on a golden tripod, issuing

---

[58] Thucydides 1.132: καὶ ὅτι ἐπὶ τὸν τρίποδά ποτε τὸν ἐν Δελφοῖς, ὃν ἀνέθεσαν οἱ Ἕλληνες ἀπὸ τῶν Μήδων ἀκροθίνιον, ἠξίωσεν ἐπιγράψασθαι αὐτὸς ἰδίᾳ τὸ ἐλεγεῖον τόδε:

"Ἑλλήνων ἀρχηγὸς ἐπεὶ στρατὸν ὤλεσε Μήδων,
Παυσανίας Φοίβῳ μνῆμ᾽ ἀνέθηκε τόδε."

[59] Demosthenes 59.97: ἐφ᾽ οἷς φυσηθεὶς Παυσανίας ὁ τῶν Λακεδαιμονίων βασιλεὺς ἐπέγραψεν ἐπὶ τὸν τρίποδα <τὸν> ἐν Δελφοῖς, ὃν οἱ Ἕλληνες οἱ συμμαχεσάμενοι τὴν Πλαταιᾶσι μάχην καὶ τὴν ἐν Σαλαμῖνι ναυμαχίαν ναυμαχήσαντες κοινῇ ποιησάμενοι ἀνέθηκαν ἀριστεῖον τῷ Ἀπόλλωνι ἀπὸ τῶν βαρβάρων,

"Ἑλλήνων ἀρχηγός, ἐπεὶ στρατὸν ὤλεσε Μήδων, Παυσανίας Φοίβῳ μνῆμ᾽ ἀνέθηκε τόδε,"

ὡς αὑτοῦ τοῦ ἔργου ὄντος καὶ τοῦ ἀναθήματος, ἀλλ᾽ οὐ κοινοῦ τῶν συμμάχων.

Trans. DeWitt 1949, modified: "Pausanias, the king of the Lakedaimonians, puffed up by this, inscribed a distich upon the tripod at Delphi, which the Greeks who had jointly fought in the battle at Plataia and in the sea-fight at Salamis had made in common from the spoils taken from the barbarians, and had set up in honor of Apollo as a memorial of their valor. The couplet was as follows: 'Pausanias, supreme commander of the Greeks, when he had destroyed the host of the Medes, dedicated to Phoibos this memorial.' He wrote thus, as if the achievement and the offering had been his own and not the common work of the allies."

[60] Trans. Oldfather 1989. Gauer 1968: 93 suggests that the two inscriptions were placed on either side of the golden bowl.

[61] There is no reason to suppose, as does Barron 1988: 599, that the epigram would have been on the limestone base.

[62] An elegy for the dead of Plataia, ascribed to Simonides, contains praise for Pausanias, suggesting it was composed before this reinscription. However, it need not have been commissioned by Pausanias. See Boedeker 1995: 224–5.

[63] See, for example, the painted *hydria* in the Vatican Museums, by the Berlin Painter, illustrated as Papalexandrou 2005: fig. 64 and also 190–1, and 204–8 for the Pythia as a living tripod attachment following her appearance, dated to the end of the seventh century. She is nowhere mentioned in the *Homeric Hymn to Apollo*.

oracles to the mortals from your lie-less mantic throne."⁶⁴ Figural attachments on the handles of Archaic tripod cauldrons anticipated this divine epiphany, and placed before the god representations of birds or bulls sacrificed to the god, and later of warriors and horses, the dedicators and their marks of status.⁶⁵ These bronze statuettes that have been discovered in numerous excavations, detached from their original contexts, and frequently rededicated, for example a middle Geometric miniature known as the "Mantiklos Apollo" (ca.700 B.C.).⁶⁶ Nassos Papalexandrou has argued that this was originally a tripod ornament, intended to represent the dedicator rather than the god.⁶⁷ But the famous kouros discovered in the sanctuary at Delphi (somewhat later, from ca. 650 B.C.), he argues, was Apollo himself, appearing upon the tripod.⁶⁸ Apollo had usurped the place of the dedicator, even as the tripod became his sacred symbol.⁶⁹

The possibility that a god might enter into a cult statue is suggested in one of the older Greek words for statue, *hedos*, "dwelling place."⁷⁰ There are many clear indications that Greeks admitted the possibility that, like Hephaistos' self-propelling tripods, sculptures might become animated. Pausanias, in his tour of Greece, pointed out those statues that were chained down, not so that they would not be stolen—"The feet of Saturn's image at Rome were fastened with woolen bands, which were only taken off at the Saturnalia"⁷¹—but in order to prevent them from running away. From late antiquity, if not earlier, rites were performed with the specific intention of animating statues, although these were not considered necessary by most, who understood that the gods could move at will between heaven and earth.⁷²

On cauldrons in the seventh century, we find also mythic creatures functioning as apotropaia, protective devices, for example famous griffin protomes,

---

⁶⁴ Euripides, *Iphigeneia in Tauris*, 1254–5: τρίποδί τ' ἐν χρυσέῳ θάσσεις, ἐν ἀψευδεῖ θρόνῳ μαντείας βροτοῖς θεσφάτων νέμων.

⁶⁵ Maass 1978: 105–10, pl. 40, 41, 42, 43; Papalexandrou 2005: 99–148.

⁶⁶ Boston, MFA 03.997 (700–675 B.C.), inscribed by the worshipper Mantiklos and found (probably) at Thebes. See Mitten 1967: 15–17; Ridgway 1993: 103; Rolley 1994: I, 129.

⁶⁷ Papalexandrou 2005: 83–7; Papalexandrou 2010: 42–3, 48.

⁶⁸ Papalexandrou 2005: 192–3; Rolley 1969: 111–13, no. 172 (= Delphi inv. 2527, of Cretan origin); Rolley 1994: I, 135–6; Jacquemin 1999: 170, n. 87, who notes also a Lakonian kouros: Rolley 1969: 125–9, no. 182 (= Delphi inv. 1663), dating from 530–520 B.C.

⁶⁹ Papalexandrou 2005: 65–97.

⁷⁰ Iles Johnston 2008: 448.

⁷¹ Frazer 1898: III, 336, in a longer consideration of "chained images." See also Spivey 1995: 442–3, 446: "Socrates likens sophistical arguments to the statues (*agalmata*) of Daedalus: 'If they are not fastened they will run away like fugitive slaves.'" However, see also Spivey 1995: 455, for tales where "Devotees pick statues from their bases and retire with them for intercourse."

⁷² Spivey 1995: 453 observes that if priests could not effectively summon the god, "by various devices and implants statues could be made to sweat and to weep." Iles Johnston 2008 argues that "ritualized animation developed only late ... [under] the Platonizing religious system called theurgy," because theurgists recognized "firm boundaries between each of the different ontological realms of their cosmos."

FIGURE 3.5 Griffin protome, sixth century B.C., Lakonia. Director's and Rebecca Darlington Stoddard Funds, 1977.56. Yale University Art Gallery.

mouths agape, their fury captured in bronze (fig. 3.5).[73] The horror provoked by their shrieking was harnessed and redirected for apotropaic ends, protecting the vessel and its contents. A similar apotropaic function is served by serpents on vessels that were designed to bear liquids, including tripod cauldrons, for example the serpent protomes depicted on the Axos *mitra*. This *mitra*, a semicircular belt attachment of hammered bronze, contains in its central panel an incised depiction of two roaring lions, their heads and tails raised, flanking a tripod. Behind the central handle on the rim of the tripod, partly obscured, perches a man with long hair, perhaps braided. Surely this is Apollo's epiphany, as imagined in Crete in the eighth century B.C.[74]

Both the form and content of the epigram placed on the lofty golden bowl of the Plataian tripod were intended to engage Apollo in truthful dialogue upon

---

[73] Mitten and Doeringer 1967: 72–3; Rolley 1983: 70–5; Gauer 1991: 13–18, and passim on the Orientalizing style.
[74] Levi 1945: 293–313; Hoffmann 1972: 23–4, plates 43–5; Papalexandrou 2005: 191, 210, n. 13, with references. However, Boardman 1961: 141 considered the figure "too insignificant to be a divine epiphany."

his epiphany: the quality of the verse attested to the truth of the statement, in the same manner that Apollo's own oracular pronouncements, divine truth, were presented in hexametric verse.[75] Moreover, the epigram would be intoned to lyre-playing Apollo, the god of *mousike*, of singing, dancing, and the performance of epic poetry. All dedicatory inscriptions were to be read aloud for and by the god, not only those by victors in musical competition, who dedicated tripods to Apollo inscribed with the evidence of their virtuosity and eloquence.[76] In the reading, the original dedicatory act was recalled and renewed. Mantiklos knew this when he had inscribed on the legs of his statuette a pair of hexameters, an epigraphic prayer to Apollo, placing his own name first, to be read by those who came after him into the sanctuary at, we believe, Thebes.[77]

Pausanias, Archegos *of the Greeks*

Placed upon the elevated golden tripod at Delphi, Pausanias' dedication could be read only by Apollo himself, who intoned their names together: "Pausanias to Phoibos." When the first epigram on the Plataian tripod was replaced, the memory of its dedicatory ritual was erased. It was shown to have been false by the performance of the new dedication and the quality of the new elegiac couplet, which later tradition ascribed to the same author. That is to say, the original couplet was also, like most epigrams of the period, later ascribed to Simonides and recorded in its Doric version in the *Greek Anthology*.

Ἑλλήνων ἀρχηγὸς, ἐπεὶ στρατὸν ὤλεσε Μήδων,
Παυσανίας Φοίβῳ μνῆμ᾽ ἀνέθηκε τόδε [78]

Of Greeks the chief, when the army he destroyed of the Medes
Pausanias to Phoibos in memory dedicated this

Ἑλλάδος εὐρυχόρου σωτῆρες τόνδ᾽ ἀνέθηκαν,
δουλοσύνης στυγερᾶς ῥυσάμενοι πόλιας[79]

Of Greece far-flung the saviours this dedicated

From slavery's bonds having saved the cities

---

[75] Papalexandrou 2005: 9–63. We do not wholly follow Papalexandrou's interpretation of the Plataian tripod, with which he begins and ends this compelling first chapter. See also Maurizio 1995.

[76] Day 1994; Papalexandrou 2005: 111; and Day 2010, for a full and rich exploration.

[77] Day 1994: 40–6, 63; Day 2010: 33–48.

[78] See *Greek Anthology*: 6.197:

Ἑλλάνων ἀρχαγὸς ἐπεὶ στρατὸν ὤλεσα Μήδων
Παυσανίας Φοίβῳ μνᾶμ᾽ ἀνέθηκα τόδε

My translation is overly literal in order to retain the word order, thus showing the balancing of names. A more flowing translation is offered above, and also by Petrović 2010: "As chieftain of the Greeks, who demolished the army of the Medes, Pausanias dedicated this in remembrance to Phoebus." The attribution to Simonides is less unlikely than many, since according to Cartledge 2001b: 183, Simonides is known to have been attracted to Sparta, writing a "a wholly functional couplet on the Spartan dead at Thermopylae in 480 ... [and] a neo-epic laudation of the Spartans' yet greater military achievement at Plataia in 479."

[79] A more fluid translation: "The saviors of spacious Hellas set up this offering, having saved their cities from hateful slavery." See Green 2006: 90.

The second couplet does not, however, have the same balance or force as the first, which employs the Greeks and Persians as counterweights, and pairs Pausanias with Apollo. It is striking, moreover, that Pausanias engages with the god as *archegos* of the Greeks, not as regent of the Spartans. Pausanias does not claim to have been simply the *strategos*, "general," of the Greeks, which would have fit the meter of the couplet just as well. Rather, he entitles himself *archegos*, which has a range of meanings including "tutelary hero," "originating power," and "founder," but might best be translated as "preeminent leader" of the Greeks. If we attribute it to the epigrammatist in 479 B.C. rather than to Thucydides, then it is the earliest recorded use of the term *archegos*.[80]

The promotion in status implied by the title suited the monument on which it was inscribed, which in its quality and scale marked a new tier of achievement on the eastern terrace at Delphi for a society that constructed and reinforced hierarchy through competitive display. A principal function of the Panhellenic sanctuaries at Delphi and Olympia was to provide spaces for such competitive display between individuals, and later, from the mid-seventh century onwards, between poleis.[81] It is striking that Spartans are not known to have had dedicated anything substantial at Delphi before this event, engaging in competitive dedications almost exclusively at Olympia. The placement of the Plataian tripod on the eastern terrace of the temple at Delphi, therefore, had profound significance. It engaged a series of prior dedications, notably those by *barbaroi* from the east made prior to a fire at the temple, and its reconstruction and expansion after 548 B.C. The Lydians had favored the eastern side of the sanctuary at Delphi, raising there various statues and dedications in bronze, silver, and gold. According to Herodotos, the first Lydian to dedicate at Delphi was Gyges, whose usurpation was confirmed by an oracle that also predicted that his house would fall in its fifth generation. This was unknown to his descendant Kroisos, who erected a statue of a bull and another of a lion on solid golden ingots and had placed golden and silver bowls at either side of the temple's entrance, seeking Apollo's judgement as to whether he should make war against the Persians.[82] Herodotos enumerated Kroisos' dedications at Delphi and at other temples to Apollo, and accordingly:

> When the Lydians came to the places where they were sent, they presented the offerings, and inquired of the oracles, in these words: "Kroisos, king of Lydia and other nations, believing that here are the only true places of divination among men, endows you with such gifts as your wisdom deserves. And now

---

[80] LSJ, s.v. ἀρχηγὸς, and a word frequency search conducted on Perseus. Plutarch, *De Herodoti malignitate* 873c, equates ἀρχηγὸς simply with ἡγεμών, while willfully misrepresenting Herodotos.

[81] Snodgrass 1986; Morgan 1990; Scott 2010.

[82] Herodotos 1. 92, noting Kroisos' other dedications in Greece and Asia Minor; Jacquemin 1999: 72–4; Scott 2010: 45–8, 311–12.

he asks you whether he is to send an army against the Persians, and whether he is to add an army of allies." Such was their inquiry; and the judgment given to Kroisos by each of the two oracles was the same: namely, that if he should send an army against the Persians he would destroy a great empire. And they advised him to discover the mightiest of the Greeks and make them his friends.[83]

The Spartans, Kroisos had determined, were the mightiest of the Greeks, and so he had marched against the Persians with what he believed to be Apollo's sanction, having forged an alliance with the Spartans. But the Spartans were preoccupied with the Argives when Kroisos was captured by the Persian king Kyros II. In defeat, Kroisos asked Kyros to allow him to send the chains in which he was held captive to be placed on the same eastern terrace of the Delphic temple. Intended as a rebuke to the god who had failed to support him in war, but who by Herodotos' telling rescued him from death on a pyre, the chains might be read as a sign that the Greeks of Asia Minor, whom the Lydians had first enslaved, were now subject to the Persians. Seventy years later, the Plataian tripod, towering over what remained of Kroisos' dedications, promised an end to Persian mastery in Asia Minor, even as it signaled the expulsion of Persians from Hellas.[84] It was also a different type of monument: whereas Kroisos' dedications had all been made to secure oracular responses, Pausanias' was to celebrate victory.

Subjection to Pausanias rather than to a distant Persian king or his satraps held little appeal for many Greek poleis, including those which had fought on the Spartan side. But it was not the Greek alliance, but rather the Spartans themselves, wary of Pausanias' hubris, who replaced the epigram on the golden tripod of Plataia and additionally ordered that the names of all the victorious Greek cities be scratched onto the tripod.[85] Exactly when this took place is unclear, but it may have been up to a decade after the monument's erection, and it would certainly have been accompanied by a ritual performance of rededication. Pausanias had been accused by the Spartan ephors of "Medizing," acting as if he were a Persian satrap, by parading forth with an entourage of Egyptians and Persians and dining in the Persian fashion. He acted without moderation and self-restraint, without *sophrosyne*, therefore in the manner of a Persian. Moreover, he was suspected of conspiring with the Persians, and for that reason was first accused and acquitted, but later pursued by the ephors until he died (in ca. 470), presumably of exposure and thirst, holed up in the Brazen House,

---

[83] Herodotos 1.53.

[84] It remains to mention a serpentine omen reported by Herodotos (1.78), that snakes swarmed into Sardis before Kroisos was besieged there by Kyros, and were eaten by horses. An answer was provided by an oracle of Apollo at Telmessos that the snakes were of the earth, and hence native to the land, but the horses were beasts of war.

[85] Thucydides 1.132.

a Spartan temple to Athena.[86] Certainly, if we believe Thucydides' account, Pausanias had acted proudly in his dedication at Delphi, displaying no moderation in addressing Apollo, the god whose oracle commanded *sophrosyne*.[87] His downfall, therefore, was to be expected. Still, the behavior of the Spartan ephors, as it is recorded by Thucydides, is remarkable. They erased the memory of their regent's greatest victory at some distance from their city, in Delphi, ostensibly to promote the spirit of Panhellenism and the universal Greek value of moderation. Their actions, therefore, might have been calculated to find favor with Athenians in the latter half of the fifth century, but lacking any alternative contemporary viewpoint, we cannot dismiss Thucydides' account.

Spartans would have expected that a victorious general would dedicate a votive offering in his own name. Indeed, originally tripods were raised only by individuals as a mark of membership of an elite stratum which was demarcated by success in competition, including athletic and poetic contests, but also war.[88] Papalexandrou expresses this rather well: "Each tripod was meant to represent a specific individual by referring to the circumstances that prompted its deposition to the sanctuary. Each tripod was a 'site' or 'performance arena' visited for its informative role in the dissemination of *kleos*, that is, the poetically enshrined fame ... and social prestige of its dedicant."[89] Through the seventh and sixth centuries, collective dedication of tripods became a custom, notably in Athens.[90] At Delphi, communal rituals incorporated the tripods from an early date, as is revealed in a paian by Alkaios.[91] However, the tripod as a symbol of collective victory was not known before 480 B.C. Nor were any known monuments to military victory dedicated at Delphi before the onset of the Persian wars.[92] Even afterwards, there appears to have remained an aversion to depositing the arms and armor of an enemy at Delphi,[93] which was in stark contrast to the practice at Olympia, where so much armor was deposited in the sanctuary that it was periodically removed and buried in the banks of the stadium, or tossed into wells.[94] Victors would tailor their dedications accordingly,

---

[86] Thucydides 1.132–4.

[87] Castriota 1992: 17–28, offers succinct commentary on the role of *hybris* and *sophrosyne* in Greek political thought and literature at the time of the Persian wars.

[88] Wilson Jones 2002: 474–7 is an overview with references to earlier literature. See also Neer 2001: 295–7. Tripods excavated at Olympia are investigated at length by Maas 1978 and Gauer 1991.

[89] Papalexandrou 2005: 109.

[90] Papalexandrou 2005: 149–88.

[91] Papalexandrou 2005: 194–200.

[92] Jacquemin 1999: 84–7; Scott 2010: 75–7.

[93] Jacquemin 1999: 86 and Scott 2010: 33 point to a possible ban on such depositions from the middle of the fifth century.

[94] Scott 2010: 155, 169–78, esp. 171, provides references, notably to the excavation reports by E. Kunze. Even Militiades' helmet ended up in the earth of the stadium bank, which was fortunate for its excavators. Snodgrass 1986: 54–5 drew attention to the practice as a key element of competitive display, and Morgan 1990: 203–5 urged caution in identifying evidence for "peer-polity interaction" before the mid-seventh century.

for example, following victory at Marathon in 490 B.C., Miltiades of Athens dedicated his helmet at Olympia even as the corporate nature of the victory was emphasized in the construction and elaboration of a new Athenian treasury at Delphi.[95]

Pausanias took credit for the Plataian tripod, since it is likely that he was principally responsible for its construction and dedication, and he was acting in a manner established through centuries as appropriate for a general and a victor. His action would have been appropriate at Olympia, where Spartans were accustomed to dedicate their war spoils, and where the names of both victor and vanquished were always inscribed on the dedication.[96] However, it was not appropriate to the sanctuary at Delphi, where victory monuments were a new feature, where they were initially the preserve of poleis rather than individuals, and where inscriptions listing the victor and vanquished appeared only decades later, during the Peloponnesian War. The modification of the dedication on the Plataian tripod by the Spartan ephors should be read in this context, but also as a feature of the struggle between rival groups in Sparta, which led to Pausanias' ouster and death.

More broadly, an understanding of the dedication and rededication of the Plataian tripod throws into relief certain familiar, perhaps well-worn, themes in Greek history at the end of the Archaic period, such as the competitive production and display of votive structures within and between the Greek poleis, notably at the Panhellenic sanctuaries, and competition between advocates of different political systems, namely rule by one, by several, and by many (i.e., tyranny, oligarchy, and democracy). In a similar manner, a treasury that was dedicated by the Corinthian tyrant Kypselos in the seventh century was renamed the Corinthian treasury according to the wishes of the citizens of Corinth following the fall of the tyranny in ca. 540 B.C.[97] The Corinthian treasury had survived the great fire of 548, but the Siphnian treasury had not. Shortly before 525 B.C., it was rebuilt, and its carved marble friezes have been interpreted as emblematic of the struggle between the many and the few for political control of Siphnos.[98] The builders of the adjacent Sikyonian treasury made a similar point more bluntly, reusing every stone block from earlier Sikyonian foundations, but placing the sculptures associated with earlier tyrants face down as the building's foundations.[99]

---

[95] Neer 2004; Scott 2010: 77–81, 168, 170, with further references. Miltiades was later imprisoned by the Athenians and died of wounds sustained in battle. See also Aymard 1949: 63–4.

[96] Scott 2010: 170: "From the end of the sixth century to the middle fifth, there is no surviving dedication to celebrate military victory at Olympia that does not have the name of both adversaries, whether it is Greek against Greek or Greek against barbarian. In contrast, at Delphi, it is only after the middle of the fifth century ... that the vanquished is usually named."

[97] Herodotos 1.14; Aymard 1949: 63; Jacquemin 1999: 54; Scott 2010: 41–5.

[98] Neer 2001; Scott 2010: 11–12, 63–6.

[99] Scott 2010: 62–3, with references.

Dedications following the Battles of Salamis and Plataia

The victories at Salamis and Plataia were together a remarkable moment in Greek history, captured in literature and art at the time and reimagined frequently thereafter.[100] In 472 B.C., decades before Herodotos wrote his account of the war, the playwright Aischylos presented a fictionalized account, ostensibly from the Persian viewpoint. Aischylos, who had fought for the Athenians at Salamis, set his *Persians* at Xerxes' court following that defeat. Aischylos advanced no condemnation of Persian autocracy, nor a promotion of democracy. Rather, his was the fundamental concern of dramatists: the exploration of human folly, driven by overweening pride, and divine retribution.[101] The hubris of Xerxes drives him to seek "to restrain the current of the sacred Hellespont, the Bosphoros, a stream divine . . . he thought in his folly he would gain mastery of all the gods, yes even over Poseidon."[102] These are the words given to the shade of Darius, who proceeds to relate his son's violation of temples and the destruction or theft of votives, which would result in the defeat at Plataia.

> For, on reaching the land of Hellas restrained by no religious awe, they ravaged the images of the gods and set fire to their temples. Altars have been destroyed, statues of the gods have been thrown from their bases in utter ruin and confusion. Therefore, since they wrought such evil, evil they suffer in no less measure; and other evils are still in store: the spring of their woes is not yet quenched, but it still wells forth. For so great will be the mass of clotted gore spilled by the Dorian lance upon Plataian soil that heaps of dead will reveal, even to the third generation, a voiceless record for the eyes of men that mortal man should not vaunt himself excessively. For presumptuous pride, when it has matured, bears as its fruit a crop of calamity, from which it reaps an abundant harvest of tears.[103]

In victory, the Greeks acknowledged their debt to the gods in the reconstruction of temples and the raising of new votives, among them the Plataian tripod.

The dedication of *agalmata*, works of art or craft that evoked wonder, as votive offerings to the gods is recorded by several writers.[104] Chief among the dedications following the sea battle at Salamis was a bronze statue of Apollo, described by Herodotos as clutching a ship's prow (*akroterion*).[105] Later

---

[100] Morris 1992: 290–5. The fullest later account is included in Plutarch, *Aristeides*.

[101] Gruen 2011: 9–21. A warning to this effect is placed in the mouth of Darius' brother, Xerxes' uncle Artabanus, according to Herodotos 7.10.

[102] Aischylos, *Persians* 745–50.

[103] Aischylos, *Persians* 809–22.

[104] Day 2010: 85–129 on *agalma*, its meaning and function, and what the term does not necessarily mean before the fifth century B.C. (i.e., "statue").

[105] Herodotos 8.121. See also Pausanias 10.14.5.

identified simply as the "Big Statue" (*megas andrias*), he stood twelve cubits (5.9 m/19.4 ft) tall on an inscribed stone base formed from several blocks.[106] The inscription appears to have included the first reference to a unified Greek people, "Hellenes" (*Hellanes* in Phokian).[107] In fact, the Hellenes responsible were a select group, an alliance of Athens, Aigina, Kerkyra, and Chios. As we have earlier noted, Aigina additionally erected a votive to its own role in the form of a bronze mast supporting three stars.

Following the land battle at Plataia, in addition to the bronze column and golden tripod dedicated to Delphic Apollo, tithes of the spoils were converted into votive statues to two other gods: a bronze statue of Olympian Zeus (4.6 m/ 15 ft), dedicated at the Panhellenic shrine at Olympia, and a bronze statue of Poseidon (2.9 m/9.5 ft), dedicated at Isthmia.[108] Six centuries later, Pausanias (5.23.3) records that the Zeus was created by Anaxagoras of Aigina, and for that reason we might suppose that the same Anaxagoras was responsible for the mast and three golden stars erected by Aigina at Delphi after Salamis. The Plataian Zeus is described as standing on a base that was inscribed, like the serpentine bronze pillar of the Delphic tripod, with the names of the Greek cities that fought the Persians, listed and grouped similarly, if not identically.[109] The inscription on the bronze column at Delphi was possibly intended to emulate that on the Olympian Zeus, since it was added later and is connected to the demise of Pausanias, the Spartan general.

It is a logical conjecture that as the spoils were distributed after the battle, responsibility for dedicating the votive statue at Delphi was claimed by Pausanias. It is also reasonable to suppose that the task of creating three large bronze statues in short order required that each work be assigned to a different workshop. These workshops might be located in particular cities or at the sanctuaries.[110] One might further suggest that the leading cities other than

---

[106] Laroche and Jacquemin 1988; Jacquemin 1999: 170–1, 336, no. 309. The association between the statue and an inscription at Delphi referring to a μέγας ανδριάς was made by G. Roux, and is accepted by Laroche and Jacquemin 1988: 245; and more recently by Scott 2010: 83–4. In fact, there was a considerably larger statue of a man on the terrace, dedicated by Alexander I of Makedonia.

[107] That is to say, a lacuna in the inscription allows for a word of eight letters, which must have been a nominative plural noun, and which Laroche and Jacquemin 1988: 245, recreate as ΗΕΛΛΑΝΕΣ. The formulation Ἕλληνες is accepted by all later writers describing the events of 480–79 B.C., including Herodotos, writing in the 440s B.C. about the allied forces at Salamis, and Thucydides. For the broader context, see Hall 2002: 125–228, esp. 128–9, 182–3.

[108] Herodotos 9.81: καὶ τῷ ἐν Ὀλυμπίῃ θεῷ ἐξελόντες, ἀπ' ἧς δεκάπηχυν χάλκεον Δία ἀνέθηκαν, καὶ τῷ ἐν Ἰσθμῷ θεῷ, ἀπ' ἧς ἑπτάπηχυς χάλκεος Ποσειδέων ἐξεγένετο. See Gauer 1968: 96–8; Scott 2010: 173.

[109] Pausanias 5.23.1–2. See above, table one.

[110] See Rolley 2002 on the bronze workshop at Delphi; for workshops in Lakonia, and elsewhere manned by Lakonians, see Stibbe 2000a. Morgan 1990: 30–9, 137–46 collates and interprets the earliest evidence for bronze working at Olympia and Delphi, concluding that tripods were always cast elsewhere before the seventh century, whereas many smaller bronze votives, notably statuettes of animals, could be produced in large enough numbers to satisfy those attending the festival by traveling craftsmen working in situ.

Sparta, Athens, and Corinth would have taken the lead role in commissioning and producing the other votives. If so, then Corinth probably was responsible for the Poseidon for nearby Isthmia, leaving to the Athenians the colossal Zeus for Olympia.[111] These conjectures proceed far beyond what the sources tell us, but intersect with the recorded observations that the votive offerings at Olympia and Isthmia took anthropomorphic forms, in marked contrast to the Plataian tripod.[112] They echoed more closely, therefore, the votive statues that had been erected at Delphi to mark the victory at Salamis, apart from the stellar mast of the Aiginetans. However, there were strong naval associations in other votives after Salamis that might be compared to the Aiginetan mast. The Salamis Apollo, raised at Delphi by the Athenians and their allies, including the Aiginetans, clutched a ship's prow. In addition, three Phoenician triremes, ships captured in battle, were raised as monuments, one each at Poseidon's sanctuaries at Isthmia and Sounion, and the third dedicated at Salamis itself to the local hero Ajax.[113]

Even as the Plataian tripod was raised, many cities chose to dedicate their own, smaller statues both at home and also to Apollo at the same location, the eastern terrace of the temple at Delphi, engaging as ever in competitive demonstrations of piety.[114] They offered representations of land animals, including cows, calves, and oxen, probably to represent the sacrifices conducted to honor Apollo after Plataia, and perhaps to signify that the victory had been a *land* battle, after which there were hopes that livestock might once again flourish on the lands devastated by the Persian army.[115]

Allowing for this competitive piety in minor votives, the major monuments dedicated to Delphic Apollo after Salamis and Plataia describe a moment in Greek history of immense significance: the time when disparate poleis came together as one people, Hellenes, allied against a common enemy, the Persians. But even then, there were leaders and followers, winners and losers. The inscriptions and dedications at both Delphi and Olympia made clear not only that the listed poleis fought together, but also that they did so under Spartan and Athenian leadership. That the ultimate victory took place under the

---

[111] Similarly, it is purely conjecture to suggest that the Zeus was manufactured at Olympia, although a good deal of support is offered by the ubiquity of Zeus statues at Olympia at this time, on which see Scott 2010: 172–5.

[112] Jacquemin 1999: 169: "Que les vainqueurs de Salamine aient offert un Apollon à Delphes et ceux de Platées un Zeus à Olympie et un Poséidon à l'Isthme montre bien l'importance de l'image du maître du sanctuaire."

[113] Herodotos 8.121. See Gauer 1968: 71–3. Also Raubitschek 1949: 198–201, no. 172; Morris 1992: 289–90, noting that another ship may once have been placed on marble blocks found before 1853 on the Athenian acropolis.

[114] For statues to the Persian wars at other locations throughout Greece, as recorded by Pausanias, see Hall 2002: 183.

[115] Jacquemin 1999: 207–9; Scott 2010: 87; Day 2010: 11–2. In the same manner, individual poleis had dedicated smaller versions of the "big statue" following Salamis.

leadership of the Spartans at Plataia, a land battle, is telling, since unity would be shattered by the continued rise of the Athenians, whose "wooden walls" had numbered half the fleet at Salamis. The struggle for supremacy between Sparta and Athens, masters of land and sea, would define the second half of the fifth century.[116] Furthermore, the citizens of those poleis that had sided with the Persians were, by implication, not properly Hellenes. Thebes, Sparta's traditional foe in central Greece and the most powerful polity in Boiotia, where Plataia is located, was in this manner excluded. According to Plutarch, eighty talents were set aside from the booty taken at Plataia to set up a sanctuary to Athena at Plataia, adorned with frescoes.[117] The Plataians were the only Boiotians to have fought on the Greek side, and the frescoes have been interpreted as mythic condemnation of the "Medizing" Boiotians, notably the Thebans. A representation of the epic story of the "Seven against Thebes" was included, with emphasis placed upon an episode that was not known before the Persian wars, namely a heroic stand against the Thebans by the Athenians to recover the bodies of Adrastos' fallen soldiers for burial at Eleusis.[118] This episode was cited by the Athenian commander before the battle of Plataia, in arguing for command of the second wing, and in securing that position, the Athenian forces were drawn up against the Thebans.[119] The paintings in the Plataian sanctuary, which were still visible, and indeed vibrant, when Plutarch (d. AD 120) wrote, were of Athenian inspiration and execution, celebrating in mythic fashion the Athenians' defeat of the Thebans. But since the dedication of the Plataian sanctuary was, in origin, a Corinthian suggestion, "both the Spartans and Athenians set up their own trophies."[120]

As more time passed following the victories over the Persians, Greek art took a new direction. For the first time, from around 470 B.C., depictions of historical events rather than mythical scenes were produced. The first known is a painting of the battle of Marathon in the Stoa Poikila at Athens, although gods and heroes still appeared alongside real Athenians. If we may trust a much later scholiast on Gregory of Nazianzos, there was also a painting of the battle of Salamis. At the Temple of the Athenians at Apollo's sanctuary on Delos, a depiction of the battle of Artemision featured the god Boreas, the north wind, who had destroyed much of the Persian fleet.[121]

---

[116] Thucydides 3.57: "Shocking indeed will it seem for Spartans to destroy Plataia, and for the city whose name your fathers inscribed upon the tripod at Delphi for its good service to be by you blotted out from the map of Hellas, to please the Thebans." A Byzantine scholion to this passage: "The [tripod] from the spoils of the Medes, which Pausanias made." See Frick 1857–60: 501, and below at chapter four.

[117] Plutarch, *Aristeides* 20.3; Castriota 1992: 63–76.

[118] Castriota 1992: 65–73.

[119] Herodotos 9.27.

[120] Plutarch, *Aristeides* 20.3.

[121] Neils 2013: 596, 610.

Seven Centuries at Delphi

In the years following the erection of the Plataian tripod, the eastern terrace of the temple at Delphi became increasingly crowded with Greek monuments to victory, projecting the achievements of individual poleis, confronting those of others, overshadowing in scale or surpassing in style or grandeur those they were placed beside or before. The poleis of Magna Graecia, which had not participated in the defense of Hellas, were major players in this escalation, and also in the new trend of displaying captured booty in creative forms at Delphi rather than simply depositing captured arms, as was standard at Olympia. For example, after 473 B.C., the western Greek polis of Taras (modern Taranto, and notably a Spartan colony), dedicated a bronze statue group consisting of women and horses, representations of the living loot cast from the arms and armor of the defeated Messapians.[122] Gelon, the tyrant of Syracuse (in modern Sicily), whose city had a long association with Delphi, wished to link his victory at Himera over the Carthaginians with the Panhellenic monuments.[123] He did so by erecting a bronze column with a statue of Nike, goddess of victory, her head surmounted by a golden tripod, emulating the Plataian trophy.[124] The artist responsible for the monument is identified by an inscription as Bion, son of Diodoros of Miletos.[125] Hieron, Gelon's brother and successor as tyrant at Syracuse, erected a similar column and tripod, perhaps to mark his victory at Cumae in 474 B.C.[126] A scholion to Pindar's first *Pythian Ode* states that Simonides wrote six lines for the dedication inscribed on this golden bowl.[127] There was also a statue of Hieron himself on the eastern terrace, and to the north of the temple a new area was dedicated by the installation of the stunning bronze chariot and charioteer, who today stands again at Delphi holding his reins.

---

[122] Jacquemin 1999: 70; Scott 2010: 75. See also Herodotos 7.170.

[123] Herodotos 7.165–6; trans. Godley: "Accordingly Gelon sent the money to Delphi, because he could not aid the Greeks. They add this tale too—that Gelon and Theron won a victory over Amilcas the Carchedonian in Sicily on the same day that the Greeks defeated the Persian at Salamis."

[124] Diodoros Sikeliotes 11.26.7; trans. Oldfather: "After this incident Gelon built noteworthy temples to Demeter and Core out of the spoils, and making a golden tripod of sixteen talents value he set it up in the sacred precinct at Delphi as a thank-offering to Apollo." The bell-shaped base of this monument was more than a meter high, suggesting that it at least matched in height the Serpent Column and golden tripod. See Amandry 1987: 81–92; Jacquemin 1999: 176, 353, n. 446; Scott 2010: 88.

[125] Perdrizet 1896; Homolle 1897: 589: Τὸν τρίποδα καὶ τὲν νίκεν ἐργάσατο/Βίον Διοδόρο υἱὸς Μιλέσιος.

[126] Amandry 1987: 90; Morris 1992: 291.

[127] Oldfather 1989, in a note on Diodoros Sikeliotes 11.26.7, states: "The Scholia to Pindar P. 1.152 give the inscription, which has been attributed to Simonides." The text and translation are to be found at *Lyra Graeca*, trans. Edmonds 1924: II, 384–5: "I say that Gelo, Hiero, Polyzalus, and Thrasybulus, sons of Deinomenes, dedicated these tripods out of fifty talents and a hundred litres of the gold of Damarete, being a tithe of the tithe of the booty they had of their victory over the Barbarian nations when they gave a great army to fight beside the Greeks for freedom." See also Green 2006: 82–3.

The polis of Kroton (in modern Calabria) also erected a tripod at about this time, perhaps a belated dedication to its victory in 510 B.C. over the Sybarites. Certainly, the statue postdated the Plataian tripod, for it was placed beside it and emulated its form as closely as the Syracusan tripods. Only a few years after their erection, therefore, for a worshipper approaching the Temple of Apollo from below, as one must at Delphi, the view of the monuments both to Salamis and Plataia was obscured by the Krotonate tripod.[128] The practice of dedicating columns and tripods continued well into the fourth century when, in ca. 330 B.C., the Acanthus Column, also known as the Column of the Dancers, was dedicated, probably by the Athenians. This pillar had an acanthus leaf capital, the earliest of its type to survive, which supported three sculpted marble dancing-girls, which in turn supported on their heads one version of the omphalos, a conical stone representing the earth's navel. A golden tripod similar to that which sat atop the twisted bronze serpents framed the dancing girls. At fourteen meters tall, this monument would have dwarfed the Plataian tripod.[129]

On a far smaller scale, it does not seem unreasonable to suggest that a striking serpent protome, produced at some time in the first half of the fifth century B.C. and discovered at Delphi, was the work of a local artist familiar with the Plataian tripod. The protome (fig. 3.6) measures 26 cm in length, from nose to base, and appears to have been fashioned to connect to a vertical pole, perhaps a candleholder.[130] The serpent's ridged eyebrow and round eye socket are strikingly similar to those of the upper jaw presumed to belong to the Serpent Column (above, fig. 1.10, above). Additionally, the mouth is slightly open, a tongue visible within, and the lower jaw sports a striking beard, as later depictions suggest was also the case with the Serpent Column's snake heads. No teeth are visible on the smaller bronze, but its neck is covered with incised lozenges, delicately mimicking a serpent's skin.

According to Pausanias, the golden tripod that had surmounted the Plataian monument was stolen by the Phokians when they seized the sanctuary at Delphi in 356 B.C.[131] We know almost nothing more of the bronze pillar

---

[128] A point made by Scott 2010: 89, in his compelling study of spatial politics at Delphi and Olympia. It is possible that the Krotonate tripod was decorated with a scene of Apollo fighting the Python, although at this time there was no developed iconography of that encounter. See Laroche and Jacquemin 1990; Luce, Laroche, Déroche, and Petridis 1993: 631–41; Jacquemin 1999: 71, 173, and no. 126.

[129] Jacquemin 1999: 132–3, 163–4, 177, 357 no. 489. The Acanthus Column was discovered at Delphi in 1894 in 260 fragments. The virtual reconstruction of the monument is reported at Thibault and Martinez 2008; online at http://www.insightdigital.org/entry/index.php?option=com_content&view=article&id=146.

[130] Delphi, Museum inv. 9420. See Rolley 1983: 146, fig. 138.

[131] Pausanias 10.13.9: "The bronze part of the offering is still preserved, but the Phokian leaders did not leave the gold as they did the bronze." See the extensive commentary by Frazer 1898: V, 299–307. It seems probable that the golden tripods that adorned other columns, including that of Kroton, were also stolen at this time, although this is not expressly stated.

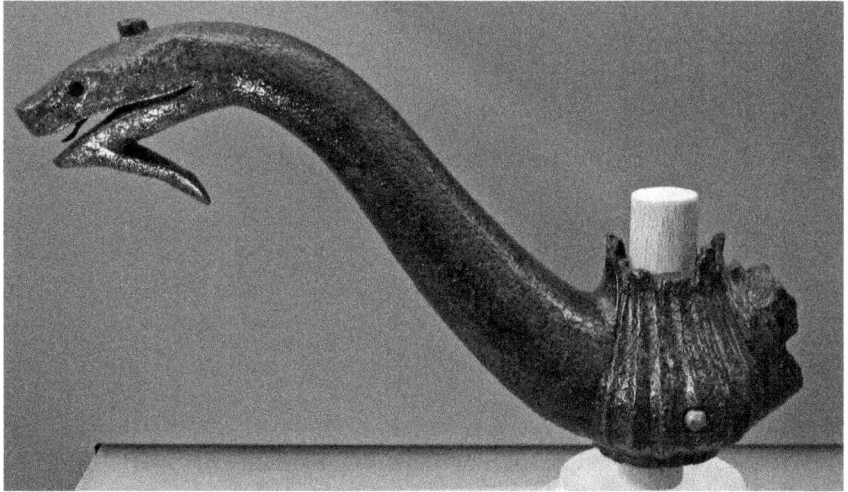

FIGURE 3.6 Serpent protome, bronze, possibly from a candleholder, fifth century B.C., Delphi, Museum inv. 9420. Photo: Dan Diffendale, with permission.

that had supported the tripod until, almost 700 years later, it was moved to Constantinople. However, there are indications that this striking monument to the Greek victory at Plataia, like those to other victories of the Persian wars and to those who fell in them, remained features of a ritual landscape cultivated by Greeks and appropriated by Romans.[132] Certainly, the mythic significance of the Persian wars appealed greatly to Octavian, later Augustus, as he fought in the east and then transformed the city of Rome into an imperial capital. Following the Battle of Actium, on 31 September B.C., Octavian's victory at sea over the forces of Mark Antony and Cleopatra, Octavian had the bronze prow mounts of his enemies' ships melted down and formed into four bronze pillars, which he erected in Rome, on the Campus Martius.[133] This appears to have been in emulation of Greek actions following Salamis, and Augustus rather later, in 2 B.C., staged the battle of Salamis on an artificial lake created for the purpose, once again equating Actium and Salamis for a Roman audience.[134] The bronze pillars were later transferred to the Capitoline by Domitian, and were seen by Servius in around A.D. 400. Following victory over the Parthians in 23 B.C. and the subsequent recovery of lost eagles from Syria, Augustus emulated the Greek victors at Plataia, erecting two huge bronze tripods on sculpted marble bases, one at Rome in his new temple complex to Apollo on the Palatine

---

[132] Alcock 2002: 74–86; Spawforth 2012.
[133] Blaauw 2001: 142–3 supplies references and commentary.
[134] Alcock 2002: 182. See now also Spawforth 2012: 103–6, 130–5 on the significance of the Persian wars, notably the battles of Marathon, Salamis, and Plataia, for Augustus and his regime, within a broader study of the role of Greece in Augustan culture.

and the second at Athens, which Pausanias (1.18.8) would later observe.[135] Augustus understood the form of the tripod to signify victory over eastern barbarians, and consistently projected the parallelism between his victories in the east and those of his Greek forebears over the Persians.[136] Additionally, following Actium, the future Augustus established on the coast by the site of the sea battle a victory city, Nikopolis, which he adorned with a temple and statuary. The significance of a notable statue, of an ass and its keeper, is explained by Plutarch and Suetonius: they were Eutyches (Prosper) and his donkey Nikon (Victory), who had wandered into Octavian's camp on the eve of battle. This statue Constantine took from Augustus' Nikopolis to place in his own, among much else, as we shall see in the following chapter.

---

[135] Schneider 1986: 50–97 discusses these tripods in a rich manner and identifies surviving elements of the marble sculpture, of kneeling Persians, that supported them. This form of representation evoked the well-known Caryatids and Persian Porch, as described by Vitruvius (1.1), and also the statues bearing tripods described by Pausanias (3.18.8), discussed elsewhere.

[136] I thank Anthony Kaldellis for drawing my attention to Schneider 1986, and other literature on this important topic.

4}

Constantinople in Late Antiquity

Victory City – Furnishing Constantinople – Heroes and Monsters – Draco Standards – The Delphic Tripods after Constantine – Depicting the Hippodrome in Late Antiquity – The Epigram of the Medes and the Dragon Statue

On 25 December 323, the "Day of the Sun," which was also the *dies natalis* of Christ, Constantine I, Roman emperor in the West, issued a law exempting all Christians from participation in lustral rites throughout the empire. "Soon after that," according to the *Origo Constantini*, "war broke out again between Licinius and Constantine." Licinius was Constantine's fellow Augustus and last remaining rival, ruling over the eastern Roman Empire. Constantine prepared for war at Thessalonike, which offered a splendid natural harbor for his fleet. Licinius, based on the Sea of Marmara and shuttling between the cities of Nikomedia and Byzantion, sent orders across the eastern Mediterranean that warships be sent to the Hellespont. The decisive war between the two emperors took place in summer 324, culminating in the Battle of Chrysopolis on 18 September 324. Zosimos relates that "a sharp battle took place between Chalkedon and Hieron, which Constantine won convincingly ... And as soon as this was known to the inhabitants of the city of Byzantion, they threw open their gates to welcome Constantine, and the Chalkedonians did the same."[1] Licinius withdrew from the battlefield to Nikomedia with his remaining forces. Although Constantine proceeded to set a siege, the war had by now been won. Having too few men to resist, Licinius surrendered. He sent his wife, Constantine's half-sister Constantia, to beg for his life, and when that was granted he came in person to relinquish his purple cloak. Having sent Licinius as a private citizen to Thessalonike, Constantine had him murdered in the spring of 325.

When Constantine, seeking a heavenly sign from his divine patron, looked to the heavens on the night before the Battle of Chrysopolis, he would have seen to his south and west, in the direction of his enemy, that the night sky

---

[1] Zosimos 2.26.

in the hours after sunset was dominated by the spiraling tails of the Milky Way, and beside it the constellations Serpens and Ophiuchus (fig. 4.1). Above his own position, just before the sun rose, Draco completed its circuit across the northern sky, its head plunging towards the horizon and further down to the underworld (fig. 4.2). As the sun's solar chariot ascended, its brilliance obliterated the dragon's writhing tail. The night sky above the battlefield, and above the nearby city of Byzantion, was almost identical to that seen at Plataia some eight centuries earlier, although surely Constantine could not have known of this remarkable coincidence. It is not impossible, however,

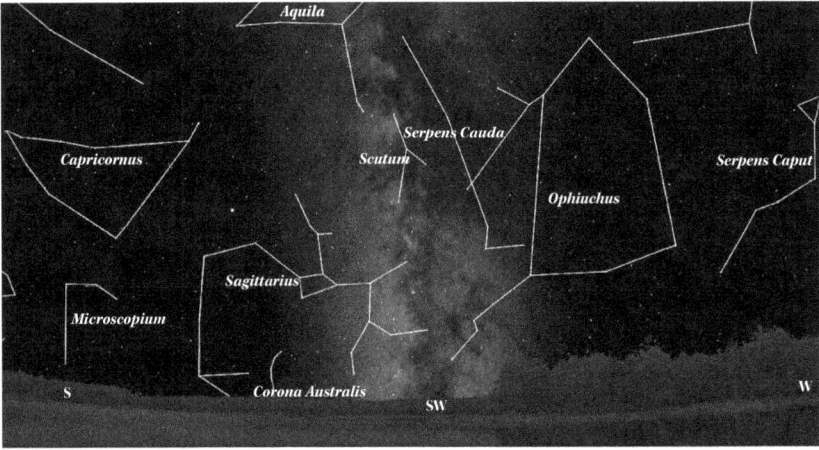

FIGURE 4.1 The night sky above Byzantion at sunset before the Battle of Chrysopolis, 17 October A.D. 324. Produced by David Pankenier using Starry Night Pro 6.4.3.

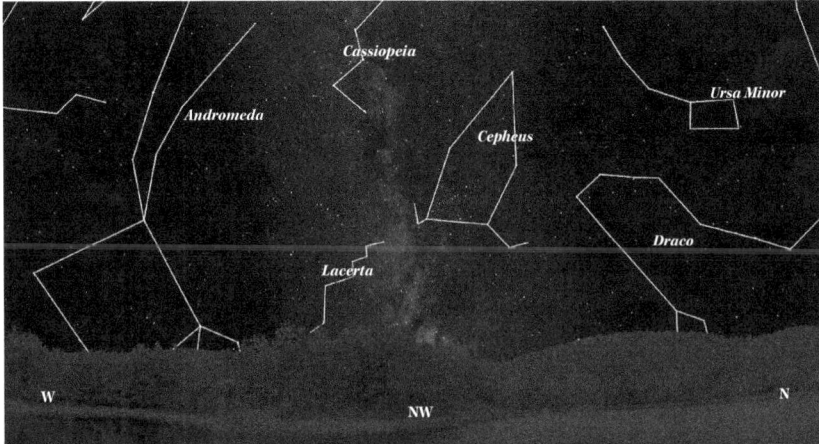

FIGURE 4.2 The night sky above Byzantion at sunrise before the Battle of Chrysopolis, 18 October A.D. 324. Produced by David Pankenier using Starry Night Pro 6.4.3.

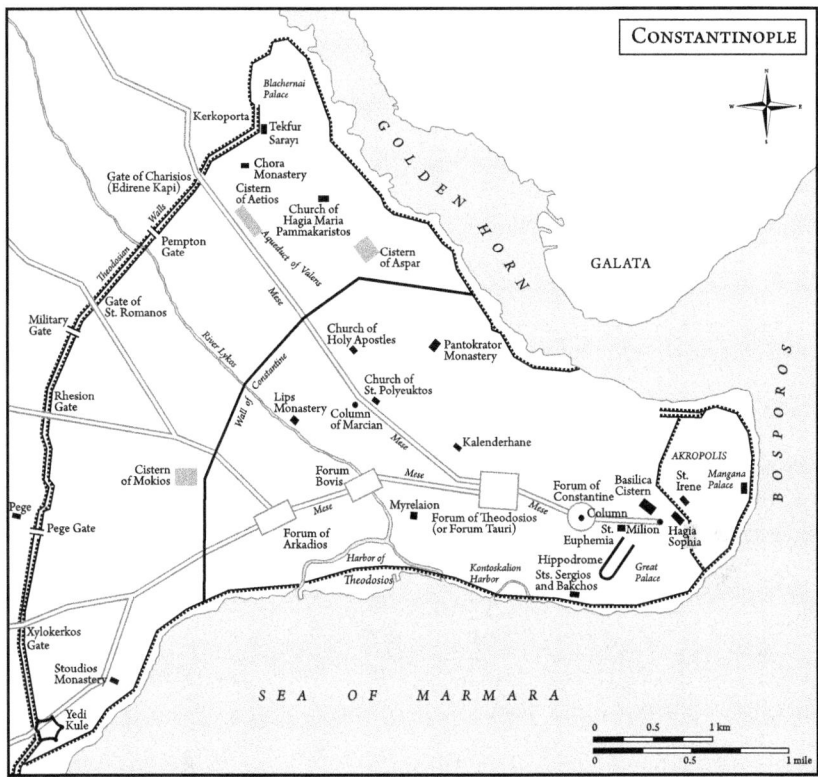

MAP 5 Byzantine Constantinople.

that he saw in the sky an image of entwined serpents. Shortly afterwards his agents brought him just such an image in bronze from Apollo's temple, among the Delphic Tripods, which were placed in his hippodrome facing the box in which he would sit to celebrate the founding of his victory city, Constantinople.

Victory City

Constantine retired from the battlefield to Nikomedia, which had been a capital both for Licinius and before him the emperors Diocletian and Galerius. It was there that a great persecution of Christians had commenced two decades earlier, when Constantine had been present at the court. Constantine, therefore, had several reasons to wish not to reside permanently in Nikomedia. He required a new capital, close enough to continue to benefit from Nikomedia's felicitous location, between west and east on the major lands routes and with access to the Mediterranean through the Sea of Marmara and Hellespont, but without associations with the persecuting emperors. Constantine also desired a victory city, a stage to celebrate his greatest triumph and his mastery of the whole Roman world, a city suited to the majesty of the Augustus, a new Nikopolis. Constantine wished, in other words, to emulate Augustus.

According to Sozomenos, writing in the middle years of the fifth century, Constantine first considered the site of Troy, known to him but not to us until its rediscovery by Frank Calvert, and later by Heinrich Schliemann, near modern Çanakkale in Turkey. Troy was the chosen progenitor of Rome, and the story of Rome's foundation had been retold and fixed in tradition by Virgil's *Aeneid*. Small wonder that the city of Constantine was to have returned to the source, in the tales of those who experienced its rise and wished to appropriate the common past of the two cities, Old and New Rome. Moreover, Troy lay close to the site of a victory won by Constantine's son Crispus against Licinius' fleet, echoing Nikopolis' proximity to the site of the battle of Actium. But if work at Troy did begin, why was a decision taken to relocate? An answer may well be related to the fate of Crispus. By the end of 326, the emperor's oldest son had been tried and executed for an obscure crime relating to Constantine's wife, Fausta, who was shortly afterwards also dead. Constantine had embarked on a process of damning their memories, and to build a great new city near the site of Crispus' greatest victory may no longer have appeared auspicious.

Constantine chose Byzantion for the site of his victory city. It was equidistant from the Rhine and the Euphrates and sat at the end of the Via Egnatia, the great land road across the Balkans, and of the military road east. But such strategic thinking was not unique to Constantine. It had long been apparent, and the city had suffered as a consequence. The walls of Byzantion and much within them had been razed by Septimius Severus in A.D. 196, as punishment for the inhabitants having supported the pretender Pescennius Niger. According to Cassius Dio, writing only six or seven years after the episode, the city had resisted a siege for three years. It did without land walls for as many decades afterwards. However, by the 320s much had been rebuilt, and a new hippodrome and bath complex supplied. Later legend assigned these to Septimius Severus, safely distant and already identified as the destroyer of much of the older city. But that contradicts the testimony of Herodian, an author of the third century, who saw the city's walls still in ruins in 240. Recently, it has been suggested that the hippodrome, at least, postdates 260. Thus, Septimius Severus seems an unlikely refounder. The most likely candidates are emperors who were based at nearby Nicomedia: Diocletian, Galerius, and Licinius. Constantine's actions in Rome, following the defeat in 312 of Maxentius at the Battle of the Milvian Bridge, provide a template for his behavior. Everything that Maxentius had built, and that was a great deal, was appropriated by Constantine. Constantine took Byzantion as his own and remade it in his honor, placing at its heart the Delphic Tripods.

Furnishing Constantinople

According to Jerome, writing in 334, "Constantinople was dedicated by denuding almost all other cities." That is to say, for the dedication of his eponymous city, his victory city, Constantine brought statues in bronze and marble, columns, pillars, and obelisks from across the late Roman world.[2] These were displayed in the major public spaces he established, refurbished, and rebuilt, notably his new palace, the adjoining hippodrome, and the eponymous Forum of Constantine.[3]

It has been suggested that Constantine's interest in the Serpent Column was related to his desire to conquer Persia.[4] This is a compelling suggestion, as Constantine died in 337, having just begun his march to the east to confront the Zoroastrian Sasanians, who had just begun to persecute Christians.[5] Moreover, we have seen that Augustus took a particular interest in the Persian wars and sought to cast his own victories, and several monuments to them, as related to that earlier existential struggle between the West and East.[6] Constantine certainly was inspired by Augustus' actions. However, Constantine's interest appears to have been in Delphi generally, the Delphic Tripods as a group, and other Apollonian *agalmata*, cult statues, rather than in one item that had particular associations with victory over Persia. At the heart of his new imperial palace, Constantine established a large court, the Tribunal (*tribounalion*), surrounded by meeting and dining halls. The Tribunal was early on given another name, which features in writings until the tenth century: Delphax. Occasionally written Delphix, Delphax was recognized to be a corrupted form of *delphikos*, Delphic, since the court's colonnade featured columns of various colours brought from Delphi.[7]

Eusebios of Caesarea, whose life of Constantine was completed shortly after 337, provides an early report on the adornment of the new city, dwelling on the Apollonian *agalmata* and claiming that Constantine's aim was to "confute the superstitious error of the heathens":

> To this end he stripped the entrances to their temples in every city, so that their doors were removed at the emperor's command.[8] In other cases the roofs were

---

[2] There are many works devoted to Constantinople's foundation and its monuments. The seminal paper on the city's antique statuary, Mango 1963, must now be read alongside Bassett 2004 (with references to the most important works of the intervening four decades) and the essays collected in Pitarakis 2010.

[3] Stephenson 2009: 190–211; Bardill 2012: 151–8.

[4] See Stichel 1997: 319–20; Dell'Acqua 2013.

[5] Barnes 2011: 166–7 is the latest to consider Constantine's efforts against the Persians a form of "holy war." But see Stephenson 2009: 248–51.

[6] See above, chapter three.

[7] Guilland 1950: 293–306; Guilland 1969: I, 70–80.

[8] The fate of the bronze doors from the Artemision at Ephesos will be discussed below.

ruined by the removal of cladding. In yet other cases the haughty works of bronze, which in error the ancients had for a long time exalted, he displayed to everyone in all the public spaces of the imperial city, so that in one place the Pythian [Apollo] was displayed to the viewers as a contemptible spectacle, and in another the Sminthian [Apollo], in the hippodrome itself the Delphic Tripods, and at the palace the Muses of Helikon. The city named after the emperor was filled throughout with objects of skilled artwork in bronze dedicated in various provinces. To these in the name of gods those sick with error had for long ages offered countless sacrifices and burnt offerings, but now they at last learnt sense, as the emperor used these adornments for the laughter and amusement of spectators.[9]

To believe the information Eusebios provides, we need not accept his interpretation of Constantine's motivations for transplanting statuary. A principal objection, that Constantinople was not exclusively a Christian city from its refoundation, has some merit, since the desire to edify and impress both pagan and Christian subjects offers a more convincing explanation for the collection and display of statuary than Eusebios' contention that these were objects solely of contempt and ridicule. The city was furnished with at least one new temple, perhaps two, and only a few churches.[10] Moreover, Constantine had been a devotee of Apollo, in his guise as Sol Invictus, the Unconquered Sun, whose image appeared on Constantine's coins after his victory at the battle of the Milvian Bridge in 312 until the early 320s.[11] According to a panegyrical oration, a speech in praise of Constantine delivered in Gaul in 310, the emperor had at that time recently experienced a vision of Apollo, who had appeared accompanied by the goddess of victory, Victoria, to offer Constantine laurel crowns.[12] The collection of Apollonian *agalmata* with which Constantine furnished Constantinople may be read in that context, and the solar significance accorded to hippodromes and their furnishings in the Roman world would also favour this contention.[13]

Recently, however, support for Eusebios' interpretation has been identified in the epigrams of Palladas. The fate of pagan bronze sculpture is spelled out, albeit somewhat obliquely, in an epigram attributed to Palladas and preserved in the *Greek Anthology*: "Having become Christian, owners of Olympian palaces dwell here unharmed; for the melting pot that produces the life-giving *follis*

---

[9] Eusebios, *Life of Constantine* 3.54; trans. Cameron and Hall 1999: 143, 301–2. See also Bassett 2004: 230–1, 245–6.

[10] A precious documentary record of A.D. 425, the *Notitia urbis Constantinopolitanae*, ed. Seeck 1876: 242, lists fourteen churches in the city a full century after its foundation.

[11] Stephenson 2009: 127–40, 151–8, 172–4, 330–9, for commentary and references to the large bibliography on this subject.

[12] Stephenson 2009: 127–31; Bardill 2012: 84–104.

[13] Bardill 2012: 154, for comments and bibliography.

will not put them in the fire."[14] By this he means that statues of the gods were either placed in Christian contexts, and thus appropriated, or were melted down for the minting of the basic bronze coin, *follis*. Palladas was hitherto believed to be writing in the later fourth and early fifth centuries, and hence describing the fate of pagan idols at that time. However, Kevin Wilkinson has suggested that Palladas was writing during the reign of Constantine.[15]

According to this interpretation, antique sculpture that was not melted down for coin would "become Christian" in the city's public spaces. But how could a cult statue, an idol, become Christian? When placed in Constantinople, ancient works of art shared in the intended polysemy that characterized the Constantinian moment: they meant different things to "pagans" and Christians.[16] Christian exegetes now understood that the New Testament was prefigured in the Old, and just as the true meanings of its stories could be drawn out, so monuments of ancient art revealed their true meanings in Christian settings. Origen in his *Contra Celsum* and Eusebios in his *Preparatio Evangelica* both employ profound erudition in their polemics, establishing and reinforcing the Christian position that Greek myths derived from Phoenician tales, which were themselves corruptions of the truths revealed in Scripture. Origen (*Contra Celsum*, 6.42) summed up the attitude of early Christian apologists to cognate mythologies succinctly: "It is the writings of Moses, which are not only far older than Heraclitus and Pherecydes, but even earlier than Homer, which taught the existence of this wicked power that fell from heaven. Some such ... doctrine is hinted at in the story that the serpent, the origin of Pherecydes' Ophioneus, was the cause of man's expulsion from the divine paradise, and deceived the female race with a promise of divine power and of attaining to greater things."

Constantine had recognized that Christ was the true sun (*Christus verus sol*), and his veneration of Apollo had been a stage on his path to recognizing the one true God. It was this God whose solar power was focused on the emperor in his hippodrome, where the imperial box faced the current location of the Serpent Column.[17] According to several writers, the Delphic Tripods, once sacred to Apollo, were immediately placed in the hippodrome, the heart of Constantine's Nikopolis, where the dedication ceremony for the city took place on 11 May 330. The dedication of Constantinople marked the reunification of the Roman Empire under a single sovereign and the end of persecution of

---

[14] *Greek Anthology* 9.528 = Palladas, *On the House of Marina*; trans. Paton 1916–18: III, 294–5. See also Barnes 2011: 130; Wilkinson 2009: 54–6; Wilkinson 2010a: 180–1; Wilkinson 2010b: 298–302.

[15] Wilkinson 2009, 2010a, 2010b; Barnes 2011: 13–16. If Palladas retains his traditional place in the fifth century, then the context for his observations is the Christian transformation of Constantinople's ritual topography, both in fact and in retrospect, at that time.

[16] Stephenson 2009: 196–203.

[17] The original location of the Serpent Column when brought to Constantinople, and even the date of its translation, have been disputed. Most recently, see Dagron 2011: 90–4; and Bardill 2012: 144, 362.

Christians. The Great Persecution of Christians had commenced in 302 under Diocletian and Galerius when the Tetrarchs consulted the oracle of Apollo at Delphi.[18] When persecution of all Christians was ended by Constantine's victory, the same temple was stripped of its tripods. Constantine was by 324, and certainly before 330, a committed Christian. The last war that Constantine fought against Licinius was presented as a clash of gods, a war that pitted the Christian god, who had revealed himself to Constantine, against lesser manifestations of divinity.

Constantine may himself have alluded to the presence of the Serpent Column among the Delphic Tripods. We have little knowledge of Constantine's own thoughts, but within his *Oration to the Saints*, a sermon that he delivered on a Good Friday of uncertain date, the emperor refers to the "priestess of Apollo, wearing a diadem on equal terms with the god whom she worshipped, in charge of the tripod round which the snake was coiled."[19] No serpent was involved in the Pythia's oracular process, and the association here would appear to be with Apollo's slaying of Python and its representations, where a snake might appear coiled around a tripod, or in the case of the Serpent Column among a proliferation of tripods.[20]

Heroes and Monsters

Like the bishops Constantine addressed, the learned citizens of Constantinople knew their own mythologies well.[21] Not only had these been written and rewritten through centuries, transmitting the Greek texts to us in those manuscripts that have survived, but comparative mythology had been debated ferociously by early Christian writers and their opponents. The myth of Kadmos and Drakon, for example, was well known in Constantine's time, and Ovid's description of a triple-tongued serpent may well have formed in the minds of those who

---

[18] According to Lactantius, *Deaths of the Persecutors* 11.7, the oracle at Didyma was consulted. Eusebios *VC* 2.50–1, 3.54; Cameron and Hall 1994: 245; Barnes 2011: 3, 129–31.

[19] *Oration to the Saints* 18; trans. Edward 2003: 41. Edwards assigns the sermon to the year 315 and suggests it was delivered to the citizens of Rome, but most others have favoured a later date, including 321, 324, 325, and 328. The oration was delivered when Constantine had progressed considerably with his Christian education, because it greatly resembles Lactantius' *Divine Institutes* in thought and terminology. Therefore, it was probably delivered in the later 320s. See Stephenson 2009: 171–2, 335–9, with references, and now also Bardill 2012: 140–1, 362.

[20] The description also brings to mind the carving of the goddess Hygieia among the Liverpool ivories, where her familiar serpent is entwined around a tripod (and observe the two smaller serpents above) (See fig. 7.8.). However, this is thought to be modelled on a cult statue in Rome, where the ivory was carved in ca. A.D. 400. Hygieia's companion is her father Asklepios, with his familiar motif, the serpent entwined around his staff; and this is certainly modeled on a statue which is now in the Palazzo Massimo in Rome. See Gibson 1994: 10–15, and below, chapter seven.

[21] Weitzmann 1951 is the seminar study and remains essential. See also his many other studies, notably Weitzmann 1981. However, for a new direction see now Maguire 2011.

observed the triple-tongued Serpent Column.²² The destruction of the dragon was the necessary precondition for the foundation of the city, or indeed its second foundation, for the city of Thebes, like Constantinople, enjoyed two foundations and competing foundation myths.²³

The citizens of Constantinople, including Christians, would have recognized the heroes of myth in the works of art that adorned their city. Adjacent to the Delphic Tripods on the median of Constantinople's hippodrome one could see several statues of heroes who encountered serpentine beasts. Herakles was to be seen in several guises including, perhaps, with the Hesperides,²⁴ certainly fighting the Nemean Lion,²⁵ and most famously sitting exhausted from cleaning the Augean stables.²⁶ As the Nemean Lion was a version of the land beast Mot/Behemoth, so Herakles fought also his own Yam/Leviathan, the Lernean Hydra, daughter of Typhon and Echidna. His victory cast Herakles as a new Apollo and Zeus, among the greatest of dragon-slayers. But Herakles fought also the triple-bodied giant Geryon and slew him along with his fierce sheepdog, Orthros, also the offspring of triple-bodied Typhon and brother of Kerberos, the triple-headed dog-monster that Herakles also tamed. Christ-like Herakles fought death itself, Thanatos, who ascended from Hades to claim the soul of Alkestis.²⁷

The protagonist of another myth cycle, that of the returning hero, Odysseus confronted many monsters. In Constantinople's hippodrome he was depicted watching in horror as the Skylla devoured six of his companions.²⁸ The Skylla group was well placed on the *euripos*, within one of its water basins, as similar sculpture groups had earlier been placed in artificial water features in Roman villas and grottos, imperial and aristocratic, notably in Italy. Most famously, a fragmentary marble version of the Skylla group was discovered in 1957 at Sperlonga, at a villa held to have been owned by the emperor Tiberius.²⁹ It was

---

²² Ovid, *Metamorphoses* 3.34: tres vibrant linguae, triplici stant ordine dentes. See above, in chapter two.

²³ Berman 2004 has shown that the Kadmos foundation myth was later than the myth which attributed Thebes' foundation to the twins Amphion and Zethos. One might also think of Laokoon, attacked with his two sons by sea serpents sent by Apollo, and recall that the myth came to be associated with the destruction of Troy and, consequently, the foundation of Rome. See Andreae 1988.

²⁴ Bassett 2004: 63, 218: "In the Roman period, Herakles is often shown with the sisters beside the apple tree around which a snake coils."

²⁵ Bassett 2004: 218–19.

²⁶ See below, at the start of chapter five.

²⁷ Fontenrose 1959, 1980: 358: "Yet there is something distinctive about Herakles: he is specifically cast as the conqueror of death; it is Thanatos whom he meets again and again under many names and forms."

²⁸ The placement of the Skylla group in the hippodrome is discussed below. The references to Skylla in medieval Greek sources are collected by Andreae 1988: 108–11; Bassett 2004: 218–19; and Berger 2010: 197–8.

²⁹ Notably by Andreae in various publications since the discovery of the fragments in 1957, including at 1988: 69–70; 1999: 205–6. See also Stewart 1977, with a lengthy argument for Tiberius' ownership. Salza Prina Ricotti 1987:140, fig. 2; 168–9 observes, to the contrary, that the grotto should not be understood to have been owned by Tiberius simply because he is known to have been dining there during a tragic rockfall in A.D. 26.

placed on an island in the central pool of a grotto facing a *triclinium*, or dining area.[30] The group was reconstructed by the sculptor S. Bertelin, advised by Bernard Andreae and Baldassare Conticello.[31] Skylla emerges from the water beside Odysseus' ship, its stern rising up near her right hand, which is clasping the head of the steersman; in her left is a steering oar, which she wields above her head as a weapon. Her two writhing fish tails grasp Odysseus' traveling companions, pulled from the boat, which the dogs around her waist are mauling and biting. Odysseus stands behind the doomed steersman holding his sword and shield.[32] This is the not the form of the Skylla described by Homer, but rather follows a later type, which had emerged by the fifth century B.C., as a terracotta from Melos now in the British Museum demonstrates (fig. 4.3).[33] It was the preferred Roman form, as described by Virgil (*Aeneid* 3. 427–8) and Ovid (*Metamorphoses* 13. 898–968).[34] Andreae and Conticello identified the composition as the Sperlonga–Constantinople type, which they held was based on a Hellenistic bronze original, probably from Rhodes, and perhaps the very one later installed in Constantinople.[35]

A further serpentine image deserves our particular attention. According to Eusebios of Caesarea, for the dedication of Constantinople "a panel was set high above the entrance to the imperial palace for the eyes of all to see." The image Constantine selected to place in this premier location is highly suggestive. For Eusebios, it was the godless tyrant Licinius shown as the crooked dragon-serpent of the deep, Leviathan, set under the *labarum*, Constantine's battle standard topped with the Savior's sign, the chi-rho.[36]

---

[30] Kuttner 2003: 121 has suggested that the beast devouring men might be seen as a humorous allusion to dining, and might have said the same for nearby Polyphemos and the wine-sack. See also Robinson 2011: 240–2.

[31] Andreae 1988: 69–134. See also Säfland 1972. A digital recreation by A. Tayfun Öner can be seen at Berger 2010: 198, fig. 11.1, and Pitarakis 2010: end, Folder 2, and online at http://www.byzantium1200.com/hipodrom.html.

[32] Andreae 1988: 76–86, provides expansive description and analysis of the Sperlonga fragments, reprised more briefly but with better photos at Andreae 1999: 205–15.

[33] According to Homer, *Odyssey* 12.85–110, who tells the tale first, the beast had six necks and heads, each with three rows of teeth that would seize a man. She was hidden in a grotto up to her middle. This form is shown, albeit with only three of the six necks, in the Chiusi ivory (dated to ca. 600 B.C.). See Buitron 1992: 136–49; Andreae 1999: 303–4; Robinson 2011: 239.

[34] It was this form of the Skylla that would re-appear in the Latin west, in a rare, perhaps unique fresco at Corvey, dated to ca. 850–900. Here Skylla is not slaying Odysseus' men, but rather being slain by Odysseus, who pierces her with a spear in the manner of a warrior saint. See Hanfmann 1987.

[35] Andreae 1988: 100–1, 115–17, 118–21. For criticism of Andreae's theories, see Ridgway 1989. A second type, a sculptural group reconstructed from marble fragments preserved from Hadrian's villa at Tivoli, lacked a boat. Nonetheless, it was placed on an island in a scenic artificial lake. Similarly, Domitian placed a Skylla group in a round pool in the gardens of his villa at Castel Gandolfo. For the extensive literature on the Roman villas, notably at Tivoli and Sperlonga, see now Kuttner 2003 and Robinson 2011: 239–45, with notes.

[36] Eusebios, *VC*: 1.28–32; Grabar 1936: 43ff.; Stephenson 2009: 182–9; Bardill 2012: 361–2.

FIGURE 4.3 Skylla, terracotta from Melos, 5th century B.C., now in the British Museum. Photo: author.

> [The picture showed] the Saviour's sign placed above his own head, and the hostile and inimical beast, which had laid siege to the Church of God through the tyranny of the godless, he made in the form of a dragon borne down to the deep. For the oracles proclaimed him a "dragon" and a "crooked serpent" in the books of the prophets of God . . .; therefore the Emperor also showed to all, through the medium of the encaustic painting, the dragon under his own feet and those of his sons, pierced through the middle of the body with a javelin, and thrust down in the depths of the sea. In this way he indicated the invisible enemy of the human race, whom he showed also to have departed to the depths of destruction by the power of the Saviour's trophy which was set up over his head.[37]

Eusebios records Constantine's own description of Licinius as a dragon, in a letter he sent to all the empire's Christian bishops: "liberty [is] restored and that dragon driven out of the public administration through the providence of the supreme God and by our service."[38]

When Leviathan is depicted in fourth-century art, it is frequently as a highly stylized whale which enjoys a coiling, twisting tail. On the Brescia Casket,

---

[37] Eusebios, *VC*: 3.3; trans. Cameron and Hall 1999: 122, 255–6.
[38] Eusebios, *VC*: 2.45; trans. Cameron and Hall 1998: 111, 244.

FIGURE 4.4 Ivory casket, carved in the late fourth century, showing the *ketos* as the beast that swallowed Jonah. Museo di Santa Giulia, Brescia. Photo: Emilie van Opstall, with permission.

carved in the late fourth century, the *ketos* (Jonah 1:17; Matthew 12:40) is no longer Leviathan, but the beast that swallowed Jonah. However, the familiar twisting body of the beast ends in a tripartite tail (fig. 4.4). The bronze tubes that formed the Serpent Column, forged like Behemoth's bones, resembled Leviathan, Behemoth's pair, the sea monster; and as Leviathan was Pharaoh for Ezekiel, so he was Licinius for Eusebios, "a wild beast, a twisting snake, coiling up on itself, breathing wrath and menace of war with God."[39] It was Eusebios' habit to compare Constantine's defeated enemies to Pharaoh, for in his *Life of Constantine* the bishop had cast his hero in the role of Moses, whose life in three cycles of forty years is mirrored in Constantine's reign, broken up by his decennial celebrations.[40] The reworked version of Constantine's vision may be seen as a parallel to Moses' vision of the burning bush (Exodus 3). Elsewhere, Constantine's palace upbringing is compared to that of Moses, who was likewise destined to free his people.[41] When Constantine fled a secret plot hatched by Galerius, he was "in this also preserving his likeness to the great prophet

---

[39] Eusebios, *VC* 2.1:

καὶ δὴ οἷά τις θὴρ δεινὸς ἢ σκολιὸς ὄφις περὶ ἑαυτὸν ἰλυσπώμενος, θυμοῦ τε καὶ ἀπειλῆς θεομάχου πνέων . . .

[40] Later sources record the transfer of the staff of Moses by Constantine to his new capital, where it was placed in a church of the *Theotokos tou rabdou*, the "Mother of God of the Staff," and subsequently transferred to the imperial palace. In this light, Eusebios' account of the manufacture of the *labarum* can be seen to echo that of the Ark of the Covenant (Exodus 25–7), while its use parallels that of Moses' staff (in Septuagint Greek, *rabdos*), the power of which was revealed to him by God (Exodus 4:2–6; 17:8–13).

[41] Eusebios, *VC* 1.12.

FIGURE 4.5 Small bronze coins Constantine minted exclusively at Constantinople in 327–8 showing a serpent pierced by a military standard. Trustees of the British Museum.

Moses."[42] The most sustained comparison comes when Eusebios recounts the downfall of Maxentius, whom Constantine defeated in 312 at the Battle of the Milvian Bridge, near Rome. Maxentius is transformed into a tyrant who oppressed the people of Rome, which reflects the disinformation disseminated after Constantine's victory. But it also demonstrates Eusebios' mature reflection on the episode, casting Maxentius as Pharaoh both in his revision of the *Ecclesiastical History* and in the *Life of Constantine*.[43]

The picture that Constantine set up above the palace gate has not survived, but a similar, if greatly simplified image is preserved on small bronze coins Constantine minted exclusively at Constantinople in 327–8 (fig. 4.5).[44] These coins feature on their obverse a bust of Constantine wearing a garland of victory within the legend CONSTANTINUS MAX AUG, "Constantine, Greatest Augustus." The reverses display a rendering of Constantine's battle standard, the *labarum*, which is a pole surmounted by a chi-rho sign, beneath which is a flag marked with three disks, representing the busts of three emperors, Constantine and his sons. The *labarum* is stands on the middle of, and appears to be piercing, a serpent that lies on the ground. Beneath the serpent is the mint-mark for Constantinople, and either side of the shaft of the standard is the legend SPES PUBLIC, "Hope of the people." The coin's design is a development of an earlier and common bronze type, for example that struck at Ticinum in 319–20, showing a *vexillum*, a military flag standard, planted

---

[42] Eusebios, *VC*: 1.20; Stephenson 2009: 206–11.

[43] Eusebios, *VC* I.38; *HE* 9.9. Forsyth 1987: 90–104, explores how the story of the parting of the Red Sea develops from a realistic storm in the early "Song of the Sea" (Exodus 15.1–18) to become a variation of the combat myth.

[44] RIC 7, Constantinople 19; Bruun 1962; Ramsköld 2010 discusses recent forgeries of this coin, even while noting that it is far less rare than hitherto imagined, with at least twenty reverse dies used, each capable of minting thousands, if not tens of thousands, of coins.

between two bound captives, with the inscription VIRTUS EXERCIT ("the Valour of the Army").

Draco Standards

If some Christians understood the coin as a representation of Constantine slaying Licinius/Pharaoh/Leviathan, in the same way that Eusebios understood the image about the palace gate, for many non-Christians the message would have been quite different. For reasons we have outlined, it would have evoked Apollo slaying Python, or Kadmos slaying Drakon, both of which acts also led to the foundation of a city, or indeed the refoundation of a city, since Delphi like Constantinople enjoyed a second foundation. We should not, however, neglect to mention a further association that may have been drawn by those whose familiarity with ancient myth was less developed or less immediate than their acquaintance with contemporary military standards. As the emperor had once defeated his enemies under the *vexillum*, so he now triumphed in war under his new battle standard, the *labarum*. But what of the serpent that had replaced the bound captives? Did this suggest that Constantine's standard was more powerful than the *draco*, or dragon standard, carried by "Skythians," northern peoples, including Licinius' auxiliary troops?[45]

The first description of the dragon standard is by Arrian, in the mid-second century A.D., who places it in the hands of Skythian horsemen.[46] It is generally understood that Arrian is referring to Sarmatians. However, dragon standards (*aždahā-peykar*) were also carried by Persians, and Lucian (*De historia conscribenda* 29) refers to these as the banners of each division of one thousand Parthians.[47] During Roman cavalry exercises, enemy units were designated by their carrying the *draco*, a beastly head with a gaping mouth through which wind passed, emitting a howling sound and aerating an attached purple streamer, akin to a modern windsock (see fig. 6.15, below, for a possible depiction).[48] By the middle years of the third century,

---

[45] The *draco* head appears to have taken many forms, including that of a wolf or hound, as depicted on Trajan's column in the hands of defeated Dacians. *Draco* standards feature on the Arch of Galerius, which was raised in Thessalonike to mark Galerius' victory over the Persians. The only surviving Roman *draco*, found at Niederbieber, Germany, is clearly a stylized dragon.

[46] Arrian, *Ars tactica*: 35. The treatise was composed in A.D. 136–7, while Arrian was commander of two Roman legions in Cappadocia. See Hyland 1993: 17, 73, 102.

[47] *EI*, s.v. Aždahā: 193.

[48] One is reminded, somewhat fancifully, of the now familiar combat myth in its Babylonian variation, where Marduk fights Tiamat. Cylinder seals depict Tiamat with a dragon's head and long serpentine tail, and *Enūma Elish* relates that Tiamat uttered "wild, piercing cries [as she trembled]." And when Marduk had Tiamat enmeshed in his net, she opened her jaws to swallow him, but he sent the storm winds into her open mouth and belly, keeping her mouth jammed open so that he could pierce her insides and destroy her. See *Enūma Elish* 4.89–105. See King 1902: 105–6; Fontenrose 1959, 1980: 150.

draco standards were taken into battle by auxiliary cavalry cohorts in the Roman army.[49] In spring 323, while preparing for his confrontation with Licinius, Constantine dealt with an invasion across the Danube by an army of Sarmatians led by Rausimodus, who had plundered Moesia and Thrace and taken many captives. To mark his victory over Rausimodus, Constantine took the title *Sarmaticus Maximus* and issued coins announcing SARMATIA DEVICTA, "Sarmatia has been conquered." Such coins were struck at Trier, Arles, Lyons, and Sirmium, all mints under Constantine's control. None were struck by Licinius, who instead melted some down as a public statement and asserted that in repelling the Sarmatians, Constantine had violated the border between their lands in Thrace. Having dispensed with Licinius, Constantine marched once again against his enemies to the north, defeating first the Goths and then, once again, the Sarmatians, in campaigns that commenced in 328. Although the date of the SPES PUBLIC coins do not correlate well with victories over Sarmatians, still one cannot rule out the possibility that many who saw the coins recognized the *draco* standard of barbarians pierced by the emperor's *labarum*.

Dragon standards remained a standard of the imperial entourage certainly until the tenth century. In the *Kleterologion*, a precedence book compiled in A.D. 899, dragon-standard bearers appear at certain ceremonial events or festivities, notably games in the hippodrome. At the chariot races held annually on the day after Epiphany, dragon-standard bearers (*drakonarioi*) were invited to dine with the emperor in the Hall of the *Kathismata*, a room attached to the imperial *kathisma*, in other words facing the Serpent Column.[50]

The Delphic Tripods after Constantine

It has been observed that we cannot know certainly when the Serpent Column was brought to Constantinople, since no author refers to it unambiguously.[51]

---

[49] Ammianus Marcellinus, 16.10.7 reveals that in 357, when Constantine's son Constantius processed in triumph through the city of Rome in a golden chariot, "he was surrounded by dragons (*dracones*), woven out of purple thread and bound to the golden and jeweled tops of spears, with wide mouths open to the breeze and hence hissing as if roused by anger, and leaving their tails winding in the wind."

[50] *Kleterologion*, ed. Oikonomides 1972: 191.

[51] Berger 2010: 203 would appear to be the most circumspect, suggesting it may not have been placed on the *euripos* until after 1261. Mango 2010: 38–9 is also ambivalent: "The kathisma [imperial box] was built into the east wing [of the hippodrome] more or less opposite the Serpent Column, although it is by no means certain that the latter, converted at some time into a fountain, stood originally at the spot it occupies today." However, Stichel 1997: 316–21 provides excellent critical scrutiny, showing that while none of the references is unambiguous, our preferred solution, that the column was placed in the hippodrome in ca. 330, is indeed the most likely scenario, largely on the basis of Sozomenos, and a posited common source for the information he provides that must predate Eusebios' *Life of Constantine*. Dagron 2011: 93 concurs.

The earliest unambiguous written reference to the Serpent Column in the hippodrome takes the form of a scholion, an explicatory note copied from a ninth-century original into an eleventh-century manuscript containing Thucydides' history. The scholion on passage 1.132—on the creation of the golden tripod and Serpent Column, quoted above—explains: "The tripod: not that with which Apollo divined, but another one which the Roman emperors took and moved to the hippodrome of Byzantion."[52] It is our contention, however, as set out above, that the Serpent Column was brought to Constantinople for the city's foundation, placed in the hippodrome before May 330, and has remained there from then until today.

Christian and non-Christian sources from the fourth century onward concur that the "Delphic Tripods" were placed in the hippodrome in the reign of Constantine I.[53] Modern skeptics are correct to note that Delphic Tripods need not refer to the Serpent Column. We agree. It is our contention that the phrase Delphic Tripods refers to a group of monuments that included the Serpent Column. Rather than seek to isolate the Serpent Column by identifying it as *the* Delphic Tripod, we must follow the sources, which are not concerned only with the column, but with a group of sculptures and tripods brought from Delphi.[54]

As we have seen, Eusebios of Caesarea was the earliest to record that Delphic Tripods were placed in the hippodrome, in his *Life of Constantine*, which was completed shortly after Constantine's death in 337, and before Eusebios' own death in 339.[55] Eusebios was followed in his description of Constantine's actions by two church historians, who both endeavored to continue his *Ecclesiastical History* in the first half of the fifth century. Sokrates Scholastikos wrote that to destroy pagan superstition, Constantine "at that time set up cult statues (*agalmata*) publicly as ornament for the city of Constantinople, and set up the confiscated Delphic Tripods in the hippodrome."[56] Eusebios' suggestion that the finer statues were subject to ridicule is here emended. Sozomenos provided

---

[52] Frick 1857–60: 501, n.4, 513; Hude 1927: 96–7: ἐπὶ τὸν τρίποδα: οὐκ ἐν ᾧ ἐμαντεύετο ὁ Ἀπόλλων, ἀλλ᾽ ἕτερόν τινα, ὃν ἔλαβον οἱ Ῥωμαίων βασιλεῖς καὶ μετέθηκαν ἐπὶ τὸν ἱππόδρομον τοῦ Βυζαντίου. Stichel 1997: 321–2 explained that the original note may have been considerably earlier, perhaps of the fifth century. Another scholion in the same manuscript, glossing passage 3.57 (referring to the Spartan destruction of Plataia, "a city inscribed upon the tripod at Delphi") clarifies that this is "The [tripod] from the spoils of the Medes, which Pausanias made." See Frick 1857–60: 501; Hude 1927: 200: τὸν ἐκ τῶν Μηδικῶν σκύλων, ὃν Παυσανίας ἐποίησε.

[53] Relevant quotations are gathered by Frick 1857–60: 513–20; Stichel 1997.

[54] Later Greek authors very frequently use plural forms for singular items or individuals, which further complicates this vexed issue.

[55] Eusebios, *Life of Constantine* 3.54; trans. Cameron and Hall 1999: 143, 301–2.

[56] Sokrates Scholastikos, 1.16:

Τὰ γοῦν ἀγάλματα κόσμον τῇ Κωνσταντίνου πόλει προὐτίθει δημοσίᾳ, καὶ τοὺς Δελφικοὺς τρίποδας ἐν τῷ ἱπποδρομίῳ δημοσιεύσας προὔθηκε.

greater detail than his principal source, Sokrates Scholastikos, and echoed Palladas' epigram:

> Such of the images as were constructed of precious material, and whatever else was valuable, were purified by fire, and became public money. The bronze images which were skillfully wrought were carried to the city, named after the emperor, and placed there for decoration, where they may still be seen in public places, in the streets, the hippodrome, and the palaces: those [statues] of Apollo from the Pythian oracle, and likewise the statues of the Muses from Helikon, the tripods from Delphi, and the much extolled Pan (ὁ πάν ὁ βοώμενος), which Pausanias the Spartan (Παυσανίας ὁ Λακεδαιμόνιος) and the Greek cities had devoted after the war against the Persians.[57]

The phrase "which Pausanias the Spartan and the Greek cities had devoted after the war against the Persians" proves that Sozomenos recognized the Serpent Column as the *agalma* described by Thucydides, who alone of ancient authors used exactly Παυσανίας ὁ Λακεδαιμόνιος to describe the Spartan general only shortly before his description of the dedication of the Plataian tripod.[58] The insertion of a statue of Pan, otherwise unattested rather than "much extolled," between the Delphic Tripods and the dedication is surely a misreading of ὁ πάνυ βοώμενος, meaning simply that the Plataian tripod and its dedication were extremely well known.[59] We have then what appears to be a clear reference to the Serpent Column in the hippodrome from an author who had read Thucydides and who worked as a lawyer in Constantinople in the early

---

[57] Sozomenos, 2.5:

> τῶν δ' αὖ ξοάνων τὰ ὄντα τιμίας ὕλης καὶ τῶν ἄλλων, ὅσον ἐδόκει χρήσιμον εἶναι, πυρὶ διεκρίνετο καὶ δημόσια ἐγίνετο χρήματα, τὰ δὲ ἐν χαλκῷ θαυμασίως εἰργασμένα πάντοθεν εἰς τὴν ἐπώνυμον πόλιν τοῦ αὐτοκράτορος μετεκομίσθη πρὸς κόσμον· καὶ εἰσέτι νῦν δημοσίᾳ ἵδρυνται κατὰ τὰς ἀγυιὰς καὶ τὸν ἱππόδρομον καὶ τὰ βασίλεια τὰ μὲν τοῦ Πυθίασι μαντικοῦ Ἀπόλλωνος καὶ Μοῦσαι αἱ Ἑλικωνιάδες καὶ οἱ ἐν Δελφοῖς τρίποδες καὶ ὁ Πὰν ὁ βοώμενος, ὃν Παυσανίας ὁ Λακεδαιμόνιος καὶ αἱ Ἑλληνίδες πόλεις ἀνέθεντο μετὰ τὸν πρὸς Μήδους πόλεμον.

Trans. Schaff 1890: 6, 46, 372, here modified. See also Stichel 1997: 318, and Bassett 2004: 150–1, which discusses the statues of the Muses, at least one set of which appear to have been destroyed before Sozomenos wrote.

[58] Thucydides 1.128: ἐπειδὴ Παυσανίας ὁ Λακεδαιμόνιος τὸ πρῶτον μεταπεμφθεὶς ὑπὸ Σπαρτιατῶν ἀπὸ τῆς ἀρχῆς τῆς ἐν Ἑλλησπόντῳ.

[59] Madden 1992: 112, n.5 makes a similar suggestion. Stichel 1997: 318 also suggested ὁ πάν βοώμενος as an alternative reading. The phrase ὁ πάνυ βοώμενος appears at Eusebios, *VC* 3.7, and Sokrates Scholastikos, 1.8, as a description of Ossius of Cordova, "the very famous" Spanish bishop at the council of Nicaea. Bassett 2004: 248 records only the passage in Sozomenos as evidence for a statue of Pan in Constantinople. However, before Pan is removed from the list of known statues, it is important to note the following epigram attributed to Simonides, recorded in the *Greek Anthology* 16.232: "Goat-hoofed Pan, the Arkadian, foe of the Medes, friend of the Athenians, Miltiades erected me." This would suggest that a statue of Pan was dedicated by Miltiades after Marathon, which may later have been brought to Constantinople. See Gauer 1968: 117.

part of the fifth century. In this role, it is rather likely that Sozomenos would have seen the Delphic Tripods close up, for legal cases were arbitrated from the tribunal below the *kathisma*, hence immediately across from the Serpent Column in the hippodrome.

Early in the sixth century, Zosimos, drawing on a fourth-century source, Eunapios, recounts that Constantine "even placed somewhere in the hippodrome the tripod [singular, *ton tripoda*] of Delphic Apollo, which had on it the very image [*agalma*] of Apollo."[60] *Agalma*, the Greek term used by Zosimos, by now meant quite specifically a cult statue, but it also might be translated more simply as image.[61] The Serpent Column did not have an image of Apollo on it, nor did a cult statue of Apollo stand upon it. There is no indication in any source that the golden tripod which once topped the column had been embossed with an image of Apollo, nor that a replacement had been furnished. What, then, does Zosimos mean? It is probable that Zosimos has introduced an error in condensing information he drew from his source. First he has rendered the Delphic Tripods in singular form, rather than the familiar plural. Second, he has conflated this reference to the tripods with another to a separate statue of Apollo. It is our conjecture that Zosimos' source, in the same manner as Sozomenos, referred to both the Delphic Tripods and a statue of Apollo, meaning a bronze statue from Delphi or elsewhere, including those described by Eusebios as "pompous statues of brass ... here a Pythian, there a Sminthian Apollo."[62] Of course, it is also possible that Zosimos is referring to another tripod adorned with an image of Apollo. We know that other inscribed tripods from Delphi survived into the tenth century in the hippodrome.[63]

---

[60] Zosimos 2.31:

> ἔστησεν δὲ κατά τι τοῦ ἱπποδρόμου μέρος καὶ τὸν τρίποδα τοῦ ἐν Δελφοῖς Ἀπόλλωνος, ἔχοντα ἐν ἑαυτῷ καὶ αὐτὸ τὸ τοῦ Ἀπόλλωνος ἄγαλμα.

Trans. Ridley 1982: 38; Frick 1857–60: 515–16. The problem of identification was noted by Mendelssohn 1887, who in his edition of Zosimos, the first to properly employ the sole surviving manuscript, wrote: "[hic] non est donarium, quae fuit Frickii aliorumque sententia: illius enim forma similis quidem erat, sed hic tripus fulcrum medium non serpentium spiras sed ipsius Apollonis simulacrum habebant."

[61] On earlier meanings of *agalma* see above, chapters two and three.

[62] Wieseler 1864: 249–50 suggests that this might have been the Salamis Apollo, or "Big Man." Others have wondered whether Zosimos is referring mistakenly to the statue Constantine raised on a porphyry column in his eponymous forum, which showed the emperor as Sol. See Fowden 1991; Mango 1993; Bassett 2004: 201–04; Stephenson 2009: 191, 196, 198, 201. Barnes 2011: 23–5 argues that this statue was not of Sol at all, but of the emperor without a radiate crown. There were also three statues of Apollo placed in the Zeuxippon, if we can trust Christodoros: see Bassett 2004: 165–6.

[63] *Patria* 2.79. For example, the Tripod of Croton, to which we have referred above, may have been decorated with a scene of Apollo fighting the Python, on which see Laroche and Jacquemin 1990: 321; Scott 2010: 89.

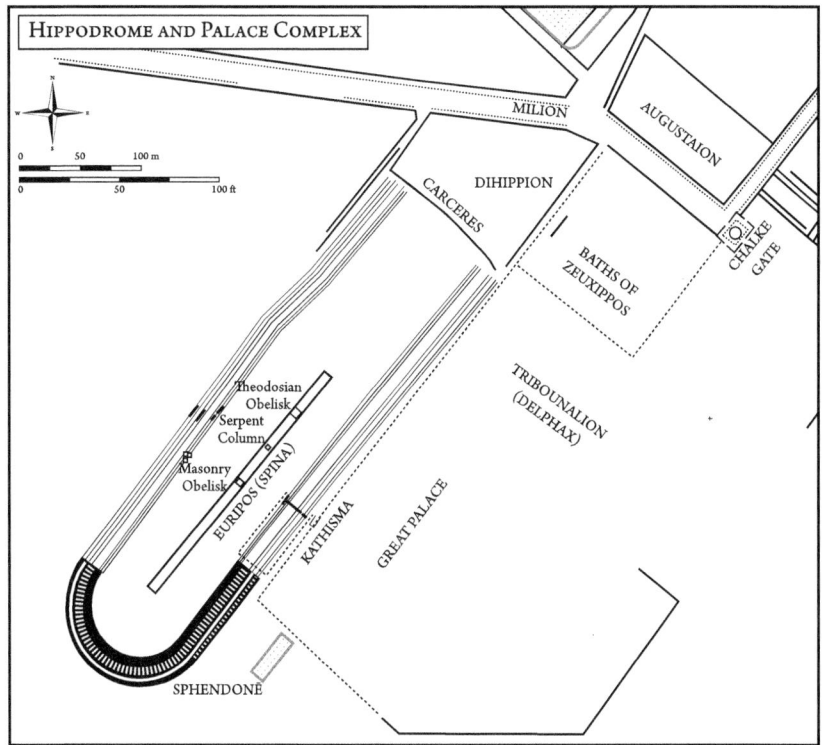

MAP 6 The Hippodrome in Constantinople.

Depicting the Hippodrome in Late Antiquity

One looks in vain for Late Antique illustrations of the Serpent Column. Notably, it cannot be identified carved onto the lower base of the Theodosian Obelisk.[64] This tall granite obelisk, which still stands in Istanbul, was raised up under Theodosios I (d. 395). Inscriptions on two faces of the lower marble base upon which the obelisk sits attest to its erection after the defeat in 388 of the pretender Maximus; that the raising took thirty (in Latin), or thirty-two (in Greek) days; and that it was the work of Proklos, who was then *eparchos*, or mayor of the city.[65] Since Proklos was put to death in 392, there is only a short period within which the obelisk could have been raised. On the third, northeastern face of the lower marble base, the obelisk is shown on its side, being raised (fig. 4.6); on the fourth, southeastern side, the obelisk is shown in place

---

[64] Pace the tentative suggestion by Newton 1865: II, 37.
[65] Pitarakis 2010 collates the latest views. The association between the two obelisks from Karnak is sustained in their inscriptions, because the Latin inscription in Constantinople echoes a longer dedication on the base of the Lateran Obelisk, alluding to the defeat by Constantius of "the vilest of tyrants," meaning the pretender Magnentius.

FIGURE 4.6 Northeastern face of the lower marble base of the Theodosian Obelisk, also known as the Egyptian Obelisk, a granite monolith carved for Pharaoh Thutmose III (r. 1479–25 B.C.). Photo: author.

in the hippodrome, where a chariot race is taking place (fig. 4.7). The inscriptions on the marble base do not reveal that the obelisk was broken during its erection, so that its height is 19.6 m (64.3 ft) rather than the original 34.8 m (114 ft), known from comparing the surviving portion with a detailed depiction of the full obelisk that survives at Karnak.[66] A second marble base was carved, therefore, to accommodate the smaller footprint of the shorter obelisk, which was placed on the original inscribed marble base, supported by four bronze cubes at its corners (fig. 4.8). This ad hoc measure has been invaluable to historians and art historians, because on the four carved faces of the obelisk's upper base the emperor and his entourage are depicted in the *kathisma*, the imperial box in the hippodrome.

Clearly the artists responsible for the bases did not sketch everything that existed in the hippodrome at the end of the fourth century. Moreover, the relief is now badly abraded, far more so than in 1574, when an anonymous German artist sketched it, and much else (fig. 4.9). His drawings, now collated in the Freshfield Album, in the library of Trinity College, Cambridge, do not show the Serpent Column among the statues, pillars and obelisks on the *euripos*, the hippodrome's central reservation. A pillar (fig. 4.10) which some today imagine depicted the Serpent Column is revealed to be a column supporting a winged statue. The anonymous artist's sketches are extremely accurate, when we are able to check them against what survives. Notably, his rendering of the hieroglyphs on the Theodosian Obelisk, which have barely weathered since, are accurate rather than allusive.

---

[66] Indeed, the disaster is masked in the depiction of the obelisk being raised, since only the shorter section is shown. That is to say, the hieroglyphics on the obelisk reproduced by the carver correspond with those visible today. The broken portion of granite may well have been placed elsewhere in the city, perhaps at the Strategion. See Bardill 2010a: 155–64.

FIGURE 4.7 Southeastern face of the bases of the Theodosian Obelisk. Photo: author.

FIGURE 4.8 Theodosian Obelisk standing on two marble bases carved for its erection in Constantinople in ca. 390. Photo: author.

Early depictions of the hippodrome are far less concerned with accurate renderings of its furnishings than with conveying the excitement of staging the games and displaying the dominating presence of the emperor, consul, or champion (see the Porphyrios bases, below and fig. 4.13). Ivory consular diptychs of the fourth to sixth centuries frequently represent the hippodrome,

FIGURE 4.9 Drawing of the Theodosian Obelisk, as it appeared in 1574. Freshfield Album, Wren Library, Trinity College, Cambridge, MS 0117.2. Master and Fellows of Trinity College Cambridge.

where a consul is illustrated presiding in the *kathisma* over the games commencing on 1 January of his consular year. On the Lampadii diptych, now in Brescia, the consul Flavius Lampadius is shown seated centrally between two other robed officials (fig. 4.11). He presides over a race between four chariots, two shown on either side of the *euripos*, upon which the Theodosian Obelisk is shown centered, immediately beneath the consul. This would, in reality, have been the location of the Delphic Tripods, which are not depicted. Rather, one sees only two *tropaia*, cruciform trophies bearing captured arms and armor, and four seated figures, one either side of each *tropaion*. These are presumably intended to represent statues, at least one of which resembles Herakles, sitting exhausted from having cleaned the Augean stables.[67]

The unique "Kugelspiel"—a game designed to simulate the fun and gambling of a day at the track, and therefore forbidden by a law of the pious Justinian— is a marble block carved with a zigzagging ramp down which a small ball would

---

[67] Volbach 1976: 50–51, no. 54, pl. 28; Daim 2010: 203–4, no. 130; Dagron 2011: 68, ill. 26. See also below, chapter five.

FIGURE 4.10 Detail of carving of the *euripos* on the southeastern face of the lower marble base of the Theodosian Obelisk. Photo: author.

roll in a game of chance (fig. 4.12). Discovered in 1834 near the hippodrome, it has hippodrome scenes on all sides.[68] The front of the block is carved into an arch, through which the gambler would shove his hand to drop the ball through an opening. Above the arch a row of figures is carved, perhaps intended to depict the *kathisma*. Two chariots race across the lowest register on the back of the block, from the viewer's right to left, chasing a third, victorious chariot on the right-hand side, and chased by a fourth on the left-hand side. The lower corners are carved into the turning posts that marked the ends of the *euripos*. There are two further carved registers on the block's sides, featuring figures and scenes from the staging of the games. In the upper registers, partisans hold banners aloft and musicians play flutes, while the middle register on the left features the lot-drawing machine, by which the charioteers' lanes were assigned, its handle turned by one figure while another, an unmounted charioteer, cracks his whip. The middle register on the right side shows a victorious charioteer on horseback and a viewer watching him from an opened window, placed above the winning chariot. However, no statues are shown.[69]

---

[68] It was published by Texier 1845, who took it for a fountain. See also Bourquelot 1865: 33.
[69] For a series of photos and commentary, see Cameron, Al. 1973: 32–9, pl. 15–18; Effenberger 2007; Daim 2010: 206–8.

FIGURE 4.11 Ivory diptych of the Lampadius family, Constantinople, fifth century A.D. Museo di Santa Giulia, Brescia. Photo: Emilie van Opstall, with permission.

The Epigram of the Medes and the Dragon Statue

By the ninth century, when the aforementioned scholion proves that the Serpent Column was in the hippodrome, it was one of many monuments on an increasingly crowded *euripos*. The *euripos* now featured numerous statues of victorious charioteers. The version of the *Greek Anthology* preserved by Planoudes supplies fifty-four separate epigrams, each copied from a charioteer's statue base in the hippodrome before the end of the ninth century, and perhaps far earlier.[70] Of these, thirty-two are dedicated to Porphyrios, two of which have been preserved on one surviving statue base, and four on a second. The two statue bases of Porphyrios were both unearthed in Istanbul and are named the "old base," discovered in 1845, and the "new base" of 1963 (fig. 4.13).[71] Another six Porphyrios bases have been lost, as have bases which once supported statues of

---

[70] Cameron, Al. 1973: 7–8, 96–116. Twenty-seven of the epigrams are also recorded in the Laurentian version of the anthology, and ten are preserved in a later addendum to the Palatine version of the anthology, MS Parisinus gr. 23, 707–9.

[71] Cameron, Al. 1973, passim; Bardill 2010: 171–9.

FIGURE 4.12 Kugelspiel, carved game of chance showing hippodrome scenes, sixth century A.D. Photo: bpk/Skulpturensammlung und Museum für Byzantinische Kunst der Staatliche Museen zu Berlin/Jürgen Liepe.

Faustinos, Constantine, Ouranios, and Ioulianos. Who dedicated the statue is significant, as this determined its location. Each statue was placed on a section of the *euripos* that faced the named faction's seats, which were located in the stand facing the *kathisma* in order—Blues, Whites, Reds, then Greens—from the starting gates (*carceres*) to the curved banked end of the stadium, called the *sphendone*.[72] All twelve charioteer statues would have had similar dimensions and reached a similar height, around 4.5 m (14 ft) above the *euripos*.[73]

In this crowd, the Serpent Column appears to have escaped the attention of many we would expect to have observed it with wonder. It is all but impossible to find in texts of the period. Recalling the reign of Michael III (d. 867), Theophanes Continuatus wrote of a three-headed statue among those erected on the *euripos* in the hippodrome, but the rest of the story makes clear that this was not the Serpent Column. Rather, it was a composition of three barbarian chieftains, two of whose heads have been removed with hammers to avert a barbarian invasion.[74] The hammering features on a miniature in the illuminated

---

[72] Cameron, Al. 1973: 180–7.

[73] Cameron, Al. 1973: 12–14, where it is explained that although the "new base" is some 3.57 m tall, and the "old base" only 2.85 m tall, the bases would have been sunk into the *euripos* to equalize their heights at ca. 2.30 m. Below that distance from the top of each base, the stone is untreated. The bronze statues are presumed to have been the same height as each other and something more than life-size, as indicated by the fixing holes on top of the bases.

[74] Theophanes Continuatus, ed. Bonn 1838: 155:

ἐν τοῖς εἰς τὸν εὔριπον τοῦ ἱπποδρομίου ἱδρυμένοις χαλκοῖς ἀνδριάσιν ἐλέγετό τις εἶναι ἀνδριὰς τρισὶ διαμορφούμενος κεφαλαῖς, ἃς κατά τινα στοιχείωσιν πρὸς τοὺς τοῦ ἔθνους ἀρχηγοὺς ἀνῆγεν. σφύρας οὖν μεγίστας σιδηρᾶς ἰσαρίθμους ταῖς κεφαλαῖς προσέταττε γενέσθαι, καὶ ἀνδράσιν ἐγχειρισθῆναι αὐτὰς τρισίν, ἐπὶ χειρῶν γενναιότητι διαφέροντας.

Young 1983: 313, n.59 makes an astute association, but appears to misplace this episode to the reign of Michael IV and suggests that he removed two heads from the Serpent Column.

FIGURE 4.13 Two extant statue bases of Porphyrios, both excavated from the Topkapı Palace, now in Istanbul Archaeological Museums. Photo: author.

Madrid Skylitzes. Cyril Mango suggested that this was a statue of Hekate. However, the only known statue of Hekate was at the Milion (Constantinople's milepost) and fashioned from porphyry.[75] In a famous woodcut by Pieter Coecke Van Aelst (1502–50) showing the hippodrome, one can see in the background a statue of three figures, apparently naked and standing back to back (fig. 8.7, below).[76] However, they all have heads.[77] It seems likely that this is the three Graces, brought with the nine Muses by Constantine from the Mouseion at Mount Helikon to Constantinople.[78] The Muses were placed in the senate

---

[75] Mango 1963: 61, who corrected Brehier 1904.

[76] Pitarakis 2010: I, 282 is among the more recent reproductions; Cameron, Al. 1973: 6–7 identifies two statueless bases in the picture as those which once supported statues of Porphyrius. These are clearer in Banduri's drawing.

[77] Casson 1928: fig. 3, 15 reproduces a version of Van Aelst's engraving from the Ashmolean Museum in Oxford, and refers also to a manuscript illumination in the "Serai Library" which shows a helmeted figure with two children. This is named in Casson 1929: 1–4 as the *Hünername* by Lokman, a two-volume illustrated history of the first Ottoman sultans, which was then unpublished. We shall return to this work below, chapter seven. We do not see any of these three-headed compositions in the catalogues of statues compiled by Bassett 2004 and Bardill 2010: 180–2.

[78] Bassett 2004: 73–4, 139, 150–1, 239–40, discusses the statue of Hecate at the Milion, as described in the *Parastaseis*.

house by the Augusteion (adjacent to the imperial palace) and were destroyed far earlier than the ninth century.[79]

Searching further, one encounters two promising passages from separate tenth-century texts, both of which turn out to be dead ends. A tenth-century Arabic account, by Harun ibn Yahya, is too precise to be taken as a reference to the Serpent Column. The statue in question was not in the hippodrome, but was said to stand near the imperial gate; perhaps it was near the Chalke Gate of the palace, where there were four snaky gorgon heads, or on the city walls, where statues were lined up to ward off threats from various beasts and barbarians.[80] Moreover, it depicted "four snakes made of brass whose tails are in their mouths," rather than three entwined snakes. It was considered a talisman against snake-bites.[81]

The *Parastaseis Syntomoi Chronikai*, a semimythical account of Constantinople and its landmarks, devotes six chapters to the statues of the hippodrome, but does not mention the Serpent Column. This is not as striking an absence as one might think, for it states that as many as sixty statues, *eidola*, were set up, but mentions only a very few of them and fails to notice those that today we consider the most striking, such as the Theodosian Obelisk and the Rhodian Quadriga now in Venice.[82] In contrast, the *Parastaseis* twice refers to a famous Herakles as "up on high, leaning on its knee," and as "a large statue in the hippodrome which holds its hand up to its face."[83] Earlier, it is suggested that Herakles had been moved to the hippodrome, originally having been placed in the reign of Constantine at the "golden-roofed Basilika" to the north of the hippodrome, whence the city's central street, the Mese, ran to the Forum of Constantine.[84] This Herakles was believed to have been sculpted by Lysippos for the city of Tarentum and brought via Rome to Constantinople, probably in 325.[85] Two epigrams on it have been preserved in the *Greek Anthology*, one of which asks: "Why did Lysippos mold you thus with dejected face and alloy your bronze with pain?"[86]

---

[79] We also note at Weitzmann 1974: 407–8, pl. 127 two compositions of three figures, golden idols, supported on double columns, which are illustrations in Jerusalem Cod. Taphou 14 (folio number not cited).

[80] Bassett 2004: 186.

[81] Vasiliev 1932: 161 and Casson et al. 1928: 13 believe this is the Serpent Column. However, this is not the case, as demonstrated by Dawkins 1924: 234, n. 51; Madden 1992: 113; and Bassett 2004: 227. For talismans, see below, chapter seven.

[82] *Parastaseis* 60, ed. and trans. Cameron and Herrin 1984: 138–9, 249–50; Bassett 2004: 212–32 provides a thoroughly annotated but incomplete list of thirty statues, pillars, and obelisks in place in Late Antiquity. Bardill 2010: 180–2 supplies a simple list of forty-eight statues, including twelve charioteer statues and bases that Bassett omits.

[83] *Parastaseis* 64, 65, ed. and trans. Cameron and Herrin 1984: 142–3, 146–7, 255–6.

[84] *Parastaseis* 37, ed. and trans. Cameron and Herrin 1984: 100–1, 214.

[85] Bassett 2004: 152–4, following *Parastaseis* 37, ed. and trans. Cameron and Herrin 1984: 100–1, 214, which relates that a statue of Herakles "was brought from Rome to Byzantion under the *hypatos* Julian with a chariot, a boat and twelve statues."

[86] *Greek Anthology* XVI. 103 and 104. The epigrams are not assigned to this statue by Bassett 2004: 152–4, who provides excerpts on it from three Byzantine texts: the *Souda*, Constantine Manasses, and Niketas Choniates.

The *Parastaseis* records some statues only partially, for example a bronze hyena, failing to notice the wolf also suckling Romulus and Remus.[87] It also includes numerous enigmatic allusions to monuments that cannot easily be identified, including the so-called "Thessalian statue," the "Epigram of the Medes" (τῶν Μήδων τοῦ ἐλεγείου) and the "Dragon Statue" (τὸ δρακονταῖον). The last two have both been identified as the Serpent Column, but neither of these identifications can be sustained.[88] The "Epigram of the Medes" must refer to an inscribed object that makes reference to the Persians, which would certainly describe the Serpent Column, although its inscription is not an epigram. As we have seen, the golden bowl once supported by the snakes' heads was inscribed with an epigram by Simonides, although the bowl had disappeared long before the column was moved to Constantinople. Other Delphic Tripods were similarly inscribed with verses by Simonides, and these may have been numbered among those that joined the Serpent Column in the hippodrome. An ancient *agalma* inscribed with an epigram alluding to the Persian wars would appear to suit the description "Epigram of the Medes" more aptly than a list of Greek poleis.

Similarly, the *drakontaion* does not refer to the Serpent Column.[89] The *Parastaseis* states the following of the "Dragon Statue":

> Philip the dynast expounded many things, in the course of which he passed this on: that while the dragon statue (*drakontaion*) is an erection [ἐκτύπωμά] of Arcadius ..., it is a display (epideixis [ἐπίδειξις]) of his brother Honorius ... reigning in Rome.[90]

It has been suggested that the *drakontaion* refers to the Skylla group, and therefore that it was installed on the *euripos* by Arkadios (*ektypoma* being either his "erection" or "likeness"). "Likeness" seems a perfectly sensible translation in the context of this work, because the authors of the *Parastaseis* set themselves the task of identifying for each statue both its historical and prophetical meanings, only some of which had hitherto been revealed.[91] For example, a statue of an elephant in the Basilika was revealed to have been a metaphor for Justinian II's use of barbarians to regain the throne, but also for his subsequent inability to control them. By the same reasoning, the "likeness" of the Skylla may have been taken as a metaphor for Arkadios' victory over the Goths in 401, as well as for the decapitation of the Gothic king Gainas, whose head was sent to the

---

[87] See Niketas Choniates, ed. van Dieten 1975: 650; trans. Magoulias 1984: 359; Bassett 2004: 219, 231.

[88] *Parastaseis* 61, ed. and trans. Cameron and Herrin 1984: 138–9, 250, 252.

[89] Dagron 2011: 375, n. 67.

[90] *Parastaseis* 62, ed. and trans. Cameron and Herrin 1984: 138–41, 250, 252.

[91] Anderson 2011, suggests that the "philosophers" of the city, who compiled the work as a dossier through the eighth century, were compelled by those objects that would reveal their true meanings through time, like the elephant that had revealed the fate of Justinian II.

emperor.⁹² Skylla, as we have noted, was gripping the head of the steersman in one hand, while she wielded his steering oar as a weapon, as if to behead him.⁹³

The identification of the *Parastaseis*' *drakontaion* as the Skylla is plausible, therefore, but far from certain.⁹⁴ Indeed, the identification appears to be undermined by the fact that the *Parastaseis* has just described the Skylla group, referring to it not as a dragon but as "among the female statues ... giving birth to wild beasts that devour men," referring thus to the serpents and dogs issuing from parts of the she-beast. The group is "accompanied also by a boat" and it "reveals the story of the godless Justinian," meaning the second reign of Justinian II (705–11).⁹⁵ However, if one accepts that the *Parastaseis* was a compilation that reflected various opinions on the same objects, and notes that we are expressly told that the *drakontaion* was interpreted by "Philip the dynast," then this duplication need not be an obstacle to identification.

The Skylla was certainly on the *euripos* in ca. 500, when a satirical poem preserved in the *Greek Anthology* (XI.271) reveals that an iron statue of Anastasios was placed near to it. Another epigram has been preserved in the *Greek Anthology*:

> On Skylla in Bronze. Unless the bronze glistened and betrayed the work to be a product of Hephaistos' cunning art, one looking from afar would think that Skylla herself stood there, transferred from sea to land, so threatening is her gesture, such wrath does she exhibit, as if dashing ships to pieces in the sea.⁹⁶

It is clear that the Skylla here described was accompanied by a boat, and therefore was of the type identified by Andreae and Conticello as the Sperlonga–Constantinople type.⁹⁷ There is clear evidence that a Skylla group was known in Constantinople in the fourth century, and perhaps as early as A.D. 330.

---

⁹² Zosimos 5. 22.

⁹³ The Column of Arkadios, which depicted the celebration of that emperor's victory over Gainas and was completed in the early decades of the fifth century, featured, on the lowest spiral of its winding narrative frieze, illustrations of the Forum of Constantine and its statues as they must have appeared at the end of the fourth century. It has frequently, and mistakenly, been stated that this is the hippodrome. On the eastern side of the Column of Arkadios, depicted immediately to the left of the schematic sketch of the circular forum, is a male upper torso wielding a club, who in the place of legs has two writhing serpents. This is a typical depiction of a giant, at least since the Hellenistic period; he appears to be engaged in combat with another male figure, around whose arm a beast, or a living pelt, is wrapped. This is clear in a high-resolution illustration supplied by Trinity College Cambridge (The Freshfield Album, Trinity College Library Cambridge, MS 0117.2), although many have followed Freshfield in interpreting the lowest spiral as depicting the hippodrome rather than the forum, and therefore have misinterpreted the giant as a depiction of Skylla. See Bardill 2010: 168, 181, and Bassett 2004: 229. Both follow Freshfield 1922 and Giglioli 1953.

⁹⁴ *Parastaseis* 62, ed. and trans. Cameron and Herrin 1984: 138–9, 140–1, suggesting that the Skylla may be the *drakontaion*. Bassett 2004: 215–16, 227–9 has provided reasons to support this identification.

⁹⁵ *Parastaseis* 61, ed. and trans. Cameron and Herrin 1984: 138–9, 250–1.

⁹⁶ *Greek Anthology*: 9.755. See also Becatti 1960: 200–2; Cameron, Al. 1993: 94; Berger 2010: 204, n. 15. Clearly, this is distinct from the earlier Latin epigram and its Greek original attributed to Palladas.

⁹⁷ This is addressed earlier in this chapter.

A epigram attributed to Palladas, but preserved only in a Latin translation collated in ca. A.D. 400 in the *Epigrammata Bobiensia*, is entitled "On the Skylla in the circus at Constantinople":

> There is fear that the gnashing Skylla has been set up in this manner near the coast, O Caesar; fashion restraints before (she strikes). For the excellence of the breathing bronze has the power to deceive, that she might seize the sailor before he is on his guard.[98]

The hippodrome is, perhaps, sufficiently close to the sea to justify the rhetorical claim that real sailors would join those cast in bronze in falling victim to the Skylla. Certainly, the Sphendone, but not the *euripos*, might have been visible from the shore of the Sea of Marmara. However, it may also be taken to indicate that the Skylla was placed first "near the coast" (*prope littoram*), when the epigram was composed, and subsequently "in the circus" (*in circo*), when it was copied into the collection and given an identifying title.

Whether or not the author of the *Parastaseis* intended the Skylla group when using the term *drakontaion*, this is how it was understood two centuries later by the compiler of the *Patria Konstantinoupoleos*, which incorporates and expands upon the *Parastaseis*. The *Patria* describes "another [statue] which includes a boat: some say it is Skylla who devours men from Charybdis. And there is Odysseus, whose head she holds in her hand. Others say this is the Earth and the Sea and the seven ages which are devoured by the deluge, and the present age is the seventh."[99]

The *Patria* is the last source to mention the Delphic Tripods. Compiled at the end of the tenth century, during the reign of Basil II, but employing many far earlier sources, it did so in the following manner: "Similarly, both the tripods of the Delphic three-legged cauldrons and the equestrian statues have inscriptions (γράφουσιν), and for this reason they were set up and signify something."[100] The *Patria*, by its reference to the inscription, would appear to refer to the Serpent Column, but as we have already noted, several other tripods, "three-legged cauldrons" brought from Delphi, were probably inscribed with dedicatory epigrams.

---

[98] *Epigrammata Bobiensia*, ed. Speyer 1963: 62, no. 51: In Scyllam Constantinopolitanum in circo: Frendentem Scyllam metus est prope litoris oram/sic sisti, Caesar: vincula necte prius./nam potis est virtus spirantis fallere aeni,/ut prius astringat [arripiat?], navita quam caveat. Wilkinson 2010a: 181 provides the translation. See also Cameron, Al. 1993: 93–5.

[99] Patria II.77; ed. Preger 1901–7:190. See now Berger 2013: 100–3, 302.

[100] *Patria* 2. 79, ed. Preger 1907; 1975: II, 191: Ὁμοίως καὶ οἱ τρίποδες τῶν Δελφικῶν κακκάβων καὶ αἱ ἔφιπποι στῆλαι γράφουσιν, δι' ἣν αἰτίαν ἔστησαν καὶ τί σημαίνουσιν. See now Berger 2013: 102–3. This is in the tenth-century P recension, dated to 989/90, on which see Berger 1988: 61–70. Preger 1895 dated this compilation of texts to ca. 995. It is the second of four books within the *Patria* relating to the antiquities. See also Cameron and Herrin 1984: 4.

5 }

Constantinople in the Middle Ages

Depicting the Serpent Column – Animate Statues – The Particular Judgment – Snakes and Ladders – The Last Judgment – Destroying Statues – Three Strands Twisted

Scholars have long discussed whether it was common practice for Byzantine artists to use model books. Only one such book, from late-twelfth- or early-thirteenth-century Cyprus, has been identified.[1] Nevertheless, it seems certain that drawings were made of Constantinople's statues, including those in the hippodrome. Recently, for example, Anthony Cutler has invited readers to make a connection between a statue of Herakles in the hippodrome, sitting exhausted from cleaning the Augean stables, and the same scene preserved on three bone plaques: two on an ivory casket in the St. Viktor Dom Museum, Xanten, of the late tenth century, and a third panel of the late tenth century, now in Munich.[2] It has long been known that the Xanten ivory casket depicts this colossal Herakles, and it is also thought that the Xanten depiction is indirect, thus transmitted to the artist by a drawing.[3] Similarly, Henry Maguire has suggested that an ivory plaque, now in the Walters Art Museum in Baltimore, is modeled closely on Herakles in the hippodrome (fig. 5.1). This plaque depicts not Herakles but Adam, identified by an inscription, seated on a basket facing to the viewer's left. His head rests on a hand, the elbow propped on one knee. Only Herakles' lion pelt is missing from Adam's pose.[4]

---

[1] Hutter 1999. The only comprehensive model book that is extant is significantly later, the seventeenth-century "Painter's Manual" by Dionysus of Fourna, ed. Hetherington 1978.

[2] Cutler 2010: 208: "Yet their kinship with the Hippodrome statue rather than any other version is assured by the fact that, other than these examples, Herakles's pose does not appear on any other object, Late Antique or Byzantine." Cutler does not mention the seated figures on the Lampadii diptych, to which we refer in chapter four.

[3] The statue is described by Niketas Choniates, ed. Van Dieten 1975: 649–50.

[4] Maguire 1977: 135–40; Maguire 2004: 12, figs. 5 and 6; Maguire 2011: 274–5. Maguire has also postulated that the Gigantomachy depicted on the bronze doors of the senate house has been preserved in an illustration in a tenth-century manuscript, an illuminated copy of Nikandros' *Theriaka* (Paris, B.N. gr. 247, fol. 47r.). See Maguire and Maguire 2007: 7, with earlier references, including Omont 1929: pl. LXVIII. For a contrasting view, see Weitzmann 1981:142–3. We shall return to these doors shortly.

FIGURE 5.1 Ivory plaque depicting Adam in the pose of an exhausted Herakles, Walters Art Museum, Baltimore, Byzantine, tenth century. Photo: author.

It is striking that Adam is identified by an inscription but Herakles is not. The reason for this difference is that even for the erudite, the classical past provoked apprehension as well as admiration. Robert Ousterhout has recently argued that it is for this reason that Byzantine authors ignored the colossal nude statue of Constantine in the guise of a solar deity, which dominated that emperor's eponymous forum, focusing instead on the column on which it stood and the Christian relics held to be buried beneath it.[5] While knowledge of the classical past, its literature, mythology, and art, was preserved and for long periods flourished through the Byzantine centuries, non-Christian images were systematically denied labels. The difficulties scholars have encountered in identifying classical scenes and motifs in Byzantine art arise from this simple fact. Fear of the power of such images is also a reason why relatively few classical scenes survive from more than a millennium of artistic activity in Christian Constantinople. Following the end of iconoclasm, formally the "Triumph of Orthodoxy" in A.D. 843, the efficacy of images as channels to their prototypes, of their power, was affirmed. Henceforth, it was imperative that holy images should be correctly identified, and although they did not deviate from established types and were easily recognized by the devout, such images were always accompanied by an inscription, which served both as confirmation and guarantee of identity.[6] For this reason, when images from classical art were co-opted into Christian contexts, they enjoyed clear labels, for example Adam in a pose copied from Herakles (fig. 5.1). But when Herakles himself was shown in the same pose, exhausted from having cleaned the Augean stables, he had no label.[7]

---

[5] Ousterhout 2014.
[6] Maguire 1996: 100–45; Maguire 2011.
[7] Maguire 2011: 273–4.

Depicting the Serpent Column

The only extant work of middle Byzantine art that appears to depict the Serpent Column is a silver inkpot, produced in Constantinople in the tenth century, which is now in the cathedral treasury in Padua (figs. 5.2, 5.3, 5.4, 5.5,).[8] The relief on the inkpot places four mythological figures, resembling statues, between four entwined serpentine columns. Each pair of snakes forms a twisted pillar ending in two heads. The four figures, which bear no inscriptions, have been identified as Eros bringing arms (fig. 5.2) to a seated shield-bearing Ares (fig. 5.3), Apollo standing beside a tripod holding a lyre (fig. 5.4),[9] and a river god (fig. 5.5). The lid of the pot bears a striking bust of Medusa, and below it, running around the rim of the pot, is a metrical dedicatory epigram: "The holder of ink [is] for Leon every means of livelihood." On the base of the pot is a second inscription: "Leon, the delightful marvel among calligraphers."[10] The figures appear to have some relationship with Leon the master calligrapher, playing on several motifs: of the pen, and words of love, being mightier than the sword (Ares, Eros); of the power of *mousike*, of singing, dancing, and the performance of epic poetry (Apollo); and of the river of words flowing from Leon's pen. The fierce Medusa, an image of "bloody violence and stony stillness," has an apotropaic function, protecting Leon's precious ink, his lifeblood.[11] Leon became Perseus whenever he used the pot, removing Medusa's head. The serpentine columns appear to have served a similar apotropaic function.[12]

Although the classical figures portrayed resemble statues, the Padua inkpot does not depict the hippodrome, just as the earliest surviving paintings of the hippodrome of Constantinople do not depict the Serpent Column or

---

[8] The inkpot was published most recently as a catalogue entry by Spiazzi 2014. I thank Carlo Cavallo, Padua, for providing this information and the article. The pot's decoration and its inscription have been interpreted by Hörandner 1989; Maguire 1994; Maguire and Maguire 2007; and Chatterjee 2014. Guillou 1996: 43 dated the object by the form of the omega in the inscription to the later tenth century, largely by association with the inscription on the Limburger Staurothek of 985/6.

[9] But perhaps this was Dionysos, who had usurped Apollo's lyre. Indeed, at Delphi in the fourth century B.C. the Athenians appear to have lavished the temple with representations of Dionysos in the guise of Apollo clutching his lyre. It is possible that such a statue had been brought to Constantinople.

[10] The inscriptions and their date are discussed by Rhoby 2010: 241–3, Nr. Me71 and 72, with full literature. Rhoby, following both Hörandner 1989: 151 and Maguire 1994: 113–14, notes that the verses recall that on another object of the later tenth century (or somewhat later), a reliquary in Venice which he records at pp. 257–8 (Nr. Me83: "Beloved receptacle of the live-bearing blood, which flowed from the side of the undefiled Logos"), and a 102-line poem written when two pens were given to the twelve-year-old Romanos II.

[11] The phrase is Paroma Chatterjee's. I thank her for letting me read her compelling paper in draft form. See now Chatterjee 2014.

[12] See below, chapter seven. Belozerskaya 2012: 54–9 has suggested that the artist responsible for the inkpot was inspired by the *tazza farnese*, although in a lively chapter on Byzantium she offers no firm evidence that the antique gem was at Constantinople in the tenth century.

FIGURE 5.2 Detail of Eros between entwined serpents. Silver ink-pot showing stylized entwined serpents amid mythological figures. Byzantine, tenth century. Padua, Diocesan Museum, from the Canons' Sacristy of the Cathedral. Photo: Carlo Cavalli/Museo Diocesano di Padova.

FIGURE 5.3 Detail of Ares between entwined serpents. Silver ink-pot showing stylized entwined serpents amid mythological figures. Byzantine, tenth century. Padua, Diocesan Museum (from the Canons' Sacristy of the Cathedral). Photo: Carlo Cavalli/Museo Diocesano di Padova.

any other statues. Frescoes preserved in Kiev, at the Church of Saint Sophia, make no visual reference to the *euripos* or any of its statues.[13] The Kiev fresco may derive at least in part from drawings made of the carved marble base of the Theodosian obelisk base, both the lower base showing the race and the upper showing the *kathisma*. In particular, the southeastern face shows musicians in the register beneath the emperor holding a laurel wreath for the victor (fig. 4.7, above). But emphasis is placed on the starting gates (*carceres*; see above, map 6) and the mechanics of the race, with the officials signaling both

---

[13] Boeck 2009: 291. But see Grabar 1936: 68, where, in a line drawing, the figure beneath the imperial couple with his hand raised appears to be offering a wreath to the winner. The image is badly abraded, and what exactly is happening is unclear.

FIGURE 5.4 Detail of Apollo between entwined serpents. Silver ink-pot showing stylized entwined serpents amid mythological figures. Byzantine, tenth century. Padua, Diocesan Museum (from the Canons' Sacristy of the Cathedral). Photo: Carlo Cavalli/Museo Diocesano di Padova.

FIGURE 5.5 Detail of a river god between entwined serpents. Silver ink-pot showing stylized entwined serpents amid mythological figures. Byzantine, tenth century. Padua, Diocesan Museum (from the Canons' Sacristy of the Cathedral). Photo: Carlo Cavalli/Museo Diocesano di Padova.

the start and end of the race, which do not appear on the marble obelisk base. The Kiev fresco was, therefore, most likely to have been based on drawings made in the hippodrome itself on the occasion of a race and taken to Kiev by Byzantine artists charged with decorating Tsar Iaroslav's private entrance to his church. Although no such expansive scene has survived from Constantinople, the Kiev fresco reminds us that Constantine V (741–75) is said to have adorned the Milion with images of his favorite charioteers in action. According to the *Life of Stephen the Younger*, hostile to the emperor, he had substituted these for images of the ecumenical councils.[14] Constantine is derided as an Iconoclast,

---

[14] This is noted at Gero 1977: 113, n. 8. See also Cameron, Al. 1973: 205, n. 1; Moorhead 1985:176; Auzépy 1997: 215, where at n. 174 the passage is described as "celebrated"; and now Pitarakis 2010: I, 265.

but a clear distinction was drawn in his reign between secular and sacred images. Consequently, his Milion may well have included images of "idols," such as the statues and tripods on the *euripos*. The Milion was redecorated before the eleventh century.

Some tripods, perhaps from Delphi, although not the Serpent Column, appear to be illustrated in two illuminated manuscripts, one dating from the eleventh century (Vatican Cod. Gr. 1947), the other from the twelfth century (Jerusalem Cod. Taphou 14). These are copies of Pseudo-Nonnus' *historiae*, sixth-century commentaries on the classical allusions contained in four homilies by Gregory of Nazianzos.[15] These illustrations (Vat. fol. 149r., badly abraded, and Taph. Fol. 101r) both show a tripod on which sits a bowl filled with water.[16] Two fires have been set under the bowl, between the legs of the tripod, to boil the water. From the middle of the bowl rises a column, evidently a single piece of veined dark marble, supporting a capital that serves as a statue base. The statue is of Apollo, standing, nude but helmeted, holding a planted spear in his right hand and in his left a shield, also resting on the capital.[17] The association with Apollo in the illuminations is intended to confirm that this is the monument from his oracle at Delphi. Pseudo-Nonnus' commentary on sermon five, chapter fifteen, explains:

> Delphi was a city in Phocis, and Phocis a province of Greece. In this Delphi was a temple of Apollo, in which was the Pytho, (and) in which stood the bronze tripod, from which bronze tripod the oracle issued. For above the tripod was a bowl on which the oracular lots leapt and sprang whenever Apollo prophesied. It was 'three-footed' (a tripod) for this reason, because it gave prophecies about the three aspects of time. For true prophecy speaks about both those things which are past and those which are present and those that are to come.[18]

In a further illumination in the Jerusalem manuscript (fol. 313r.), we see the Egyptian gods portrayed as animals on columns. The placement of a pillar behind the tripod and cauldron shows that the earlier illumination was a

---

[15] Weitzmann 1951: 64–5, figs. 75 and 78. Contrary to his broader argument that the illuminations reflect the importance of classical models in Byzantine art, Weitzmann includes, on p. 75, the observation that these miniatures are among those "in which no classical features could be detected ... [and which] must be considered as Byzantine inventions." The commentaries are translated with an introduction by Nimmo Smith 2001.

[16] It is clear from Athonite documents that tripods (*pyrostia*) were still employed in this manner for cooking. See ByzAD, s.v. "pyrostia."

[17] Vatican Cod. Gr. 1947, fol. 149r., where the illumination is terribly abraded and only poorly visible in Weitzmann's illustration, and Jerusalem Cod. Taphou 14, fol. 101r., which is very clear. That this is a conflation of two images is suggested by fol. 313r. in the same Jerusalem manuscript, where a column supporting a statue stands behind a tripod bearing a bowl, which is Weitzmann 1951: fig. 92.

[18] Nimmo Smith 2001: 79 (5:15), 102–3 (39:13). See also Weitzmann 1974: 403, where we are told that Pseudo-Nonnus explains: "above the tripod was a brazen bowl, in which the prophetic pebbles leapt up whenever she looked at them" (or perhaps whenever the water boiled).

portmanteau, a conflation of two separate objects, perhaps indicating their relative positions in a public space in Constantinople. By chance, surely, it echoes Zosimos' conflation of a statue of Apollo and a tripod.[19]

Animate Statues

Byzantines feared the power of statues, because they understood that images were connected to their prototypes. They understood that ancient idols were repositories for supernatural powers, demonic forces that might be animated by triggers, known and unknown. Few of us find it strange that, when we touch a metal object that has been outside on a summer's day, we find that it is hot. We understand that it has been heated by the sun, and therefore that it is the sun's heat that we feel radiating from it. Many things absorb the sun's energy, but some store and conduct it better than others. So it is with supernatural energy, which some things by their nature, by contact or proximity, or by how they are fashioned, are able to store and conduct better than others.

Even looking at a statue could be dangerous. When looking at a statue, according to the theory of intromission, we absorb the atoms or energy that it emits (Plato identified the energy emitted as light rays). If one rejects this premise, preferring the theory of extramission (as did Euclid and Ptolemy), then the eye emitted energy (*pneuma*, Galen's term), which bouncing off the thing returned to the eye. In either case, it is energy that passed through the eye to imprint the statue's form in the viewer's mind. In both theories of vision available to the Byzantines, the eye engages with the thing seen, the statue, and perceives it by sharing its energy, or rather by receiving part of its matter which may have been energized by a divine or supernatural force.[20]

Statues in bronze were especially fearsome, because bronze, like other copper alloys, seems to have been considered an especially effective medium for harnessing and radiating supernatural energy. When Hephaistos fashioned bulls for Aietes, king of Kolkhis, to harvest warriors grown from a dragon's teeth, he forged their most animate parts, their feet and fire-breathing mouths, in bronze.[21] Bronze, like other metals, was held to be water-based. Plato (*Timaeus* 58d–59b) considered metals to be formed by "fusible" water "partaking of small and fine particles of earth so that it is harder [including a] particular kind of bright and solid water ... bronze." Aristotle also held that metals formed

---

[19] As we have already noted, in chapter four, Zosimos writes that Constantine "even placed somewhere in the hippodrome the tripod of Delphic Apollo, which had on it the very image of Apollo." Zosimos, II. 31; trans. Ridley 1982: 38; Frick 1857–60: 515–16.

[20] The idea of extramission was popularized in an edited collection by Nelson 2000, which addresses many aspects of premodern vision and visuality.

[21] Apollonios, *Argonautika* 3.401–21, 492–501; Ovid, *Metamorphoses* 7.120–58. I thank Benjamin Acosta-Hughes for this reference.

when waters, or potential waters, trapped in the earth, congealed: "The following are therefore composed of water: gold, silver, bronze, tin, lead, glass, and many types of stone that have no names."[22] He further explained that "in water *pneuma* is present, and in all *pneuma*, soul-heat is present so that in a way all hydrous things are charged with soul."[23] Theurgic rituals for the animation of statues were developed in late antiquity by Neoplatonists. The "revival" of this knowledge, which the Greeks had lost, according to Porphyry, was a great accomplishment of his age. In his *Philosophy from Oracles* (fr. 324F, 2–9), Porphyry reminded his readers: "The road to the gods is bronze-bound, steep and rugged, whose many paths the barbarians discovered, the Greek lost, and the ones in power already have thoroughly destroyed."[24] Porphyry was well known to Byzantine readers, and his treatise on the "ensouled statue" (*agalma empsychon*) was read by Byzantine philosophers, including Psellos and Gemistos Plethon.[25] They knew, therefore, that "the telestic art by means of symbols ... makes statues suitable for becoming receptacles for the illuminations of the gods."[26]

The "telestic art" meant the ritual animation of statues, but even those who had no knowledge of theurgy will have known of the possibility that "magic" might connect the viewer inadvertently to the thing or person represented. Popular magical interpretations and uses of statues could be many and varied, as demonstrated by the *Greek Magical Papyri*, dating from the second to fifth centuries A.D.[27] Consequently, many works of ancient art were now branded with a cross, not as an attempt to Christianize the image but rather as an *apotropaion*, a mark intended to protect the image from any demonic force that might enter it or, if that had already happened, to defend the viewer from the evil that might venture forth from within it. The emperor Basil I was not so lucky, according to the *Logothete's Chronicle*. A statue of a "bishop" holding a staff around which was entwined a snake had been placed within his New Church, newly built in the palace grounds. When, for no stated reason, Basil stuck his finger in the snake's mouth, he was bitten by a snake living within it and was sorely wounded.[28] As Adam was Herakles, the unnamed "bishop" was, presumably, in fact a statue of Asklepeios.

---

[22] Aristotle, *Meterologica* 389a. See also Cole 1999: 222,233. I thank Barbara Haeger for this reference.

[23] Aristotle, *Generation of Animals*, 762a.

[24] Quoted in translation by Tanaseanu-Döbler 2013: 71.

[25] Iles Johnston 2008, which is far more developed than a suggestion by Mango 1963: 61, citing a letter of Psellos, *Ep.* 187, ed. Sathas 1876: V, 474.

[26] Iles Johnston 2008: 454.

[27] For example, according to *PGM* 4.3125–71, a wax statue with three heads is made hollow and a lodestone inserted, in addition to a papyrus with special names. See Haluszka 2008: 492.

[28] *Logothete's Chronicle*, ed. Wahlgren 2006: 132.12; ed. Bekker 1838: 691–2. See Anagnostaki and Kaldellis 2014: 123–8, for commentary and context.

Constantinople's statues were a source of wonder, as well as fear, for its citizens, and serpentine creatures proved especially evocative. To offer but one example, the great bronze doors of the senate house in the Forum of Constantine, given by Trajan to the Temple of Artemis at Ephesus, and which had been brought to Constantinople for Constantine, were embossed with a Hellenistic depiction of the Gigantomachy, the battle between the gods and Giants.[29] Constantine the Rhodian was able to explain the scene in his tenth-century *ekphrasis* of the "seven wonders of Constantinople," relating that the viewer could observe the Giants writhing serpentine tails as they hurled rocks at the gods and demigods, who fought back with their traditional weapons:

> Apollo firing a poisoned arrow,
> and Herakles wearing the lion pelt
> and a quiver filled with arrows
> smashing their heads with a club, that is
> the giants whose feet were like serpents coiled
> beneath and turned in,
> throwing aloft fragments of the rocks
> and the serpents just like flashing tongues
> roaring terribly, fearful to look upon
> and flashing fire from their eyes.[30]

Facing the doors, standing on pillars within the circular space of the forum, Constantine had placed statues of Zeus of Dodona and of Athena of Lindos. The natives of Lindos on Rhodes, the hometown of the poet himself, had worshipped Pallas Athena, and the citizens of tenth-century Constantinople recognized her by her helmet and the symbol around her neck, the Gorgoneion entwined with snakes. A fictional madman, St. Andrew the Fool, created by a contemporary of the Rhodian poet, saw in the same scene on the senate's bronze doors a vision of judgment, divining its true Christian meaning from the snaky legs of the giants.[31]

---

[29] Henry Maguire has postulated that this very scene has been preserved in an illustration in a tenth-century manuscript, an illuminated copy of Nikandros' *Theriaka* (Paris, B.N. gr. 247, fol. 47r.). See Maguire 1989: 220; Maguire 1999:191; Maguire and Maguire 2007: 7. For a contrasting view, see Weitzmann 1981:142–3, who suggests that the illustration alludes obliquely to the very beginning of the *Theriaka*, which attests to the creation of "noxious spiders ... grievous reptiles and vipers and the earth's countless burdens from the Titans' blood." See *Theriaka*, ll. 8–10; trans. Gow and Schofield 1953: 28–9. Although they are conflated by later authors, the Titans were not the Giants.

[30] Constantine the Rhodian, ed. Legrande, 9, ll. 125–52. See Stephenson 2010. A new edition of the poem by I. Vassis, with full English translation and commentary by Liz James and others, appeared after this chapter was written.

[31] See below in this chapter, also in chapter six, and Stephenson 2010.

The Particular Judgment

The serpentine antiquities of Constantinople also fired the imagination of the apocalyptic author who, at around the time Constantine of Rhodes was writing, created the fictional *Life of St. Andrew the Fool*. Besides the hippodrome, Andrew is placed at various well-known places throughout the city. At one point he is at the Staurion, named for a cross on a column:[32]

> Now when Andrew arrived there [at the Staurion], being adorned with the gift of insight, he saw a terrible dragon coiled around his [a monk's] neck. It had three heads and its tail hung down to his feet. Of its heads, the first was that of miserliness, the second that of madness, the third that of heartlessness ... The holy man, withdrawing a little from him, saw an inscription in dark letters hovering in the air above him, saying "The dragon of greed, the root of all iniquities." When he looked behind him he saw two men who were eunuchs engaged in a trial for his sake. One of them was black with darkened eyes, the other was white, shining with brilliance eclipsing the sun.[33]

In other words, Andrew the Fool has a premonition of the particular judgment, in which demons and angels vie to snatch the soul of a person on the point of death by weighing good deeds against sins, the *psychostasis*. This is a familiar motif in tenth-century popular literature. To offer just three examples, the particular judgment is the subject of an extended episode, the vision of Theodora in the *Life of Basil the Younger*, and of two brief beneficial tales in the collection of Paul of Monemvasia.[34]

Archangel Michael is frequently identified in early Christian and medieval apocalyptical texts as holding the scales at the *psychostasis*.[35] The scales, drawing on Job 31:6 and Daniel 5:27, may have appeared in Christian art in northern Europe as early as A.D. 900, on the Muirdach Cross in Ireland. However, there is there no sign of Michael. Michael and the weighing of souls feature prominently in a twelfth-century Last Judgment at Autun, France, which shows distinct Byzantine influences (fig. 5.6). A commentator on the Autun carving, Don Denny, has drawn attention to the "demons of sticklike thinness," which is just one aspect of the tympanum that suggests a profound debt to the Byzantine type.[36] One might also draw attention to the three-headed snake

---

[32] *Life of Andrew*, ed. Rydén 1995: 142–4, ll. 1963–75; Stephenson 2010.

[33] *Life of Andrew*, ed. Rydén 1995: II, 142–4, ll. 1963–75. Magdalino 1999: 93, points out a similar miserly monk in the *Life of St. Basil the Younger*.

[34] Wortley 1996: 68–71 (BHG 1449c), 108–11 (BHG 1449k). See also Wortley 2001.

[35] Perry 1912, 1913.

[36] Denny 1982: 533, 536: "So many of the major features of the Autun tympanum are closely similar to Byzantine forms and either uncommon or unknown in earlier western Last Judgments that one may suppose the Autun artist to have had direct access to a Byzantine work, very possibly a manuscript painting." See also Smith 2008.

FIGURE 5.6 Detail from a scene of the Last Judgment, Cathedral of Saint-Lazare, Autun, France, twelfth century. Photograph: Michele Vescovi, with permission.

curled around the leg of a demon of sticklike thinness, which equally is a profoundly Byzantine image, and reminiscent of the serpent wrapped around the miserly monk's neck.[37]

On another occasion, in the middle of Lent, breaking off from running and dancing around the Forum of Constantine, Andrew the Fool is contemplating the Gigantomachy on the bronze doors of the Senate house.[38] As Andrew contemplates this scene, a passerby slaps him on the back and demands "What are you looking at, fool?," to which he replies:

> "You fool! I am staring at the visible idols, but you are a spiritual strap-leg and a serpent and of the viper's brood. Your soul's axles and heart's spiritual legs are twisted and going to Hades. Behold, Hades has opened his mouth waiting to swallow you up, for you are a fornicator and an adulterer and you sacrifice to the Devil every day." When the man heard this he was overcome by

---

[37] This would appear also to prefigure the account in the *Legenda Aurea*, where the sinner confronts three accusers: the Devil, the sin itself, and the whole world. See Perry 1912, 1913.

[38] *Life of Andrew*, ed. Rydén 1995: II, 140–1, ll. 1919–32, 1963–75; Stephenson 2010.

shudders and wondered in his heart, "Does he know this from God or from demons? But how can he know God, a foolish and crazy man?"[39]

The fool is here concerned with crookedness, a physical manifestation of wickedness.[40] The legs of the passerby are serpentine because he is a fornicator and adulterer, and by his sins he sacrifices daily to the Devil.

Specifically, the fool's allusion is to Matthew 12:34: "You brood of vipers! How can you speak good when you are evil? For out of the abundance of the heart the mouth speaks."[41] Matthew mentions the brood of vipers (γεννήματα ἐχιδνῶν) twice more (Matthew 3:7 and 23:33). Both verses concern fear of the Last Judgment. Matthew 3:7 reads: "When the crowds came to John for baptism, he said, 'You brood of snakes! Who warned you to flee God's coming wrath?'"[42] Matthew 23:33 is still clearer: "You snakes, you brood of vipers, how will you escape the judgment of Gehenna?"[43] Here, Matthew has Jesus condemn the teachers of the law and the Pharisees, for hypocrisy above all else—which is a great concern of Andrew the Fool throughout the *Life*—and for valuing the external above the internal, judging appearance not character, like the spiritual strap-leg. That such people will be damned is made clear throughout the *Life*. Indeed, the episode in the Forum of Constantine is followed immediately by an extended reflection on the Particular Judgment, the contest for the soul of the miserly monk between two "eunuchs," described in typical Byzantine fashion as a "dazzling angel" and a demon "black with darkened eyes."[44] The fool knows where the spiritual strap-leg is headed: "Behold, Hades has opened his mouth waiting to swallow you up," he warns the fornicator in the forum. In a terse but rich note to his translation of the *Life*, L. Rydén observed: "To Andrew's mind Hades has the shape of a dragon, which is how Hades appears in the iconography of the Last Judgment and therefore often also in that of the Heavenly Ladder."[45]

Snakes and Ladders

The *Heavenly Ladder*, or *Ladder of Divine Ascent*, was written in the seventh century by John Climacus (Ioannes Klimakos), abbot of St. Catherine's

---

[39] Rydén 1978: 129–55, at 137; Life of Andrew, ed. Rydén 1995: I, 140–1, ll. 1919–32, with comments at II, 325–6. The Gigantomachy is alluded to once more at *Life of Andrew*, ed. Rydén 1995: II, 274–5, l. 3987, with comment at 352, n. 62.

[40] *Life of Andrew*, ed. Rydén 1995: II, 326, n. 4.

[41] Matthew 12:34.

[42] Matthew 3:7.

[43] Matthew 23:33.

[44] *Life of Andrew*, ed. Rydén 1995: II, 144–5, ll. 1973–4. Both episodes here explored are contained in the majuscule fragment that Rydén has identified as part of the autograph manuscript, produced ca. 950.

[45] *Life of Andrew*, ed. Rydén 1995: II, 326, n. 5. Rydén perhaps still had this image in mind when translating διεσκορπίσθη τὰ ὀστᾶ αὐτοῦ παρὰ τὸν ᾅδην as "and his bones were strewn at the mouth of Hades." See also Rydén 1995, II, 169–70, ll. 2397–8.

Monastery at Mt. Sinai. The earliest Greek manuscripts to preserve the text date from the tenth century. It presents thirty chapters on virtues and vices as thirty rungs on a ladder, an image that would appear to demand illustration. The earliest extant illuminated manuscript in Greek, preserved at St. Catherine's Monastery (Sinai MS 417), dates only to the mid-tenth century, and this has only a basic illustration of two ladders (fol. 13v.), one marking the left-hand side of the page and another ascending across the page from one-third of the way up the page on the right to one-quarter of the way across the page from the top left-hand corner.[46] At the base of the diagonal ladder is a chalice.[47] At the top of the ladder is a swirl, within which are written the virtues "Faith, Hope and Love," the ultimate attainments, corresponding to rung thirty, and treated in the thirtieth chapter.[48] The earliest fully illustrated manuscripts were produced in the eleventh century, and motifs developed quickly. In a Sinai manuscript of the twelfth century, the ladder is occupied by four clambering monks whose progress is impeded by winged demons, who grab at one monk's hair and another's foot.[49] Only the most advanced is helped, by Christ himself, who offers His hand. On the ground where the ladder rests are three more figures, dressed in formal robes, evidently officials looking to leave secular life to become monks. The leaf evokes a famous Sinai panel icon of the Heavenly Ladder where souls are dragged from the ladder by black demons with chains or straps and fall into the mouth of Hades, depicted as a black human face.[50]

A manuscript in Princeton University's Firestone Library includes the earliest extant depiction of a dragon at the foot of the Heavenly Ladder (fig. 5.7).[51] The dragon, now somewhat abraded, appears to be have an entwined body, like the Serpent Column, and to have two heads, one of which points upwards, its open mouth displaying sharp teeth. The second head faces downwards, located at the end of the coiled body where one would expect to see a tail. The ladder occupies the right-hand margin of the page containing the last chapter of the work, a brief summary and exhortation that begins "Ascend, my brothers, ascend eagerly."[52] At the top of the ladder, one finds a bust of Christ, His

---

[46] Martin 1954: 186–7, figs. 1–4; Weitzmann and Galavaris 1990: 28–31, fig. 33. See also Ševčenko 2009: 42.

[47] This image is reproduced in a tenth-century Patmos manuscript, as yet unpublished and recently noted by Nancy P. Ševčenko (Patmos, Monastery of St. John, gr. 121, fol. 3v.). See Ševčenko 2009: 44–5, 47, 49, figs. 2, 4, 6.

[48] John Climacus, trans. Luibhead and Russell 1982: 286. The same manuscript has a second image of the ladder's rungs between two columns. At the top, a later hand has added a sketch of Christ, who at the end of chapter thirty appears as Love, "since that is the very name of God himself (1 John 4:8)."

[49] Sinai MS 418, fol. 15v. See Martin 1954: 187–9, fig. 179; Weitzmann and Galavaris 1990: 153–62, fig. 594.

[50] Nelson and Collins 2006: 244–7, with description by B. Pentcheva. Also Weitzmann 1975: 37–8, and 40–1 figs. 33, 34, who posited the existence of an eleventh- or twelfth-century Greek manuscript illumination, now lost, at Sinai, which served as a model.

[51] Princeton, Univ. Library Garrett MS 16, fol. 194r. See Martin 1954 fig. 66; Kotzabassi and Ševčenko 2010: 112–25.

[52] John Climacus, trans. Luibhead and Russell 1982: 291.

FIGURE 5.7. Princeton, Univ. Library Garrett MS 16, fol. 194r., includes the earliest extant depiction of a dragon at the foot of the Heavenly Ladder. Princeton University, Firestone Library.

hands projecting below the firmament offering crowns to those monks who would attain paradise. One has almost reached his goal, but is falling from the top rung, headfirst toward the mouth of the dragon. A brother falling from a lower rung will be devoured before him. Three monks remain on the ladder, heading up. The first has his right foot still on the ground and his left foot on the first rung, equating to the first chapter, "On renunciation of [secular] life." A second monk has his right foot on rung ten ("On slander") and his left on rung eleven ("On talkativeness and silence"). It is from this step that the lower of the two falling monks appears to have slipped, perhaps suggesting he is a blabbermouth. The highest of the three ascending monks has his right foot on rung twenty-two ("On vainglory") and his left on twenty-three ("On pride"). If he avoids these vices and several more, his head may be wreathed with the crown located directly above him.

There is no mention anywhere in the text of the *Heavenly Ladder* that the punishment for failing to ascend the ladder in good order, by observing virtues and avoiding vices, is to fall into the maw of Hades. However, the artist responsible for the Princeton manuscript determined to make that point by sketching the bicephalic dragon. He may be drawing on a far earlier idea: a dragon at the base of a ladder is encountered in the third-century *Passion of St. Perpetua*, where the heroine dreamt of trampling the serpent just before her death:

> I beheld a ladder of bronze, marvelously great, reaching up to heaven; and it was narrow, so that not more than one might go up at one time. And in the sides of the ladder were planted all manner of things of iron. There were swords there, spears, hooks, and knives; so that if any that went up took not good heed or looked not upward, he would be torn and his flesh would cling to the iron. And there was right at the ladder's foot a serpent lying, marvelously great, which lay in wait for those that would go up, and frightened them that they might not go up ... Slowly, as though he were afraid of me, the dragon stuck his head out from beneath the ladder. Then using it as my first step, I trod on his head and went up.[53]

Perpetua's vision of the ladder and dragon, although perhaps originally composed in Latin, was well known in the Greek milieu at the time the *Life of Andrew the Fool* was written. It appears in abridged form in two versions of the *Synaxarion of Constantinople*: the original produced during the reign of Constantine VII, and a somewhat later version preserved in the so-called *Menologion* of Basil II.[54] The latter features one of the few known Byzantine illustrations of Perpetua, showing her martyrdom with her six companions. However, there are, to our knowledge, no extant Byzantine illustrations of Perpetua's ladder and the serpent at its base.[55]

The Last Judgment

Depicting the maw of Hades as a writhing, coiled dragon at the base of a ladder was a new development. In ninth-century Byzantine psalters, Hades is portrayed as a giant with a large belly, and the entrance to his abode as a pair of gates, which Christ rends in his descent to claim the souls of Adam and Eve.[56] In a ninth-century version of the *Acts of St. Marina*, a dragon emerges from Hades to attack the saint following an earthquake, but he is not held to be the mouth of Hades, which is accessed via a crack in the corner of her

---

[53] *Passion of Perpetua*, 4.

[54] See Ševčenko 1992: 188–9. The famous illuminated *Menologion* covers only six months, September to February.

[55] White 2008: 155–7. The tale also inspired writers of other lives, notably the author of a *Passion of Polyeuktos* (BHG 1567), writing before the later tenth century, when it was abridged by Symeon Metaphrastes. As White notes, "The *Passio* goes on to develop the theme of the dragon and the ladder by connecting it with Polyeuktos' rejection of idols, and claims that his faith, like that of Thekla, extinguished fires and blocked the mouths of lions."

[56] Kartsonis 1986: 134–40.

prison cell. Marina prays to the Lord, who has bound Hades and controls who is freed from there.[57] The conception of Hades and its entrance appears to have changed in tandem with a particular and pressing interest in apocalyptic writings and predictions.[58] As Paul Magdalino has shown, there were real millennial fears and expectations in Constantinople in the later ninth and throughout the tenth century, although most modern scholars of the eastern empire have ignored them, believing that those who used a dating system that placed the Creation 5508 years before the Incarnation had little interest in the *Annus Domini* 1000. John of Patmos' *Apocalypse* (Revelation) was of marginal interest to the Greek fathers and was not used in Orthodox liturgical readings. However, it was read with far greater interest and regularity as the millennial anniversary of the Incarnation drew near.[59]

For Arethas of Caesarea, who wrote a Greek commentary on Revelation between ca. 913 and ca. 932, the thousand-year reign predicted at Revelation 20:1–3 was the period from the Incarnation to the commencement of the reign of the Antichrist, although he insisted that the calculation was not exact, and God would decide exactly when the millennium was complete (Matthew 24:36; Acts 1:7–8).[60] In this, Arethas followed Andrew of Caesarea, whose commentary on Revelation dates to an earlier period of eschatological fear, between the years A.D. 500 and 700. This period began in the middle of the seventh millennium, the seventh day, and saw the rise of Islam, which resulted in much activity, including the production of the *Apocalypse* of Pseudo-Methodios, possibly in the 690s.[61] The *Life of St. Andrew the Fool* is well placed in this tenth-century context, and not simply because it contains a long apocalyptic vision.[62] The life as a whole is concerned with sin and judgment in Constantinople, and it contributed to and drew from a rich textual environment.[63] Shortly after Andrew's life was written, in the 950s, the related *Life of Basil the Younger* appeared.[64] This contains two extended apocalyptical visions, that of Gregory of the Second Coming and the Last Judgment and that of Theodora—as recounted to Gregory in another of his visions—of her own death and the ascent of her soul through various spiritual tollbooths, at each of which her sins are assessed.

---

[57] See above, chapter two, for earlier instances of dragon combat.
[58] Instructive in this regard is Guldan 1969.
[59] Magdalino 2003: 249–56.
[60] PG 106, cols. 493–786, at 748–9; Lemerle 1986: 237–80, esp. 270–1.
[61] Magdalino 2003: 237 lists works relevant to this subject.
[62] *Life of Andrew*, ed. Rydén 1995: II, 258–85.
[63] Magdalino 1999: 83–112; Baun 2007. These works support Rydén's dating of the life against a suggestion that it originated in the seventh century.
[64] A new study with full English translation appeared after this chapter was completed (Sullivan, Talbot, and McGrath 2014). I am grateful to Denis Sullivan, Alice-Mary Talbot, and Stamatina McGrath for allowing me to read parts of that work in progress, notably translations of the two visions. I had the pleasure of participating in Dumbarton Oaks Greek reading group seminars devoted to the work in progress in 2002. See also *Life of Andrew*, ed. Rydén 1995: I, 53–4.

Besides Theodora's vision, which elaborates on a theme established by patristic writers, most notably a homily by Cyril of Alexandria,[65] one might consider the quite different *Vision of the Monk Kosmas*;[66] the *Apocalypse of the Theotokos*, which might have originated in the ninth century but circulated throughout the tenth century; and also various visions of Daniel.[67] The *Life of St. Niphon*, which is set in the fourth century but was probably written around A.D. 1000—it drew upon the *Life of St. Andrew the Fool*—also contains an extended vision of the Last Judgment.[68]

There is also the *Apocalypse of Anastasia*, which has been dated by Jane Baun and others to the reign of Basil II.[69] This seems eminently plausible, for it contains a set-piece confrontation in Hades between Nikephoros II Phokas and his murderer, John I Tzimiskes. The *Apocalypse of Anastasia* is set in the sixth century, so this is to be read as a "prefiguration." As Baun notes, the great fourth-century martyr Anastasia and the fictional sixth-century Anastasia who is treated to the tour in this apocalypse should not be equated.[70] However, they often were, and the cult of the saint was going strong in the later tenth century. Indeed it is St. Anastasia's appearance in her own church to Andrew the Fool in his first vision, at the start of four months that he spent in chains, that leads him to become a fool for Christ.[71] The church of Anastasia, which also features in the *Life of Niphon* and twice in the *Life of Basil the Younger*, seems to have been used in the later tenth century as a lunatic asylum.[72]

Monumental depictions of the Last Judgment must also have existed in Byzantium by the middle of the ninth century, if Theophanes Continuatus is to be trusted.[73] If we follow closely what Theodore the Stoudite said at the beginning of the ninth century, such representations may initially have been restricted to the separation of those to the left and right of Christ's throne, the sheep and goats of Matthew 25.[74] The *Sacra Parallela* provides a ninth-century example of this motif as a manuscript illumination.[75] Observations by C. Jolivet-Lévy may allow us to identify frescoes in Cappadocian rock churches

---

[65] Cyril of Alexandria, Homily 14, "On the departure of the soul and on the Second Coming," PG 77, cols. 1072–89.
[66] Angelidi 1983.
[67] See now generally Baun 2007: 110–29.
[68] Rydén 1990: 33–40.
[69] Baun 2007: 18; Timotin 2006: 406.
[70] Baun 2007: 118–19, "One suspects, however, that the various compilers would not have been displeased if hearers confused the fiction and the saint."
[71] *Life of Andrew*, ed. Rydén 1995: II, 18–20, ll. 96–129.
[72] *Life of Andrew*, ed. Rydén 1995: II, 306, n. 5; Magdalino 1999: 91.
[73] *Theophanes Continuatus*, ed. Bekker 1838: 163–4; trans. Mango 1972, 1988: 190–1.
[74] Theodore Stoudites, *On the Holy Icons*, I. 10; trans. Roth 1981: 31. Generally, see Brenk 1964, and now Pace 2007.
[75] Paris gr. 923, fol. 68v. The miniature is attached to a homily by John Chrysostomos, to which is barely relates. There are clear connections to Matthew 25, but also details that do not relate to this,

as dating to the later ninth century.[76] Still, the full multi-register version with which we are today familiar dates from the later tenth century or from very early in the eleventh century. Byzantine ideas and motifs were then transmitted to southern Italy, the Veneto, and even, perhaps, to Iceland, where compositions of the Last Judgment have been shown either to be the work of Byzantine artists or to have been inspired by Byzantine models transmitted by drawings and illuminations.

The earliest surviving illumination is contained in the so-called Stoudios Tetraevangelion, an illustrated gospel book produced in Constantinople's Stoudios Monastery in the eleventh century.[77] It has been argued that this reproduces an earlier model, also produced at Stoudios, which in turn influenced monumental works such as the mosaic at Torcello, Italy, where the scene of judgment forms a compositional unit with an Anastasis, and the Last Judgment at Sant'Angelo in Formis, which is believed to have been produced in the manner of a contemporary fresco which once adorned the basilica built by Abbot Desiderius at Monte Cassino in ca. 1072.[78] On a smaller scale, an ivory plaque in London's Victoria and Albert Museum, once thought to be from Venice but currently attributed to a workshop of Constantinople, depicts a similar scene (fig. 5.8).[79] One might add to this short list a Nordic Byzantine Last Judgment: a series of carvings on fir panels from Bjarnastadahlíd, Iceland, which Selma Jónsdóttir demonstrated came from a Byzantine composition, surely by an artist in possession of a drawing or icon.[80]

In each of these compositions, a male figure is depicted seated on a monster, or a monstrous throne. In the later scenes, the monstrous heads of the throne are clearly serpentine. The motif has been considered enigmatic, and deserves further study.[81] It is sufficient here to state that in eleventh-century Byzantine works this figure is not Satan but Hades, in his ninth-century guise as a fat, bald giant; and also that the serpents are not unambiguously devouring the damned, but may in fact be giving them back, disgorging them from Hades, so that they may be judged. That is to say, the motif seems to illustrate Revelation 20:13–14: "The sea gave up the dead that were in it, and death and Hades gave up the dead that were in them, and each person was judged according to what

---

which led Weitzmann to suggest that the miniature was based on a monumental Last Judgment. See Weitzmann 1979: 169–70, pl. XCVI, fig. 441.

[76] Jolivet-Lévy 2007 suggests that judgment scenes in Cappadocian churches may date from the second half of the ninth century.

[77] BN, Paris gr. 74. See Angheben 2002; also Angheben in Pace 2007: 52, 54–58.

[78] Angheben 2002: figs. 4, 5, and passim; Angheben in Pace 2007: 57–63; Kartsonis 1986:159–64.

[79] Longhurst 1926; Angheben 2002: fig. 6 and passim.

[80] Jónsdóttir 1959. I am grateful to François-Xavier Dillmann for drawing my attention to more recent treatments, notably Ágústsson 1989, which argues that the panels are of the later twelfth century and from Bjarnastadahlíd, not from Flatatunga and of the later eleventh century as Jónsdóttir maintained.

[81] For now, see the astute commentary of Angheben in Pace 2007: 55–6.

FIGURE 5.8 Ivory plaque depicting the Last Judgment, now in London's Victoria and Albert Museum, possibly Constantinople, eleventh century. Photo: author.

he had done. Then death and Hades were thrown into the lake of fire. The lake of fire is the second death. If anyone's name was not found written in the book of life, he was thrown into the lake of fire." [82]

Hell and Hades remained distinct in Byzantine thought. For Andrew the Fool, the entrance to and exit from Hades (ultimately to be cast into hell) were through the mouths of a serpent or dragon.[83] But we cannot say that the author of his life was familiar with visual representations, because none has survived that predates the *Life*. It is better to state that the graphic descriptions provided in this *Life* and others of the period contributed to the fuller visualization of such ideas, and therefore to the development of iconographical forms, like the dragon at the base of the Heavenly Ladder or the triple-headed serpent of the apocalypse.

At Yılanlı Kilise in Cappadocia, dominating the narthex is a representation of the Last Judgment.[84] In the upper register is Christ enthroned within

---

[82] Magdalino 2003 establishes clearly that Revelation had an impact in Byzantium towards the year 1000, and this motif would appear to be further evidence. Jolivet-Lévy 2001: 270–2 noted that motifs from Revelation appeared in Cappadocian wall painting of the tenth century but were not retained in Byzantine iconography.

[83] This development is parallel to that identified (Schmidt 1995) in Britain in the tenth century, associated with the monastic revival of that period. Connections between the developments in portraying the mouth of hell or Hades in northern Europe and Byzantium at this time deserve further study.

[84] Jolivet-Lévy 2001: 272–4; Brenk 1964: 123 considered this to be later, perhaps of the twelfth century, offering a correction to Thierry and Thierry 1960: 159–68, pl. XXXV–XXXIX.

a mandorla attended by angels, and along the walls the twenty-four elders of Revelation (4:4). In the middle register are the martyrs (Revelation 7:9), awaiting the completion of their number that will trigger the end of days. There are here forty martyrs, evoking the Forty Martyrs of Sebaste, who are commemorated in numerous middle Byzantine churches, including four others in Cappadocia. In the lowest register is hell. To the right-hand side, the viewer sees the damned being bitten by snakes, and to the right an angel, Michael, weighing souls. In the central panel of the lowest register is the beast, in the form of a braided serpent with three heads, each devouring the damned, whose legs protrude from the mouths. The river of fire in which the beast swims is also identified by an inscription, and one sees also the river of tar, in which the damned are sunk up to their heads.[85]

Could the Serpent Column have been a direct inspiration for the apocalyptic images of polycephalous serpents painted in distant Cappadocia? It is neither possible nor necessary to demonstrate a direct link.[86] It is enough to record that the dragon of Revelation was anticipated as keenly in tenth-century Constantinople, where the statues in the hippodrome were known to be visible idols, tempting the unwary and corrupting the hypocritical citizens of Constantinople, who on race days filled the stands rather than the city's churches. But more than this, it is revealed in the *Patria* that there was at the very end of the tenth century a common belief that the end of the city, and therefore of the world, was revealed by the statues in the hippodrome.[87]

> The remaining statues of the hippodrome, the men and the women, the various horses, the *columns of stone and bronze* and the brazen obelisks at the turning points, the representations on the obelisk, the statues of the charioteers with their bases in relief, the columns of the galleries with their capitals and pedestals, and those in the curved part, the marble revetments and reliefs, the steps and podia and *every place where an inscription can be found, especially on the brazen statues* – all these are representations of the last days and of the future [i.e. the Last Judgment].[88]

The end of the city of Constantinople, and therefore the beginning of the end times, was foretold especially on the "columns of stone and bronze," and "every

---

[85] Makarios of Egypt, *Homily* 18, "Concerning the progress of the Christian," relates: "There are the rivers of dragons, and the mouths of lions. But the fire of love burneth up all." Later, also on sin: "And yet there are dragons, and there are lions, the poisonous beasts, and all the treasures of wickedness, and there are rugged ways, and precipices."

[86] One might otherwise propose that there was no sudden, independent fascination with triple-headed coiled serpents in Cappadocia, but rather that a model book had been produced in Constantinople that contained images drawing upon the city's statues.

[87] *Patria*, II, 79, ll. 14–15, ed. Preger: 191; trans. Berger 2013: 102–3. See also Berger 1988: 543–8, passage 155/οε'.

[88] The italics are mine, but the translation is from Berger 2010: 196–8 (also in Turkish). See also Diehl 1929–30; Vasiliev 1942–3: 493–4, where the phrase is translated "the truth about the last destinies."

place where an inscription can be found, especially on brazen statues." The names inscribed in the Book of Life would be saved, but something quite different was inscribed in the Egyptian hieroglyphs on the Theodosian Obelisk and in the Phokian letters on the Serpent Column.[89]

Destroying Statues

Although never washed away completely, the cityscape of Constantinople was always in a state of flux, its furnishings damaged or destroyed by fire and earthquake, riots and imperial whims. The hippodrome was especially vulnerable, since the greatest crowds gathered there not only to cheer on charioteers, but also to raise up and bring down emperors. Anastasios (491–518) was crowned in the *kathisma*, and later appeared there, without his crown, to quell a riot.[90] Protests were common, and sometimes they became riots that damaged the hippodrome. Supporters of the Greens, a racing faction, threw rocks at Anastasios as he sat in his box, and when one of their number was killed by his guards they set fire to the hippodrome. Its colonnade was destroyed by fire as far as the *kathisma*, and beyond the stadium the Chalke gate and the public portico was burned as far as the Forum of Constantine.[91] The devastation was repaired, but again the hippodrome burned, and much else besides, during the infamous Nika riot of A.D. 532. The statue collections in the Baths of Zeuxippos and Palace of Lausos were both devastated.

Emperors might also destroy statues by choice. A number of the bronzes brought to the city for Constantine were melted down by Anastasios. Malalas attributes this act to one John the Paphlagonian, who determined to cast a colossal statue of the emperor to place on a column in the Forum of the Bull, whence an earlier statue of Theodosios had fallen in an earthquake.[92] Anastasios had a second statue of himself, apparently forged from iron, erected on the *euripos* near the Skylla.[93] Sometime later, Justinian is said to have destroyed

---

[89] In Middle Persian myth, at the end of the world the sky serpent Gōčihr, equivalent to Draco, would fall to earth and melt the ore contained in mountains and hills, creating a river of molten metal that would purify mankind. See *EI*, s.v. Aždahā: 197.

[90] Anastasios' coronation in the *kathisma* is reported by Theophanes, s.a. 5983, ed. Bonn: 136; trans. Mango and Scott 1996: 209–10. For the hippodrome in this period of unrest, see Cameron 1976: 271–96; Dagron 2011: 151–84.

[91] Malalas, 16.4, ed. Thurn 2000: 321; trans. Jeffreys, Jeffreys, and Scott 1986: 221. Anastasios' rebuilding of the Chalke is recorded at *Greek Anthology* IX. 656.

[92] Malalas, 16.13, ed. Thurn 2000: 328; trans. Jeffreys, Jeffreys, and Scott 1986: 225. Theophanes, s.a. 5999, ed. Bonn: 149; trans. Mango and Scott 1996: 228 states that this was done on Anastasios' orders.

[93] *Greek Anthology* XI.270–1, cited by Cameron, Al. 1993: 93, as *Palatine Anthology* IX. 271–2. It was earlier noted by Edward Gibbon.

or removed hippodrome statues, perhaps those marked by the fires set in 532 rather than, as stated, part of a systematic purging of pagan imagery. He also, like Anastasios, determined to raise a statue of himself on a column. Justinian's was an equestrian statue, showing the emperor in a peacock-feathered tiara, the *toupha*, which was adopted from Persian triumphal regalia. The statue was cast to celebrate a victory over the Persians from captured arms and armor, as an epigram revealed: "The bronze from the Assyrian spoils moulded the horse and the monarch and Babylon perishing. This is Justinian, whom Julianus, holding the balance of the east, erected, his own witness to the slaying of the Persians."[94]

The greatest damage to the city's statuary was done in 1204, by the forces of the Fourth Crusade. Niketas Choniates, as an addendum to his historical account of the sack, provided a threnody for the city's statues, notably those in the hippodrome. Choniates reports both what he believes to be the truth about the statues and also what others had claimed. The more fabulous accounts are drawn from the established patriographical tradition. Choniates describes many lost works of art, including Eutyches and Nikon from Octavian's Nikopolis, and reveals that the Skylla group was still in situ, terrifying all who beheld it: "the ancient Skylla [is] depicted leaning forward as she leaped into Odysseus' ships and devoured many of his companions: in female form down to the waist, huge-breasted and full of savagery, and below the waist divided into beasts of prey."[95] Choniates displays a fascination with animal statuary, notably that depicting combat. He mentions a man fighting a lion—Herakles and the Nemean lion—as well as an elephant and a hippo, and describes at length an eagle clutching a serpent, which is attributed mythographically to the first-century wonder-worker Apollonius of Tyana.[96]

---

[94] *Greek Anthology* XVI. 62 and 63. The translation given is by W. R. Paton of 63. An equestrian statue of Theodosios I had been erected in the Forum of the Bull by Arkadios. On this, see Bassett 2004: 208–11. The epigrammatic inscription was recorded in the *Greek Anthology*, XVI. 65: "You sprang from the East to mid heaven, gentle hearted Theodosios, a second sun, giver of light to mortals, with ocean at your feet as well as the boundless land, resplendent on all sides, helmeted, reining in easily, O great-hearted emperor, your magnificent horse, although he strives to break away." Clearly identifying Theodosios, this epigram may have become illegible or detached, since at the start of the thirteenth century, according to both the *History* and *De Signis* of Choniates, the statue was identified as Bellerophontes riding Pegasus, or Joshua son of Nun. See Niketas Choniates, ed. van Dieten 1975: 643 (History), 649 (*De Signis*); ed. Morisani, Gagliuolo, and de Franciscis 1960: 20; trans. Magoulias 1984: 353, 358. Niketas is repeating information from the *Patria*, II. 47. However, the correct identification was made in the tenth century by Constantine the Rhodian, 219–40, and also by a source employed by Kedrenos (I. 566) in the mid-eleventh century.

[95] Niketas Choniates, ed. van Dieten 1975: 651; ed. Morisani, Gagliuolo and de Franciscis 1960: 24; trans. Magoulias 1984: 359; Bassett 2004: 218–19. On the *De Signis*, see Cutler 1968, who was, however, unaware of the edition by Morisani et al.

[96] Niketas Choniates, ed. van Dieten 1975: 651; ed. Morisani, Gagliuolo and de Franciscis 1960: 24–6; trans. Magoulias 1984: 359–60. See also Bassett 2004: 216.

Three Strands Twisted

When in 1204 the city was sacked by the forces of the Fourth Crusade, who destroyed or stole many of its prominent works of art and buildings, the Serpent Column survived. The reason for its survival was not recorded or has not been preserved. It is clear that after 1204, with the removal of so much that had once surrounded and obscured it, the Serpent Column was now a prominent feature of the cityscape, and therefore received a great deal more attention from both locals and visitors to the city, and was named for the first time in several languages. In a thirteenth-century version of the *Synaxarion of Constantinople*, in the beneficial tale of Nicholas the monk, former soldier, a temptress is described as a τρίπλοκος ὄφις.[97] "Triplokos," as adjective or noun, is rare, being employed to refer either to triple baptism or, more frequently, to a laurel wreath braided from three strands. A plausible translation of *triplokos ophis* is "triple-braided snake," or "thrice-turned snake." The specific reference to a τρίπλοκος ὄφις seems to be unique to this Constantinopolitan text.[98] It may, therefore, reflect a local name applied to the triple-braided snake in the hippodrome. Similar terms in Latin and Slavonic were used by travelers to describe the Serpent Column. The Italian traveler Buondelmonti refers to "three bronze snakes, rising and twisted into one, with their mouths open."[99] Clavijo, a Spanish ambassador who visited the hippodrome in 1403–6, wrote similarly in Latin of "three copper figures of serpents. They are twisted like a rope, and they have three heads with open mouths."[100] Zosima the Deacon, a Russian who visited Constantinople twice in 1420 and 1421, describes the Theodosian Obelisk with wonder, and observes that next to it stands "a column of brass, with three asp heads, braided together (стоит столп, 3 главы аспидовы, мѣдены, сплетены в мѣсто)."[101]

In c. 1390, Ignatius of Smolensk, the earliest of the Russian travelers to Constantinople whose accounts have been preserved, describes the hippodrome, where "stands a brass column apparently [made of] three strands twisted; there is a serpent head on each end of the divided top."[102] An anonymous description,

---

[97] Stephenson and Shilling 2012, which offers a translation from the edition by Clugnet 1902.

[98] The τρίπλοκος ὄφις does not feature in a later version of the beneficial tale contained in a *Synaxarion* dating from the seventeenth century: Clugnet 1902: 326–8, where the temptress has become τὸν τρικέφαλον ᾠήδην, "the three-headed snake." The τρίπλοκος ὄφις reappears in a nineteenth-century version of the *Synaxarion* printed in Venice, for which see Clugnet 1902: 328–30. We shall return to this text in the next chapter.

[99] Buondelmonti, ed. Gerola 1930: 274, C: "tres eneos serpentes in unum contortique exorti stant oribus apertis." Alt. A: "tres eneos serpentes in unum contortique ercti videmus oris apertis." Alt. M: "tres eneos serpentes in unum contortos erectosque videmus oris apertis."

[100] Clavijo, trans. Markham 1859: 35.

[101] Majeska 1984: 184–5. I have slightly altered Majeska's English translation.

[102] Majeska 1984: 92–3: "и стоит тамо столп мѣдян, аки в три пряти свит, в верху разведены, а на коемждо конци по змиевѣ главѣ." I have altered the English translation slightly from Majeska's so that the word order corresponds to the Slavic.

also of ca. 1390, refers to "three brass serpents [3 змии мѣдяны]," with no mention of their being braided or twisted.[103] However, it then proceeds to relate that "these serpents turn three times a year," which appears to be a misunderstanding of their being turned, or twisted together. This is compounded in a more elaborate text based on the anonymous description, the *Dialogue on the Shrines and Other Points of Interest of Constantinople*, which relates that the column turns "when the sun enters the summer solstice, the winter solstice, and when it will be a leap year." However, one is struck by the consonance between the story of the serpents turning and a far earlier tale, reported in Pseudo-Nonnus' *historiae*, that when the Achaians came to Delphi "to the Temple of Apollo to enquire ... suddenly a voice from an invisible source was heard. After the tripod had turned three times, the prophetess offered an oracle."[104]

---

[103] Majeska 2004: 144–5.
[104] See Weitzmann 1951: 64.

6 }

Fountain

Serpentine Fountains of Constantinople – Fantastic Fountains –
Annunciation and the Second Eve – Triple Temptation – Christian
Serpent-tramplers and Dragon-slayers

There was in the Greco-Roman world an enduring association between snakes and water. The very form of the Serpent Column evoked the power of the Python, guardian of the spring of Castalia at Delphi. Snakes as fountains abounded, many inviting the observer, the listener, to imagine the hissing sound of water escaping a fountain under pressure as serpentine sibilation. Since, as we established in our first chapter, the Serpent Column served for some time as a fountain, the entwined serpents may have been understood to protect the waters. However, it also inspired abundant stories of its miraculous properties, some of which it may have acquired from the city's other serpentine fountains.

Serpentine Fountains of Constantinople

The classical association between serpents and water was retained and developed in middle Byzantium, where antique basins and fountains remained in use. In the *Vita Basilii*, written in the mid-tenth century, we read of a serpentine fountain placed outside the Nea, or New, Church by Basil I:

> On the western side, in the very atrium, stand two fountains, the one to the south, the other to the north. ... The southern one is made of Egyptian stone, which we are wont to call Roman [porphyry], and is encircled by serpents excellently carved. In the middle of it rises a perforated pine-cone supported by hollow white colonnettes disposed in circular dance formation, and these are crowned by an entablature that extends all round. From all of these [elements] water spouted forth and inundated the underlying surface of the trough.

This basin is clearly of antique manufacture, since porphyry was no longer available, and it is probably the same fountain that a later emperor, Andronikos Komnenos, moved again, to his mausoleum from the small garden of the

152 } The Serpent Column

FIGURE 6.1 Red breccia basin, with carved serpent snaking around the rim, Hellenistic (reused). Now in the outer narthex of Hagia Sophia, Istanbul. Photo: author.

imperial palace in the 1180s. According to Niketas Choniates, this was a "great porphyry basin, which has coiled together around its rim two entwined dragons, a wonder to behold."[1] No mention is made of the pine-cone finial, which perhaps was removed, since the object now was unplumbed. Laskarina Bouras identified this as the reddish breccia basin at Hagia Sophia, which has holes and a circular recess where the finial would have been mounted (fig. 6.1). However, the fact that it is clearly identified as porphyry makes this association unlikely.[2]

Another fountain sporting a carved serpent is described by Manuel Philes.[3]

> A soulful serpent and an artful lion
> Nature finds formed freely from stone
> For if not yoked by the stiffness of stone

---

[1] Niketas Choniates, ed. Van Dieten 1975: 332; trans. Magoulias 1984: 183; trans. Mango 1972: 234. On the fountains of Constantinople, see now Shilling and Stephenson 2016.

[2] Bouras 1977: 65–8. I thank Federica Broilo for reminding me of this important distinction. See also Broilo 2009: 21. Delbrueck's catalogue of porphyry objects records a porphyry fountain basin with snakes at the rim at Naples, and also a porphyry snake head now in Paris. See Delbrueck 1932: 176–9.

[3] Pietsch 2010: 108–9, no. 48: *A Fountain in the Martyrium with the Cenotaph of Sts. Florus and Laurus*.

FIGURE 6.2 Bronze *strobilion*, the only Byzantine fountain finial currently known to have survived, Great Lavra Monastery, Mt. Athos, Greece. Photo: Charalambos Bouras/Dumbarton Oaks.

> One would have seen the snakes before now slither
> Supposing them alive and desiring to stir
> But scared to death and in rigor mortis
> Perhaps from fear of slipping
> For the bold lions standing below
> Have gaping mouths hurrying to feed.

This was formerly but incorrectly understood to describe the *strobilion* or finial of a fountain that can still be seen at the Great Lavra Monastery on Mt. Athos. The bronze *strobilion*, the only Byzantine fountain finial currently known to have survived, comprises an eagle with outstretched wings, the uppermost figure (perhaps a later addition, and once surmounted by a cross); a middle tier of eight creatures—four serpents (or dragons) alternating with two winged lions and two griffins—projecting from a pomegranate or pine cone; and a third, lower tier of four serpents (or dragons), each with a bull or ram in its mouth (fig. 6.2).[4] The

---

[4] Bouras 1976, which suggests that the eagle is a later addition, since it does not feature in Byzantine illustrations of fountains. But an eagle does surmount the finial of the fountain imagined by Makrembolites, *Hysmine and Hysminias*, I.5; trans. Jeffreys 2012: 179–80.

basin beneath the finial has been dated by an inscription to 1060. A similar *strobilion* inspired an artist at Mistra, who in 1366 painted a fresco of St. Gregory of Nazianzos in the southeast chapel of the Aphendiko, comparing him to a fountain with a finial formed from four serpents projecting from a pine cone dispensing water into a hexagonal basin, from which a stream emerged through a lion-head spout.[5] The projecting serpents evoke also a model *strobilion* attributed to Philon of Byzantion, a scientist who flourished in the third century B.C.[6] Other fountains sporting finials adorned with a remarkable array of *zodia*, but lacking serpents, are described in a twelfth-century romance by Makremobolites and a fourteenth-century *ekphrasis* by Hyrtakenos.[7]

Serpentine finials adorn fountains depicted in manuscripts, especially those drawn in the twelfth century. A striking fountain with entwined serpents forming a finial can be seen in the mid-twelfth-century Seraglio Octateuch.[8] It has the shape and proportions, including the three-stepped base, of the recently mentioned breccia basin that today stands in the outer narthex at Hagia Sophia. A similar fountain with an entwined serpentine finial features in an illuminated gospel book from the end of the twelfth century now held at the Vatopedi Monastery on Mount Athos.[9] A very similar motif features twice in a manuscript of the twelfth century containing Gregory of Nazianzos' homilies. Each marginal scene depicts a fountain with a quatrefoil basin and tank and an elaborate finial (fig. 6.3, fig. 6.4).[10] From the center of each bowl rises a spout that quickly divides into three parts, the central stem rising to form an ornate pine cone–like device—or perhaps it is a nut or flower, or a pineapple—from which two jets of water fall. The left and right branches of the finial curl out like vines and then inwards to enclose a heart-shaped space divided by the central finial. The vines have three leaves, and each vine ends in a serpent's head, the mouth visibly open and emitting water.[11] Thus there are four separate streams of water. To each side of the quatrefoil bowl stands a bird drinking.[12]

---

[5] Bouras 1977: 65, illustrated at Millet 1910: pl. 109.

[6] Bouras 1976: 91, ill. B.

[7] Maguire 1994: 109; Jeffreys 2012: 179–80; Dolezal and Mavroudi 2002: 121–8, with translation of Hyrtakenos.

[8] Topkapı Sarayı Gr. 8, fol. 251v. See Lowden 1992: 21–6, and passim.

[9] Athos Vatopedi 918, fol. 10r, being the pi-shaped head-piece to the Gospel of Matthew. See Galavaris 1979: 118, and fig. 89, as cited by Stichel 1997: 324. See also Eustratiades and Vatopedinos 1924: 170.

[10] Paris, BN Cod. gr. 550, fols. 59v. and 166v. See Galavaris 1969: XC, fig. 412; XCIII, fig. 423.

[11] Style akin to that described in Maguire and Maguire 2007, where fruit is grown in a mold so that the heads seem to be those of animals. That is, the three-pronged finial of the fountain is a vine, perhaps, but ends in two serpents' heads.

[12] See also Galavaris 1969: fol. 239v., showing the *koimesis*, where two rabbits or hares try to drink from the fountain, but no serpent heads.

FIGURE 6.3 Gregory of Nazianzos' homilies, Paris, BN Cod. gr. 550, fol. 59v., Constantinople, twelfth century. Photo: Bibliothèque nationale de France.

Fantastic Fountains

It has been suggested, rather romantically, that it was because it still served as a fountain that the Serpent Column was preserved in 1204, so that jousting Crusaders might drink from it.[13] Water cascading down from more than seven meters above the floor of the hippodrome, or at least four meters above the mouth of a mounted man, would be less likely to refresh a jouster than drench him and his horse, but perhaps that was desirable after a robust joust. Reports of the Serpent Column fountain have always been fantastic, and for that reason they deserve our scrutiny.

The earliest preserved accounts of the Serpent Column fountain concur that it was once a magical device designed to spurt different liquids. The Italian traveler Buondelmonti, who visited Constantinople in the 1420s, related that on festival days each snake-head disgorged a different liquid: one water, one wine, one milk.[14] The symbolic value of such an adaptation is

---

[13] Madden 1992.
[14] Buondelmonti, ed. Gerola 1931: 274; Majeska 1984: 255–6

FIGURE 6.4 Gregory of Nazianzos' homilies, Paris, BN Cod. gr. 550, fol.166v, Constantinople, twelfth century. Photo: Bibliothèque nationale de France.

clear: water, wine, and milk all have meanings that we shall explore later.[15] It would not have been beyond the wit of a Byzantine engineer in any period to fashion a device to distribute water, wine, and milk from the mouths of the Serpent Column on certain days. This would not even have required a tower and siphons. For example, it might easily have been achieved by placing on top of the column, in the manner of the original golden tripod, a tank with its interior divided into three sections containing different liquids. Three taps emerging from the bottom of the tank might be positioned at or near each serpent's head. Securing such a device to the top of the serpents' heads might have required solder (so we might recall that a trace of hard solder was found on the upper jaw of the one remaining serpent head). There is, however, no indication that this method was ever employed, nor did Buondelmonti see such a fountain functioning. Rather, he was reporting a folk tale, which was

---

[15] See below in this chapter.

repeated in a slightly different form shortly afterwards by the Spanish traveler Pero Tafur (ca. 1435–9).[16]

> There is in Constantinople a great place made by hand, with porticoes and gateways, and arches below, where the people used in ancient times to watch the games when they celebrated their holidays, and in the center are two snakes entwined, made of gilded brass, and they say that wine poured from the mouth of one and milk from the other. But no one can remember this, and it seems to me that too much credit must not be attached to the story.

Tafur does not mention the third serpent's head, which suggests that he did not see the statue, or did not look very carefully. The former seems more likely, since he claims in the same passage to have seen in the hippodrome a statue "of brass, where merchants who could not agree on a price" would go to receive supernatural arbitration. In fact, no such statue stood in the hippodrome in the fifteenth century, and the tradition had been transferred from the bronze hands of the *modion*.[17] Giovan-Maria Angiolello would report half a century later, and more accurately, that the tradition had in fact been transferred to a marble statue of a seated man, placed within "a small building of bricks in the form of three little pillars."[18] Pero Tafur implies that he does not believe the story that the Serpent Column spouted wine and milk, and he is similarly skeptical when he reports that a nearby bath had two doors, through one of which a woman accused of adultery would be led, and as she departed through the other, if she had sinned, "her skirts raised themselves high without her noticing, so that from the middle down everything could be seen."[19] This, once more, is a tale recorded far earlier, in the *Patria*, of quite another monument, a statue of Aphrodite on a column.[20]

If the Serpent Column were such a marvelous fountain at the start of the fifteenth century, this would surely have been mentioned by Clavijo, a Spanish ambassador who visited the hippodrome in 1403–6 and described it very accurately. Clavijo saw "three copper figures of serpents . . . twisted like a rope, and they have three heads with open mouths."[21] It is notable, moreover, that the four

---

[16] Pero Tafur, trans. Letts 1926: 143. See also Majeska 1984: 256–7; and Lett's comment on p. 11 that "even the Serpent Column failed to move" Pero Tafur, "possibly because he did not know its history." It was only later that the third snake-head may have been damaged, on which see below, chapter eight.

[17] Janin 1964: 104. Tafur also misidentifies the equestrian statue of Justinian, which he sees upon leaving Hagia Sophia, as Constantine; and reports that the Theodosian Obelisk "is neither fine nor ancient," and was made for the body of Constantine.

[18] Grélois 2010: 228–9.

[19] Pero Tafur, quoted by Grélois 2010: 229.

[20] Grélois 2010: 229; Patria II.65; trans. Berger 2013: 94–7.

[21] Clavijo, trans. Markham 1859: 35.

Russian travelers who left detailed accounts of their trips to Constantinople between 1389 and 1421 fail to mention that it was, or had ever been, a fountain. Nevertheless, the tale was later reported by several travelers, including Wolf von Zühlnart in 1496, who stated that the mouths spurted wine, milk, and oil; Carlier de Pinon in 1579, who repeated Buondelmonti's account; and Reinhold Lubenau in 1588–89, who reported that water had once gushed from the three mouths.[22]

It is possible that Buondelmonti and Pero Tafur, and those who followed them in reporting on the festive gushing of various liquids, were recording a tradition which had attached to the Serpent Column far earlier. The tradition, or the fountain if it existed, may have inspired an altogether different fountain, a remarkable device spouting water, wine, mares' milk, and mead, which was observed at the court of Möngke Khan (1209–59) in spring 1254. It was described by the Franciscan William of Rubruck, who attributed it to the Parisian goldsmith Guillaume Boucher.[23]

> In the entry of this great palace, it being unseemly to bring in there skins of milk and other drinks, master William the Parisian had made for him [the khan] a great silver tree, and at its roots are four lions of silver, each with a conduit through it, and all belching forth white milk of mares. And four conduits are led inside the tree to its tops, which are bent downward, and on each of these is also a gilded serpent, whose tail twines round the tree. And from one of these pipes flows wine, from another *caracosmos*, or clarified mare's milk, from another *bal*, a drink made with honey, and from another rice mead, which is called *terracina*; and for each liquor there is a special silver bowl at the foot of the tree to receive it. Between these four conduits in the top, he made an angel holding a trumpet, and underneath the tree he made a vault in which a man can be hid. And pipes go up through the heart of the tree to the angel. In the first place he made bellows, but they did not give enough wind. Outside the palace is a cellar in which the liquors are stored, and there are servants all ready to pour them out when they hear the angel trumpeting. And there are branches of silver on the tree, and leaves and fruit. When then drink is wanted, the head butler cries to the angel to blow his trumpet. Then he who is concealed in the vault, hearing this blows with all his might in the pipe leading to the angel, and the angel places the trumpet to his mouth, and blows the trumpet right loudly. Then the servants who are in the cellar, hearing this, pour the different liquors into the proper conduits, and the conduits lead them down into the bowls prepared for that, and then the butlers draw it and carry it to the palace to the men and women.

Guillaume Boucher, the master goldsmith, had been captured at Belgrade in 1242 and taken to Karakorum, where he presided over a workshop of some

---

[22] Stichel 1997: 326 provides full references and commentary. See also Paravicini 1994–2001 for a list of late medieval travelers to the East.

[23] William of Rubruck, trans. Rockhill 1900: 207–8.

fifty artisans.[24] His "magic fountain" was unveiled at the khan's spring reception, where ceremonial, including the *proskynesis*, is held to have been modeled on that of Constantinople.[25] Möngke Khan's magic fountain would have required only that the cellar of the palace be level with the top of the tree in the reception area so that liquids could be delivered by siphons to the spouts in the serpent's mouths high in the tree. Alternatively, since he resorted to placing a slave in a trench beneath the fountain to pump wind into the angel's trumpet, he may also have employed hand pumps to propel the liquids up the tree.

In the very decade the Mongol fountain was created, Chinese writers were producing major mathematical treatises, and books on hydraulics they acknowledged were based on knowledge from "Fu-lin," i.e., Byzantium.[26] It is possible that Boucher had seen similar hydraulic devices in Constantinople, and his fountain also echoed contemporary developments in France, such as the rudimentary automata in Villard de Honnecourt's sketchbook. Functioning mechanical marvels, as is well known, had been part of Byzantine ceremonial since the ninth century. Automata were developed in competition between Constantinople and Baghdad, when ideas flowed freely. Thus, Theophilos built his Bryas Palace, which is described as "Saracen," with an audience chamber decked out with automata to rival those of the Abbasid caliph Mamun. At exactly this time, one finds described in the *Kitáb al-Hiyal*, or *Book of Ingenious Devices*, which drew upon several Greek works (Heron, Philon, Archimedes), a number of elaborate fountains which were able to flow alternately with water and wine. Mamun was surely the patron of the Banu Musa, the sons of Musa, authors of the *Kitáb al-Hiyal*. Mohammad, one of the sons of Musa, visited Constantinople before he and, principally, his brother Ahmad composed the *Kitáb al-Hiyal*.[27] Mechanical table fountains with spouts delivering different liquids are recorded in the *De cerimoniis*.[28]

Monumental fountains in Constantinople also delivered wine on certain occasions. According to the *Vita Basilii*, in the later ninth century a bronze fountain in the middle of the Sigma, a semicircular courtyard of the imperial palace, was on the occasion of receptions "filled with pistachios, almonds and pine nuts, while spiced wine flowed from its [gilded] pine cone [finial] for the enjoyment of those attending," including organists and performers in acrobatic displays staged for the emperor.[29] The *Vita Basilii* also refers to another

---

[24] Olschki 1946: 45–6.

[25] Eight years earlier, John of Plano Carpini had attended a reception in the golden tent of Kuyuk Khan, where he observed the gilded ebony throne manufactured by a Ruthenian goldsmith called Cosmas, which Olschki 1946: 17–22, considered "a monument of Byzantine style."

[26] S. Kaplan, in a review of Olschki 1946, in *Speculum* 23/ii (1948), 326–8 at 328.

[27] The mood is well captured in Magdalino 1998. See also Dolezal and Mavroudi 2002: 128–32.

[28] The ca. 1320 silver table fountain from France, now in the Cleveland Museum of Art, gives some idea of how these may have appeared: http://www.clevelandart.org/art/1924.859.

[29] Maguire and Maguire 2007: 45–6, citing the *De Cerimoniis* and Theophanes (meaning Theophanes Continuatus), on the reign of Theophilos. This passage is translated by Mango 1972: 162. The description of the waterworks continues, "Next to the fountain [which we have just considered] are set up steps of white Proconnesian marble ... also, next to the long side of the Sigma have been erected two bronze lions with gaping mouths. These spouted water and flooded the entire hollow area of the Sigma."

160 } The Serpent Column

FIGURE 6.5 The Larnaka Tympanum, Victoria and Albert Museum, London. Photo: author.

fountain, "The northern basin [which] has been fashioned from the stone called Sagarios ... one can also see cups near which in former times wine used to spout up from below, providing drink and welcome to the passers-by."[30]

There are three illustrations, all from the period ca. 1200 to 1280, that appear to depict the Serpent Column as a fountain with liquid spurting from the snakes' mouths. Two of these images depict the Annunciation to Mary at the well, where the liquid is certainly water. The earlier of these two, possibly, is a marble tympanum excavated at Larnaka, Cyprus, before 1882 and now held in London's Victoria and Albert Museum (fig. 6.5). Its central panel, dominating the upper and middle of three registers, depicts the Ascension, with Christ enthroned within a mandorla supported by the hands and feet of four angels. On the viewer's left, also occupying the upper two registers, is a crucifixion scene. On the viewer's right, balancing this, are two scenes: in the upper register, Christ is baptized in the Jordan; in the middle register, Gabriel appears to Mary, and between them is a column of twisted snakes (fig. 6.6). The three birds in the scene appear to be a conflation, or perhaps more a confusion, of two motifs, namely the birds symbolic of spring and the fecundity of nature, and in the case of the bird perched on the column, the dove representing the Holy Spirit, both shown in the famous Sinai Annunciation icon.

The Larnaka Tympanum is currently held to be a product of the period 1210–30, when Cyprus was under Latin rule, although this is on stylistic grounds and largely by analogy with the very few sculptural representations

---

[30] *Vita Basilii*, 85; trans. Mango 1972: 194–5; ed. and trans. Ševčenko 2012: 276–9.

FIGURE 6.6 Detail from the Larnaka Tympanum, Victoria and Albert Museum, London. Photo: author.

of the Ascension from Tuscany (one each from Pisa, Arezzo, and Florence).[31] Since there are very few such tympana from Tuscany, and none with scenes arranged in registers, one would wish to revisit the proposed date and discussion of stylistic influences. Paul Hetherington has suggested that the piece is a nineteenth-century pastiche, implicated in the various alleged frauds of General Cesnola, the snakes derived from a second representation of a serpentine fountain in a fresco also on Cyprus. He suggests that the object is rather too narrow to have sat above a door, and that it has damage in very odd places and is undamaged in others where one would expect it.[32]

At Moutoullas in the Troodos Mountains of Cyprus, in a small church dedicated by its Latin founders to the Panagia, there is a cycle of wall paintings that is dated precisely by a donors' inscription to A.D. 1280.[33] The conch of the apse contains a bust of the Theotokos Blachernitissa flanked by the archangels Michael and Gabriel. On either side of the apse is painted the Annunciation: to the viewer's left is Gabriel, badly damaged, and to the viewer's right, in better condition, is Mary and a fountain or well in the form of twisted serpents. Two snakes are entwined to form a fountain. Water falls from the mouths of both into a tank. The border of the tank appears to be of panels or tiles, studded with pearls, and one sees water filling the tank (fig. 6.7).

---

[31] Willis 1981. Willis, an expert in Indian art, was at the time of writing curator of the early South Asian and Himalayan collections at the British Museum.

[32] Hetherington 2000.

[33] Mouriki 1984.

FIGURE 6.7 Entwined serpent fountain in a depiction of the Annunciation, Church of the Panagia, Moutoullas, Cyprus. Photo: author.

The snake fountain in depictions of the Annunciation at the Well is an allusion to the serpent of Genesis, the tempter by whom mankind was led into sin before that sin was redeemed through Christ. Paradise lost will be regained through the waters that flow from the fountain in four streams, as they did in Eden. The snakes evoke the Fall even as they bear witness to the announcement by Gabriel that God will redeem mankind for that sin through his son, born to a woman. Any number of texts from the fourth to the thirteenth centuries might be cited in support of this proposition, and we shall turn to some later in this chapter.[34] However, unlike that of the Annunciation to Anna, the image of the Annunciation to Mary, as Henry Maguire has recently argued, does not feature a fountain in the Byzantine tradition.[35] The image at Moutoullas is located in a church built for a Latin donor, and it cannot be taken as a literal illustration of the Serpent Column in Constantinople. Rather, it might better be viewed as a representation of a story that had now become attached to the column and was told frequently to and by travelers who had visited the Byzantine capital.

---

[34] See below, "Annunciation and the Second Eve.".
[35] Maguire 2016.

Fountain } 163

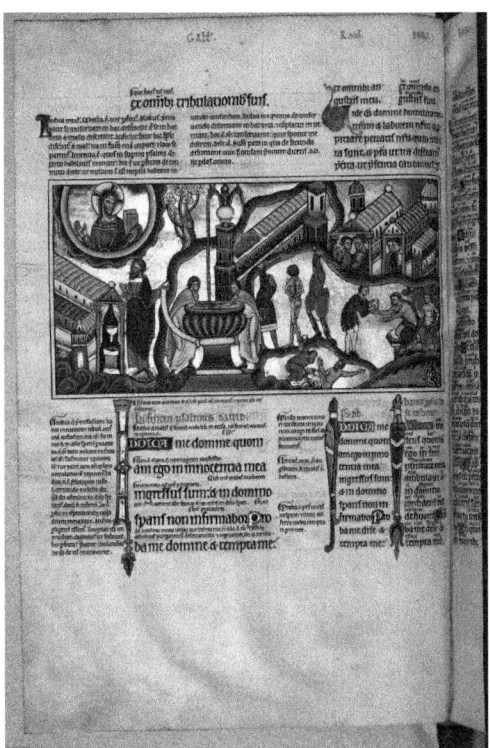

FIGURE 6.8 Great Canterbury Psalter, Paris BN Lat. 8846, fol. 43v. Photo: Bibliothèque nationale de France.

The third illustration, a remarkable illumination painted far from Constantinople, appears to show a tall serpentine fountain with two heads spouting water. A psalter produced in Canterbury around the year 1200, and completed in Catalonia more than a century later, is called variously the Paris Psalter (it is now Paris BN Lat. 8846), the Great Canterbury Psalter, and the Anglo-Catalan Psalter (fig. 6.8).[36] It is the third and last psalter produced in Canterbury to be inspired by the ninth-century Utrecht Psalter, and it drew also upon a slightly earlier twelfth-century psalter produced in Canterbury, known after its scribe as the Eadwine (Canterbury) Psalter (fig. 6.9).[37] The Utrecht

---

[36] For a description of the manuscript, see http://www.le.ac.uk/english/em1060to1220/mss/EM.P.Lat.8846.htm.
  The illustrations are reproduced at Omont 1906, as pl. 34. See also Sandler 2000: 71 and fig. 8. Eunice Dauterman Maguire drew this to my attention and offered her own interesting commentary.
[37] Stirnemann 1992: 188: "It seems reasonable to suppose that the artist of *Paris* [i.e. the Great Canterbury/Anglo-Catalan Psalter], who was one of the leading Byzantinizing artists of the day, would have wanted to compare two of the older manuscripts (*Utrecht* and *Eadwine*) at Canterbury ... *Paris* would then be a sort of visual conflation of both sources, more closely dependent upon *Eadwine* at the beginning, and later drawing upon *Utrecht*." The judgment is deliberately contrary to that of Heimann 1975, which posited a lost intermediary between *Eadwine* and *Paris*. Noel 1995: 203, warns against regarding the various Canterbury psalters as "copies" of the Utrecht Psalter.

Psalter (HS 32 dl, fol. 14v.), in illustrating Psalm 25 (26), employs a fountain to elucidate verse six, "I will wash my hands among the innocents and go around your altar, O Lord." Water cascades in a single stream into a basin from the mouth of a lion, which is shown sitting atop a column at the end of a row of arches, which appear to represent an aqueduct conveying a river from beyond a city. The city is encompassed by the three basilica churches—"I love the house where you live, O Lord"—two depicted with an altar placed outside. Nine children, the innocents—who are people, "inter innocentes" the Gallicanum version of the Vulgate clarifies—wash their hands in the basin and in a stream of water overflowing its rim.[38] The Psalmist stands off to the side of the basin looking to heaven, where Christ is to be seen among angels. The Eadwine Psalter (Trinity College Cambridge, MS R. 17. 1, fol. 43v.; fig. 6.9), produced in Canterbury in ca. 1160, offers a faithful reproduction of both the design and details of the Utrecht Psalter's illustration of Psalm 25 (26), including both the aqueduct and fountain of a seated lion on a pillar.[39] The Paris or Great Canterbury Psalter, whose artist drew upon both the Utrecht and Eadwine Psalters, echoes the composition closely, but with significant adaptations (fol. 43v., fig. 6.8). There are now two older innocents, beardless youths dressed in flowing robes. Christ is austere and alone in his majesty, the Pantokrator in heaven delimited by the firmament.[40] The fountain discharges two streams, one into a basin before it and the other into a tank within the structure behind it. This is no longer an aqueduct supplying the fountain, but a structure that resembles a large cistern and has something like the shape of a hippodrome. The finial discharging the two streams is no longer a lion but has two heads, of dogs or dragons or serpents. Between them is a third, globular shape marking the top of a pole that juts from the top of an elaborate tower with four rows of two windows. One wonders what might have inspired the artist to draw such a fabulous fountain in Canterbury at the turn of the twelfth to thirteenth century, in a psalter that displays profound Byzantine influences.

Since the Great Canterbury Psalter was illustrated at Canterbury between 1180 and 1200, its Byzantinizing artist may have seen illustrations of serpentine

---

[38] Panofsky 1943: 54–5 has a detail of the fountain from the Psalter and sets beside each other the Gallicanum and Hebraicum versions of the Vulgate Latin text of Psalm 25 (26).

[39] See Gibson, Heslop, and Pfaff 1992: pl. 1. The Eadwine Psalter employs color in the illustration and misinterprets some details, for example not showing any water flowing from the source across the aqueduct. The first Canterbury interpretation of the Utrecht Psalter, BL MS Harley 603, eleventh century, also offers a faithful reproduction of the illustration at fol. 14v. The lion fountain stands on its column at the end of the aqueduct, and nine innocents wash in the basin and its overflowing stream. This also fails to show water flowing across the aqueduct. See generally Noel 1995, although the fountain is mentioned only once and in passing on p. 192.

[40] As was observed by Tselos 1959: 145, the form and frequent presence of the Pantokrator is but one very clear indication of strong Byzantine influence on the illustration of this psalter, which distinguishes it clearly from the Utrecht Psalter. See also Heimann 1975: 314. In contrast, as Noel 1995: 109 notes, the principal artist of the Harley Psalter contented himself with rubricating the cross in Christ's nimbus.

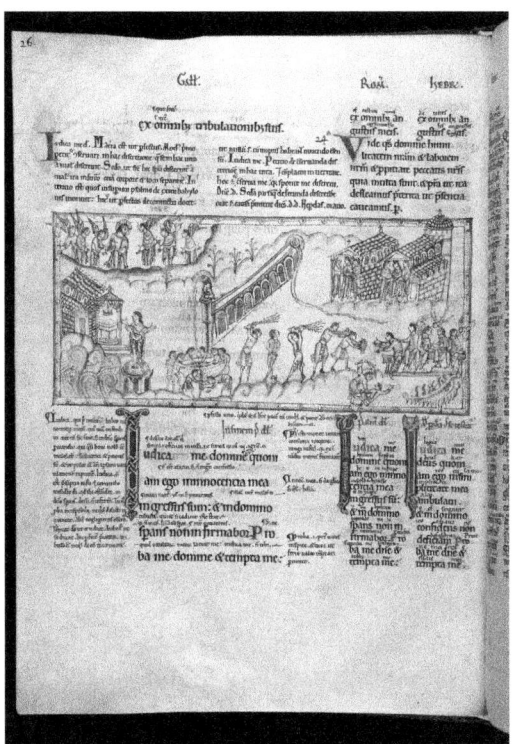

FIGURE 6.9 A lion fountain, apparently terminating an aqueduct, discharges into a basin. Eadwine Psalter, Wren Library, Trinity College, Cambridge, MS R. 17. 1, fol. 43v. Master and Fellows of Trinity College, Cambridge.

fountains by Constantinopolitan artists and adapted the fountain in his models to reflect this motif, just as he substituted the austere Pantokrator for Christ flanked by six angels. We shall look at several twelfth-century Byzantine illustrations of fountains later in this chapter. However, it is conceivable that the adaptation of the illustration for Psalm 25 (26) reflects a recent wonder still fresh in the telling. Emperor Manuel I Komnenos (1143–80) staged a grand banquet in Constantinople's hippodrome at Lent 1180, to celebrate the betrothal of his son Alexios to Agnes of France, and also the recent marriage of his daughter Maria to Renier of Montferrat. Both Alexios and Agnes were children, too young to be offered wine, and in such circumstances might they have been offered water or milk? A panegyric by Eustathios of Thessalonike preserves a description of the occasion.[41] One is obliged, therefore, still to wonder: could

---

[41] Eustathios, ed. Wirth 2000: 170–81, at 174–6. See also Magdalino 1993: 100–1, 456, writing before Wirth's edition, and hence referring to the Escorial manuscript in which the work is preserved. Stone 2001: 249, 250 suggests the date of Lent 1180. Maguire and Maguire 2007: 29–57, esp. 53–4, discuss the spectacle of dining and imperial display, including a reference to Manuel's feast.

the "magic fountain" have existed in the hippodrome after all, perhaps only briefly and for the edification of western visitors to Constantinople? This seems less likely than an alternative, that the artist illustrating the Great Canterbury Psalter kept the basic design and proportions of the lion seated on a pillar, but offered a Byzantinizing alternative, drawing on imagery developed in Constantinople through the twelfth century.

Annunciation and the Second Eve

The Larnaka Tympanum and fresco at Moutoullas (figs. 6.5, 6.6. 6.7) both depict the Annunciation to Mary taking place at a fountain formed from entwined snakes spouting water from their two mouths. The meaning of the serpentine fountain was clear to thirteenth-century viewers, as it stood in a tradition of exegesis that stretched back through the Christian millennium. Paradise lost would be regained through the living waters that flow from the fountain, in four streams, as they did in Eden. Snakes evoked the Fall even as they bore witness to the announcement by Gabriel that God would redeem mankind for that sin through his son, born to Mary, the Theotokos, the second Eve. In the words of Anastasios of Antioch, writing in the sixth century a homily on the Annunciation:

> Therefore on this day, Gabriel was sent out, proclaiming to the Virgin the uncorrupt birth, and declaring to her the impending salvation of the nations through her: at the same time as the greeting, The word became flesh, forming anew the figure, which sin spoiled, having entered along with the words of the evil snake. For it was necessary, it was necessary that flesh be corrupted by the hissing of the snake to return to incorruption by means of the greeting of the angel: and just as death was effected through a woman, so it was necessary that salvation be dispensed through a woman.[42]

Such sentiments were developed in homiletic literature before the sixth century. In the fourth century, Ephrem the Syrian wrote, "Our Lord has caused them to find the tunic of Adam again. While the Church purifies its ears of this serpent's words, which [men] heard, and which sullied them." Ephrem also wrote of fountains of milk, recalling the words of the famous *Akathistos Hymn*, and also drawing us back to a description of the Serpent Column spouting milk as well as water and wine.[43]

---

[42] Anastasius of Antioch, Sermon II, PG 89. 1376–85: Εἰς τὸν Εὐαγγελισμὸν τῆς παναχράντου καὶ Θεοτόκου Μαρίας (On the Annunciation of the all-immaculate and God-bearing Mary). This was drawn to my attention by Brooke Shilling, as was Didymus of Alexandria, *De Trinitate*, II.XIII; PG 39, cols. 692AB, cited in Peltomaa 2001: 132–3: "For she is the baptismal font of the Trinity, the workshop of salvation of all believers; and those who bathe therein she frees from the bite of the serpent and she becomes mother of all, a virgin dwelling in the Holy Spirit ..."

[43] See earlier in this chapter.

Gabriel's first appearance to Mary is held to have taken place near a well, which is often depicted in Byzantine art as a fountain, from which Mary fled in fright. The Annunciation then took place in Mary's home, where she is frequently depicted spinning, and later seated on a throne. As the Christian tradition developed, a further Annunciation scene appeared, which is first recorded in the apocryphal *Protevangelion of James*. This is the Annunciation to St. Anne, Mary's mother, an episode that came to be celebrated in the Orthodox calendar on 9 December. This too is held to have taken place beside a well, later shown within a verdant garden. This can hardly have been the case on 9 December, of course, but the fecundity of nature is the central idea, and depictions were inspired by the Song of Songs 4:12–15: "A garden enclosed is my sister, my spouse; a spring shut up, a fountain sealed … A fountain of gardens, a well of living waters, and streams from Lebanon."

A famous mosaic depicting the Annunciation to Anne can be seen at Daphni, near Athens (fig. 6.10). The fountain in the Daphni mosaic comprises five parts, from top to bottom: (1) a pine-cone finial discharging four streams of water; (2) a small bronze or gilt bowl, almost an oyster shell in design, from which two further streams fall into (3) a quatrefoil basin, filled with water, from the center of which ascends a bronze pillar which is or contains a pipe, and which is supported on (4) a pink marble pillar, which features towards its base an opening from which gushes water into (5) an ornate tank, filled with water, perhaps fashioned from bronze and embossed with a shield or shell and two vine leaves.[44] Its form resembles in some ways that of the Serpent Column as a fountain, notably the emergence of water from a hole near the base cascading into a tank.

Serpentine fountains feature in two richly illustrated manuscripts containing six homilies on the life of the Theotokos Mary by James, a monk of the Kokkinobaphos Monastery.[45] These manuscripts date from the middle years of the twelfth century (1130s–1150s). In the first homily, the Annunciation to Anne takes place in a garden. No description of the garden is provided, although its tranquility is emphasized.[46] In the Vatican manuscript, fol. 16v. (fig. 6.11), one sees a fountain very similar to that in the Seraglio Octateuch.[47] However, now the fountain expels water into a cubic tank at its base, just as

---

[44] Dolezal and Mavroudi 2002: 105–58 offer full commentary and a translation of a pertinent *ekphrasis* by Hyrtakenos. The fact that there are seven streams of water depicted is significant: they represent the same number of openings as in the human head, but more pertinently also virginity, seven being a number "without a mother" and also a virgin, since "it is the only single-digit number that can be neither divided by nor divide another single-digit number." This quality is enjoyed also by five for those who count in Arabic numerals, but not in Greek letters.

[45] Parisinus BN graecus 1208 and Vaticanus graecus 1162. See Anderson 1991. The Vatican manuscript is available in facsimile, ed. Hutter and Canart 1991. The text of the homilies is at PG 127, cols. 543–700.

[46] PG 127, cols. 556–7. See Dolezal and Mavroudi 2002: 107–8.

[47] Vat. gr. 1162, fol. 16v.

168 } The Serpent Column

FIGURE 6.10 Annunciation to St. Anne in the garden, mosaic at Daphni, near Athens, Byzantine, eleventh century. Josephine Powell Photograph, courtesy of Special Collections, Fine Arts Library, Harvard College Library.

at Daphni and in the two miniatures depicting birds drinking in Paris gr. 550 (fig. 6.3, fig. 6.4, above). In the lower register of folio 16v., four streams gush from the fountain: two from the serpents' mouths, two from the tank at its base. This reminds us of the four rivers of paradise, as does the tree depicted centrally with pine-cone-shaped hole, which also features in another illustration, fol. 35v., which features centrally the snake tempting Eve, coiled around the tree, rather like the entwined serpents of the fountain (fol. 35v., the four rivers of paradise, the serpent coiled around a tree, and the expulsion of Adam and Eve).[48] The richness of the illustration is rivalled only in the Paris example, where the fountain is now without its serpentine finials (fig. 6.12).

In the twelfth-century Codex Ebnerianus, an Annunciation to Mary is placed above the author portrait of St. Luke, whose gospel (Luke 1:24–39) is read on that feast, 25 March. The scene places Mary not in a garden, but rather on a more familiar throne before a palace. Nevertheless, a fountain is depicted

---

[48] It has been suggested, by Jacqueline Lafontaine-Dosogne 1964, 1992: I, 196–201, that an illustrated version of the *Protevangelion of James* supplied the models for the depictions of the early life of the Virgin, including both Annunciations in gardens, in the Kokkinobaphos homilies. However, we cannot know if a serpent fountain existed in this posited prototype, and it seems less likely than that it was the invention of the twelfth-century master. See also Anderson 1991: 77.

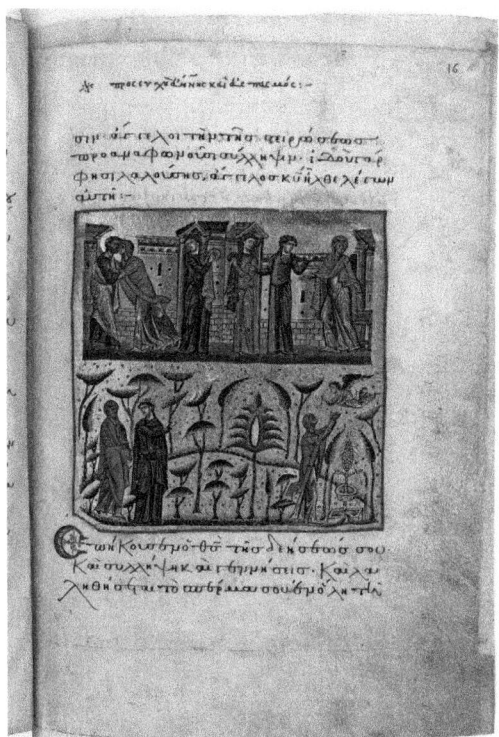

FIGURE 6.11 Annunciation to St. Anne in the garden, homilies of James, monk of Kokkinobaphos, Vat. gr. 1162, fol. 16v., Constantinople, twelfth century. Biblioteca Apostolica Vaticana.

resting on an arch. It is a simple white basin, from which emerges a pine-cone finial and two snakes. The arch, which forms part of a building and abuts Mary's throne, is supported by a spiral column.[49] This is evidently a conflation of the two Annunciation scenes.[50] A very similar fountain, with two serpent heads looking in at each other above a basin, is placed at the top of a canon table in the Vani Gospels, which manuscript was produced in Constantinople toward the end of the twelfth century by the scribe Ioane, and was sent to Queen Tamar of Georgia.[51]

---

[49] Constantinople early 12 c. Bodleian MS Auct. T. infra I. 10, fol. 178 v. There are three more such columns in the lower register, behind Luke's back. Remarkably, they appear to form a tripod, supporting a bowl of water, although this must have been intended as the form of a cupola.

[50] There are many cognate examples. Maguire 1981: 47, figs. 31 and 32, writes of the lion-head fountain, similar to that found in the Annunciation at the Kariye Mosque, in the Komnenian Annunciation to Mary at Perachorio, Cyprus. Lion-headed fountains with three stone basins also feature in frescoes at the Bogorodica Peribleptos, Ohrid; the Church of the Annunciation at Gradac; and (the earliest of this sequence) at the Church of the Holy Apostles in Thessalonike. There is no fountain in the Annunciation to Anna in the fourteenth-century fresco in the Church of the Holy Cross at Pelendri, although Anna kneels in a garden on a rocky foreground before three trees. On this, see Gerasimou at al. 2005: fig. 73.

[51] Lazarev 1948: II, pl. 207.

FIGURE 6.12 Annunciation to St. Anne in the garden, homilies of James, monk of Kokkinobaphos, Paris BN gr. 1208, fol. 21v., Constantinople, twelfth century. Photo: Bibliothèque nationale de France.

Jeffrey Anderson has argued that the same workshop in twelfth-century Constantinople was responsible for the Codex Ebnerianus, the two versions of Kokkinobaphos' homilies, and the Seraglio Octateuch. In Anderson's judgment, the Kokkinobaphos Master had several lesser artists working under him. One might surmise, therefore, that in each case we are looking at stylized versions of a small group of serpentine fountains. Perhaps the Master or another in his workshop produced sketches that informed his illuminations, and which may have traveled further afield, providing models for artists working far beyond the walls of Constantinople, in Cyprus and perhaps even as far as Canterbury.[52] Among these models was the Serpent Column, standing in the hippodrome, thought once to have been a fountain, provoking diverse reflections and reactions from all who viewed it. Although few artists would have been so bold as to depict the column directly, it appears in Christian contexts as a Christianized motif, its protective powers appropriated and directed toward those who sought redemption through Christ and the Theotokos.

---

[52] Stichel 1997.

Triple Temptation

The temptation of the first Eve by a serpent (Genesis 3), to which the second Eve, Mary, supplied the antidote, was portrayed early and often in Christian art and writings. Frequently, the serpent is a three-headed monster. Dante conjured an infernal three-headed beast, whose mouths chomped on the betrayers Judas, Brutus, and Cassius. This was not Dante's invention. Some eight centuries earlier, in the sixth century, a triple-headed serpent was identified as the agent of mankind's temptation by Romanos the Melode in his *Fourth Hymn on the Resurrection*.[53] Likewise, Eusebios of Alexandria, in his *Third Homily on the Passion*, referred to "three-headed Beelzebub (τρικέφαλε Βεελζεβοὺλ)," and the fifth-century Bishop of Ravenna, Peter Chrysologus, preached: "We have seen this beast, brethren, devouring with a triple mouth (*trino ore*) all the highly precious sprouts of the human family. Yes brethren, with a mouth that is triple: as sin this beast captures, as death it devours, and as hell it swallows down."[54] Earlier still, and far to the east of Ravenna, a three-headed dragon demon appears in the *Testament of Solomon*, where it is called Korouphe, "crest of dragons," as opposed to Tribolos ("caltrop") or Pterodrakon ("winged dragon"). It is clearly a corruption of this dragon that we meet in the *Acts of St. Marina*, where Rouphos (Rufus) is commanded by Beelzebub, who also appears as the archdemon in the *Testament*.[55] A *kanon* to Marina, praising her serpent-slaying, is found in one eleventh-century (Mess. gr. 139) and one twelfth-century manuscript (Sinait. gr. 627). "You warded off the multi-formed serpent in female form, and the fall of Eve you restored, most worthy one."[56]

In later Byzantine romance, Eros was imagined not as a cherubic deity of erotic love but as a king with three heads, or perhaps one triple-formed face, displaying the features of a small child, middle-aged man, and old man.[57] Most famously in Byzantine literature, Digenis Akrites confronts and beheads a three-headed dragon, which has been posited as being a metaphor for his own erotic passion.[58] In the Escorial version of *Digenis*, two of the dragon's three heads echo those of King Eros: "one was that of an old man, the second that of a young man, and the one in the middle was a snake's, the dragon of Gehenna." Digenis strikes off all three heads with one blow of his sword.[59] In

---

[53] Romanos the Melode, *Hymns*: 43.20.1; ed. Grosdidier de Matons 1967: IV, 524: τρικέφαλε δράκον.
[54] *Sermon* 111, "On original sin," PL 52: 506A; trans. Ganss 1953: 177.
[55] *Acta Sanctae Marinae*, ed. Usener 1886: 29; White 2008: 158–9.
[56] Ἤλεγξας τὸν πολύμορφον ὄφιν ἐν γυναικείᾳ μορφῇ καὶ τῆς Εὔας τὴν πτῶσιν ἀνώρθωσας, ἀξιάγαστε. See Shirò 1966–83: XI, 307 (this line), 310 (refers to dragon); as cited in White 2008: 161. See also dragons holding a cross in a marginal illumination, Paris gr. 375 (d. 1021), where the cross is at the "top right hand corner of a folio ... resembling an illuminated initial letter, made up of twisted strands. Two dragons hold its foot in their jaws." Here I am quoting from Walter 1997: 201.
[57] Beaton 1996: 155–8 analyzes the pertinent literature, notably quoting from Libistros, where the *trimorphoprosopos* appears.
[58] Livanos 2011: 133–4.
[59] Jeffreys 1996: 322–3.

the Grottaferrata version of the epic, the tale blends elements of classical and Christian myth, of Hades and Persephone, and of Eve and the Serpent. Digenis falls asleep beside a spring in an Edenic garden and is awoken by the cries of his girl, "the beautiful daughter of the general Doukas," who is threatened by a terrible three-headed dragon (*drakon*).[60] This serpent of the spring had transformed itself into a handsome boy in order to rape the girl, but as Digenis approached,

> he revealed a hideous apparition to me, huge and terrifying to human eyes—three gigantic heads, completely engulfed in fire: from each it gushed out flame like lightning flashes ... Thickening its body and drawing its heads into one, growing thin behind and making a sharp tail, at one moment coiling itself and then unfolding again, it launched its whole attack against me. But I, reckoning this spectacle at nothing, stretched my sword up high ... and brought it down on the ferocious beast's heads, and cut them all off at once. It collapsed on the ground, twitching its tail up and down in its last spasms. I wiped my sword and replaced it in its scabbard.[61]

Christopher Livanos has drawn attention to the phallic symbolism of this episode, and also to the fact that in a preceding episode Digenis was himself cast in the role of rapist: "the dragon is punished for attempting the very crime that Digenis has just committed."[62]

A "triple-braided snake" appears as a tempter in a thirteenth-century version of the *Synaxarion of Constantinople*, in the beneficial tale of Nicholas the monk, former soldier (BHG 2311 = *NMS*).[63] "Triplokos," as an adjective or noun, occurs infrequently, and the specific reference to a τρίπλοκος ὄφις is, we believe, unique to this Constantinopolitan text.[64] It seems likely, therefore, that the phrase is used by an author familiar with the Serpent Column and that he uses a local name for it. Nicholas' story had already appeared, inserted into the *Life* of Nicholas of Stoudios (BHG 1365 = *VNS*), written early in the tenth century. However, there one finds no mention of the triple-braided snake. In both versions of the parable, the protagonist sets out to war against the Bulgars in the army of Emperor Nikephoros I (d. 811). For one reason or another (neither version is specific), he travels apart from the army, and spends the night at an inn or hostel (according to the *VNS*, this was located in Thrace). Having been treated well and fed by the hostess (in *VNS*, she is a wealthy woman apt

---

[60] Jeffreys 1998: 152–7.
[61] Jeffreys 1998: 156–7.
[62] Livanos 2011: 133.
[63] Stephenson and Shilling 2012, which offers a translation from the edition by Clugnet 1902.
[64] The phrase τρίπλοκον ὄφιν does not feature in a later version of the beneficial tale, contained in a *Synaxarion* dating from the seventeenth century: Clugnet 1902: 326–8. Here the temptress has become τὸν τρικέφαλον φήδην, "the three-headed snake." The τρίπλοκον ὄφιν reappears in a nineteenth-century version of the *Synaxarion* printed in Venice, for which see Clugnet 1902: 328–30.

to entertain those passing by; in *NMS*, she is the innkeeper's daughter) the protagonist takes to his bed. However, during the night, on three occasions, he is woken by the woman, who is driven by a satanic lust to proposition him. On all three occasions he resists her, and he berates her for wishing to drag him down into "the depths of hell (εἰς ᾅδου πέταυρον)."[65] A telling phrase, this signals that the tale is rehearsing the message of *Proverbs* 9. The temptress, the "triple-braided snake," is Folly, who tempts passers-by into her bed, drawing them off the path to Wisdom and into the "the depths of hell."

Departing (in the *NMS* having taken time to pray), the protagonist heads toward the battlefield. In the *VNS*, but not the *NMS*, the temptress sends slaves to hide her shame by killing the protagonist, but instead the killers die, by God's grace. Arriving in the vicinity of the battle, the protagonist has a supernatural experience (in the *VNS* he is summoned to a mountaintop by a voice, whereas in the *NMS* he simply falls asleep and dreams what follows). A powerful figure appears to him (in the *VNS*, we are told further that he is aged, gigantic, and dressed in white), seated with his legs crossed, right upon left. He draws the attention of the protagonist to the battle between the Romans and Bulgars, proceeding below them, and to the fact that the Romans are winning. The seated figure then places his left leg upon his right and the Bulgars gain the upper hand (foot). The Romans are all slaughtered, but the man draws the protagonist's attention to a single bare patch on the battlefield, where no corpse lays. That, he observes, was where the protagonist would have fallen had he succumbed to the advances of the temptress (called in the *NMS* "the triple-braided snake," τὸν τρίπλοκον ὄφιν). The protagonist (having awoken in the *NMS*) withdraws from the vicinity of the battlefield and prays, but he cannot save the army, only himself. Consequently, he enters a monastery and serves God truly, becoming a holy father. It would be impossible for citizens of Constantinople familiar with this story, which was first told to and by monks of the city's own Stoudios Monastery, to have looked upon the triple-braided, three-mouthed snake in the hippodrome and not have thought of worldly temptation. If they were in the hippodrome during races, of course, it may already have been too late.

Christian Serpent-tramplers and Dragon-slayers

The serpentine tempter of Genesis 3 returned as Satan, the adversary, the deceiver, to be vanquished by Christ at Revelation 12:9: "And the great dragon was cast out, the ancient serpent, called the Devil and Satan, which deceives the whole world." There are two quite distinct retellings of the familiar combat narrative, of victory and defeat, where Christ confronted his serpentine adversary,

---

[65] *VNS*: πρὸς πέταυρον ᾅδου; *NMS*: εἰς ᾅδου πέταυρον. This phrase is used upon her third approach in the *VNS*, and her first in the *NMS*.

Satan. In one version, Christ gained the ultimate victory by knowingly granting an ephemeral win to His adversary, allowing Satan through Judas to betray Him. This version culminates in the Crucifixion.[66] In the second version, the battle was truly combat between hero and dragon, as revealed to John of Patmos and written down in his book of Revelation that entered the canon of Christian scripture definitively only in the reign of Constantine. Revelation now featured as the culmination of the Bibles that Constantine commissioned Eusebios to produce for fifty new churches in and near Constantinople.[67] Evidently, this was Constantine's preferred Christ. John's apocalypse translates the combat myth from a cosmogonic struggle for the creation of order from chaos to an apocalyptic ending of earthly order corrupted by the beast, who held sway over sea and earth. First, the heroic Archangel,

> Michael and his angels fought against the dragon, and the dragon and his angels fought back. But he was not strong enough, and they lost their place in heaven. The great dragon was hurled down, that ancient serpent called the devil, or Satan, who leads the whole world astray. He was hurled to the earth, and his angels with him.

Later, Christ returned in majesty seated on a white horse, "just in judgement and just in war," a sword projecting from his mouth to smite the nations. "For he it is who shall rule them with an iron rod and tread the winepress of the wrath and retribution of God." He is identified by the inscription on his robes as "King of kings and Lord of lords."

This was Christ as cosmic conqueror, trampling the beasts in Psalm 90 (91): 13—"You shall tread upon the lion and adder: The young lion and the serpent you shall trample under foot"—and remembered at Luke 10:19—"Behold I give unto you the power to tread on serpents and scorpions and the power to overcome all the power of the enemy, nothing will harm you."[68] A rare late antique image of this militant Christ has been preserved in a sixth-century mosaic at Ravenna's Archbishop's Chapel, which clearly emulates earlier imperial and numismatic art (fig. 6.13). Christ is dressed as a general, and a cross is slung over his shoulder as an emperor might be shown with a spear or, occasionally, a trophy (*tropaeum*). His tunic billows out like a commander's cape (*paludamentum*) fixed at one shoulder with an imperial brooch (*fibula*). Under His right foot is a cowed, crouching lion, and under His left a rather modest snake. Christ holds open a book at a verse from John 14:6: *Ego sum via veritas et vita*, "I am the path, the truth, and the life, [nobody comes to the Father but

---

[66] See below, chapter seven, for "The Brazen Serpent and the Crucifixion."

[67] Dungan 2007: 118–23.

[68] Tishpak is said (Lewis 1996: 33, n. 41) to trample on two serpents. See also Wiggermann 1989. Similarly, Marduk is described as "the one who wields the mace and tramples on the serpent/dragon." See Lewis 1996: 37.

FIGURE 6.13 Christ militant, preserved in a sixth-century mosaic at Ravenna's Archbishop's Chapel. Photo: DAI Rome (58.599).

through me]." This is a gloss on the psalm, a *balbale* to the protection offered only by the Almighty.

The scene is rare but not unique in Ravenna; a late-fifth-century stucco relief in the Orthodox Baptistery of Neon again depicts a Christ militant trampling the serpent and lion, their positions reversed (fig. 6.14). Paulinus of Nola had shortly before that identified Christ in Psalm 90 (91) as a protector against sin and false belief.[69] This militant Christ did not appeal to later Byzantine artists, but struck a chord at Charlemagne's court in Aachen, where from 800 it was painted into several books, including the Stuttgart and Utrecht Psalters, and carved into at least three ivory book covers.[70] The Douce Ivory, produced perhaps for Charles himself, places the Old Testament motif centrally, surrounded by New Testament scenes of Christ's life.[71]

Rather less dramatic than many accounts of serpent-slaying, St. Paul was able to shake into a fire the Maltese viper that bit his hand. When he did not

---

[69] Kessler 2006: 145–6.
[70] Kessler 2006; Kessler 2008:109.
[71] Oxford, Bodleian MS Douce 176, upper cover. See Brown 2006: 3089, no. 73.

FIGURE 6.14 A late-fifth-century stucco relief in the Orthodox Baptistery of Neon depicts a Christ militant trampling the serpent and lion. Photo: Mariëtte Verhoeven, with permission.

fall down dead, the Maltese considered him a god (Acts 28:3–6). Tertullian recommended serpent-trampling to early Christian martyrs: "The prison, indeed, is the devil's house as well, wherein he keeps his family. But you have come within its walls for the very purpose of trampling the wicked one under foot in his chosen abode."[72] One early martyr, St. Perpetua, dreamt of just this action before her death: "At the foot of the ladder lay a dragon ... Using it as my first step, I trod on his head and went up." That Perpetua was a woman is significant, since it was the temptation of Eve, by the serpent, which had established eternal enmity between mankind and the serpent, according to Genesis 3:15, "I will put enmity between you and the woman, and between your seed and her seed; he shall bruise your head, and you shall bruise his heel."

The struggle of a holy person against the adversary, the *diabolos*, Satan, frequently involves combat with a serpent or dragon, both literally and figuratively. The corpus of hagiography that collates the spiritual combat waged by each holy man or women to achieve sanctity provides abundant allusions to serpent-trampling and dragon-slaying. Even when one restricts this to eastern

---

[72] Tertullian, *Ad martyras*, 1:18.

Christian texts written in Greek, and to tales that will have been known in Constantinople, the number of tales is large.[73] Sozomenos, who wrote his fifth-century ecclesiastical history in Constantinople, recorded the tales of St. Arsakios, who through the power of his prayer induced a dragon to smash its own head on the ground until it died, and of St. Donatus of Evorea, who slew a dragon with the sign of the cross and a gob of his own spittle, which ancient lore held to have a similar effect on serpents as did their venom on humans. Once dead, Donatus' dragon "did not appear in size inferior to the noted serpents of India."[74]

In the seventh-century *Life of St. George of Amastris* (BHG 668), the devil is blamed for casting the blessed child George into a fire, burning his hands and feet before he was able to take up arms against the adversary.

> Even though the serpent knew that his own head would be trampled on, he plotted against the boy's feet. And even though he knew his deeds would be destroyed, he mutilated the boy's hands in the fire ... Perhaps he permitted the soldier to be struck so that in the moment of battle he might take his place in line more courageously, and so that incited by the scars of the enemy's plot he might contend against him more vigorously and direct all his wrath against the snake alone.[75]

Demons, including the Devil himself, took the form of serpents more frequently than other noxious and pestering creatures, and the snake was considered the most dangerous of all creatures. St. Thomas Dephourkinos, a tenth-century saint whose potted life (BHG 2458) is preserved in the *Synaxarion of Constantinople*, fought the devil when he took the form of mosquitoes, flies, wasps, and, ultimately, snakes.[76]

An evocative description of a dragon is offered in the *Acts of St. Marina* (BHG 1165), the earliest extant version of which dates from the late ninth century.[77] Marina has been thrown in jail for refusing to abjure Christ, and she passes her time in prayer. An earthquake strikes once she has finished her prayer, and from a crack in the corner emerges, quite suddenly,

> a great and frightful dragon (*drakon*) with a many-hued hide. His comb and beard were just like gold, his teeth flashed, and his eyes were the same as a pearl. Fiery flame and much smoke billowed from his nostrils, and his tongue was like blood. Serpents were coiling around his neck, and the arches of his eyes

---

[73] A search of the *Dumbarton Oaks Hagiography Database* using the term "serpent" gives some indication of the ubiquity of the motif.

[74] Sozomenos 4.16; 7.26. On Donatus' serpent-slaying saliva, see now Ogden 2013: 395–6, 406.

[75] *Vita Georgii*, 7; trans. Bachrach et al. 2001

[76] *Synax CP*: 293–8

[77] White 2008: 157–8, follows Boulhol in dating the original tale to the seventh century. However, the motif of the dragon emerging from Hades commends a date in the later ninth century at the earliest for the Greek text that is preserved in Paris gr. 1470.

were like silver. It was in the middle of the cell wailing and hissing. Running, it circled Marina with a naked blade, and its hissing made a terrible stink in the cell. The holy virgin was very scared, and her limbs went limp while her vision failed. Through fear she stopped praying. At her own request, the Lord acted and showed her the enemy and antagonist of all men. Falling to her knees, she began again to pray and said: "Invisible God, by whose countenance the sea and the abyss were quenched, you set the frontiers to Hades, you loosed the chains of the earth so that it does not shake. You humbled the power of the dragon who hates good. You bound Hades and freed those trapped within. Now look upon me and protect me, and do not acquiesce to let me be harmed by an evil demon."[78]

As Marina's prayer hung in the air, the dragon advanced, offering further opportunity for description. "Its head hung down to the ground and its legs were on the earth, running from its throat formed from serpents, and its mouth was wide open." St. Marina was swallowed by the dragon, but on the way down she made the sign of the cross, which pierced its belly. The ruptured dragon fell in half, dead, and she emerged, both as a living symbol of her own redemption and, like Jonah, as a metaphor for Christian resurrection.[79] It is striking that the description of the dragon appears to share so much with the Serpent Column, with its neck formed from writhing serpents and legs emerging from these. The bronze serpents' eyes were once set with stones, and perhaps still resembled pearls and silver. Each serpent head had a beard, sharp teeth, and a tongue darting from a gaping mouth. The dragon is later named by a demon who visits Marina: he was Rufus, also the name of a dragon controlled by a powerful demon, Beelzebub, in a far earlier text, the *Testament of Solomon*.[80]

Marina was armed with the power of the cross, which becomes a central motif in middle Byzantine tales of serpent combat. In the tenth-century *Life of St. Andrew the Fool*, serpentine demons are defeated with the sign of the cross.[81] For example, a demon who has taken the form of an old woman accuses Andrew of robbing and beating her. Andrew throws some mud at her, and "at the same time he breathed on her 'crosswise' (σταυροειδῶς), and at once she lost her human appearance and became a huge serpent." In a dream, before he becomes a fool for Christ, Andrew wrestles a demon in the hippodrome at Constantinople, therefore in the vicinity of the Serpent Column, throwing him to the floor with a "crosswise" move (σταυροειδῶς).[82] This would appear to be a wrestling throw, perhaps a "body-slam," the type of athletic display one might expect to see in the arena. As his reward, a man in white whom Andrew does

---

[78] *Acta Sanctae Marinae*, ed. Usener 1886: 25–6.
[79] White 2008.
[80] See earlier in this chapter.
[81] Rydén, *Life of Andrew*, II, 64–5.
[82] Rydén, *Life of Andrew*, II, 16–17, 306, n. 14.

not recognize as Christ presents him with "precious wreaths," the reward for victory in an athletic contest, but here of greater significance, because Andrew has become an athlete of Christ. A page of a Princeton manuscript, which we have explored above, and which depicts a twisting, two-headed dragon at the base of a heavenly ladder, also contains a cross on steps, placed beneath the last line of text, and surrounded by a poem and two monostichs which praise the cross as a weapon against demons (fig. 5.7, above). [83] The dragon is the entrance to Hades, whence it had emerged into Marina's prison cell following an earthquake.

The slaying of serpents from horseback by a holy rider emerged as early as the seventh century, although named warrior saints appear only centuries later. If it is genuine, a unique clay icon from Vinica that depicts and names St. Theodore is among the earliest known depictions of a named saint, and it is noteworthy that his name is recorded in Latin (fig. 6.15).[84] However, Theodore is not slaying a serpent, as is generally believed, but instead appears to be holding a *draco* standard. Henry Maguire has traced the shift from anonymous holy riders involved in household magic to the named military saints of middle and late Byzantium, and has associated the addition of inscriptions with the closer regulation of holy images, their use and nature after iconoclasm, which required the naming of all such riders.[85] The iconography of the holy rider itself was borrowed into the magical, nonmilitary household context from military iconography of an earlier era. Riders spearing serpents and boars are widely represented on Roman and earlier stelae commemorating soldiers. A votive carving from Krupac, Serbia, depicts Apollo and Asklepios as Thracian riders, offering their open hands to the serpent entwined around the tree beside an altar.[86] A votive stela of the Dioskouroi as Thracian riders, now in the Louvre, shows the twins mounted on either side of a tree of life in which one sees a serpent. They are striking at a boar with their spears.[87]

Paintings in Cappadocian rock churches, many only recently discovered and not yet fully published, show spiritual warriors and military saints confronting serpents with one, two, or three heads.[88] At the church known as Mavrucan 3, at Göreme in Cappadocia, a wall painting generally dated to the tenth century

---

[83] Garrett MS 16, fol. 194r. See Ševčenko 2009: 50, and fig. 8, noting that in the same hand, one finds marginal poems addressing demons on folios 87r., 93v., and 125r. See also Kotzabassi and Ševčenko 2010: 113, 123.

[84] Balabanov and Krstevski 1991.

[85] See above, chapter five, and Maguire 1996: 120–7. See also Maguire, Maguire, and Flowers 1989: 25–8.

[86] Dimitrova 2002: 218.

[87] Thierry 1972: 259.

[88] Catherine Jolivet-Lévy has drawn attention in several recent papers to similar images of polycephalous snakes in Cappadocia. There are also carved reliefs from Caucasian Georgia, for example a tenth-century carved relief at Martvili which depicts two mounted warrior saints attacking a bicephalous dragon. See Pancaroğlu 2004: 154.

180 { The Serpent Column

FIGURE 6.15 Clay icon of St. Theodore, discovered at Vinica, possibly sixth-seventh century. Photo: author.

portrays two holy riders and two serpents entwined around a tree.[89] The fresco is strikingly similar to the far earlier votive stela of the Dioskouroi, except that now the riders are striking at the snakes. In N. Thierry's drawing, at least, it is clear that there are two snakes with separate heads. This is not always the case in several wall paintings of the tenth and eleventh centuries in Cappadocia that illustrate entwined or polycephalous serpents.[90] In the so-called Church of the Rock 5, also at Göreme, which dates from the first part or middle of the eleventh century, we see two riders, identified as the saints George and Theodore, the former on a white horse and the latter on a brown, attacking a coiled serpent with two heads. In a somewhat later image, dating to the second half of the eleventh century, the same theme is addressed slightly differently. A wall painting in a nearby church, known as Yusuf Koç Kilisesi at Maçan-Göreme, shows George and Theodore once again, now with George on the

---

[89] Thierry 1972, who dates the fresco to as early as the seventh century. However, this seems unlikely, as it would be three hundred years earlier than any other church fresco in the region. See also Pancaroğlu 2004: 163, n. 19.

[90] Jolivet-Levy 2007: 83–4, fig. 12; Jolivet-Levy 2008.

FIGURE 6.16 Saints George and Theodore killing a polycephalous (three-headed?) serpent at Yusuf Koç church, Göreme, Cappadocia. Photo: Robert Ousterhout, with permission.

FIGURE 6.17 St. George slays a polycephalous (three-headed?) serpent at Kirkdamaltı church, Ihlara, Cappadocia, thirteenth century. Photo: Robert Ousterhout, with permission.

brown horse and Theodore on the white. Both hold spears aloft in their right hands, which are penetrating two serpents coiled together with three heads (according to Thierry, although it is extremely hard to see) (fig. 6.16).[91] Saints George and Theodore are depicted once again killing a two-headed serpent at Yılanlı Kilise (Church of the Serpent), at Ihlara, Cappadocia, which has also been dated to the second half of the eleventh century. The inscription above the serpent suggests the equation of Christ's victory over death on the cross with the defeat of evil in the form of the serpent, echoing Carolingian developments.[92] In a damaged fresco at nearby Kirkdamaltı (Kirk Damalı), a later church (thirteenth century), St. George alone on a white horse slays a beast with three heads, two of which are clearly visible at each end of its serpentine body (fig. 6.17).

---

[91] Walter 2003: 100–1, offers the clarification employed here: "In a private letter Madame Thierry modified slightly her published description. Although this is difficult to discern on the photograph there are, in fact, *two* dragons coiled together in a central knot, from which emerge *three* heads [Walter's italics]."

[92] Thierry 1963: 91; Pancaroğlu 2004: 155.

7 }

Talisman

The Copper Horse – Apotropaic Animals – Twisted and Brazen
Apotropaia – *The Brazen Serpent and the Crucifixion – Holy Powers and Health*

According to an early Ottoman report by Kemal Pashazade,

> [Constantine son of Helena] caused to be made that bronze statue in the hippodrome, which is the representation of three serpents twined together, and by making and designing that talisman he stopped up the source of the mischief of snakes whose poison is fatal to life. The narrator says: Before this talisman—which is a rarity of the age, designed on a wondrous plan—was made, it was impossible to walk in those regions for poisonous snakes. This strange fact too is reported: They say that when the bodies of those snakes, of which the jaw of one has now fallen off, were complete, no snakes were to be seen in the city.[1]

Kemal Pashazade's report, written before 1512, is the earliest to record that the lower jaw of one serpent on the Serpent Column had fallen off.[2] Later legends attributed this to a show of strength by Mehmed the Conqueror, who upon capturing the city of Constantinople in 1453 rode through to the hippodrome and threw his battle mace at the Serpent Column. This tale is reported and illustrated in a miniature contained in the *Hünername* ("Book of Skills"), two large illuminated volumes begun under Süleyman I and completed in ca. 1584 and ca. 1588. The text relates that when Mehmed attacked the column, the patriarch hurried from nearby Hagia Sophia to tell him that if he damaged the column the city would be infested with snakes; and indeed, following the removal of a jaw, there was a plague of snails.[3] A miniature (*Hünername,* fol.

---

[1] Ménage 1964: 170–1, provides a transcription of the Ottoman and the English translation reproduced here. See also Mansel 1970: 202; Dell'Acqua 2013: 332–8.

[2] Ménage 1964: 170–1; Mansel 1970: 202.

[3] Mansel 1970: 200 offers a transcription of the Ottoman text with commentary and a reproduction of the miniature (fig. 13). A larger reproduction with outdated commentary can be seen at Casson et al. 1929: 2–3, fig. 2.

FIGURE 7.1 *Hünername*, Topkapı Palace Museum Library H.1523, fol. 162v., Mehmed II throws his mace at the Serpent Column in the At meydanı. Topkapı Palace Museum Library. Photo: Robert Dankoff, with permission.

162b) shows the sultan's mace, thrown high in the air, striking the lower jaw of a left-facing serpent (fig. 7.1). The sultan, white-turbaned and riding a white horse, has twenty-one companions, eleven mounted and ten standing, all wearing turbans or military caps or helmets. Standing below and to the right of the Serpent Column is Patriarch Gennadios, shown with a long white beard and a black monastic cowl pulled over his head.

The Serpent Column was reported to be a powerful talisman against serpents and related pests by earlier visitors to Constantinople. Of the four Russian travelers who described the Serpent Column between ca. 1390 and ca. 1430, three recorded that "serpent venom is enclosed in the column."[4] This is also reported in 1403–6, by the Spanish ambassador Clavijo. The venom in the column was believed both to protect the city against infestation by snakes and to ensure that those bitten by snakes—by some accounts, only those bitten within the

---

[4] Majeska 1984: 92–3 (Ignatius of Smolensk, who visited Constantinople in 1389), 144–5 (Anonymous, ca. 1390–1400), 164–5 (Alexander the Clerk, visited ca. 1394–5), 184–5 (Zosima, visited in 1420 and 1421), 250–1.

confines of the city—would be cured by touching the column.⁵ This was also noted by Giovan-Maria Angiolello, a resident of Constantinople between 1474 and 1481, who wrote that Mehmed II, his master, preserved and repaired the column "because it was said that the thing had been made to chase all the snakes out of the city of Constantinople, for there had formerly been a time when it was uninhabitable by reason of the great number of snakes that were there. At present, however, there are no snakes at all except for those brought in by the occasional snake-charmer."⁶

It is as an *apotropaion*, or talisman against snakes and snakebites, therefore, that the Serpent Column drew the attention of the greatest number of travelers to Constantinople, and it is as a talisman that it has attracted the greatest number of scholars who have written about it.⁷ In this chapter, rather than reproduce a good amount of material that has been discussed elsewhere, I shall place the talisman in a richer context, sketching the apotropaic environment in which it was situated, both within and beyond Constantinople, before addressing the Serpent Column's qualities that were held to be especially apotropaic—principally its serpentine form, but also the fact that it was both twisted and brazen.

The Copper Horse

Some decades after Pashazade wrote, Pierre Gilles, who was resident in Constantinople from 1544 until 1548, identified a colossal bronze statue in pieces, recently removed from the sultan's palace, "where it had been preserved a long time," and which was now being melted down for ordnance. He saw a leg and a nine-inch nose, and the legs and hooves, also nine inches long, of his horse.⁸ That Mehmed II had been responsible for the statue's removal, but not its destruction, is clear from Gilles' account, although other sources appear to contradict it. According to Johannes Schiltberger, the statue still stood in front of the palace high on its column in 1427. "At one time the statue had a golden apple in the hand, and that meant that he had been a mighty emperor over Christians and Infidels; but now he has no longer that power, so the apple

---

⁵ See Dawkins 1924, Mango 1963, and most other commentators on the Serpent Column.

⁶ Pierre MacKay supplied me with his transcription and translation of this portion of Angiolello's memoir, Vicenza 413, Biblioteca Civica Bertoliana, fol. 14v.: "perche non fosse cagione di guastar il detto ediffitio per li quale si dice che fusse fatto per discasar le bisse della Citta di Costantinopoli, che gia tempo fu che la detta Citta non si poteva habitare per la gran moltitudine che vi ne era, et in questi giorni pressenti non si ne trova niuna se non fosero portato per qualch' Orbolato." We shall return to Angiolello in the following chapter.

⁷ Most recently, Dell'Acqua 2013 and Strootman 2014. I have also been fortunate to read a very good paper in draft form by Andrew Griebeler.

⁸ Gilles, II. 17; trans. Ball 1729: 129–30; cited by Mango 1959: 353; Johann Schiltberger, trans. Telfer 1879: 230, n. 5A.

has disappeared."⁹ Schiltberger's interpretation relates to the significance of the apple for the Turks: *kızıl elma*, the red apple, or golden apple, symbolized any city to be captured, and ultimately Constantinople.¹⁰ Pero Tafur clarifies that the golden orb Justinian held had fallen and was replaced, while the horse was chained down to prevent it too falling at a cost of 8,000 ducats.¹¹ The column and statue are described by the same Russian travelers as evinced a fascination with the Serpent Column, and it was sketched by Theophanes "the Greek," an artist working in Moscow at the beginning of the fifteenth century.¹² According to Angiolello, Mehmed II removed the statue because it was considered a symbol of Greek power and a talisman against the Turks. This was on the advice of astrologers. Angiolello called the statue "Santo Agostino," using a name given to the monument because it stood in the Augusteion.¹³ No western source, however, confirms that the statue was destroyed. That information is provided only in Ottoman sources, which consider the destruction an element in the purging of Christian symbols. According to Şemeddin, whose late-fifteenth-century work is one of various legendary tales of the construction of Hagia Sophia, "The copper horse (*bakır at*) [survived in its original form] until the present day. Story-mongers gossiped about it and on their words Sultan Mehmed Han Gazi . . . had it pulled down; and from the copper of those statues he had splendid canons made, but the column is still standing, as it had been opposite Ayasofya."¹⁴ The column was indeed left standing, until it fell, according to Gilles, thirty years before his visit, so in around 1515–20.¹⁵

If Islam could not easily tolerate anthropomorphic statuary, and many Turks might be offended by its public display, still the Copper Horse with its imperious rider was regarded with especial suspicion as a talisman of the Christians. Therefore, it is no surprise that Mehmed wished it to be known that he had dismembered and melted it down, along with Christian bells and crosses, to forge cannons, which would be directed against Christians during the siege of Belgrade in 1456.¹⁶ On the other hand, Hartmann Schedel, in his *Liber*

---

⁹ Johann Schiltberger, trans. Telfer 1879: 80. In 1432, Bertrand de la Brocquière mistook the statue for Constantine. See Wright 1848: 339.

¹⁰ See Tolan, Laurens, and Veinstein 2012: 181–4, citing research by S. Yerasimos.

¹¹ Pero Tafur, trans. Letts 1926: 140–1; Mango 1959: 353.

¹² Pyatnitsky 2011: 322 and fig. 1. Majeska 1984: 29, 35, 135–7, 185, 237–40.

¹³ Raby 1987: 308 provides a full quotation from the Caparrozzo edition of Angiolello. See also Mango 1959: 354, although Mango was unable to consult an edition of Angiolello directly.

¹⁴ Quoted in translation by Raby 1987: 309. Raby (311, n. 17) notes that the author writes of statues, plural, and this corresponds to a later account by Sadeddin, although there is no indication of what other statues Mehmed may have melted down.

¹⁵ Gilles, trans. Ball 129: According to Doukas, ed. Bonn, 300, during the capture of the city a head was pinned to the tall column on which the statue stood, and reports were spread that it belonged to Constantine XI. See Mango 1959: 354; Raby 1987: 306, n. 1, and 310 for Ottoman sources for the column's collapse.

¹⁶ This second piece of information is provided by Aşıkpaşazade, cited by Raby 1987: 309.

FIGURE 7.2 Hartmann Schedel, *Liber Chronicarum* (1493), woodcut showing the column and equestrian statue of Justinian. Photo: author.

Chronicarum of 1493, reports that the statue was still standing on its column when on 12 July 1490 it was struck by lightning but refused to fall, providing a woodcut of the incident by way of confirmation (fig. 7.2).[17] These contradictory accounts would both appear to be pious fictions, seeking to harness the symbolic horse-power of the *bakır at*. Therefore, a middle path suggests itself, that Mehmed wished it believed that he had destroyed the Copper Horse, but in fact took the statue's parts into his New Palace, whence they were removed only a century later, when Gilles saw them. This interpretation receives support from a late source, Patriarch Jeremias (d. 1595), who claims that Mehmed sought to have the statue reassembled, giving as his reason the belief that the Copper Horse was a talisman against the plague. This talismanic function is also reported in the Ottoman *Anonymous Chronicles* tradition.[18] By the middle of the seventeenth century, Evliya Çelebi would apportion a talismanic function to each of the hippodrome's standing objects, and to many others besides.[19]

Çelebi, an Ottoman traveler and native of Constantinople, listed the talismans held to protect his city, which he called Islambol ("full of Islam"), in the seventeenth century. Most of these *apotropaia* were columns, or forged from bronze, or both in the case of the Serpent Column, the seventeenth talisman.

> A sage named Surendeh, who flourished in the days of error under King Puzentin, set up a brazen image of a triple-headed dragon in the At meydanı

---

[17] Raby 1987: 308, fig. 2; Berger and Bardill 1998: 4, 15–24. The statue was also represented in a Buondelmonti map of ca. 1481: Kafescioğlu 2009: 152; Necipoğlu 2010: 267, fig. 6.

[18] Raby 1987: 312, with full references.

[19] See now Strootman 2011: 190.

[the hippodrome]. This was to destroy all serpents, lizards, scorpions and other similar poisonous reptiles. And there was not a poisonous beast in the whole of "Makedoniyyah." It has now the form of a twisted serpent, measuring ten cubits above and as many below the ground. It remained thus buried in mud and earth from the building of Sultan Ahmed's Mosque, but uninjured till Selim II, surnamed "the Sot," passing by on horseback, knocked off with a mace the lower jaw of that head of the dragon which looks to the west. Serpents then made their appearance on the western side of the city, and since that time have become common in every part of it. If, moreover, the remaining heads should be destroyed, Islambol will be completely eaten up with vermin. In short, there were 366 talismans like those [17] we have described, which are all that remain.[20]

Çelebi proceeded to describe a second "triple-headed bronze dragon, spitting fire, and burning all the enemies' ships," which sat at the Seraglio point facing out to sea. This was one of six talismans against attacks from the sea that were all cast down in a great earthquake on the night of the Prophet's birth.[21]

Apotropaic Animals

It was believed across the medieval Mediterranean world that the material traces of the past were invested with special powers. For example, in both Damascus and Aleppo columns bearing spheres were believed to make donkeys urinate. Columns and stones bearing inscriptions in non-Arabic scripts were considered especially powerful, and were often removed to gates or city walls, to defend against threats.[22] Representations of the creatures whose threats were to be deflected were commonly hung near gateways, notably lions, scorpions, and serpents. San'a in Yemen was reported in the tenth century to be "surrounded by talismans against vipers and snakes, so that vipers and snakes can barely harm anyone, and a person stung who has died from that has never been heard of ... One of these talismans is of iron and the other of brass."[23] From the Crusader period, serpentine columns were reported to have been used for an apotropaic purpose at the Holy Sepulcher complex in Jerusalem. According to al-'Ulaymī, an Arabic writer of the fifteenth century, the entrance to the Mosque of Umar had for centuries been guarded by two stone columns with capitals carved with the image (*sūra*) of serpents, a talisman (*tilsam*).[24]

---

[20] Çelebi, trans. Hammer 1834: 19. See also Dell'Acqua 2013: 337–8, who in a personal note reminded me that the word here used for dragon is *azhderha*, derived from *aždahā*, on which see *EI*, s.v. Aždahā.
[21] Çelebi, trans. Hammer 1834: 20.
[22] Flood 2006: 148.
[23] The historian al-Rāzī, cited by Flood 2006: 149.
[24] Flood 2006: 145.

Animal statues appeared to the citizens of Constantinople to possess magical powers related to the creatures they represented, including those depicting serpents.[25] The principle was simple and is still familiar from modern homeopathy: *similia similibus curantur*, "like is cured by like."[26] We have earlier noted that Harun ibn Yahya, an Arab hostage in Constantinople between 911 and 913, referred to a statue near "the imperial gate" that comprised "four snakes made of brass whose tails are in their mouths," and which was considered a talisman against snakebites.[27] Niketas Choniates reported the fanciful tale of the first-century wonder-worker Apollonius of Tyana, who "once, while visiting the citizens of Byzantion, was entreated to bring them relief from the snakebites that plagued them . . . set up on a column an eagle [with] . . . a coiled snake clutched in its claws . . . It was said that the very sight of this snake uncoiled and incapable of delivering a deadly bite frightened away by its example the remaining serpents in Byzantion."[28] This description can be compared to an element in the surviving sixth-century peristyle mosaic floor of Constantinople's Great Palace, where a snake is entwined around both the body and talons of an eagle (fig. 7.3),[29] and to a fountain placed by Constantine VII in the porphyry guardhouse before his chamber,

> wherein he contrived a receptacle of water surrounded by marble columns shining smooth. And what else did his noble mind [invent]? He set upon the water pipe a silver eagle, looking not ahead but sideways, his neck high and proud as if he had caught a prey, while stifling a serpent that was coiled round his feet.[30]

In his description of the eagle and serpent sculpture and its meanings, Choniates contributes to a tradition that dates back at least to the early sixth century, when Hesychios of Miletos recorded the important role that serpents and snakebites had played in the foundation of Constantinople. Hesychios deserves to be quoted at length in Anthony Kaldellis' recent translation.[31]

> After this victory, Byzas was driving his enemies into Thrake when Odryses, the king of the Skythians, crossed the Istros river and came up to the very walls of the city, laying siege to those inside. Against him was ranged the wife of Byzas, the amazing Phidaleia, who was not in the least terrified by the multitude of the enemy host but rather brought a feminine touch to the contest, outwitting

---

[25] See here Maguire 1987: 368–72 on Adam and the animals, including serpents, which in his former state of grace could not harm Adam, and which are neutralized again through Christ.
[26] Flood 2006: 154; Kessler 2009: 129; Kuehn 2011: 23, 39, 170, 174, 206.
[27] See Madden 1992: 113; Bassett 2004: 227.
[28] Niketas Choniates, ed. van Dieten 1975: 651; ed. Morisani, Gagliuolo, and de Franciscis 1960: 24–6; trans. Magoulias 1984: 359–60. See also Bassett 2004: 216; Flood 2006: 154.
[29] Nicely illustrated in Grabar 1967: fig. 106. See also Jobst, Erdal, and Gurtner 1997: 42–3.
[30] Theophanes Continuatus, ed. Bonn, 451; trans. Mango 1972, 208.
[31] Hesychios, trans. Kaldellis, Brill's New Jacoby, available at http://brill.nl/bnjo; Kaldellis 2005, suggests that Hesychios' *Patria* is excerpted from his *Roman and General History*, written in the early sixth century.

FIGURE 7.3 Eagle and snake motif, mosaic floor of the Great Palace of Constantinople, Byzantine, sixth century. Photo: author.

> the barbarian by making an alliance with serpents. She gathered together the snakes of the city in one spot and guarded them there; then, appearing suddenly before the enemy, she would hurl the beasts at them in the manner of arrows or spears. By harming a good many in this way she saved the city. This, then, was the origin of the ancient commandment that it is necessary not to kill snakes that are captured in the city, given that they were its benefactors.

Snakes were integrated into the mythical foundation of the city of Byzantion, later Constantinople, serving to protect the city against invaders. When Byzas died, Hesychios continues, snakes became a danger rather than an asset. A certain Dineos came to the city's rescue not with a magical remedy but with storks, which can still be seen nesting in Istanbul.

> A short while afterwards, he [Dineos] crossed over to the city and repelled the barbarians, becoming *strategos* over the people of Byzantion. It was in those days that a multitude of serpent species came to dwell in the city to the point where its inhabitants were being injured. In response, and with the assistance (as they say) of Poseidon, they took advantage of the species of bird called storks, which have a tendency to attack snakes. But not long afterwards the birds too adopted a hostile attitude and became the cause of death among them, both by hurling the snakes that they captured into the water-cisterns and by dropping them, from unseen heights, onto citizens in the streets. They were at a complete loss.

An image that is both consonant and contemporary with Hesychios' story has survived as a sixth-century carving, an apotropaic device on the Kurşunlugerme aqueduct, which brought water from Thrace to Constantinople. An eagle, rather than a stork, is shown clutching a writhing serpent, protecting the water supply, essential to the health of all who lived in the city.[32]

Twisted and Brazen Apotropaia

The Serpent Column was believed to be a talisman against snakes and snakebites, therefore, because it was serpentine. However, it was distinct from many other such talismans in that it was also twisted and brazen, both qualities that offered additional protection. Columns have been accorded an apotropaic function in Judeo-Christian tradition since the establishment of the first temple.[33] Two hollow bronze columns named Jachin and Boaz protected the entrance to the Temple of Solomon. The fullest description, at 3 Kings 7: 15–22 in the Septuagint, recounts elaborate ornamentation that is rather obscure, but included rows of chains and pomegranates (ῥοῶν), which might mean knots resembling pomegranates. Additionally, there was fashioned a bronze basin ("the sea") standing on a dozen bronze oxen, and ten bronze stands.[34] Knotted columns were carved in marble to be placed in some churches on the iconostasis and flanking windows in apses, thus guarding against intrusion into the sanctuary. Representations of knotted columns can be seen in a number of middle Byzantine manuscripts, frequently flanking canon tables, for example, in the Vani Gospels. Even if they were relatively common, only a few knotted columns have survived.[35] However, one can see the apotropaic knot, formed from entwined acanthus leaves, repeated along the marble band that forms part of the entablature in the gallery at Hagia Sophia (fig. 7.4).

In a condensation of the description of Jachin and Boaz at 2 Chronicles 3:16, the *rhoai* of 3 Kings have become ῥοΐσκοι, which the Byzantine dictionary, the *Souda*, defined as "gold-woven embellishments, like pomegranates,

---

[32] Crow, Bardill, and Bayliss 2008: 159–60, 167, 175–6 offer illustrations and commentary, but misidentify the serpent as a victor's wreath with ribbons, despite following suggestions at Maguire 1991–2. This leads to the suggestions that the eagle represents the emperor's victory over his enemies, and also "evokes the struggle with evil and ultimately the triumph of Christ." Maguire 2012: 6 notes a wader holding a snake in its bill in the mosaics of the sanctuary vault at San Vitale, Ravenna; 32, 34 alludes to an earlier discussion (Maguire 1991–2) of an eagle clutching a serpent in an early Christian marble relief at Kavalla, with the observation that "Early Church writers linked the image of the eagle and its prey both with the eucharist and with baptism."

[33] The inverse was also true, and columns could not protect temples to false gods, as Samson demonstrated when he pressed his hands against the two central columns of the temple of the Philistines: Judges 16: 29.

[34] In the KJV, this is 1 Kings 7:15–22, 41–2. The king stands by the columns, according to custom, when renewing the covenant (2 Kings 11:14; 23:3).

[35] Kalavrezou 1985, for commentary and a list of examples, although omitting the Vani Gospels.

FIGURE 7.4 An apotropaic knot, formed from entwined acanthus leaves, repeated along the marble band which forms part of the entablature in the gallery at Hagia Sophia, Istanbul. Photo: author.

intended to decorate the robe of the priest."[36] The Byzantines understood this ornament to be the Herculean knot, used by Herakles to tie the lion pelt around his shoulders, and so by others to fasten their capes to ward off danger, and also to tie bandages for its perceived healing powers. We know it as the reef knot. Roman travelers, notably merchants, might pray to Mercury to ensure successful commerce and for his protection. Mercury's caduceus was made from a wand and two serpents forming a figure eight, their heads confronted and their tails entwined. A remarkable second-century silver statue discovered at Berthouville shows the serpents attached to Mercury's staff by a short spiral of curling tails and, at the middle, by a Herculean, or reef, knot (fig. 7.5).[37]

The form of the knotted column could not be mistaken for twisted serpents. However, an early Christian interpretation of Solomonic columns more closely resembles the form of the Serpent Column. According to the *Liber Pontificalis*, Constantine sent six "viney columns from Greece [*columnae vitineae de grecias*],"

---

[36] Suidas, ed. Adler 1928–38: IV, 214, 298 = rho, 191, rho 214; cited by Kalavrezou 1985: 99, 102, n. 25. See now Souda Online, s.v. Rhoas, Rhoïskoi.

[37] Frothingham 1916 demonstrated that the caduceus was found as early as the fourth millennium B.C. on Babylonian cylinder seals, but took its form as an emblem of Hermes, later Mercury, rather late in his development.

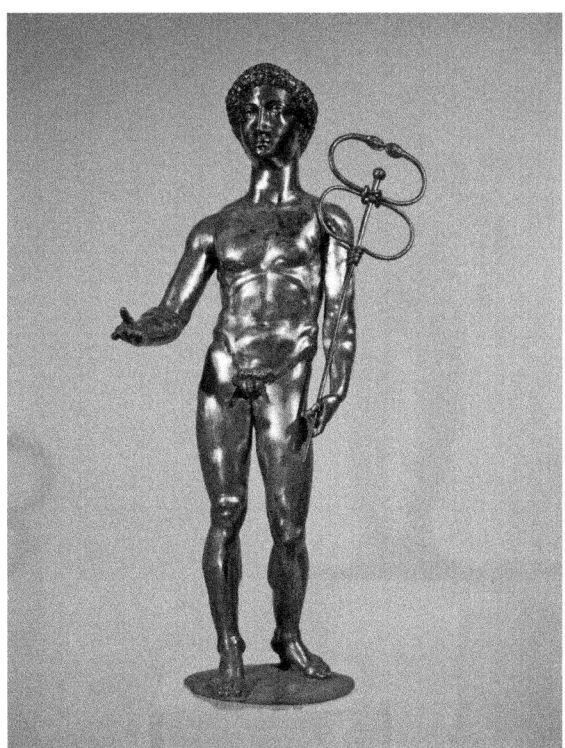

FIGURE 7.5 Silver statue of Mercury holding a serpentine caduceus, where the snakes are attached to the staff by forming a reef knot, A.D. 175–225. Discovered in 1830 at Berthouville, France. Cabinet des Médailles, Bibliothèque nationale de France

which were placed around the tomb of St. Peter.[38] The disposition of these spiral columns, decorated with scenes of vintaging, can be seen on the fifth-century Pola Casket. To these, six more spiral columns were added in the eighth century, translated from Ravenna, a gift of the Byzantine exarch. Eleven of the twelve columns remain at St. Peter's, where since the later Middle Ages some gazing upon them have claimed that they were all originally part of Solomon's Temple. Four columns modeled on these marble originals, fashioned in bronze like Jachin and Boaz, are incorporated into Bernini's famous baldachin above St. Peter's tomb.[39] In contrast to these very rare twisting columns, spirally fluted column are relatively common. Perhaps the earliest was uncovered at Stabiae, near Pompeii, where it was buried in A.D. 79. Straight columns and smaller colonnettes were carved with a spiral design known from many sites in Greece and

---

[38] *Liber Pontificalis*, c. 33–4: Sylvester, at 34.16, ed. Duchesne 1955–7. See Ward-Perkins 1952. Blaauw 2001 notes that Constantine surely supplied another four bronze pillars to his basilica, St. John in Lateran, to support the so-called *fastigium*.

[39] Ward-Perkins 1952: 21–33.

Cyprus, where they have survived in several sizes and marbles, as composites and monoliths.[40] Spirally fluted columns appear to have shared the apotropaic function of knotted columns, protecting the sanctuary and altar, by their incorporation into ciboria and chancel screens. Single twisted poles, of turned wood or brass, appear as book stands in illustrations of evangelists. Peacocks with necks twisted together are found, notably in Armenian manuscripts produced in Cilicia in the thirteenth century. And, as we have seen in an earlier chapter, serpentine finials adorned manuscript illustrations of fountains produced in Constantinople in the twelfth century.

The Brazen Serpent and the Crucifixion

Bronze appears to have been considered an especially effective medium for harnessing supernatural holy powers. This was true in the classical tradition, as we have seen in an earlier chapter, and also in the Judeo-Christian tradition, in which manufactured bronze columns like Jachin and Boaz, as well as bronze doors for temples and churches and bronze amulets and rings (and later bronze crosses) to be worn by individuals, were all held to deflect harm and cure illness. The Lord himself made Moses aware of this when he had him set up a bronze statue of a serpent on a column (Numbers 21:6–9):

> And the Lord sent fiery serpents among the people, and they bit the people; and much people of Israel died. Therefore the people came to Moses, and said, We have sinned, for we have spoken against the Lord, and against you; pray to the Lord, that he take away the serpents from us. And Moses prayed for the people. And the Lord said to Moses, Make you a fiery serpent, and set it on a pole: and it shall come to pass, that every one that is bitten, when he looks on it, shall live. And Moses made a serpent of bronze, and put it on a pole, and it came to pass, that if a serpent had bitten any man, when he beheld the serpent of bronze, he lived.[41]

The brazen serpent sanctioned by God came to be called Nehushtan, and later was worshipped as an idol in the Tabernacle. Hezekiah, king of Judah, broke it into pieces to prevent its further adoration (2 Kings 18:4). However, it was not as a cult statue that the brazen serpent was manufactured, but as an apotropaion. It is, in fact, the only bronze image mentioned in the Old Testament, where idols were usually fashioned in wood or other precious metals, usually silver or gold, laid over wood, for example the Golden Calf fashioned by Aaron

---

[40] Benson 1956; Benson 1959.
[41] The KJV offers "brass" where we have written bronze, but there is no indication that Moses has access to zinc, necessary for making brass. Hence modern English translations adopt a more scientific approach.

(Exodus 32:4, 8; Deuteronomy 9:12, 16), or Jeroboam's two calves (2 Kings 17:16).[42]

Nehushtan was rehabilitated by John 3:14: "As Moses raised up the serpent in the wilderness, even so must the Son of Man be lifted up, so that whosoever believes in him shall have eternal life."[43] Early Christian commentators took up this typology swiftly, for example Augustine of Hippo, who asked:

> What are the biting serpents? Sins, for the mortality of the flesh. What is the Serpent lifted up? The Lord's death upon the cross. For as death came by the serpent, it was figured by the image of the serpent. The serpent's bite was deadly, the Lord's death is life-giving. A serpent is gazed on that the serpent may have no power. What is this? A death is gazed on, that death may have no power.[44]

Augustine's principle is the familiar "like is cured by like."[45] As the Israelites were cured of their physical maladies by gazing upon its cause, a snake, so Christians would be cured of their spiritual ills by gazing upon the Crucifixion, fixing it in their mind's eye or their eyes upon an image of it.

The Crucifixion can be read as a Christian inversion of the combat myth, just as the *tropaium*, a cruciform symbol of Roman victory and Rome's instrument of torture, was inverted, becoming the ultimate Christian sign. In defeat, Christ achieved the greater victory, over death itself, so "that through death He might destroy him that had power over death, that is, the devil, and deliver them who through fear of death were all their lifetime subject to bondage" (Hebrews 2:14–15). This message was disseminated in the Pauline epistles, where the Crucifixion is treated, in the words of Neil Forsyth, "as a brilliantly paradoxical transformation of the old eschatological hope: death has been overcome by Christ's death and resurrection." The paradox of victory through defeat troubled many early Christian thinkers. Origen wished to place Satan on the cross in Christ's stead: "The Son of God was visibly crucified in the flesh, but invisibly it was the devil who was fixed to the cross with his principalities and powers." Origen is alluding to Paul, at Ephesians 6:12, and proceeds to quote from Colossians 2:14–15: "What was opposed to us, he has removed from the way, fixing it to the cross."[46] The principalities and powers of Rome continued to persecute and would make a martyr of Origen himself.

The Roman Good Friday liturgy stipulated the reading of Psalm 90 (91) after a recitation of Habakkuk's prayer, where "Death shall go before his face,

---

[42] Hurowitz 2006: 4, n. 2, distinguished between the bronze apotropaion and idols of wood and precious metals, with references also to scholarship on the composition of the Golden Calf. This is similar to the *sphyrelaton* technique employed in the manufacture of Archaic Greek cult statues. I thank Carolina López-Ruiz for this reference.

[43] Kessler 2009.

[44] *Tractatum in Iohannem* 12.11; quoted in fuller translation by Kessler 2009: 122.

[45] Flood 2006: 154; Kessler 2009: 129.

[46] Origen, *Homilies on Joshua* 8:3, quoted by Forsyth 1987: 364.

and the devil shall go before his feet" (Habakkuk 3:5).[47] However, during the ninth century this was replaced in the Carolingian church by the reading of Psalm 139 (140), which invokes God's aid against evil men, who "have sharpened their tongues like a serpent; adders' poison is under their lips."[48] This had been elucidated by St. Augustine, who identified the devil with the serpent-tongued men and echoes the appearance in Carolingian art of a serpent at the base of Christ's crucifix, the writhing Satan pierced and defeated by the cross, for example in a ninth-century ivory now in the Walters Art Museum (fig. 7.6).[49] The Carolingians recognized the power of objects fashioned in bronze and revived the art of lost-wax casting, as a cast inscription on a leonine door-knocker created for the cathedral at Trier reveals: "That which the wax gives, the fire removes, and the bronze returns to you."[50] Charlemagne had made not only bronze knockers but whole doors, each cast as a single piece with integrated lion handle, for his palatine church, the Cathedral of St. Mary at Aachen. These doors were formed with eight rectangular panels, but were otherwise unadorned, quite unlike the doors of Solomon's Temple, which were of juniper wood carved with cherubim, palms, and flowers and gilded, set within olive-wood frames (1 Kings 16). Their bronze stood, and still stands, in place of Jachin and Boaz, protecting the entrance to the palatine church.

Although the Byzantines did not read Augustine, they were intimately familiar with Moses' brazen serpent and knew as well that Christ's Crucifixion gave Christians power over death. Photios, in his ninth-century *Bibliotheke* (51), records a long work "On the Brazen Serpent" by a certain Hesychios, presbyter of Constantinople, full of speeches "put into the mouth of Moses."[51] The error of the Israelites was not to have created their brazen serpent, but rather to have worshipped it as a god. Christ had since then appeared as man to take upon himself the sins of mankind, but those who worshipped the image of the crucified Christ were not in error. This was determined by the Second Council of Nicaea, which in 787 declared: "We believe that gazing on the brazen serpent freed the Israelites from disaster, should we doubt that looking at and venerating pictures of Christ our Lord and his saints might save us?"[52] In a twelfth-century Byzantine Octateuch, a manuscript containing the first eight books of the Old Testament, an illustration of Moses raising the brazen serpent leaves the viewer in no doubt that he is witnessing also the Crucifixion: the serpent is stretched out straight, forming a crossbar for the wooden pole on which he

---

[47] Chazelle 2001: 261; Saxon 2011a: 264.
[48] Chazelle 2001: 261; Kessler 2006: 145; Saxon 2011: 157–8; Saxon 2011a: 264–5.
[49] Saxon 2011a: 265: "Christ, the brazen serpent, here defeats the devil/snake and heals the sins of those who look upon him with faith and will receive eternal life. Here, the exegesis is Augustine's [*Tractatus in Iohannem* 12:11]," which is quoted above. See also Kessler 2009.
[50] Weinryb 2012: 69.
[51] I thank Anthony Kaldellis for this reference.
[52] Quoted by Kessler 2009: 127.

FIGURE 7.6 Christ crucified, his cross piercing a serpent. Ninth-century ivory, Frankish, now in the Walters Art Museum, Baltimore. Photo: author.

is hoisted and bound by Moses' rope.[53] A contemporary poem by Theodore Prodromos affirms that "The bronze serpent was stretched crosswise on the erect wood, opposed to evil living serpents."[54] The connection is implicit in the long tradition of fashioning bronze pectoral crosses, *enkolpia*, from bronze.[55]

When in the reign of Basil II (d. 1025) the Milanese archbishop Arnulfus II visited Constantinople and was invited to select a gift from the imperial treasury, he chose a Hellenistic bronze serpent. Upon his return to Milan, this

---

[53] Istanbul Seraglio Octateuch, fol. 359r., reproduced with comments by Maguire 1977: 137, fig. 23.
[54] Quoted by Maguire 1977: 137.
[55] Weinryb 2012: 72.

was erected in the Basilica Sant'Ambrogio. Like Moses' bronze serpent, it was placed high on a pillar, and following John 3:14 it sat opposite its equivalent, a cross also raised on a pillar. The desire to identify the bronze serpent of Sant'Ambrogio as Moses' miraculous snake was strong, despite the evidence of 2 Kings 18:4 that is had long ago been destroyed, and a later legend held that both objects had been cast in a single mold.[56]

On the Pala d'Oro, the remarkable golden altarpiece of San Marco, Venice, created in part from enamels by middle Byzantine artists, one sees only the cross on a column, not the brazen serpent. In an enamel illustrating the baptism of Christ, the nude Christ stands in the River Jordan, looking toward John the Baptist above him to the left, affixing Christ's nimbus (fig. 7.7). Opposite the Baptist are two angels. The Holy Spirit, a dove, hovers immediately above Christ, within a smaller river of grace connecting his nimbus to the firmament. Within the river, reclining at Christ's right foot, is a representation of Jordan, his flow spilling from an upturned jug. At Christ's left foot stands something far less classical, and entirely out of place: a spiral column on three bejeweled steps, reaching only from beneath Christ's foot to his knee. Atop the small twisted pillar is a capital that appear to be formed from two serpentine heads supporting a golden cross.[57] However, this is an illusion. A closer inspection reveals that there is a blue vein of enamel running through a white capital, to give the impression of marble. A similar spirally fluted column features in another enamel, where St. Mark pulls down an idol that stands atop the capital. The golden cross on a spiraling pillar, while seeming to evoke the original golden tripod on the Plataian Tripod, proclaims the triumph of Christianity and the destruction of fallen idols, including the brazen serpent of Moses, now understood as prefiguring the Crucifixion.

Holy Powers and Health

As Nehushtan cured ills caused by snakes, so Christ who took the form of man saved man from himself. Christ healed moral infirmities, sins, but also physical infirmities and illnesses of human flesh, including those caused by other animals. Christ offered mundane protection: his trampling of the lions and snakes protected his faithful against their deadly bites. "He will deliver you from the snare of the fowler and deadly disease, He will cover you with his feathers. He will shelter you with his wings" (Psalm 90 (91): 3–4). Christ

---

[56] Dell'Acqua 2013: 331 explores this idea inventively, citing an eleventh-century Milanese chronicle (Landulphus senior). However, I have found no evidence that the bronze serpent consigned to the treasury was equated by the Byzantines with that of Moses in Constantinople, and consider it unlikely that such a precious relic would have been given away.

[57] Strootman 2014: 443–4, fig. 3, mistakes the column capital for serpent heads.

FIGURE 7.7 Enamel plaque showing the baptism of Christ in the River Jordan, incorporated into the Pala d'Oro, St. Mark's, Venice, Byzantine, twelfth century. akg-images/De Agostini Picture Library/M. Carieri.

himself is said to have glossed the psalm for his seventy-two disciples: "I have given you power to trample on snakes and scorpions, and upon all the strength of the enemy [i.e., the devil], so that he will not be able to harm you" (Luke 10:19).

But faith in Christ alone proved insufficient for many Christians, who turned to tangible things, objects, often fashioned from bronze—the aforementioned *enkolpia* following in this tradition—to protect them in their daily lives. Christians knew the envy of Satan and his demons wrought evil in the world, often through humans or animals, bringing pollution, illness, and disease. A rich and fearful variety of demons was known to the Byzantines through such popular texts as the *Testament of Solomon*, and the means for repelling demons were also known, through magical incantations, spells, seals, rings, and amulets, all of which were prescribed by the *Testament*. Many demons took serpentine form. Amulets and rings, therefore, might feature a serpent—like cures like—or instead might have magical inscriptions and designs. Armbands, jugs, and flasks featured holy riders, who would wield a lance to pierce a serpent demon in the manner of earlier, and later, dragon-slayers. Holy riders, like pagan deities but in contrast to later military saints, were generally unnamed, as for example on several small, copper water jugs dated to the sixth or seventh century.[58] The anonymity of the holy rider made him multivalent: he might be effective against any number of demons, including Korouphe and Tribolos, both three-headed dragon demons.[59] However, Saints Solomon, Sisinnios, and Sisinnarios might all be invoked by name to serve particular functions, for example protecting a child or pregnant woman. In an image at the Monastery of St. Apollo, at Bawit in Egypt, dated to the sixth or seventh century, St. Sisinnios slays the demoness Alabasdria, while her snake-tailed daughter is shown hovering above. Alabasdria is identified in the *Testament of Solomon* as the demon responsible for the deaths of children during child-birth.[60]

Nikandros' *Theriaka*, a poem of the second century B.C., is replete with Greek serpent lore that was copied by the Byzantines, who will have learned from it which herbs and ointments would repel snakes and how to create salves and herbal remedies if bitten. A tenth-century illuminated manuscript illustrates a rich array of the serpents that Nikandros lists by attributes and behavior.[61] The illness by which Job (2:7) was afflicted by Satan, an ulcer from his head to his feet, was the greatest of all the tests to his faith, and was imagined by the Byzantines to have taken the form of a polycephalous reptilian beast. The Book of Job was a popular text among Byzantines, and a number of illuminated copies have survived.[62] The earliest illustration, in the mid-ninth-century Vatican Job, depicts the ulcer as a creature with three heads, taking the form of the first letter of the Greek world for ulcer, *elkos*. The top head is that of a dragon, the middle head of a lion, the bottom head of a snake.[63] Later illuminators developed the motif. In a twelfth- or thirteenth-century manuscript (Barocci 201, fol. 32v.), the three-headed beast bites at Job's head, feet, and hand as he reclines. The topmost part of the beast, formerly its dragon head, is now formed by the Devil himself, who does not ride the beast but emerges from it wielding a sword.[64]

Serpents brought illness and disease, and as a preferred guise adopted by demons they afflicted communities across the Mediterranean and Near

---

[58] Examples of these jugs can be found in the Walters Art Museum, Baltimore (53.155), the Metropolitan Museum of Art, New York (67.200.2), and the Victoria and Albert Museum, London (M.434–1910), and others have been found as far apart as Essex (UK) and Gaza.

[59] See Maguire, Maguire and Flowers 1989: 25–8. Consider also Glykon, and the snake-tailed giants in Nikandros, *Theriaka*, illustrated in the Paris BN, cod. Supll. Gr. 247, fol. 47r., which is discussed by Weitzmann 1971: 142–3, and fig. 117.

[60] See generally Vikan 1984; Maguire, Maguire, and Flowers 1989. In Maguire 1995, fig. 15, one can pick out a three-headed snake. In the same article, Maguire explores early silks showing dragon-slayers in Philadelphia and Lyons.

[61] Nikandros, *Theriaka*, illustrated in the Paris BN, cod. Supll. Gr. 247. See Stephenson 2010: 62–3.

[62] Evangelatou 2009: 19, records fifteen illuminated codices, many of which remain unpublished.

[63] Vatican MS gr. 749, fol. 25. See Evangelatou 2009: 19–21, figs. 1–3.

[64] Evangelatou 2009: 29.

Eastern world. But serpents had an equally long tradition of healing in the same broad region.[65] Ninĝišzida, whom we have met as a Mesopotamian dragon-slayer with serpentine properties, was also a god of healing.[66] Healers had long used venom in healing, and serpentine motifs were employed to protect against specific maladies well into the Christian period. A rayed serpent guarded the stomach, and a form of Chnoubis (Cnouphi), a serpent with a lion's head, was associated with the womb.[67] It has been suggested that a sixth-century A.D. silver and gilt plaque, a votive to St. Symeon the Stylite, by depicting a snake coiling up his pillar alludes to the healing power of the *locus sanctus*, the site of the saint's *askesis* and of his relics.[68] Most famously, healing serpents were associated with the cult of Asklepios, the Greek god of healing, which remained vibrant from his appearance of the son of Apollo in the *Homeric Hymn to Asklepios* well into Late Antiquity. The staff of Asklepios came to be depicted with an entwined serpent, although the healing powers of the serpent remained distinct from the staff, and the giant snake was known variously as Asklepios' pet, symbol, and embodiment. Asklepios himself took the form of a giant serpent as he moved between his healing sanctuaries, Asklepieia, notably when extending his powers from Epidauros to other temples at their foundations.[69] The best-attested episode involves the establishment of an Asklepieion on the Tiber Island in the city of Rome in 291 B.C. Asklepios' serpentine epiphany is reported at length by Livy, Ovid, and many others into the fourth century A.D.[70] One is struck by a carving of the goddess Hygieia ("health"), daughter of Asklepios, among the Liverpool ivories, where her own serpent is entwined around a tripod with two smaller serpents above (fig. 7.8). This was modeled on a cult statue raised in Rome, where the ivory was carved in ca. A.D. 400. Hygieia's companion is her father, with a serpent entwined around his staff, modeled on a statue which is now in the Palazzo Massimo in Rome.[71] When Zeus slew Asklepios for raising the dead, he was placed in the sky as the constellation Ophiuchus, the serpent-bearer, which, as we have seen, appears in the night sky to the northwest of the center of the spiraling Milky Way.

---

[65] Ogden 2013: 310–46, 347–82.

[66] Ogden 2013: 310, n. 1 confronts earlier claims that Asklepios derived his form and symbols from Ninĝišzida (Nigizzida) with the observation that more than 1,500 years passed between known representations of Ninĝišzida and the earliest depictions of Asklepios. On mooted connections between Ninĝišzida, the Gudean vase, and Hermes' caduceus, see Frothingham 1916.

[67] Vikan 1984; Maguire, Maguire, and Flowers 1989: 7–8, 196–202, 211–13. See also Ogden 2013: 306.

[68] Mundell Mango 1986: 240–1, no. 71. But see Vikan 1998: 231, 233; and for a related design on a stela, see Vikan 1982: 36–7.

[69] Pausanias 2.10.2–3; Ogden 2013: 313.

[70] Ogden 2013: 311–12 provides a detailed summary of Ovid's account and a list of further references.

[71] Gibson 1994: 10–15.

FIGURE 7.8 Ivory carving of the goddess Hygieia, "health," daughter of Asklepios, among the Liverpool ivories, where her serpent is entwined around a tripod with two smaller serpents above. Photo: Liverpool Art Museums/Nathan Pendlebury.

Siphnos

The talismanic powers of the Serpent Column appear to have been well known far away from Constantinople and well into the nineteenth century. A carved stone plaque, 33 cm high and 25 cm wide, now in the Benaki Museum in Athens is believed to have been produced in the nineteenth century on the island of Siphnos, which sent a trireme to Salamis and later was rewarded with a line in the dedicatory inscription on the Plataian tripod (fig. 7.9). The plaque bears a magical cryptographic inscription above a carved image of a man dressed in priestly costume holding a cross staff. He stands between two striking monuments, an obelisk standing on an inscribed base and a twisting stump, also on a carved base, but broken at the top. The man is Constantine, the first Christian Roman emperor and an Orthodox saint, who is shown standing in his hippodrome in Constantinople. Faces can be seen in the stands, beneath pediments marked with crosses. All three objects that identify the man and his location are out of time, anachronisms in stone. The cross staff that Constantine holds is not his famous scepter, the *labarum*, which was topped with the chi-rho, the

FIGURE 7.9 Carved plaque with cryptographic inscription, showing Constantine between the Theodosian Obelisk and a headless Serpent Column, now in the Benaki Museum, Athens, originally from Siphnos, nineteenth century. Photo: Thomas W. Gallant, with permission.

first two letters of Christ in Greek. It is the true cross, which according to a legend first told at the end of the fourth century was discovered by Helena, Constantine's mother. The Theodosian Obelisk, shown to the emperor's left, was raised half a century after Constantine's death, around the time that the legend of the true cross emerged. The obelisk now dwarfs the twisted stump of the Serpent Column, shown to Constantine's right. However, the column's shaft was not broken until 1700.

There is a tradition of carving on Siphnos, which became rich in antiquity from its silver mines and demonstrated its wealth to rival cities and its gratitude to Apollo by the construction of a magnificent treasury at the Panhellenic shrine at Delphi. But why would a Greek artisan on Siphnos in the 1800s, in support of his magical invocation, portray a long-dead emperor and two ancient monuments in a distant city no longer in Greek hands? It is unlikely that the carver knew that Constantine, in his *Oration to the Saints*, had observed that many believed the Apollonian Sibyl, "in charge of the tripod around which the serpent was coiled," prophesied the coming of Christ and his ultimate judgement in a lengthy acrostic oracle, which began: "In sign of coming judgment earth shall sweat; Eternal monarchy shall come from heaven Straightway to judge the flesh and all the world."[72] Could the carver have known of the work of archaeologists and epigraphers from the 1850s? This is possible, for his carving suggests a familiarity with the column in its excavated state, notably showing a marble base on which the column stands. This would have lain under the earth before Newton's dig of 1855. However, the actual marble base is not carved with figures, so it may be that the artist was simply replicating his impression of the base of the obelisk, which famously shows a hippodrome scene, with faces in the stands and obelisks. Is this a clever circular reference, since the Siphnos plaque itself is a hippodrome scene? Had the artist visited Constantinople? This is possible, but unnecessary, since he may instead have seen photographs of the hippodrome, which circulated after 1850. On one of the earliest, by James Robertson, the still half-buried Serpent Column is barely visible, but one can see the carved base of the Theodosian Obelisk (fig. 8.16, below). After its excavation, the Siphnian artist would have known that the name of his own people was inscribed on the newly uncovered base of the Serpent Column. If he knew tales of Constantine, then surely he also knew of the Persian Wars, and how this monument, the Plataian tripod, stood as a symbol of Greek resistance to oriental overlordship. The Siphnians were closely involved in resistance to the Ottomans during the nineteenth century, as the new kingdom of Greece was established and gradually expanded across the Aegean. Here, then, one might detect the desire for emancipation for all Greeks from "Persian," that is Turkish domination, and perhaps even the dream of liberating the city of Constantine.[73] Such a political interpretation is possible, as this dream was alive when the Siphnos plaque was carved, possibly as late as the 1890s, when the Orient Express was traveling as far as Istanbul, bringing visitors who returned with postcards showing the Serpent Column as we see it today.

However, the Siphnos plaque need not convey an overtly political message. The composition may be informed by modern photography and archaeology, but its purpose was surely protective, harnessing the power of the cross, certainly, but also that of a saintly king and the powerful *apotropaia* he wielded. The plaque is the perfect size to be placed beside a door or window. As the Serpent Column was created to thank Apollo for victory and ensure his continued favor for the Greeks, and just as it was imagined to protect the city of Constantine through centuries, so it might provoke divine assistance to protect the occupants of a Siphnian house from misfortune, perhaps the venomous blunt-nosed Milos viper (*Macrovipera schweizeri*), native to the Cyclades. We cannot know for certain when or why the Siphnian plaque was produced, nor where or how it was employed, but we can state with certainty that to the craftsman who carved it, the Serpent Column retained potency after 2,500 years.

---

[72] *Oration to the Saints* 18; trans. Edwards 2003: 41–2. The acrostic, and Edwards' inventive translation, spell out *Iesous Chreistos Theou Huios Soter Stauros*. See also Bardill 2012: 362.

[73] Alcock 2002: 3–5.

8 }

Istanbul

Mehmed the Dragon-Slayer – Mehmed the Antiquarian – Sketching the Serpent Column – Ottoman Miniatures – Beheading the Serpents – The Modern Hippodrome

The hippodrome of Constantinople attracted comment from visitors impressed that horsemanship could be admired in the city center. In 1322, Sir John Maundeville considered it "a fair place for joustings or for other plays and sports." He also observed the benefits of the tiered seating.[1] In 1427, Johannes Schiltberger described it as "a fine square for tilting and all kinds of pastime that might be desired in front of the palace." Shortly afterwards, in 1432, Bertrandon de la Brocquière described a "large and handsome square surrounded with walls like a palace" where he saw "the brother of the emperor, the despot of the Morea, exercise himself with a score of other horsemen. Each had a bow, and they galloped along the enclosure throwing their hats before them, which, when they had passed, they shot at."[2] This sport, Bertrandon determined, they had adopted from the Turks. The hippodrome in its early-fifteenth-century condition is captured in a famous sketch, later published by Panvinio. This fine square for tilting the Turks called At meydanı, "the open place for horses," when they captured Constantinople in May 1453.

Mehmed the Dragon-Slayer

The world of Rūm, the Roman Empire, and its remarkable capital was well known to the Ottomans long before they took the city. Tales of visitors to the city will have enhanced far earlier tales, frequently retold and illustrated, in versions of the *Shahnama* (*Shahnameh*), "Book of Kings," completed by Firdowsi in 1010, which was derived from a late Sasanian work. A good deal of early Ottoman prestige was built on the use of Persian at court, and copies of

---

[1] Sir John Maundeville, in Wright 1848: 135. Maundeville is also known as Mandeville.
[2] Johann Schiltberger, trans. Telfer 1879: 80, 228; Wright 1848: 339.

the *Shahnama* allowed this new dynasty to project itself into the past through appropriation of epic, establishing historical (in fact, historiographical) roots. A seminal late-fifteenth-century versified *Shahnama*-style Persian history, Malik Ummi's *Shahnama*, drew directly upon Firdowsi. Further books of kings were produced at court in the early sixteenth century, all consciously modeled on Firdowsi, with the most prestigious versions in Persian *mesnevi* verse form.[3] One of the richest illuminated copies of the Persian epic was given in 1568 to Selim II by the Safavid ruler Tahmasp I, and it remained for the following three centuries at the New (Topkapı) Palace. It surely served as an inspiration for the richly illuminated *Shahanshāhnāma*, the "King's Book of Kings," composed in 1581 to eulogize the reign of Murad III. We shall return to these richly illustrated volumes and their artists shortly.

In the fourth book of Firdowsi's *Shahnama*, Gushtasp, son of Shah Luhrasp, despairs of his life at court and sets out for Rūm.[4] Dwelling with a village chief, he is summoned with all the noble youths of the land to the court of Caesar, whose eldest daughter, Katayun, would choose a husband. She chooses Gushtasp for a husband, but they must live away from the city in Gushtasp's adopted village. Subsequently, a Roman noble named Mirin, who wishes to marry the second daughter of Caesar, is charged with killing a wolf. Mirin seeks out Gushtasp to entrust him with the task, at which Gushtasp succeeds. Ahran, a younger Roman noble, wishes to marry the third daughter of Caesar. He is charged with killing a dragon that dwells on Mount Sakila. Ahran asks Gushtasp to undertake the task, as he has heard of his recent wolf-slaying on behalf of Mirin. Gushtasp commissions a mighty new sword, and with it slays the dragon in the land of Rūm. The scene of dragon-slaying is frequently illustrated.[5] Like Kadmos who slew Drakon, Gushtasp removes the dragon's teeth. The carcass of the beast is taken to Caesar, the emperor, whose daughter is then married to Ahran. In Constantinople, both new sons-in-law of the Caesar are held in high esteem, displaying their skills of horsemanship and archery on the riding ground overlooked by a balcony in the Caesar's palace. That is to say, the men ride and shoot in the hippodrome, while the imperial party watch from the *kathisma*. But when Gushtasp comes to the Caesar's riding ground and surpasses all others, Caesar recognizes the man who must have slain the wolf and dragon. Gushtasp produces the dragon's teeth that he carries with him as proof of his achievement.[6]

---

[3] Woodhead 2007.

[4] *Shahnama*, "Luhrasp," cc. 9 (marriage) 10 (wolf) 12 (dragon); trans. Warner, IV: 333 41, 346–9. Gushtasp's son, Isfandiyar (Esfandiyar), also fights a dragon. This is his third labor, fighting the dragon after fighting two land beasts (wolves, then lions).

[5] See, for example, Rizvi 2012: 233. A database of images can be found at the *Cambridge Shahnama Project*:

http://shahnama.caret.cam.ac.uk/new/jnama/page.

[6] *Shahnama*, "Luhrasp"; trans. Warner, IV: 318–52. This is also illustrated, although far less widely than the dragon-slaying.

The tale of Mehmed II striking off the jaw of a serpent in the hippodrome, which we explored in the previous chapter, cast him in the role of Gushtasp, even as he was himself now Caesar, new ruler of the Roman world. We discussed a miniature (*Hünername,* fol. 162b), which shows the sultan's mace, thrown high in the air, striking the lower jaw of a left-facing serpent (fig. 7.1, above). Victory, the city, and the empire had been bestowed by God on Mehmed, son of Murad II. Mehmed, like Gushtasp, stood in the boots of the Mesopotamian conquering hero-god Marduk, who smashed the skull of Serpentine Tiamat with his battle mace to establish cosmic order.[7] At the same time, Mehmed was placed in an iconographical tradition that stretched back millennia to Pharaonic Egypt, where rulers including Narmer (ca. 3100 B.C.) and Den (ca. 2900 B.C.) were portrayed smiting their enemies with a battle mace.[8] In the Persian tradition, on which the Ottomans drew, the dragon was Aži Dahāka, a demonic creature known in Zoroastrian scripture to have three heads, three mouths, and six hands.[9] At the top of the *Hünername* illustration (fig. 7.1), pressed against the upper frame, are four boxes resembling the form of painted hoardings, which contain written verse offering a gloss on the scene:

> Lord of the club and the heavy mace.
> Lord of the sword, the spear, and the spearhead
> Lord of justice and lord of judgment
> He whose head is raised above all, Sultan Murad.
> O God, may he endure until resurrection
> The sultan, mighty as the heavens, strong as the sun.[10]

The calligrapher of the *Hünername* reminds the reader that while Mehmed is depicted, now the wielder of the sultan's heavy battle mace is Murad III (1574–95), grandson of the conqueror's great-grandson. Each sultan is Gushtasp,

---

[7] *Enūma Elish*, 5; trans. Dalley 2009: 254. Compare with Psalm 74.12–14: "But you, O God ... broke the heads of the monster in the waters. It was you who crushed the heads of Leviathan and gave him as food to the creatures of the desert." See also Noegel 2007: 19, and above at chapter two.

[8] Noegel 2007: 14–15, figs. 1.1, 1.2, being the Label of Den (British Museum, EA 55586) and Narmer Palmette (Cairo, Egyptian Museum, JE 32169 [CG 14716]), with commentary and a reference to a fuller study by E. Swan Hall 1986.

[9] *EI*, s.v. Aždahā: 190–205, at 194. This essay provides a full and rich exploration of the dragon in Old and Middle Iranian, Persian literature, Iranian folktales, and Armenian literature, including the *Shahname* tradition.

[10] Hudâvend-i kûpâl u gürz-i girân

Hudâvend-i şimşîr u rümh u sinân
Hudâvend-i 'adl u Hudâvend-i dâd.
Kamunun ser-efrâzı Sultân Murâd
İlâhî ola haşre dek ber-karâr
Felek-kadr hâkân-ı mihr-iktidâr

Robert Dankoff kindly supplied both the transliteration and translation, through Jane Hathaway. I thank them both.

Marduk, Narmer, and Den, a conquering hero, "mighty as the heavens, strong as the sun."

For Mehmed II, the dragon stood for the Christian empire he had conquered. For Christians observing the conquest, Mehmed was the serpent and his empire Satanic. In around 1470, Mehmed acquired a portrait, one of sixteen prints attached to the so-called Fatih Album now held in the Topkapı Palace Library (Hazine 2153, 2160). This portrait depicts the sultan wearing a dragon-crested helmet and sporting the epithet "El Gran Turco," the Great Turk. Attributed to the Master of the Vienna Passion, possibly inspired by Antonio del Pollaiuolo, and perhaps acquired from Florentine merchants, "El Gran Turco" was drawn after an earlier, famous portrait medal of John VIII Palaiologos by Pisanello (fig. 8.1).[11] Pisanello's John faced right, wearing a distinctive peaked helmet, almost a mirror image of his pointed beard, with between the two an aquiline nose. Mehmed sponsored the production and circulation of similar medals of himself, both in Constantinople and in Italy for distribution in the West, including examples by Gentile Bellini (from 1480), Bertoldo di Giovanni (1480), and Costanzo da Ferrara (1481, fig. 8.2).[12] On these bronzes, in place of Palaiologos' peaked cap, Mehmed wore a turban, and his face with bearded chin and equally aquiline nose looked left, as if facing west from Istanbul. "El Gran Turco" was quite different (fig. 8.3). Mehmed's helmet, unlike Palaiologos', features a rampant dragon, with two clawed feet raised and his arched neck fringed with a scalloped fin. From the dragon's nose a horn protrudes, and from its mouth dart three tongues of flame. Evidently, since he acquired and preserved the portrait, Mehmed appreciated his representation as a dragon-slayer. The image impressed others too, in Florence, where majolica storage jars were manufactured and decorated with the same image, although the fierce dragon became a rather limp plume, while the Great Turk's long hair is rust and his beard and cheeks blue (fig. 8.4).[13]

For Felice Feliciano of Verona, the humanist collector and calligrapher, disciple of Ciriaco d'Ancona and friend to the Bellinis and Mantegna, the Great Turk did not tame the dragon but was the beast itself, threatening Italy and enslaving the Church.[14] In a collection of poems assembled by Feliciano in 1471 or 1472, in a section entitled *Stramoti Amorosi*, one finds an anonymous poem with the title "Pronostico overo prophetia dela venuta del turcho," *Prediction,*

---

[11] Raby 2000: 64–5; Campbell and Chong 2005: 66–9. For a consideration of the attribution to Pollaiuolo, and the suggestion that this was a stylized image only later captioned "El Gran Turco," see Wright 2005: 129, 513. Also Kafescioğlu 2009: 159.

[12] Examples of all three can be seen by searching the Victoria and Albert Museum's collections online. See also Campbell and Chong 2005: 70–3 for illustrations. Commentary at Raby 1981; Raby 1982: 5; Raby 2000: 67–9; Rodini 2011: 24–5.

[13] Campbell and Chong 2005: 67. The British Museum description maintains the association with Antonio Pollaiuolo.

[14] Mitchell 1961.

FIGURE 8.1 Bronze portrait medallion, John VIII Palaiologos by Pisanello, ca, 1438–43. Trustees of the British Museum.

FIGURE 8.2 Bronze portrait medallion, Mehmed II by Costanzo da Ferrara, 1481. Victoria and Albert Museum.

or rather prophecy on the coming of the Turk.[15] The verse is obscure, but "nota" follow, and an illustration (Harvard University, Houghton Library, MS Typ 0157, fol. 96v.), perhaps by Feliciano himself, offers illumination. The image depicts a dragon, a rooster perched on its rump, and a writhing serpent bound around the neck and front leg of a griffin (fig. 8.5). The serpent is identified as the *dux mediol[anum]*, "Duke of Milan," being the Visconti viper, a favored emblem of Galeazzo Maria Sforza. The griffin that it chokes, clutching a key in its beak, is *Rex Siculus*, the "King of Sicily," one title of John II of Aragon. Beneath the griffin's hind legs are eggs labeled "Florentines." The rooster, sporting a crown-like comb atop its head, is identified as the King of France, who dominated Savoy. The green dragon, *basilisco* or *drago*, is the dominant beast, filling the central space, its tail wound around a sword, and a sack of money

---

[15] Mazzi 1901–2: 62–4.

FIGURE 8.3 "El Gran Turco" (Hazine 2153, 2160), etching contained in the Fatih Album, ca. 1470. Topkapı Palace Museum Library.

labeled *pecunia magna* ("a lot of money") is suspended above the sword, hanging from the dragon's neck. In its mouth the dragon holds a bishop's crozier, within its curved top the words *eclesia dei* [*sic*], "God's Church." On the dragon's face, beneath its eye, is a six-pointed star, and on its haunch a crescent moon is shown in blue and white. To reinforce the identification, above its head, between a pointed snout and long curved ears, is the designation *magnus teucrus*, "the Great Turk."[16] As the apocalyptic poem reveals, "Truly this dragon is full of wickedness, tearing with his teeth the pastoral calm, clutching in his

---

[16] Mazzi 1901–2: 57. See also Raby 2000: 64.

FIGURE 8.4 "El Gran Turco" on a majolica storage jar manufactured in Florence, ca. 1470. Trustees of the British Museum.

claws all justice."[17] This is the beast of John's Apocalypse, come in the form of the Ottoman sultan who attacked but preserved the Serpent Column.

Mehmed the Antiquarian

Mehmed the Conqueror, twenty-one-year-old sultan of the Ottoman Turks, paid a good deal of attention to the hippodrome, but unlike the conquerors of the city in 1204, his interest was in preserving and collecting rather than destroying. A remarkable note on Mehmed efforts to preserve the Serpent Column is supplied by Giovan-Maria Angiolello, who was captured at the Siege of Negroponte in 1470, learned Turkish well, and served the sultan directly from 1474 until Mehmed's death in 1481. In his memoir, which was later used

---

[17] Mazzi 1901–2: 63: Verrà quel drago colmo di nequitia/e roderà con denti el pastorale/tenendo fra le graffe ogni iustitia.

FIGURE 8.5 An illustration, perhaps by Felice Feliciano, ca. 1471–2, depicting a dragon, a rooster perched on its rump, and a writhing serpent bound around the neck and front leg of a griffin. Harvard University, Houghton Library, MS Typ 0157, fol. 96v. Reproduced from Digital Scriptorium under a Creative Commons license.

by the author of the better-known *Historia Turchesa*, Angiolello reports the following.[18]

> (Folio 14r., l. 21) In the middle of the aforesaid place, running lengthwise, there are four fine structures. First, in the direction of the aforementioned columns there is a line of stone blocks formed into a wall, and these blocks are as perfectly fitted together as could ever be. After them are three bronze serpents, twisted together very tightly, with their heads and their tongues (f. 14v) pointing out in three directions. In the center of these three serpents, a mulberry tree (*more rose*) began to grow which produced reddish exudations, and as it swelled, the main shaft began to separate and open out, but the Sultan had it cauterized with hot irons so that it should not destroy the whole structure. This

---

[18] MacKay 2006. I am profoundly grateful to Pierre MacKay for supplying me with his own transcription and translation of the pertinent part of Angiolello's memoir, MS Vicenza 413, Biblioteca Civica Bertoliana, which is otherwise extremely difficult to access in the first and best edition by Caparrozzo (1881).

was because it was said that the thing had been made to chase all the snakes out of the city of Constantinople, for there had formerly been a time when it was uninhabitable by reason of the great number of snakes that were there. At present, however, there are no snakes at all except for those brought in by the occasional snake-charmer.[19]

Mehmed thinned out the remaining monuments of the Byzantine hippodrome when he began construction at the Seraglio, once the Byzantine acropolis, of his New Palace, his second in the city, which would far later be called the Topkapı Palace.[20] The New Palace consisted of two inner courtyards comprising residential and administrative buildings, surrounded by hanging gardens encircled by a wall and outer court, the first court or Court of Processions, which linked the palace to the city.[21] The first gate, or imperial gate, has an extant inscription attesting to its completion, and therefore to the completion of the first court, in 1478. To the second courtyard, where the business of state was conducted, Mehmed had transported a collection of antiquities taken from two notable sites: from the Church of the Holy Apostles, which he had dismantled in 1461 to replace with the Fatih Mosque, and from the hippodrome. Additionally, according to a list compiled by an Italian on the orders of Bayezid II, Mehmed's son and successor, there was a great collection of Christian relics "in the palace of the Grand Signor, in which the Great Turk, the late father of [the sultan] placed them when he took Constantinople."[22]

Mehmed wished to preserve objects of art and devotion in his private space, where they might neither offend nor provoke those who did not share his own love of classical art and architecture, literature, and history.[23] Mehmed had, as a young man, produced his own sketches, some of which have been preserved

---

[19] The following is MacKay's transcription of Angiolello, (fol. 14r., l. 21): Ancora per mezzo il predetto luogo, cio e per longeza vi sono quattro belli ediffiti; prima verso le predette colone vi sono una filla di quadri di pietra murata in un muro, et sono tanto bene acconci quanto mai sia possibile. Dietro gli sono tre bisse di metallo tortigliate tutte insieme, et molto strette, et le teste di quelle con le lingue guar (f. 14v.) da [\a] tre parti, et per lo mezzo delle dette tre bisse [vi] era nato un Moraro di quelli che fano le more rose et per esser ingrossato il troncho cominsciava a separarle et aprirle, et lo Gran Turco lo fece afocare con feri caldi, perche non fosse cagione di guastar il detto ediffitio per li quale si dice che fusse fatto per discasar le bisse della Citta di Costantinopoli, che gia tempo fu che la detta Citta non {non} si poteva habitare per la gran moltitudine che vi ne era, et in questi giorni pressenti non si ne trova niuna se non fosero portato per qualch' Orbolato. MacKay observes that "more rose" may refer, instead, to a corrosive bronze disease. However, "mulberry tree" is a possible translation, and was preferred by Raby 1987: 311. The symbolic aspects of the mulberry tree, which may be pertinent here, are addressed by Jane Hathaway, and I thank her for referring me to her book, Hathaway 2003: 135–42.

[20] The name Topkapı was given to a summer palace built in the palace's grounds in the early eighteenth century, and came later to refer to the whole palace complex. See Raby 1980: 243.

[21] A dynastic law code compiled for Mehmed II was the first to codify court ceremonial, which continued to develop and become more elaborate thereafter: Necipoğlu 1991: 16–22.

[22] Quoted by Raby 1982: 5.

[23] Raby 1980 suggests this was not inspired by Ciriaco d'Ancona, but nonetheless it was genuine and instilled by other tutors. Raby 1982.

in a school notebook. His face appeared on numerous medallions produced by Italian artists.[24] His collection of antiquities could be observed only by those whom he invited into the palace, which in time included Gentile Bellini, apparently commissioned to produce some erotica for the sultan, and an icon of the Virgin and infant Christ to accompany the remarkable collection of Christian relics. Nine benches from the hippodrome stands were provided so that his guests might rest between perusing his antiquities, which included several porphyry sarcophagi that once housed the bodies of Byzantine emperors, two huge capitals which once supported bronze statues (fig. 8.6), and the two extant statue bases of Porphyrios, both excavated from that site, albeit more than a century apart (fig. 4.13, above).[25] On the occasion when the "old base" of Porphyrios was dug out, in excavations conducted between 1845 and 1847, several large objects would not pass through the gateway from the courtyard, that is the second or middle gate, proving that they must have been relocated there before the gate itself was built, certainly by the end of the fifteenth century.[26] The collection also included the equestrian statue of Justinian, removed from its tall column in the Augusteion overlooking the hippodrome, perhaps in pieces.

The New Palace's second courtyard as it appeared in the later sixteenth century is depicted frequently in the *Hünername*, completed around a century after the palace complex was completed. Its gardens are clearly illustrated, although one cannot pick out individual monuments.[27] Pierre Gilles, who made a meticulous study of the city during his four years in Istanbul, was not fortunate enough to be invited into the palace's second courtyard, and so he failed to notice that many of the hippodrome's furnishings had been transported there.[28] He was otherwise well informed about these, not least from his reading of the *Greek Anthology*, of which five editions had been published before Gilles' arrival at Istanbul in 1544.[29] His description of the hippodrome and its surviving furnishings is both carefully observed and informed by his reading in Greek sources.[30]

> Modern historians, as Zonaras and others, write that the hippodrome was built by Severus following his reconciliation with the Byzantines. Zosimus, a

---

[24] Raby 1982; Raby 2000: 67–9, 86–9; Rodini 2011.

[25] Raby 1987: 311.

[26] Cameron, Al. 1973: 4–12; Müller-Wiener 1977: 39, 68; Necipoğlu 1991: 6–8, 50–1. The middle gate, beyond which only the sultan could ride a horse, is depicted already in the woodcut illustration of Schedel's *Liber Chronicarum* (1493). An inscription on the doors relates their replacement in 1524–5, not the construction of the gate.

[27] Tükel 2010: 97–8, warns against expecting a "bird's-eye view."

[28] On Gilles, for full references, see Paravicini 1994–2001: II, 187–8.

[29] Gilles II.13; trans. Ball 1729: 114, "I have not time to take notice of the numberless statues of all the combatants, wrestlers, charioteers, formerly placed in the hippodrome; of which, though there is nothing remaining at present, the memory of them is still preserved in a small poem of three hundred verses, in which some chariot-racers are mentioned with particular honours . . ."

[30] Gilles, II.11–13; trans. Ball 1729: 103, 110 (revised).

FIGURE 8.6 A huge capital in the grounds of the Topkapı Palace which once supported a statue, perhaps the equestrian statue of Justinian that stood in the Augusteion. Photo: author.

> more ancient writer, tells us it was built . . . by Constantine the Great . . . About the middle of the hippodrome, among a strait range of small obelisks, stand seven pillars. One of these, made of Arabian marble, is seventeen feet and eight digits in circumference, and one Abraham [Ibrahim], a Pasha, erected on top of it a statue of Hercules in bronze, made from the spoils he had taken from Hungary. But upon the death of Abraham, Hercules . . . was at last forced to submit and was torn to pieces by the Turks, the most inveterate enemies to statuary . . .

Not all Muslim Turks were offended by images in the round. Evidently both Mehmed II and, eighty years later, Ibrahim Pasha, the Grand Vizier born to Greek parents in Epirus, favored anthropomorphic statues. Unlike Ibrahim Pasha, who was murdered on the order of Süleyman I, the conqueror feared no man's opprobrium, although he appears to have earned that of his own son, Bayezid II, who questioned his father's devotion to Islam.[31] In a letter of 1519 sent to Michelangelo from Turkey, Tommaso di Tolfo lamented that Bayezid took "no delight in figures of any sort; indeed he hated them."[32] Nevertheless, the Serpent Column stood untouched in a highly visible location throughout

---

[31] Raby 1982.
[32] Quoted in translation by Raby 1982: 8.

Bayezid's reign, and also that of his son, Selim I, "The Stern," before it earned a long description from Gilles, writing under Süleyman I, "The Magnificent."[33] The reason for its survival appears to be related to its status as a talisman.

Sketching the Serpent Column

The surviving ancient monuments of Constantinople held travelers enthralled, including Ciriaco d'Ancona, who traveled to the city on at least four occasions, latterly to sketch Hagia Sophia shortly before its capture by Mehmed II.[34] Although his own sketches have not been preserved, Giuliano da Sangallo reimagined Ciriaco's description of Hagia Sophia and its many columns of porphyry and serpentine, the latter being a green marble rather than serpentine in form.[35] For a Christian after 1453 to enter the Ayasofya Mosque required permission and close supervision—the Freshfield Album artist, to whom we turn below, managed only two rushed and uncharacteristically inaccurate sketches of the interior[36]—but all travelers had access freely to the At meydanı, which had become a place to exercise horses, a destination for stately processions, and the location of various service buildings around the open space, including a stable, a menagerie, an armory, an archive, and various workshops.[37] In the empty grounds between these, the Serpent Column was left in place between the two obelisks of masonry and granite. Consequently, standing on a virtually bare median which had not yet been robbed of its masonry, the column could be seen by all and came to be reported on and sketched by visitors.

The Serpent Column does not appear in some famous panoramas and conspectuses of the city, images that were produced for the first time in the fifteenth century. It cannot be seen in the earliest versions of Buondelmonti's bird's-eye view of the city, first drawn in 1422 and subsequently produced in thirteen versions. Each of these maps, becoming more elaborate, has its own perspective, and it is striking that the hippodrome, its obelisks, and between them a column, not obviously serpentine, are clearly visible in a drawing of ca. 1481, in a Düsseldorf manuscript of Buondelmonti (Universitäts- und Landesbibliothek MS G 13, fol. 541). This map, unlike its predecessors, acknowledges the Ottoman presence in the city, and features all the major architectural projects undertaken by Mehmed II and his viziers.[38] The Serpent Column is not depicted in Vavassore's woodcut *Byzantium sive Costantineopolis*, dated to 1535, although

---

[33] Gilles II. 13, quoted above. The translation at Ball 1729: 111–12, is rather too free to be useful.

[34] This was probably after 1440, according to Smith 1987.

[35] Brown and Kleiner 1983; Stichel 1997: 328.

[36] Freshfield 1922: 89; Mango 1965: 306.

[37] Necipoğlu 1991: 46.

[38] Kafescioğlu 2009: 148–50, esp. fig. 111. That the column between obelisks is not the Serpent Column is clear from a detail of the Düsseldorf map reproduced at Necipoğlu 2010: 267, fig. 6.

Constantine's Column is entitled "Colona Serpentina."[39] There is no sign of the Serpent Column in any of the woodcuts in Hartmann Schedel's *Liber Chronicarum*, which first appeared in 1493, although the *sphendone* of the hippodrome and the two obelisks between are shown.[40] Nor is the column to be found in the grand 1559 panorama of the city by Melchior Lorichs (Lorck), where structures can be picked out from a viewpoint on the walls or tower of Galata across the Golden Horn (the artist is shown standing to the left in panel 11). Surviving Byzantine monuments, including Hagia Sophia (panel 6) and Constantine's Column (panel 8), are exaggerated in scale by Lorichs, as by others.[41] Surely, therefore, the hippodrome would have featured in the seventh panel (of twenty-one), which has suffered extensive damage, and perhaps the Serpent Column once appeared there.[42]

Pieter Coecke van Aelst's famous woodcut *Les moeurs et fachons de faire de Turcs* offers the earliest unequivocal sketch of the Serpent Column in situ, at least in the form of the original sketch made in 1533, although the woodcut blocks were not produced until two decades later (fig. 8.7). In its final blocks, the composite picture captures the appearance of the At meydanı in 1533, during the long reign of Süleyman I. At that time, a statue taken from Buda stood before the palace of Ibrahim Pasha. This mythical statue group stood for less than a decade, and was removed by those it offended shortly after the Grand Vizier's assassination, as Pierre Gilles described. The Serpent Column can be seen clearly in its correct location, between the obelisks to the right of the picture, immediately above the rump of the sultan's horse. However, the monuments of the hippodrome are rearranged to fit the composition. The viewpoint is from the south, with the walls and Tower of Galata framing the upper register of buildings. However, the hippodrome is reoriented from southwest to northeast, so that the viewer's eye is drawn from the sultan's procession along the line of the *euripos*, ending at the banked, curved *sphendone*. The heads of the serpents are rounded and project only slightly from the twisted column. Two heads are depicted in profile, the third from behind. The upper jaws of the two visible heads are drawn to resemble beaks, and it is possible that one or both lack lower jaws. The dolphin-like creatures are as impressionistic as the base of the Theodosian Obelisk, which is shown standing on its bronze corner supports and two bases. However, the upper base is here blank and smaller than the lower base, on which one can discern some human figures, perhaps engaged in a race, perhaps representing statues. Two sides of each obelisk are visible, and the hieroglyphs of Thutmose III are rendered freely, including another dolphin-like creature swimming above two waves beneath a crescent

---

[39] Kafescioğlu 2009: 154–64, 251–5. For a zoomable image of Vavassore's map, see the online version of Westbrook, Dark, and van Meeuwen 2010: fig. 4.
[40] Berger and Bardill 1998; Kafescioğlu 2009: 164–7.
[41] Mango and Yerasimos 1999; Westbrook, Dark, and van Meeuwen 2010.
[42] Westbrook, Dark, and van Meeuwen 2010: 72.

FIGURE 8.7 Pieter Coecke van Aelst's woodcut, *Les moeurs et fachons de faire de Turcs*. The Serpent Column can be seen clearly in its correct location, between the obelisks to the right of the picture, immediately above the rump of the sultan's horse. Trustees of the British Museum.

moon and an owl. One cannot, therefore, imagine that the Serpent Column is rendered exactly as it then appeared. However, and remarkably, the opening at the base of the column through which water once flowed can be seen, and the coils become slacker as one moves up the column. There are twenty-six coils beneath the necks, and a robed figure standing beside the column, as if to offer a sense of scale, reaches to the top of the sixteenth coil, a little under half the height of the column, therefore more than three meters tall.

The Serpent Column can be seen in a woodcut map of Constantinople that illustrates Salomon Schweigger's travels, on page 102 of the Nuremberg edition, and in a separate illustration of four monuments (page 123), where it is marked as C alongside the Column of Constantine (A), the Theodosian Obelisk (B), and the Column of Arkadios (D). Each monument earns its own description. Schweigger's journey took place in 1578, but the book was printed only thirty years later.[43] Further descriptions and representations are well covered in an important article by Rudolph Stichel, including those of the Hungarian Johannes Belsius, who counted the column's thirty spirals, and Jérôme Maurand of Antibes, whose sketch shows two snakes winding loosely around a third snake, his straight body forming a central pillar.[44] The Serpent

---

[43] Schweigger 1613; Ménage 1964: 170.
[44] Stichel 1997: 330–1.

FIGURE 8.8 Hagia Sophia and monuments of the hippodrome, as they appeared in 1574. Freshfield Album, Wren Library, Trinity College, Cambridge, MS 0117.2, fol. 21. Master and Fellows of Trinity College Cambridge.

Column was illustrated in several editions of works by the French cosmographer André Thevet, rather similarly in woodcuts published in 1555 and 1617, but rather differently in a more splendid illustration of 1575.[45]

In 1574, an anonymous artist, occasionally identified as Lambert de Vos from Mechelen, sketched the Serpent Column twice.[46] Both sketches are contained within the Freshfield Album, held in the Wren Library, Trinity College, Cambridge (MS 0117.2).[47] In the first instance (fol. 21), the column is placed between the two obelisks, which together form the right-hand portion of a composite sketch juxtaposing the key monuments of the hippodrome with Hagia Sophia and adjacent buildings (fig. 8.8). The viewpoint is as if from the west, looking from the location of Ibrahim Pasha's palace (see below) back across the At meydanı towards Ayasofya, with the distance between the two

---

[45] Stichel 1997: 334–6, reproduces all three with commentary (figs. 3, 4, 5)

[46] Freshfield 1922: 89 identifies the artist by a note he wrote on the back of one sketch as a German who traveled with David Ungnad, the imperial envoy of Maximilian II to Constantinople. Freshfield suggests the sketches were made by or for Ungnad's chaplain, Stefan Gerlach. Lambert de Vos, a Flemish artist who visited Istanbul at exactly this time, produced a costume book, now in the University Library of Bremen. See Stichel 1997: 337–8; Artan 2011: 152, 201; Faroqhi 2012: http://www.turksestudies.ugent.be/node/10

[47] I am extremely grateful to Sandy Paul, Sub-Librarian, for discussing the Freshfield Album and Dryden Costume Book with me and supplying several high-resolution images. See Madden 1992: 132–5. E. H. Freshfield (1922: 87), who donated the manuscript to Trinity, was unsure when and where his father acquired it, noting that he first referred to it in 1900. It is likely that it was purchased in 1883, when it was among the Towneley collection of manuscripts removed from Towneley Hall, Lancashire and sold at auction in London by Sotheby, Wilkinson, and Hodge, 27 June 1883. See http://www.towneley.org.uk/downloads/mss_1883sale.pdf.

locations telescoped dramatically. There are two headings in Latin, the first to the left of Hagia Sophia, which is depicted with two minarets, above a complex of buildings rendered in red brick and tile with several brown wooden balconies: "Part of the building of St. Sophia where now lions are kept, to the northern flank of the hippodrome" (*Pars aedificii S. Sophia ubi nunc leones seruantur. ad Hippodromi latus septentrionale*). This corresponds to Gilles' description of a menagerie housing the Sultan's lions, which has been identified as the former Church of St. John of the Diippion.[48] The second heading is placed centrally, above the hippodrome, whose northern flank is delimited by a long building with tiled roof and two doors, above each of which is a balcony, gable, and chimneys, extended by a long wall: "Location of the obelisk, of the three-headed bronze column, and the colossus in the hippodrome" (*Situs obelisci columnæ æneæ tricipitis et colossi in Hippodromo*).[49] Once again, the terms used correspond closely to those employed by Gilles, and beneath the sketch one finds a reference to "Gilles, Book 2, chapter 11" (*Gil: lib: 2. cap: ii*), where a description of the hippodrome's monuments begins. The relative heights of the three monuments are rendered accurately, with the Masonry Obelisk, the so-called "colossus," overtopping the Theodosian Obelisk, and the Serpent Column reaching to around half the height of the latter. The sketches of both the west-facing hieroglyphs and the scene of submission on the obelisk base are identifiable and accurately rendered, leading one to give great credence to the depiction of the Serpent Column. Again, the opening at the base of the coils is shown, extending up to the top of second coil from the right, which is the third coil counting from the right, exactly as it is today (fig. 1.3, above). Thirty coils are shown before the neck of the rightward-looking serpent projects out from the column, with its pair to the left forming a gentle U-shape bisected by the central neck, such that one appears to see the Greek letter Ψ. Each serpent sports a beard formed from small spikes, an arched eyebrow over an eye, and an open mouth.

The form of the Serpent Column as seen by the anonymous artist in 1574 is clarified in a second, far more detailed, sketch (fol. 6, fig. 8.9). Once again, the column is colored gold and seems almost to shimmer, but otherwise the rendering appears to be realistic and replete with important details. There are thirty coils, at first in a tight spiral but relaxing gently as they ascend to the three heads and as the column narrows. The serpent necks project to around three times the width of the column, each ending in an open-jawed head. The

---

[48] Gilles II.23: "ubi iam leones Regis stabulantur"; it in unclear why Ball 1729: 153 translates this as "[this was the church] where the elephants of the Grand Seignor are now stabled." See Mango 1950; Mango 1986: 59; Bardill 1997: 89–95; Westbrook, Dark, and van Meeuwen 2010: 71–2; Artan 2011: 158–66.

[49] In fact, the word "aeneae" is partly hidden within the fold of the page and damaged, although the term, here in the genitive, can be determined by comparison with the larger sketch and the "æne" can be seen clearly.

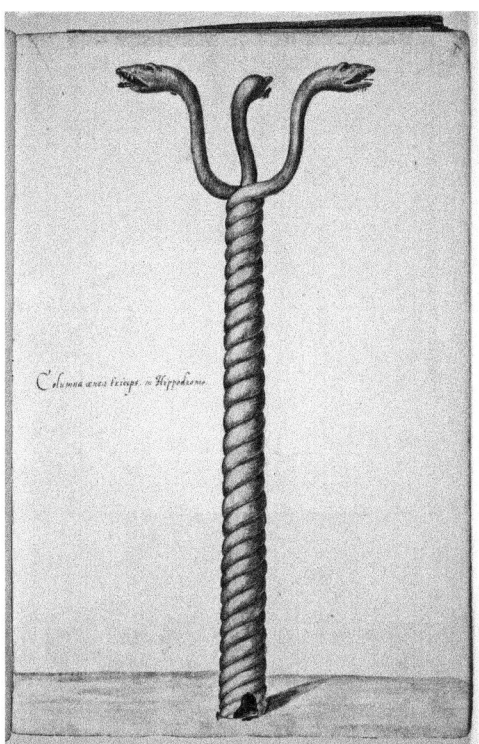

FIGURE 8.9 Drawing of the Serpent Column, as it appeared in 1574. Freshfield Album, Wren Library, Trinity College, Cambridge, MS O117.2, fol. 6. Master and Fellows of Trinity College Cambridge.

snake-head looking to the right is complete, with a lower jaw sporting three bristles or barbs as a beard and three teeth on either side of the upper jaw. What appears to be a tongue projects from the mouth, painted in a darker shade and not obviously attached to the mouth. A similar but less delicately rendered tongue darts from the serpent looking to the left. Once again, three sharp teeth descend from each side of the upper jaw, although the end of the lower jaw, with its barbed beard, is missing. The arch of the serpent's eyebrow and the eye beneath is also less distinctly drawn that that on the right, and no eyebrow is visible on the third head, which looks backwards and resembles a duck more than a snake, albeit with three strands of a beard on its extant lower jaw. A label identifies the "Three-headed bronze column in the Hippodrome" (*Columna ænea triceps. in Hippodromo*).

A far more fanciful column also stands alone on a green hillock in the pages of the Dryden Costume Album, Trinity College, Cambridge (MS R 14.23, sixteenth century).[50] Painted in blue with golden and black accents on the coils and up the necks and snouts of the serpents, the monument is named as "The

---

[50] See Stichel 1997: 339–40.

FIGURE 8.10 Fantastic sketch of the Serpent Column. Dryden Costume Album, Trinity College, Cambridge, MS R 14.23, sixteenth century. Master and Fellows of Trinity College Cambridge.

Pillar of ye 3 serpents in Constantinople (of copper)" (fig. 8.10). Each serpent head sports two pointed ears, and a golden barb, almost a small tusk, ends each snout. Both upper and lower jaws, all shown intact, have two teeth, although that on the left-facing head has three on its upper jaw. From each open mouth thrusts a prominent red tongue, licking upwards. Only the right-facing serpent has a clear eye, with a white pupil distinct, whereas the right and central heads have only black dots and eyebrows. Slightly less fantastic is a watercolor of the Serpent Column in Ludolphus Stockheim's *Stammbuch*, where twelve coils can be seen decreasing in size towards three bird-like beaked serpent heads. A musical annotation on the same page, a fragment of a canon identified as added in Munich on 2 December 1594, provide a solid terminus ante quem for the illustration. Although German in origin and once in collections in Kiel, Hamburg, and Reetz, the *Stammbuch* is now in the Hermitage and has been associated with a number of works by Russian travelers to Constantinople's hippodrome recently studied by Yuri Pyatnitsky.[51]

---

[51] Pyatnitsky 2011, which offers a useful overview of manuscripts in the Hermitage collection that are not easily accessible with original translations from them. I am grateful to Paul Magdalino for drawing this article to my attention and supplying me with a copy.

Ottoman Miniatures

The At meydanı, and within it the Serpent Column, can be picked out clearly in a miniature map of Constantinople and Pera in the manuscript of *Mecmu-ı Menazil*, "Compilation of the halting places" of Süleyman I on his eastern campaign of 1535–7.[52] Known more fully as *Beyan-ı Menazil-i Sefer-i Irakeyn* (Istanbul University Library, T. 5964), the manuscript, with 107 illustrations, is generally dated to 1537–8. The accuracy of detail in many of the maps has commended it to scholars of architecture as well as historians and art historians, and the map of Istanbul features more than 200 edifices, most of which can be identified.[53] However, an architectural shorthand is employed, such that many Byzantine buildings are rendered according to type, for example Hagia Irene resembles the idea of an Orthodox church. The artist aimed for topographical accuracy generally, and specific accuracy for mosques and other unique monuments, such as those in the At meydanı.[54]

From the middle years of the sixteenth century onwards, an increasing number of richly illustrated books were produced by an official court historian, the *şehnameci*, an office introduced by Süleyman I.[55] The earliest *şehnameci*s composed in Persian, modeling their compositions on Firdowsi's *Shahnama*, an eleventh-century epic in Persian *mesnevi* form. His works were, therefore, called *şehname*s, "Books of Kings," after their model, but also because they were produced for the sultans as records of their deeds. Drafts were produced by the *şenameci* to be approved by a committee prior to the production of lavishly illuminated copies for the exclusive use of the sultan and his court. Each book might take a full decade to produce. There is no evidence that the *şehname*s circulated at all beyond the confines of the palace, and certainly they did not influence early Ottoman historiography.[56] From 1569, the *şehnameci* was Seyyid Lokman, whose works have been preserved at the Topkapı Palace Library. The chief illuminator of Lokman's *şehname*s was Nakkaş Osman, although other illustrators have been identified.[57] Lokman wrote and oversaw the illustration of several of the most remarkable surviving Ottoman illuminated works, notably the *Shahanshahnama* (*Şehinşehname*), the "King's Book of Kings," composed to eulogize the reign of Murad III, and *Hünername*, the "Book of Skills," recording imperial deeds stretching back to the conquests by Mehmed II. Both works feature depictions of the Serpent Column in the At meydanı.

---

[52] Gabriel 1928: 337, no. 3k; Denny 1970: 57, no. 21 (who identifies the Serpent Column as Gabriel 3n, a "colonne votive"). See also Avcıoğlu 2008.
[53] Gabriel 1928 and Denny 1970 both provide catalogues.
[54] Denny 1970: 50–1. Both Atasoy 1974: II, 750–1; III, pl. 243, and Yenişehirlioğlu 2010: 112, fig. 1, offer details highlighting the At meydanı. Tükel 2010 commends Denny's study and notes that the third courtyard of the Topkapı Palace has been relocated across the Golden Horn.
[55] Woodhead 2007, summarizing her earlier work on the office; Fetvacı 2013: 15–20, 65.
[56] Woodhead 2007.
[57] Fetvacı 2013: 65–74, on authors and teams.

The *Hünername*, a work in two volumes commenced under Süleyman I but completed only in 1584 and 1588 (Topkapı Palace Museum Library H.1523, 1524), features several illustrations of the At meydanı. What appears to be an aerial view of the imperial city, fol.158b–159a, is in fact two vistas, from the walls at Galata in the north and, presumably, aboard a ship off the southern coast, both looking towards the promontory. Where the viewpoints meet, a horizontal axis that runs just to the north of the hippodrome, the orientation of the buildings depicted flips. The map offers tiny representations of the defining monuments of the At meydanı, namely the two obelisks and, between them, the Serpent Column (fig. 8.11). These are far less clear than the many minarets and domes of mosques picked out in gold leaf. However, the monuments are illustrated frequently in the *Hünername* in larger format in scenes set in the At meydanı. In a scene depicting festivities staged in 1530, to mark the circumcisions of the sultan's sons, a scramble for dishes takes place at the At meydanı. The foreground of the miniature is dominated by both obelisks, with men clambering to their tops. A tall pole has been planted next to the Theodosian Obelisk so that a third climber can ascend it. Between the obelisks stand two pillars, their capitals empty, and the Serpent Column, which is shown with its three snake heads rising, earless, high above the coiled pillar, pointing outwards and upwards, each mouth open, and the lower jaw of the right-facing serpent

FIGURE 8.11 *Hünername*, Topkapı Palace Museum Library H.1523, fol.158b–159a, offers tiny representations of the defining monuments of the At meydanı, namely the two obelisks and, between them, the Serpent Column. Photo: author.

apparently missing.⁵⁸ The Serpent Column is also depicted several times in the second volume of the *Shahanshahnama* (*Şehinşehname*), whose two volumes were completed in 1581 and 1592; for example, a distribution of coins by the sultan, and a display of fireworks, both in the At meydanı in 1582 by the fifth vizier Mehmed Pasha (Topkapı Palace Museum Library B. 200, vol. 2, fols. 51a and 59a).⁵⁹ Folio 46a shows vizier Siyavuş Pasha's fireworks. The Serpent Column is placed front and center between the two obelisks and surrounded by statuesque confections ready to explode with light and sound. The serpent heads have open jaws and ears.⁶⁰

The festivities of summer 1582 are placed in their fullest context in the *Surname-i hümayun* ("Book of Imperial Festivals"), also known as the *Surname* of Murad III (Topkapı Palace Museum Library H.1344, an illuminated copy, one of four known versions).⁶¹ The *Surname* was begun in 1582 but completed only in 1589, to record and illustrate the festivities that attended the circumcision of Murad's son, the future Mehmed III. The illustrated manuscript, which is now missing around seventy pages, features 427 illuminations (215 double folios) detailing the events that took place over more than fifty days in early summer 1582, consisting of many and varied processions in the At meydanı by the imperial party and their subjects, including the janissaries and the city's various orders of merchants and craftsmen.⁶² Dignitaries from courts across Europe were invited to attend the events that commenced late in May 1582, and several left eyewitness accounts to compare to the panegyrical *Surname*. The fullest account, by Nicholas van Hanoulth, reports on diverse ritual performances in the At meydanı, including on each day the circumcisions of up to 150 Christian converts to Islam,⁶³ and entertainments, including mimes and puppetry, conjuring and juggling, strong men and animal acts, and much music and noise.⁶⁴ Every night there were displays of fireworks, including on one occasion a show devised by the enslaved English gunner Edward Webbe, who recounts that "I my selfe was there constrained to make a cunning peece of fire work framed in form to like to ye Arke of Noy, beeing 24 yardes high, and eight yardes broade, wherein was placed 40 men drawen on 6 wheeles, yet no man seene, but seemed to goe alone, as though it were onely drawen by two Fiery Dragons, in which shew or Ark there was thirteene thousand seuerall peeces of fire worke."⁶⁵

---

⁵⁸ See Pitarakis 2010: II, 76.

⁵⁹ Terzioğlu 1995: figs. 8 and 2.

⁶⁰ Illustrated at Fetvacı 2013: 182, fig. 4.19.

⁶¹ Traditionally ascribed to Lokman, but a note in epilogue identifies the author as from Foča in Hercegovina, whereas Lokman was from Urmiya, Azerbaijan: see Terzioğlu 1995: 97, n. 3. Woodhead 2007: 75 calls the author "anonymous." Fetvacı 2013: 70–1, 176–7, identifies him as the chancery scribe Intizami under instruction and direction by Mehmed Agha, the chief black eunuch, and Zeyrek Agha.

⁶² Stout 1966; Terzioğlu 1995; Yerasimos 2000.

⁶³ Nicolas von Hanoulth: 476, cited at and quoted from Stout 1966: 14, 269–70.

⁶⁴ Stout 1966: 106–205.

⁶⁵ Edward Webbe, ed. Arber 1895: 28–9

There were many spectacles staged, including, on the evening of 14 June 1582, a duel between St. George and the Dragon. The *Surname* offers an account of the fire-snorting dragon; according to Hanoulth, this was performed by the Christian slaves of the late Sokullu Mehmed Pasha, grand vizier until his murder in 1579. They "presented the knight St. George, whom they also consider a saint ... Then came the dragon, which spat fire, carried by one man, of whom one could see only his legs."[66] As the denouement of the duel, according to another German visitor's *Particular Beschreybung*, a virgin (*jungefräwlin*)—presumably a Christian man in drag—emerged from the split belly of the dragon, a veritable St. Marina, no longer saved by her own piety and the sign of the cross.[67] Ottoman, and especially imperial, onlookers may have interpreted the tableau differently, recognizing in it an allusion to the murder by stabbing of the Grand Vizier, who had lost the sultan's favor for opposing his war with the Safavids of Persia. Others may have recalled a tale from the fourth book of Firdowsi's original *Shahnama*, where Gushtasp slew the dragon and won the hand of the daughter of the Caesar of Rum, celebrating with a display of his mounted skills before Caesar's box in the hippodrome. As a circumcision gift, the third vizier Siyavuş Pasha had presented to Murad and Mehmed two illustrated copies of Firdowsi's *Shahnama*.[68]

The sultan and prince also marveled, like Caesar, at acts of horsemanship in the hippodrome. On 11 July, according to a letter preserved in the state papers of Elizabeth I sent by Her Majesty's Ambassador in Constantinople, "After midday appeared in the field 100 horsemen," who set up balls on masts as targets.

> The horseman rode straight for them, and at the beginning of the course drew his sword, aimed a blow at the log, at once replaced his sword, shot an arrow at the ball on the mast, and at once taking another from his quiver shot it at the other mark, almost as the course was ending ... Two others in several courses did wonderful things. They threw darts standing upright on the saddle, and then with their head on the saddle and their feet in the air. Then they turned somersaults from the croup to the saddle and back. The courses were all at full speed; and those who bore themselves thus honourably had many presents from his Majesty, who was all the time intent upon all these things.[69]

The spectacles all took place in the shadow of the Serpent Column beneath the imperial balcony.[70] Illustrations that accompany the descriptions of the

---

[66] Nicolas von Hanoulth: quoted from Stout 1966: 210–12. See also Terzioğlu 1995: 99, n. 55.

[67] *Particular Beschreybung*, a German account published in 1583, which can be seen at: http://aleph.library.uu.nl/F?func=direct&doc_number=000978258.

[68] Woodhead 2007: 73. The dragon, which was depicted at *Surname* fol. 351a, uniquely has been obliterated by a later reader of the work. See Atasoy 1997: 113.

[69] *Calendar of State Papers, Foreign Series, May–December 1852*: 170–88. The scene is illustrated at *Surname* fol. 42b–43a. See Atasoy 1997: 42–43, 116–17.

[70] See chapter five for St. Marina and some further instances of dragon combat.

FIGURE 8.12 Palace of Grand Vizier Ibrahim Pasha, built 1524, under renovation, opposite the Serpent Column in Istanbul. Photo: author.

festivities in Murad III's *Surname* show the sultan, attended by the prince and two attendants, seated in his loggia, placed in the upper left-hand corner of the composition. The sultan's balcony was opposite the former location of the imperial *kathisma*, that is to say facing the Serpent Column now from the west. Since 1524, this had been the site of a palace constructed for Grand Vizier Ibrahim Pasha (fig. 8.12).[71] For that reason, in many of the *Surname's* illustrations the Serpent Column is depicted in the foreground, a constant feature of the sultan's view of the festivities, and also of the view of the onlooker gazing at the events in the At meydanı from ground level, and watching the sultan and dignitaries as they watched from above.

At fol. 14b–15a, the Seyyids, descendants of the Prophet, arrive in the At meydanı wearing their distinctive green turbans, with long robes, their sleeves reaching to the ground, the oldest sporting white beards.[72] An inversion of this scene is offered at fol. 276b, where fools mock the Safavids, enemies of the sultan, and defile their white turbans, placing them on the buttocks of a bent-over buffoon. A more obvious juxtaposition is shown at fol. 390a, where a solemn performance of the Mevlevi ritual is placed beside a *çengi* dance, performed by

---

[71] Atasoy 1974: 753–4, pl. 252. Today the palace is home to the Turkish and Islamic Arts Museum.
[72] Atasoy 1997: 30–1.

a boy dressed as a woman. All take place around the Serpent Column beneath the sultan's gaze. At fol. 367a, the space between the sultan and Serpent Column is occupied by a model of a coffee shop on wheels, highlighting the introduction of these enterprises into the city as recently as the 1550s. At fol. 57a, fruit-sellers, a more traditional enterprise, are in the place of the coffee-sellers, with no such wondrous and newfangled shop-on-wheels. At fol. 327a, bird-sellers carrying cages process between the Serpent Column and the imperial balcony, whither one escaping bird flies; a child on the balcony reaches out to grab it (fig. 8.13).[73] Fol. 338b–339a shows the grand procession with birds fashioned from paper above banners, the works of *peshtamal* makers.[74] Equally elaborate confections, now edible, dominate fol. 24b, with sugar sculptures in the forms of birds, wildcats, and mythical creatures.[75] At fol. 205b, jugglers and conjurers perform beneath the Serpent Column, no longer a fountain, although one conjurer "set a bowl on a stool and then by conjury caused it to spout water left and right like a fountain."[76]

Each composition in the volume comprises two parts: that on the left shows the sultan's pavilion, a tented balcony of the Ibrahim Pasha palace, and activities before it; that on the right shows the galleries raised for visiting dignitaries, who sit in order of precedence to observe the festivities. Emphasis is placed on the ever-changing activity by framing devices: the constant imperial presence in the left-hand corner of each composition is balanced by an unseen presence, that of the mothers of both Murad and Mehmed behind grilled or mesh windows in a separate tented pavilion, whose appearance changes frequently, but which always occupies the top right corner of the left-hand folio, pressing up against the central margin.[77] Balancing the sultan and sultanas, the Masonry Obelisk occupies the lower left corner beneath the imperial loggia, and in most, but not all, illustrations the Serpent Column is depicted in the lower right corner of the composition. The sultan is pictured seated in the center of his pavilion in an array of costumes, while his constant companions, the prince to his left and to his right two beardless eunuch attendants, stand, partially obscured, marginalized, their heads slightly bowed towards the sultan. On one occasion only, fol. 46b, the sultan stands to throw coins, and a skirmish ensues below him. This scene of disorder serves to highlight the order elsewhere.[78] The volume and its illustrations reflect the Ottoman ideal of order and hierarchy under the rightful ruler, an idea they shared with the Byzantine emperors they succeeded. In the three-tiered

---

[73] Terzioğlu 1995; Atasoy 1974: 754; Atasoy 1997: 110.
[74] Atasoy 1997: 78–9.
[75] Atasoy 1997: 34–5.
[76] Atasoy 1997: 66–7, with partial translation quoted here.
[77] Tükel 2010: 99 warns against reading these changes literally. "For example, the types of trees can change; the number of windows in the wall or the choice of color can vary. I[t is] a system where the same *signified* can be expressed with different *signifiers* on every page."
[78] Fetvacı 2013: 178–9.

stand that dominates the upper register on the right-hand folios, the guests are stacked according to their ranks, with Christians evident from their colored hats, not white turbans, always placed in the lowest tier nearest to the door.

Although in the foreground, the Serpent Column is never drawn to scale. Frequently individuals are shown as almost the same height, drawing the viewer's gaze. The artist had considerable freedom to emphasize elements of his composition. The form of the Serpent Column is consistent but not identical in each of the scenes in which it appears. Two snake-heads always point toward the imperial balcony, another away from it. Generally it has eighteen, nineteen, or at most twenty tight, flat coils between the ground and the start of its three necks, which are shown rising high in a gentle arc almost echoing the shape of a tulip (fig. 8.13). The heads and jaws of the serpents are far more carefully drawn in the scene with buffoons and turbans (fol. 276b) than it that with coffee-sellers (fol. 367a), for example. Occasionally the serpents' teeth can be discerned, such as at fol. 290a, a procession of beggars and invalids, although here the coils, generally shown as tight and relatively flat, are loose and more vertical. There are only thirteen coils. The Serpent Column is most often painted as golden in color, but on occasion it is shown in green. Its changes of color echo those of the surface of the At meydanı, which is at times various shades of blue and green, pink and purple. This does not seem to reflect changes in lighting, for example darker hues later in the day. The column appears golden both in day scenes and in evening scenes, for example where one expects fireworks. The color changes are most simply explained as a further example of the freedom allowed to the artist. Thus, the hieroglyphs on the Theodosian Obelisk are always shown, and always shown differently.[79]

While the imperial presence is constant, there are several instances where the Serpent Column is absent.[80] On fol. 19a, musicians and singers are placed where the column would normally stand. The column is depicted neither at fol. 30a, a scramble for dishes, nor at fol. 33a, with glass-makers, nor at fol. 81b, with bath-cloth weavers, nor at fol. 245b, with coppersmiths. Frequently, where it is absent it is because the artist needs space to insert a magnificent confection, such as the glass-makers' mobile kiln, the copper-smiths' float, or the cloth-weavers' huge loom on wheels. Likewise, and most impressively (fol. 190b), those carrying a huge replica of the Süleymaniye Mosque are not obscured by the Serpent Column. Yet the coffee-house on wheels (fol. 367a) and the paper-glazers' (fol. 99b) wheeled platform both trundle past the column. In some cases, evidently, we are confronted with the artist's perspective, because the herdsmen (fol. 138b) gathered at the base of the Masonry Obelisk seem closer to the viewer and the sultan more distant, suggesting that the artist's viewpoint was between the column and obelisk. Hence, we do not expect to

---

[79] Tükel 2010: 106.
[80] Tükel 2010: 102–3, 110, fn. 16 explains the omissions as deliberate "arbitrariness."

230 } The Serpent Column

FIGURE 8.13 *Surname-i hümayun*, Topkapı Palace Museum Library H. 1344, fol. 327a, bird-sellers. Topkapı Palace Museum Library. Photo: After Atasoy 1997.

see the column as we do in other scenes. Yet the column appears in most scenes where animals are depicted, including those of mule-drivers (fol. 209b–210a) monkey-trainers (fol. 304a), dog-trainers (fol. 371a, 373a), bird-trainers (fol. 391a, 392b), and the roasting of an ox (fol. 19b–20a).[81]

Snake-charmers are depicted at fol. 103b–104a (fig. 8.14), which the *Surname* describes thus:

> Each one was the sort who could cajole a snake out of a hole. A skillful performer appeared with an arm full of snakes. They also brought in a huge barrel into which they stuffed handfuls of snakes. A man stripped to the waist and dressed in a waist-cloth then climbed into the barrel. He became as flesh and bone with those cold-blooded snakes as they in turn ringed his neck and body. Next the wardens rolled the barrel a distance with kicks and the snakes began to chase one another about. Then they opened the barrel and the man climbed out, still enveloped with snakes that writhed like demons there in the field. The people were astounded.[82]

---

[81] Atasoy 1997: 70–1, 109–10, 120.
[82] Atasoy 1997: 54–5.

FIGURE 8.14 *Surname-i hümayun*, Topkapı Palace Museum Library H. 1344, fol. 103b–104a, snake charmers. Topkapı Palace Museum Library. Photo: After Atasoy 1997.

The Ottoman court had moved to Edirne for much of the seventeenth century, returning to Istanbul only in 1703. Shortly afterward, the *Surname-i Vehbi* (Topkapı Palace Museum Library A.3593), the last illustrated Ottoman manuscript of its type, was commissioned for a sultan.[83] Produced between 1720 and 1730 for a celebration of the circumcisions of the sons of Ahmed III, the festivities lasted not fifty but fifteen days in 1720. The manuscript—written in Turkish, no longer Persian, by the poet Vehbi and illuminated by Abdülcelil Çelebi, better known as Levni ("Colorful")—has 137 illustrations in its 175 folios. It was copied by followers of Levni shortly after its completion, and today, quite unlike earlier *surname*s, it survives in twenty-five copies, two of which are fully illustrated. The festivities all took place away from the At meydanı, at the Ok meydanı, archery grounds overlooking the Golden Horn,

---

[83] Atıl 1993.

which were bedecked with tents, or in pavilions and on boats along the Golden Horn. Consequently, no depictions of the Serpent Column are presented, although by now it would have appeared quite different, for in 1700 the serpents had lost their heads.

Beheading the Serpents

We have read that Mehmed II was held to have attacked a single serpent with his battle mace. A version of this story circulated at least as early as 1550, and it continued to be reported by credulous travelers, including Salomon Schweigger (who visited in 1578), Jean de Thévenot (1655–6), and Gerard Hinlopen (1670), along with reports on the column's talismanic function.[84] By this time, the act of vandalism had also been attributed to another lover of bronze statuary, Ibrahim Pasha.[85] Further mutilators would be identified in local and travelers' accounts: Süleyman "the Magnificent" (r. 1520–66), Selim "the Sot" (r. 1566–74), and Murad IV (1623–40).[86] Süleyman is named by Pierre de Canaye, Selim by Evliya Çelebi, and Murad by some of the last travelers to see the heads attached, including Spon and Wheler.[87] Wheler was troubled by the name given by its inscription to the Masonry Obelisk, ΧΑΛΚΟC ΘΑΜΒΟC, "the brazen wonder," and conjectured that the bronze serpents may once have stood upon it, and thus would have "made a wonderful show." A schematic illustration of the Serpent Column, entitled the "brazen pillar," is supplied with a cross reference.[88] By this time, following the building of the Sultan Ahmed Camii ("Blue Mosque"), completed in 1609–10, so much soil had been piled up in the At meydanı that the Serpent Column projected only around 3.5 meters above the surface.[89] It would have been, in other words, far easier to imagine it atop the Masonry Obelisk, and also possible for a tall man to reach the base of the necks with a long axe or pick.

The last foreigner to see and report on the intact Serpent Column was Aubrey de la Mottraye, who referred to the conjecture, evidently a local tale, that the column may once have topped the so-called ΚΑΛΚΟC ΘΑΜΒΟC, translated as "Miracle of Brass" in the 1723 English version of Mottraye's travels. The author was aware of the account by Spon and Wheler, referring to absences in their work immediately before his description of the column. He offers also the correct solution to the brazen puzzle, that the Masonry Obelisk was formerly

---

[84] Schweigger 1613: 124; Ménage 1964: 169–70; Dell'Acqua 2013: 332–3; Strootman 2014: 440–1.
[85] Ménage 1964: 171, citing the legendary history as recast by Ali (ca. 1600).
[86] For the Ottoman accounts generally, see Frick 1857–60: 519–20; Casson et al. 1929: 1–4; Ménage 1964; Mansel 1970; Yenişehirlioğlu 2010. Strootman 2014: 440 reports that Hinlopen favored Murad IV.
[87] Ménage 1964: 172.
[88] Spon and Wheler 1682: 185.
[89] Müller-Wiener 1977: 68–9, 470; Stichel 1997: 345, 348.

clad with bronze plaques.⁹⁰ Mottraye observed the column's "three unfolded Heads, which form a Triangle on the Top of it, make some think it was made to sustain a *Tripos* of *Apollo*; and *Herodotus*, who says that the Golden *Tripode* at *Delphos* was supported by three Serpents Heads, confirm them in this Belief."⁹¹ An etching by Hogarth, plate 15 of the edition of Mottraye's work published in London in 1723, shows a "Procession through the hippodrome," passing the intact Serpent Column (fig. 8.15). Hogarth did not personally visit Istanbul.⁹²

"At the time of evening prayer," on a Wednesday evening, after sunset on 20 October 1700,

> all three of the bronze serpents in the At meydanı, which had stood firm for 1500 years, broke all together at their necks and fell to the ground; yet there is no question of their being struck, for there was nobody nearby. They broke with a noise as if a powerful man were chopping down trees and people who heard the noise reported what had happened.

This passage, translated by Ménage in a concise but rich study of the column in Ottoman sources, is taken from a detailed record of events, notably those in Istanbul, written by Fındıklılı Mehmed.⁹³ Evidently, reports that the heads had fallen reached those responsible for the public space only after the heads had been spirited away, and if the tale is to be believed, the serpents fell from metal fatigue, probably a weld failing after it had held for more than 2,000 years.⁹⁴ Yet if nobody was nearby, one might suggest, then nobody could deny that the ancient weld was given a little help. Certainly, when one inspects the upper jaw of a serpent preserved today in Istanbul Archaeological Museums, there are indications that the fracture was preceded by several blows with a sharp object, perhaps an axe (fig. 1.11, above). This may have happened as the heads all lay on the ground, and one can imagine locals appearing to grab what they could of the bronze. Quite how the surviving jaw ended up buried a short distance from the hippodrome, outside Hagia Sophia, also remains an unsolved mystery.⁹⁵

How the heads fell became a matter of speculation and rumor, and Mottraye reported a story that has been often misinterpreted. He begins with the arrival at the beginning of April 1700 of Count Lisinsky, Ambassador Extraordinary of the King and Republic of Poland, with a train of 600 men dressed in the chain mail taken from Turks defeated at the Siege of Vienna, in 1683. "Some

---

⁹⁰ Mottraye 1723: 196, spelling *chalkos* with a kappa in place of chi.
⁹¹ Mottraye 1723: 196, with italics, capitals, and grammar retained.
⁹² Stichel 1997: 341.
⁹³ Ménage 1964: 173, referring to the Silahdar named Fındıklılı Mehemmed, also called Mehmed Ağa.
⁹⁴ See Mansel 1970; Yenişehirlioğlu 2010: 126, fn. 26.
⁹⁵ Stichel 1997: 346–7, rightly questions a report of 1739 that fragments were taken into the palace. We do not follow the suggestion that an explosion may later have moved the extant serpent jaw.

FIGURE 8.15 William Hogarth, *A Procession through the Hippodrome*, plate 15 in A. de La Mottraye, *Travels through Europe, Asia, and into Part of Africa*, 2 vols. London 1723. Victoria and Albert Museum.

old *Spahis*," who had fought at Vienna, were offended by the spectacle, which one might imagine took place in the At meydanı, since the count was lodging at the Ibrahim Pasha palace. A second, graver offense was then given when a Muslim Pole, formerly in the count's service, who could not "renounce the love of wine and brandy" and twice visited his compatriots, on the second occasion was beheaded on the count's order and his body tossed into the At meydanı. Since the Turks could not prove the crime, they took the body and buried it quietly.[96]

> Some little time after, the two Heads remaining on the *Serpentine Pillar* were broken off, and carried away one dark Night, of which the *Turks* took no more Notice, than they had done of the Death of their Proselyte; and indeed I wonder their Antipathy for the Figures of any living Creatures had not made them take away the whole Column some Ages since, to melt it down for a Piece of Artillery. The *Franks* suspected that some of the Ambassador's Train had carried them off, and that was all.[97]

Mottraye's account is allusive. He does not say that the Serpent Column was damaged by the Poles, but merely that this was the interpretation of "some

---

[96] Mottraye 1723: 205–6.
[97] Mottraye 1723: 206.

Franks." He implies that one head had already disappeared, which no other source recounts (unless this is an allusion to the damaged lower jaw of one head), and that the damage to the remaining two heads was deliberate, although this is not stated unambiguously. Only carrying off the heads is clearly an active construction, and those who made off with them need not be those who committed the violent act. Indeed, since the episode is offered to mirror the murder and surreptitious burial of a Muslim Pole, the reader might follow the Franks in inferring that the Poles beheaded the snakes and the Turks spirited away the evidence. Certainly, greater credence was accorded by later writers to the rumor spread by Mottraye's "Franks," who had blamed the followers of Count Lisinsky, than to the older tale of Mehmed's mace-blow.[98] According to the testimony of Anton Korfiz von Ulfeld, in 1739, two heads had been transferred to the sultan's palace. But this report also attributes the loss of the first head to Mehmed's mace-blow, and therefore is not to be taken as reliable.[99]

The Modern Hippodrome

The modern condition of the Serpent Column was remarked upon by Edward Daniel Clarke in 1800. "There is nothing grand or beautiful in the remains of the Brazen Column, before mentioned, consisting of the bodies of three serpents twisted spirally together." Its base was buried at that time beneath the surface layer of the At meydanı, so that it seemed to be "about twelve feet in height: being hollow, the Turks have filled it with broken tiles, stones, and other rubbish."[100] Clarke had an artist sketch the hippodrome in its current state, since, in his opinion, "no accurate view of it had been engraved." The engraving published in the second volume of his travels, in 1813, is a view from the western side of the At meydanı, apparently from just south of the Ibrahim Pasha Palace. It depicts a low wooden building of one or two stories erected in the center of the At meydanı, which appears almost to abut the Serpent Column.[101] Clarke stresses the accuracy of this new depiction, and the wall of the Sultan Ahmed Camii is indeed accurately depicted, although some decades later, when the first photographs of the At meydanı were taken, the wooden house to the east in Clarke's sketch had disappeared and houses crowded the three monuments from the west. In a photograph from 1850, taken by James D. Robertson (fig. 8.16), which is a view from the northeast, apparently from just outside the perimeter wall of the Sultan Ahmed Camii, houses are only a few meters from the Serpent Column, of which only the top thirteen or fourteen coils are visible

---

[98] Clarke 1813: 58; Newton 1865: 26; Grueber 1887. In an argumentative footnote to the second edition of his travels, Clarke scolds a reviewer who had attempted to correct his recounting of Mottraye.
[99] Stichel 1997: 347.
[100] Clarke 1813: 57.
[101] The engraving is inserted between pages 56 and 57 of Clarke 1813.

FIGURE 8.16 Photograph from 1850, taken by James D. Robertson, showing the Serpent Column, of which only the top fourteen coils are visible above the surface. Musée d'Orsay, Paris/Art Resource.

above the surface. Fifteen coils were, therefore, submerged.[102] The lower base of the Theodosian Obelisk is also partly submerged beneath the dusty ground, although the upper base is clear, while the base of the Masonry Obelisk is mostly beneath earth.

In 1855, C. T. Newton obtained permission to dig in the hippodrome. In a letter dated 26 November 1855, later incorporated into his *Travels and Discoveries in the Levant*, Newton observes: "Since I began this letter, I have been engaged in an excavation round the base of the famous brazen serpent in the Atmeidan, or Hippodrome. This serpent is a relic dating from remote antiquity, and has a very curious history," which he proceeds to recount in brief. Passing swiftly from Herodotos to Pausanias to Zosimos, Newton notes that,

> A succession of travellers, from the fifteenth century to our own day, have described the bronze serpent as standing in the Hippodrome; and the testimony in proof of its identity so completely satisfied the sceptical mind of Gibbon, that he declares that "the guardians of the most holy relics would rejoice if they were able to produce such a chain of evidence."

---

[102] Frick 1859: 491.

> The serpent was triple, being composed of three snakes intertwined … Signor Fossati, the architect who restored St. Sophia, in digging near the church found a bronze serpent's head without a lower jaw, which is believed to belong to the Delphic monument, and which is now preserved in the Museum of St. Irene, in the Seraglio.[103]

The Church of Hagia Irene, enclosed within the first court of the Topkapı Palace, was at that time used as a museum for antiquities, and two imperial porphyry sarcophagi remain in its environs. Permission to dig required an imperial firman, which Newton obtained through the longtime British ambassador to the Sublime Porte, Stratford Canning.[104] The digging, which took three days, was undertaken by "twelve lusty Croats, with picks and wooden shovels."[105] By uncovering the marble base of the pillar, Newton established that "the entire height of this monument from plinth to the highest spiral is nearly 18 feet."[106] The hole was later preserved by a retaining wall and surrounded by iron railings, which remain in place today.[107]

Newton was at that time British vice-consul in Mytilene, with a responsibility to identify, excavate, and, where possible, acquire classical treasures, many of which were brought to the British Museum. A leading Hellenist of his day, and founding member and first chairman of the Society for the Promotion of Hellenic Studies in the United Kingdom, Newton's interest was in all aspects of Hellenic history and culture, but more particularly in its material remains, notably epigraphy. Thus, Newton relates, "the idea of making the excavation in the Hippodrome was suggested to me by Lord Napier [first secretary to the ambassador in Istanbul], who thought that some inscription relative to this monument might be found on its base."[108] However, since Newton was rushing off to join a cruise, he did not find time to examine the base properly, and did not notice the inscription.[109] His trip led him to his greatest discovery, the Mausoleum of Halikarnassos, which he excavated in 1856–8. In January 1856, Otto Frick and P. A. Dethier examined the inscription at the base of the Serpent Column, making a plaster cast, and found that it "contains exactly what the statements of Thucydides and Herodotus would lead us to expect: the names of those Greek states which took an active part in the defeat of the Persians."[110]

---

[103] Newton II: 25–7.

[104] Unfortunately, no copy of the firman or any additional information on the excavation has been preserved among Newton's papers at the British Museum and British Library. I thank Graham Stewart for searching for them so diligently.

[105] Newton 1865: II, 27.

[106] Newton 1865: II, 28.

[107] Frick 1859: 489. The bases of the two obelisks were also cleared and treated in the same manner as the work continued, supervised by Lord Napier. Bourquelot 1865: 27, substitutes forty English soldiers for Newton's Croats.

[108] Newton 1865: II, 27. See also Frick 1859: 488.

[109] Newton 1865: II, 29.

[110] Newton 1865: II, 29.

So began the scientific study of the Serpent Column and its inscription, the history of which is sketched in our first chapter. As "a relic dating from remote antiquity," the headless column became once more compelling to travelers, who, with the advent of mass tourism, came in ever greater numbers. In the later nineteenth century, travel accounts, with their woodcuts and engravings, aimed at readers who would never replicate the adventures of the authors, gave way to guidebooks inviting tourists to board the new direct train link between western Europe and the exotic orient. The first Express d'Orient departed the Gare de l'Est of Paris in 1883, but terminated at Vienna until, from 1 June 1889 until 19 May 1977, the Orient Express connected Paris directly to Istanbul's Sirkeci station, a short uphill walk from Hagia Sophia and the hippodrome. To accommodate tourists, the area around the three monuments was transformed.[111] In 1890, *La Turquie* announced an imperial plan to create a public park with kiosks in each wing. Although this did not happen, in 1899 a new fountain was placed at the north end of the At meydanı, a gift of Kaiser Wilhelm II.[112] Finally, an approach was made to the French architect Joseph Antoine Bouvard, who was from 1900 inspector general of the architectural department of the city of Paris.[113]

The refurbishment of the At meydanı was to be part of the grand scheme for Istanbul, which was provoked by a tourist's complaint. The Ottoman ambassador to France reported the Sultan Abdulhamid II's feelings thus:

> This has been bothering me ... It is the translation of an article written on Istanbul by a European traveler ... [who] criticizes us vehemently for not planning and improving the places that catch a traveler's eye ... which could be made even more attractive than the shoreline of Nice and that of the Italian seaside cities; and for not cleaning and repairing the streets of the city.[114]

Bouvard was commissioned to produce a grand plan to satisfy the sultan and future European travelers to Istanbul. He accepted, although he professed to be far too busy to visit Istanbul, and rather than a master plan he produced impressionistic sketches from gazing at large photographs, which ignored the topography of the city. Pleasing to the sultan, Bouvard's sketches were presented as a gift of the French government. His recommendation to lower the surface to the level of the Byzantine hippodrome, with steps leading to a surrounding boulevard, was not implemented, but the central, symmetrical landscaped garden, evoking both the Place de la Concorde and the Byzantine *euripos*, was realized.[115] The emergence of the new vista can be seen in photographic

---

[111] It is a trope of modern tourism studies that "the purity of the monument must not be compromised by untidy surroundings." See Nelson 2003: 63.

[112] Çelik 1984: 343; Çelik 1986: 111.

[113] Nelson 2003: 66–8.

[114] Quoted in translation at Çelik 1984: 342; and Çelik 1986: 110. Also Nelson 2003: 67.

[115] Çelik 1984: 344; Çelik 1986: 112 reproduces the sketch, which also would have required the demolition of the Ibrahim Pasha Palace.

postcards produced for tourists. Whereas on early cards the bronze stump in the At meydanı was paired with local street merchants and fez-wearing urchins, later the well-dressed perambulated by, arm-in-arm or in vehicles, both horse-drawn and motorized.[116]

Tourists still gather in the hippodrome, frequently called Sultanahmet Square. Many disembark from coaches parked in the former Augustaion, in front of Hagia Sophia, and process towards the "German Fountain." On 12 January 2016, a suicide bomber targeted a group of tourists. Reports and photographs indicate that he detonated his bomb between the Serpent Column and Theodosian Obelisk, killing twelve people and injuring another fourteen.

---

[116] Ousterhout and Başgelen 1995: 58–61, 64–6.

Conclusion

The form of the Serpent Column, I have argued, is a Greek understanding and representation of the Near Eastern primordial combat myth: it is Typhon, a dragon defeated by Zeus, and also Python, the dragon-serpent slain by Apollo. The column was created after a battle where the sky was dominated by serpentine constellations and by the spiraling tails of our galaxy, the Milky Way, which may have inspired the form given to Typhon-Python. The column was erected as a votive, a thank-offering to Apollo at Delphi, and as a monument to the victory of the united Greek poleis (independent city-states) over an invading army of Persians. It is as a victory monument, I suggest, that the column was transplanted to Constantinople and erected opposite the Roman emperor's box in the hippodrome. The enduring meaning of the column as a monument to cosmic victory—not just any victory, but the defeat of the Persians by the Greek poleis; the defeat by Constantine of Licinius, his last pagan rival, and the foundation of Constantinople; the capture of Constantinople by the Ottomans—evoked for observers through centuries variants of the combat myth, in which a hero-god slays a dragon-serpent. Once located in Constantinople, the column took on many additional meanings. Through the Byzantine centuries, these interpretations were fundamentally Christian, drawing upon serpentine imagery in Scripture, patristic, and homiletic writings. When Byzantines saw the monument, they reflected upon this multivalent serpentine symbolism, but also upon the fact that it was a bronze column. For these observers, it evoked the Temple's brazen pillars Jachin and Boaz, Moses' brazen serpent, the serpentine tempter of Genesis (Satan), and the beast of Revelation, while also evoking Yahweh's struggle with Leviathan (Lotan). The column could thus be inserted into Christian sacred history, symbolizing creation and the end of chaos even as local lore held that it foretold the coming end times. The most enduring interpretation of the column, which is unrelated to religion and therefore survived the Ottoman capture of the city, is as a talisman against snakes and snakebites. It is this tale that was told by travelers to Constantinople throughout the Middle Ages, and it is this story that is told to tourists today who visit Istanbul.

BIBLIOGRAPHY

Throughout this book, authors and their works have been cited according to *OCD* and *ODB* conventions. The names of authors, and other individuals, are generally given in the forms cited in these standard reference works. However, I have always used an English form for a name that is in common usage (e.g. Apollo, not Apollon). For less common names, I have preferred a Grecized form for Greek names (e.g., Arsakios, not Arsacius) and a Latinized form for Latin names (e.g., Donatus not Donatos). I have not aimed for absolute consistency. I have not provided references to classical authors whose works appear in many editions, for example Herodotos, since there is a standard method of citation. The same cannot yet be said of early Christian and Byzantine writers. Translations are my own unless a modern translated is listed below or cited in a footnote. Occasionally, I have modified published translations into English, and indicate this on each occasion in a footnote. In a book that covers so much ground, it has proven impossible to cite every primary source fully. However, the list of secondary literature is intended to be comprehensive.

Abbreviations

AB	*The Art Bulletin*
AJA	*American Journal of Archaeology*
ANRW	*Aufstieg und Niedergang der römischen Welt*
BCH	*Bulletin de correspondance hellénique*
CP	*Classical Philology*
CQ	*Classical Quarterly*
CT	*Cuneiform Texts from Babylonian Tablets in the British Museum*, London 1896
DOP	*Dumbarton Oaks Papers*
DOS	*Catalogue of Byzantine Seals at Dumbarton Oaks and in the Fogg Museum of Art,* 6 vols., eds. N. Oikonomides and J. Nesbitt, Washington, DC
EI	*Encyclopaedia Iranica*, ed. E. Yarshater, London and New York, 1982–: http://www.iranicaonline.org/
GRBS	*Greek, Roman, and Byzantine Studies*
IDD	*Iconography of Deities and Demons in the Ancient Near East*: http://www.religionswissenschaft.uzh.ch/idd/index.php
JAOS	*Journal of the American Oriental Society*
JDAI	*Jahrbuch des Deutschen Archäologischen Instituts*
JNES	*Journal of Near Eastern Studies*

JRA   *Journal of Roman Archaeology*
LIMC   *Lexicon Iconographicum Mythologiae Classicae*, 8 vols., Zurich, Munich, and Düsseldorff, 1981–99
OCD   *Oxford Classical Dictionary*, 3rd ed., eds. S. Hornblower and A. Spawforth, Oxford 2005
ODB   *Oxford Dictionary of Byzantium*, 3 vols., eds. A. Kazhdan and A.-M. Talbot, Oxford 1991
PLRE   *The Prosopography of the Later Roman Empire*, 3 vols., eds. A. H. M. Jones and J. R. Martindale, Oxford
RE   *Realencyclopädie der classischen Altertumswissenschaft: Neue Bearbeitung*, eds. A. Pauly, H. Wissowa, et al., Stuttgart, 1894–1980

Partial List of Principal Primary Sources

Acta S. Marinae et S. Christophori, ed. H. Usener, *Festschrift zur fünften Säcularfeier der Carl-Ruprechts-Universität zu Heidelberg* (Bonn, 1886)

Analecta hymnica graeca e codicibus eruta Italiae inferioris, 13 vols., ed. I. Shirò (Rome, 1966–83)

Choniates, N. *Nicetae Choniatae Historiae*, ed. J.-A. Van Dieten, CFHB (Berlin and New York, 1975); trans. H. J. Magoulias, *O City of Byzantium: The Annals of Niketas Choniates* (Detroit, 1984)

Clavijo, R. *Narrative of the Embassy of Ruy Gonzalez de Clavijo*, trans. C. R. Markham (London, 1859)

Climacus, J. *The Ladder of Divine Ascent*, trans. C. Luibhead and N. Russell (New York, 1982), 286

Constantine the Rhodian. *Description des oeuvres d'art et de l'église des Saints Apôtres de Constantinople*, ed. E. Legrand (Paris, 1896)

Çelebi, E.. *Narrative of Travels in Europe, Asia, and Africa in the Seventeenth Century by Evliya Efendi*, trans. J. von Hammer (London, 1834)

Easter Chronicle. Chronicon Paschale, ed. L. Dindorf, CSHB (Bonn, 1832); trans. M. Whitby and M. Whitby, *Chronicon Paschale, 284–628 AD* (Liverpool, 1989)

Edward Webbe, Chief Master Gunner, His Travailes, 1590, ed. E. Arber (London, 1895)

Enūma Elish: The Seven Tablets of Creation, trans. L. W. King (London, 1902); trans. S. Dalley, *Myths from Mesopotamia*, rev. ed. (Oxford, 2009)

Enūma Anu Enlil: Enūma Anu Enlil, Tablets 50–51, eds. E. Reiner and D. Pingree (Malibu, 1981)

Epigrammata Bobiensia, ed. W. Speyer (Leipzig, 1963)

Giese, F. *Die altosmanischen anonymen Chroniken. Teil 1, Text und Variantenverzeichnis* (Breslau, 1922); *Teil 2, Übersetzung* (Leipzig, 1925).

Gilles, P. *Petrus Gyllius, De Topographia Constantinopoleos* (Lyon, 1562); *The Antiquities of Constantinople . . . written originally in Latin by Petrus Gyllius, a Byzantine historian*, trans. J. Ball (London, 1729)

Greek Anthology, ed. and trans. W. R. Paton, 5 vols. (Cambridge, MA and London, 1916–18)

Hesychios of Miletos. *Patria of Constantinople*, in Preger, *Scriptores*; trans. A. Kaldellis, Brill's New Jacoby: http://brill.nl/bnjo

Johann Schiltberger. *The Bondage and Travels of Johann Schiltberger*, trans. A. J. Buchan Telfer (London, 1879)

Kleterologion of Philotheos. N. Oikonomides, *Les listes de préséance Byzantines des IXe et Xe siècles* (Paris, 1972)

Liber Pontificalis, ed. L. Duchesne, 2nd ed., 3 vols. (Paris, 1955–7)

The Life of St. Andrew the Fool, ed. and trans. L. Rydén, 2 vols. (Uppsala, 1995)

The Life of St. Stephen the Younger: M.-F. Auzépy, *La vie d'Étienne le Jeune* (Aldershot, 1997)

Logothete's Chronicle: *Symeonis Magistri et Logothetae Chronicon*, ed. S. Wahlgren (Berlin and New York, 2006); ed. I. Bekker (Bonn, 1838)

Lyra Graeca, ed. and trans. J.M. Edmonds, 3 vols.(London and New York, 1924)

Malalas, J. *Ioannis Malalae Chronographia*, ed. J. Thurn, CFHB 35 (Berlin and New York, 2000); trans. E. Jeffreys, M. Jeffreys, and R. Scott, *The Chronicle of John Malalas* (Melbourne, 1986)

MUL.APIN. *MUL.APIN. An Astronomical Compendium in Cuneiform*, eds. H. Hunger and D. Pingree (Horn, 1989)

Nikandros. *Nicander, The Poems and Poetical Fragments*, ed. and trans. A. S. F. Gow and A. F. Schofield (Cambridge, 1953)

Oration to the Saints, trans. Mark J. Edwards, *Constantine and Christendom* (Liverpool, 2003)

Pseudo-Nonnus. A Christian's Guide to Greek Culture: The Pseudo-Nonnus Commentaries on Sermons 4, 5, 39 and 43 by Gregory of Nazianzus, trans. J. Nimmo Smith (Liverpool, 2001)

Panegyrici Latini. C. E. V. Nixon and B. T. Rodgers, *In Praise of Later Roman Emperors: The Panegyrici Latini* (Berkeley, Los Angeles, and Oxford, 1994)

Parastaseis. Constantinople in the Early Eighth Century: The Parastaseis Syntomoi Chronikai, eds. A. Cameron and J. Herrin (Leiden, 1984)

Patria. Preger, T. *Scriptores Originum Constantinopolitanarum, II: Pseudo-Codini Origines Continens* (Leipzig, 1907; repr. 1975). A. Berger, trans., *Accounts of Medieval Constantinople: The Patria* (Cambridge, MA, 2013)

Schweigger, S. *Ein newe Reiss Beschreibung auss Teutschland nach Constantinopel und Jerusalem* (Nuremberg, 1613)

Spon and Wheler. *A Journey into Greece, by George Wheler Esq; in company of Dr Spon of Lyons* (London, 1682)

Theodore Stoudites, *On the Holy Icons*, trans. C. P. Roth (New York, 1981)

Theophanes Continuatus, ed. I. Bekker, CSHB (Bonn, 1838)

William of Rubruck: *The Journey of William of Rubruck to the Eastern Parts of the World, 1253–55, as narrated by himself, with two accounts of the earlier journey of John of Pian de Carpine*. Trans. W. W. Rockhill (London, 1900)

Secondary Literature

Alcock, S. (2002) *Archaeologies of the Greek Past: Landscape, Monuments, and Memories*, Cambridge

Alföldi, A. (1943) *Die Kontorniaten*, 2 vols., Budapest; rev. ed. (1976, 1990) *Die Kontorniat-Medallions*, Berlin and New York

Anagnostakis, I., and A. Kaldellis (2014) "The Textual Sources for the Peloponnese, A.D. 582–959: Their Creative Engagement with Ancient Literature," *GRBS* 54: 105–35

Anderson, B. (2011) "Classified Knowledge: The Epistemology of Statuary in the *Parastaseis Syntomoi Chronikai*," *BMGS* 35: 1–19

Anderson, J. (1982) "The Sergalio Octateuch and the Kokkinobaphos Master," *DOP* 36: 83–114

Anderson, J. (1991) "The Illustrated Sermons of James the Monk: Their Date, Order, and Place in the History of Byzantine Art," *Viator* 22: 69–120

Andreae, B. (1988) *Laokoon und die Gründung Roms*, Mainz

Andreae, B. (1999) *Odysseus: Mythos und Errinerung*, Mainz

Angelidi, Ch. (1983) "La version longue de la vision du moine Cosmas," *Analecta Bollandiana* 101: 73–99

Angheben, M. (2002) "Les jugements derniers des XIe–XIIe siècles et l'iconographie du jugement immédiat," *Cahiers archéologiques* 50: 105–34

Amandry P. (1987) "Trépieds de Delphes et du Péloponnèse," *BCH* 111: 79–131

Amiet, P. (1973) "Glyptique Élamite, à propos de nouveaux documents," *Arts asiatiques* 26: 3–64

Ando, C. (2008) *The Matter of the Gods: Religion and the Roman Empire*, Chicago

Artan, T. (2011) "The Making of the Sublime Porte near the Alay Köşkü and a Tour of a Grand Vizierial Palace at Süleymaniye," *Turcica* 43: 145–206

Atasoy, N. (1974) "The Documentary Value of Ottoman Miniatures," in *Mansel'e Armağan— Mélanges Mansel*, Ankara, II, 749–53; III, pl. 243–54

Atasoy, N. (1997) *Surname-i Hümayun, 1582: An Imperial Celebration*, Istanbul

Atıl, E. (1993) "The Story of an Eighteenth-Century Ottoman Festival," *Muqarnas* 10: 181–200

Avcıoğlu, N. (2008) "Istanbul: The Palimpsest City in Search of its Architext," *RES: Anthropology and Aesthetics* 53/54: 190–210

Aymard, A. (1949) "Sur quelques vers d'Euripide qui poussèrent Alexandre au meutre," *Annuaire de l'Institut de philologie et d'histoire orientales et slaves* 9: 43–74 = *Mélanges H. Grégoire*, I, Brussels

Ágústsson, H. (1989) *Dómsdagur og helgir menn á Hólum*, Reykjavík

Balabanov, K., and C. Krstevski (1990) *Terakotni ikoni od Vinica*, Skopje

Bardill, J. (1997) "The Palace of Lausus and Nearby Monuments in Constantinople," *AJA* 101: 67–95

Bardill, J. (2010), "The Monuments and Decoration of the Hippodrome in Constantinople," in Pitarakis (2010), 149–84

Barnes, T. D. (2011) *Constantine: Dynasty, Religion and Power in the Later Roman Empire*, Oxford

Barnett, R. (1987) "The Serpent-Headed Tripod Base," in *Michael Avi-Yonah Memorial Volume*, ed. D. Barag, G. Foerster, and A. Neger, *Eretz-Israel* 19, Jerusalem

Barron, J. (1988) "The Liberation of Greece," in *The Cambridge Ancient History* IV, New Edition, Cambridge, 592–622

Bass, G. (1986) "A Bronze Age Shipwreck at Ulu Burun (Kaş): 1984 Campaign," *AJA* 90: 269–96

Bassett, S. (1991) "The Antiquities in the Hippodrome of Constantinople," *DOP* 45: 87–96

Bassett, S. (1996) "*Historiae custos*: Sculpture and Tradition in the Baths of Zeuxippos," *AJA* 100: 491–506

Bassett, S. (2004) *The Urban Image of Late Antique Constantinople*, Cambridge

Baun, J. (2007) *Tales from Another Byzantium: Celestial Journey and Medieval Community in the Medieval Greek Apocrypha*, Cambridge
Beaton, R. (1996) *The Medieval Greek Romance*, 2nd ed., London
Becatti, G. (1960) *La colonna coclide istoriata: Problemi storici, iconografici, stilistici*, Rome
Belozerskaya, M. (2012) *Medusa's Gaze: The Extraordinary Journey of the* Tazza Farnese, Oxford
Berger, A. (1988) *Untersuchungen zu den Patria Konstantinoupoleos*, Bonn
Berger, A. (2010) "Hippodrome in Folklore and Legend," in Pitarakis (2010), 194–205
Berger, A., and J. Bardill (1998) "The Representations of Constantinople in Hartmann Schedel's *World Chronicle*, and Related Pictures," *BMGS* 22: 2–37
Blaauw, S. de (2001) "Imperial Connotations in Roman Church Interiors. The Significance and Effect of the Lateran Fastigium," in *Imperial Art as Christian Art, Christian Art as Imperial Art*, eds. J. R. Brandt and O. Steen, Rome, 137–46
Boardman, J. (1961) *The Cretan Collection in Oxford: The Dictaean Cave and Iron Age Crete*, Oxford
Boardman, J. (1968) *Archaic Greek Gems*, London
Bock, C. (1857) "Zur Schlangensäule in Constantinopel," *Denkmäler, Forschungen und Berichte als Fortsetzung der Archäologischen Zeitung* 90, 1857: *Denkmäler und Forschungen* 100, 101, 102, April to June 1857: 48
Boedeker, D. (1995) "Simonides on Plataea: Narrative Elegy, Mythodic History," *Zeitschrift für Papyrologie und Epigraphik* 107: 217–29
Boeck, E. (2009) "Simulating the Hippodrome: The Performance of Power in Kiev's St. Sophia," *AB* 91: 283–301
Bouras, L. (1975–6) "Some Observations on the Grand Lavra Phiale at Mount Athos and its Bronze Strobilion (πίν. 44–51)," *Deltion tes Christianikes Archaiologikes Etaireias* 2: 85–96, pl. 43–51
Bouras, L. (1977) "Dragon Representations on Byzantine Phialae and Their Conduits," *Gesta* 16: 65–8
Bourquelot, F. (1865) "La colonne serpentine à Constantinople," *Mémoires de la Société Impériale des Antiquaires de France*, 3rd series, 8: 20–47
Boutsikas, E. (2011) "Astronomical Evidence for the Timing of the Panathenaia," *AJA* 115: 303–9
Boutsikas, E., and C. Ruggles (2011) "Temples, Stars and Ritual Landscapes: The Potential for Archaeoastronomy in Ancient Greece," *AJA* 115: 55–68
Brenk, B. (1964) "Die Anfänge der byzantinischen Weltgerichtsdarstellung," *BZ* 57: 106–26
Broilo, F. (2009) "'*Cleanses the sins with the water of the pure-flowing font*': Fountains for Ablutions in the Byzantine Constantinopolitan Context," *Revue des études sud-est européenes* 47: 5–24
Broodbank, C. (2013) *The Making of the Middle Sea: A History of the Mediterranean from the Beginning to the Emergence of the Classical World*, Oxford and New York
Brown, B., and D. Kleiner (1983) "Giuliano da Sangallo's Drawings after Ciriaco d'Ancona: Transformation of Greek and Roman Antiquities in Athens," *Journal of the Society of Architectural Historians* 42: 321–35
Brown, D. (2000) *Mesopotamian Planetary Astronomy-Astrology*, Cuneiform Monographs 18, Groningen
Brown, M. P. (2006) *In the Beginning: Bibles before the Year 1000*, Washington, DC

Bruns, G. (1935) *Der Obelisk und seine Basis auf dem Hippodrom zu Konstantinopel*, Istanbuler Forschungen 7, Istanbul

Bruun, P. (1966) *The Roman Imperial Coinage*, ed. C. Sutherland and R. Carson, vol. 7: *Constantine and Licinius, A.D. 313–337*, ed. P. Bruun, London

Buitron, D., B. Cohen, and N. Austin (1992) *The Odyssey and Ancient Art: An Epic in Word and Image*, Annendale-on-Hudson, NY

Cameron, A. (1973) *Porphyrius the Charioteer*, Oxford

Cameron, A. (1976) *Circus Factions: Blues and Greens at Rome and Byzantium*, Oxford

Cameron, A. (1993) *The Greek Anthology from Meleager to Planudes*, Oxford

Cameron, A. (2006) "Constantine and Christianity," in E. Hartley et al., eds., *Constantine the Great: York's Roman Emperor*, York, 2006, 96–103

Carpenter, R. (1945) "The Alphabet in Italy," *AJA* 49: 452–64

Cartledge, P. (2001a) "Spartan Kingship: Doubly Odd?" in P. Cartledge, *Spartan Reflections*, Berkeley and Los Angeles, 55–67

Cartledge, P. (2001b) "The Mirage of Lykourgan Sparta: Some Brazen Reflections," in P. Cartledge, *Spartan Reflections*, Berkeley and Los Angeles, 169–84

Cartledge, P. (2013) *After Thermopylae: The Oath of Plataea and the End of the Graeco-Persian Wars*, Oxford

Casson, S., et al. (1928) *Preliminary Report upon the Excavations Carried Out in the Hippodrome of Constantinople in 1927 on Behalf of the British Academy*, London

Casson, S. et al. (1929) *Second Report upon the Excavations Carried Out in and near the Hippodrome of Constantinople in 1928 on Behalf of the British Academy*, London

Chamoux, F. (1970) "Trépieds votifs à caryatides," *BCH* 94: 319–26

Chatterjee, P. (2014) "The Gifts of the Gorgon: A Close Look at a Byzantine Inkpot," *RES: Anthropology and Aesthetics* 65: 212–23

Chazelle, C. (2001) *The Crucified God in the Carolingian Era: Theology and Art of Christ's Passion*, Cambridge

Chazelle, C. (2011) "The Eucharist in Early Medieval Europe," in I. Levy, G. Macy, and C. Van Austall, eds., *A Companion to the Eucharist in the Middle Ages*, Leiden, 205–50

Cole, M. (1999) "Cellini's Blood," *AB* 81: 215–35

Cook, A. B. (1914–25) *Zeus: A Study in Ancient Religion*, 3 vols., Cambridge

Corvisier, J. N. (2011) *La bataille de Platées, 479 av. J.C.*, Clermont

Crow, J., J. Bardill, and R. Bayliss (2008) *The Water Supply of Byzantine Constantinople*, Journal of Roman Studies Monograph 11, London

Curtius, E. (1856) untitled ["Mittheilung über die Ausgrabung der Schlangensäule auf dem Hippodrom zu Constantinopel,"], *Monatsberichte der Königlichen Preussische Akademie des Wissenschaften zu Berlin*, 1856: 162–81

Cutler, A. (1968) "The *De Signis* of Nicetas Choniates: A Reappraisal," *AJA* 72: 113–18

Çelik, Z. (1984) "Bouvard's Boulevards: Beaux-Arts Planning in Istanbul," *Journal of the Society of Architectural Historians* 43: 341–55

Çelik, Z. (1986) *The Remaking of Istanbul: Portrait of an Ottoman City in the Nineteenth Century*, Berkeley

Dagron, G. (2011) *L'hippodrome de Constantinople: Jeux, peuple, politique*, Paris

Daim, F., ed. (2010) *Byzanz: Pracht und Alltag*, Bonn

Day, J. (1985) *God's Conflict with the Dragon and the Sea*, Cambridge

Day, J. W. (1995) "Interactive Offerings: Early Greek Dedicatory Epigrams and Ritual," *Harvard Studies in Classical Philology* 96: 37–74

Day, J. W. (2010) *Archaic Greek Epigram and Dedication*, Cambridge
Dark, K., and F. Özgümüş (2002) "New Evidence for the Byzantine Church of the Holy Apostles from Fatih Camii, Istanbul," *Oxford Journal of Archaeology* 21 (2002): 393–413
Dawkins, R. (1924) "Ancient Statues in Mediaeval Constantinople," *Folklore* 35: 209–48
Delivorrias, A. (2009) "The Throne of Apollo at the Amyklaion: Old Proposals, New Perspectives," in *Sparta and Laconia from Prehistory to Pre-modern*, eds. W. G. Cavanagh, C. Gallou, and M. Georgiadis, London, 133–5
Dell'Acqua Boyvadaoğlu, F. (2013) "Constantinople 1453: The Patriarch Gennadios, Mehmet the II and the Serpent Column in the Hippodrome," in *Synergies in Visual Culture: Bildkulturen im Diaog. Festschrift für Gerhard Wolf*, Munich, 325–38
Denny, W. (1970) "A Sixteenth-Century Architectural Plan of Istanbul," *Ars Orientalis* 8: 49–63
Denny, D. (1982) "The Last Judgment Tympanum at Autun: Its Sources and Meaning," *Speculum* 57: 532–47
Dethier, P., and A. Mordtmann (1864) "Epigraphik von Byzation und Constantinopolis," *Denkschriften der Kaiserlichem Akademie der Wissenschaften, Phil. Hist. Klasse* 13: 20–8
Diehl, C. (1929–30) "De quelques croyances byzantines sur la fin de Constantinople," *BZ* 30: 192–7
Dimitrova, N. (2002) "Inscriptions and Iconography in the Monuments of the Thracian Rider," *Hesperia* 71: 209–29
Dodd, E. C. (1968) "Byzantine Silver Stamps: Supplement II, More Treasure from Syria," *DOP* 22: 141–9
Downey, G. (1951) "The Builder of the Original Church of the Apostles at Constantinople: A Contribution to the Criticism of the *Vita Constantini* Attributed to Eusebius," *DOP* 6 (1951): 51–80
Doyle, J. (2009) "The Rocky Statue: 1980–2009," *PopHistoryDig.com*, 20 July 2009: http://www.pophistorydig.com/topics/tag/rocky-statue-philadelphia-art-museum/
Ducat, J. (1964) "Périrrhantèria," *BCH* 88: 577–606
Dungan, D. L (2007) *Constantine's Bible: Politics and the Making of the New Testament*, Minneapolis
Edwards, R. B. (1979) *Kadmos the Phoenician: A Study in Greek Legends and the Mycenaean Age*, Amsterdam
Edwards, K., G. Chase, H. Fowler, and D. Robinson (1933) "Coins, 1896–1929," *Corinth* 6: 1–172
Eldem, E. (2012–13) "The Archaeology of a Photograph: Philipp Anton Dethier and His 'Group for the History of Greek Art,'" *JDAI* 127–8: 499–530
Elsner, J. (2003) "Iconoclasm and the Preservation of Memory," in Nelson and Olin (2003): 209–31
Fabricius, C. (1886) "Das plataïsche Weihgeschenk in Delphi," *JDAI* 1: 175–91
Faustoferri, A. (1993) "The Throne of Apollo at Amyklai: Its Significance and Chronology," in *Sculpture from Arcadia and Laconia: Proceedings of an International Conference Held at the American School of Classical Studies at Athens, April 10–14, 1992*, eds. W. Coulson and O. Palagia, Oxford, 159–66
Fears, J. R. (1981) "The Theology of Victory at Rome: Approaches and Problems," *ANRW* II.17.2: 736–826
Fetvacı, E. (2013) *Picturing History at the Ottoman Court*, Bloomington and Indianapolis

Flood, F. B. (2006) "Image against Nature: Spolia as Apotropaia in Byzantium and the dār al-Islām," *The Medieval History Journal* 9/i:143–66
Flower, M. (1998) "Simonides, Ephorus, and Herodotus on the Battle of Thermopylae," *CQ* 48: 365–79
Flower, M., and J. Marincola (2002) *Herodotus, Histories, Book IX*, Cambridge
Fontenrose, J. (1959; 1980) *Python: A Study of Delphic Myth and its Origins*, Berkeley
Forsyth, N. (1987) *The Old Enemy: Satan and the Combat Myth*, Princeton
Fowden, G. (1987) "Nicagoras of Athens and the Lateran Obelisk," *JHS* 107: 51–7
Fowden, G. (1991) "Constantine's Porphyry Column: The Earliest Literary Allusion," *JRS* 81: 119–31
Frazer, J. G. (1898) *Pausanias's Description of Greece*, vol. 5, *Commentary on Books IX, X, Addenda*, London
Freshfield, E. H. (1922) "Notes on a Vellum Album Containing Some Original Sketches of Public Buildings and Monuments, Drawn by a German Artist Who Visited Constantinople in 1574," *Archaeologia: Miscellaneous Tracts Relating to Antiquity* 72: 87–104
Frick, O. (1856) "Die Inschriften der Schlangensäule im Hippodrom zu Constantinopel," *Archäologischer Anzeiger* [zur Archäologischen Zeitung 14, 1855] 90, June 1856: 217–24
Frick, O. (1857), photographic presentation to the Berlin Academy noted in "Wissenschaftliche Vereine," *Archäologischer Anzeiger* [zur Archäologischen Zeitung 15, 1856] 90, October–November 1857: 97–100
Frick, O. (1857–60) "Das plataeische Weihgeschenk zu Konstantinopel," *Jahrbücher für classische Philologie, Dritter Supplementband*, Leipzig
Frothingham, A. L. (1888) "Early Bronzes Recently Discovered on Mount Ida in Krete," *AJA* 4: 431–49
Frothingham, A. L. (1916) "Babylonian Origins of Hermes the Snake-god, and of the Caduceus, I," *AJA* 20: 175–211
Gabriel, A. (1928) "Les étapes d'une campagne dans les deux Irak d'après un manuscrit turc du XVIe siècle," *Syria* 9: 328–49
Galavaris, G. (1979) *The Illustrations of the Prefaces in Byzantine Gospels*, Vienna
Garrison, M. (2009) "God on a Serpent Throne," in *IDD*
Gauer, W. (1968) *Weihgeschenke aus den Perserkriegen*, Istanbuler Mitteilungen Beiheft 2, Tübingen
Gauer, W. (1991) *Die Bronzegefässe von Olympia: Mit Ausnahme der geometrischen Dreifüsse und der Kessel des orientalisierenden Stils*, Olympische Studien 20, Berlin
Gebele, E. (1932–3), "Die Pilgerreise des augsburger Domherrn Wolf von Zülhart nach dem Heiligen Lande 1495/96," *Zeitschrift des historischen Vereins für Schwaben und Neuburg* 50: 51–180
Gee, E. (2013) *Aratus and the Astronomical Tradition*, Oxford and New York
Georgoulaki, E. (1994) "Le type iconographique de la statue culturelle d'Apollon Amyklaios: Un emprunt oriental?" *Kernos* 7: 95–118
Gerasimou, C., D. Myrianthefs, K. Papaioakim, and Ch. Hadjichristodoulou, eds. (2005) *The Churches of Pelendria: History, Architecture, Art*, Nicosia
Gerhard, E., and E. Curtius (1856), untitled ["Nachträgliche Mittheilung"], *Monatsbericht der Königlichen Preussische Akademie des Wissenschaften zu Berlin*, 1856: 286–7
Gero, S. (1977) *Byzantine Iconoclasm during the Reign of Constantine V*, Louvain

Gibson, M. (1995) *The Liverpool Ivories: Late Antique and Medieval Ivory and Bone Carving in Liverpool Museum and the Walker Art Gallery*, London

Gibson, M., T. Heslop, and R. Pfaff, eds. (1992) *The Eadwine Psalter: Text, Image and Monastic Culture in Twelfth-Century Canterbury*, London and University Park, PA

Golvin, J.-C. (2003) *L'Antiquité retrouvée*, Paris

Gomme, A. W. (1913) "The Legend of Cadmus and the Logographi," *JHS* 33: 53–72

Grabar, A. (1936) *L'empereur dans l'art byzantin*, Paris

Graf, F. (2009) *Apollo*, Abingdon and New York

Graeven, H. (1902) "Mittelalterliche Nachbildungen des Lysippischen Herakleskolosses," *Bonner Jahrbücher* 108–9: 252–77

Green, P. (2006) *Diodorus Siculus, Books 11–12,37.1: Greek History 480–431 B.C.—The Alternative Version*, Austin

Greswell, E. (1862) *Origines kalendariae hellenicae; or, the history of the primitive calendar among the Greeks before and after the legislation of Solon, in six volumes*, I, Oxford

Grueber, H. A. (1887) untitled, *Proceedings of the Society of Antiquaries*, 2nd series 12: 39–41

Gruen, E. (2011) *Rethinking the Other in Antiquity*, Princeton

Grundy, G. B. (1894) *The Topography of the Battle of Plataea*, London

Guilland, R. (1950) "Le Delphax," *Annuaire de l'Institut de Philologie et d'Histoire Orientales et Slaves* 10: 293–306

Guilland, R. (1969) *Études de topographie de Constantinople byzantine*, Berlin and Amsterdam

Guillou, A. (1996) *Recueil des inscriptions grecques médiévales d'Italie*, Rome

Guldan, E. (1969) "Das Monster-Portal am Palazzo Zuccari in Rom: Wandlungen eines Motivs vom Mittelalter zum Manierismus," *Zeitschrift für Kunstgeschichte* 32: 229–61

Gunter, A. (2009) *Greek Art and the Orient*, Cambridge

Hall, J. (2002) *Hellenicity: Between Ethnicity and Culture*, Chicago

Haluszka, A. (2008) "Sacred Signified: The Semiotics of Statues in the *Greek Magical Papyri*," *Arethusa* 41: 479–94

Hammond, N. (1956) "The Battle of Salamis," *JHS* 76: 32–54

Hansen, D. (1963) "New Votive Plaques from Nippur," *JNES* 22: 145–66

Hathaway, J. (2003) *A Tale of Two Factions: Myth, Memory, and Identity in Ottoman Egypt and Yemen*, Albany

Heimann, A. (1975) "The Last Copy of the Utrecht Psalter," in *The Year 1200: A Symposium*, New York, 313–38

Heimpel, W. (1981) "The Nanshe Hymn," *Journal of Cuneiform Studies* 33: 65–139

Hemingway, S. (2004) *The Horse and Jockey from Artemision: A Bronze Equestrian Monument of the Hellenistic Period*, New York

Henten, J. W. van (2009) "Typhon," in *IDD*

Hinz, W. (1965) "The Elamite God d.Gal," *JNES* 24: 351–4

Hoffmann, L. (1997) *Imports and Immigrants: Near Eastern Contacts with Iron Age Crete*, Ann Arbor, MI

Homolle, T. (1897) "Le trépied de Gélon," *BCH* 21: 588–90

Homolle, T. (1898) "Communication: Exposé des travaux de l'École française en 1898," *BCH* 22: 558–66

Hörandner, W. (1989) "Poetic Forms in the Tenth Century," in *Constantine VII Porphyrogenitus and His Age*, ed. A. Markopoulos, Athens, 135–53

Hude, C., ed. (1927) *Scholia in Thucydidem, ad optimos codices collata*, Leipzig
Hunger, H., and D. Pingree (1989) *MUL.APIN: An Astronomical Compendium in Cuneiform*, Horn.
Hunger, H., and D. Pingree (1999) *Astral Sciences in Mesopotamia*, Leiden
Hunt, P. (1997) "Helots at the Battle of Plataea," *Historia: Zeitschrift für Alte Geschichte* 46: 129–44
Hurowitz, V. A. (2006) "What Goes in Is What Comes out," in G. Beckman and T. J Lewis, eds., *Text, Artifact, and Image: Revealing Ancient Israelite Religion*, Providence, RI, 3–23
Hurwit, J. M. (1999) *The Athenian Acropolis: History, Mythology and Archaeology from the Neolithic Era to the Present*, Cambridge
Hutter, I. (1999) "The Magdalen College 'Musterbuch': A Painter's Guide from Cyprus at Oxford," in N. P. Ševčenko and C. Moss, eds., *Medieval Cyprus: Studies in Art, Architecture and History in Memory of Doula Mouriki*, Princeton, 117–46
Jacobsen, T. (1968) "The Battle between Marduk and Tiamat," *JAOS* 88: 104–8
Jacobsen, T. (1976) *The Treasures of Darkness: A History of Mesopotamian Religion*, New Haven
Jacquemin, A. (1999) *Offrandes monumentales à Delphes*, Athens
Janin, R. (1964) *Constantinople byzantine: Développement urbain et répertoire topographique*, 2nd ed., Paris
Jeffery, L. H. (1962) *The Local Scripts of Archaic Greece: A Study of the Origin of the Greek Alphabet and its Development from the Eighth to the Fifth Centuries B.C.*, Oxford
Jeffreys, E. (1998) *Digenis Akritis: The Grottaferrata and Escorial Versions*, Cambridge
Jeffreys, E. (2012) *Four Byzantine Novels*, Liverpool and Chicago
Jenkins, R. (1947) "The Bronze Athena at Byzantium," *Journal of Hellenic Studies* 67: 31–3
Jenkins, R. (1951) "Further Evidence Regarding the Bronze Athena at Byzantium," *Annual of the British School at Athens* 46: 72–4
Johnston, S. I. (2008) "Animating Statues: A Case Study in Ritual," *Arethusa* 41: 445–77
Jolivet-Lévy, C. (2001) *La Cappadoce médiévale: Images et spiritualité*, Saint-Léger-Vauban
Jolivet-Lévy, C. (2007) "Nouvelles données sur le IXe siècle en Cappadoce: L'église d' İçeridere," *ZRVI* 44: 73–86
Jolivet-Lévy, C. (2008) "Saint Theodore et le dragon: Nouvelles données," in *Puer Apuliae: Mélanges offerts à Jean-Marie Martin*, ed. E. Cuozzo et al., Paris, 357–70
Jolivet-Lévy, C. (2009) "Les cavaliers de Karbala," *Zograf* 33: 19–31
Jónsdóttir, J. (1959) *An 11th Century Byzantine Last Judgement in Iceland*, Reykjavik
Jung, M. (2006) *Marathon und Plataiai: Zwei Perserschlachten als 'lieux de mémoire' im antiken Griechenland*, Göttingen
Kafescioğlu, Ç. (2009) *Constantinopolis/Istanbul: Cultural Encounter, Imperial Vision, and the Construction of the Ottoman Capital*, University Park, PA
Kalavrezou, I. (1985) "The Byzantine Knotted Column," *Byzantina kai Metabyzantina* 4: 95–103, 4 plates
Kaldellis, A. (2005) "The Works and Days of Hesychios the Illoustrious of Miletos," *GRBS* 45: 381–403
Kartsonis, A. (1986) *Anastasis: The Making of an Image*, Princeton
Kasak, E. (2001) "Understanding Planets in Ancient Mesopotamia," *Folklore* 16: 6–33
Kessler, H. (2006) "Margin and Metaphor," in *Pictorial Languages and Their Meanings: Liber Amicorum in Honor of Nurith Kenaan-Kedar*, eds. C. Verzár Bornstein and G. Fishhof, Tel Aviv, 141–52

Kessler, H. (2008) "Evil Eye(ing): Romanesque Art as a Shield of Faith," in C. Hourihane, ed., *Romanesque Art and Thought in the Twelfth Century*, Princeton, 107–35

Kessler, H. (2009) "Christ the Magic Dragon," *Gesta* 48: 119–34

Kiilerich. B. (1993) *Late Fourth-Century Classicism in the Plastic Arts: Studies in the So-Called Theodosian Renaissance*, Odense

Kiilerich, B. (1998) *The Obelisk Base in Constantinople: Court Art and Imperial Ideology*, Rome

Kluge, K. (1929) "Die Gestaltung des Erzes in der archaisch-griechischen Kunst," *JDAI* 44:1–30

Kopytoff, I. (1986) "The Cultural Biography of Things," in A. Appadurai, ed., *The Social Life of Things: Commodities in Cultural Perspective*, Cambridge, 64–91

Kotzabassi, S., and N. P. Ševčenko (2010) *Greek Manuscripts at Princeton, Sixth to Nineteenth Century: A Descriptive Catalogue*, Princeton

Kuehn, S. (2011) *The Dragon in Medieval East Christian and Islamic Art*, Leiden

Kunze, E. (1931) *Kretische Bronzereliefs*, 2 vols, Stuttgart

Kuttner, A. (2003) "Delight and Danger in the Roman Water Garden: Sperlonga and Tivoli," in M. Conan, ed., *Landscape Design and the Experience of Motion*, Washington, DC, 103–56

Laroche, D. (1989) "Nouvelles observations sur l'offrande de Platées," *BCH* 113: 183–98

Laroche, D., and A. Jacquemin (1988) "Une base pour l'Apollon de Salamine à Delphes," *BCH* 112: 235–46

Laroche, D., and A. Jacquemin (1990) "Une offrande monumentale à Delphes: Le trépied des Crotoniates," *BCH* 114: 299–323

Lazarev, V. (1948) *Istoriia vizantiiskoi zhivopisi*, Moscow

Lemerle, P. (1986) *Byzantine Humanism*, Canberra

Levi, D. (1945) "Gleanings from Crete," *AJA* 49: 270–329

Lewis, T. (1996) "CT 13.33-34 and Ezekiel 32: Lion-Dragon Myths," *JAOS* 116: 28–47

Livanos, C. (2011) "A Case Study in Byzantine Dragon-Slaying: Digenes and the Serpent," *Oral Tradition* 26: 125–44

Longhurst, M. (1926) "A Byzantine Ivory Panel for South Kensington," *Burlington Magazine* 280 (July 1926), 38, 42–3

López-Ruiz, C. (2010) *When the Gods Were Born: Greek Cosmogonies and the Near East*, Cambridge, MA

Luce, J.-M., D. Laroche, V. Déroche, and P. Petridis (1993) "Delphes," *BCH* 117: 619–44

Maass, M. (1978) Die geometrischen Dreifüsse von Olympia, Olympische Forschungen 10, Berlin

MacKay, P. (2006) "Giovan-Maria Angiolello," http://angiolello.net/GIovan-Maria.htm

Madden, T. (1992) "The Serpent Column of Delphi in Constantinople: Placement, Purpose and Mutilations," *BMGS* 16: 111–45

Magdalino, P. (1998) "The Road to Baghdad in the Thought-World of Ninth-Century Byzantium," in L. Brubaker, ed., *Byzantium in the Ninth Century: Dead or Alive?* Aldershot, 195–213

Magdalino, P. (1999) "'What we heard in the Lives of the saints we have seen with our own eyes': The Holy Man as Literary Text in Tenth-Century Constantinople," in J. D. Howard-Johnston and P. Hayward, eds., *The Cult of Saints in Late Antiquity and the Middle Ages: Essays on the Contribution of Peter Brown*, Oxford, 83–112

Magdalino, P. (2003) "The Year 1000 in Byzantium," in P. Magdalino, ed., *Byzantium in the Year 1000*, Leiden, 233–70
Maguire, H. (1977) "The Depiction of Sorrow in Middle Byzantine Art," *DOP* 31: 123–74
Maguire, H. (1987) "Adam and the Animals," *DOP* 41: 363–73
Maguire, H. (1989) "Style and Ideology in Byzantine Imperial Art," *Gesta* 28: 217–31
Maguire, H. (1991–2) "An Early Christian Marble Relief at Kavala," *Deltion tes Christianikes Archaiologikes Etaireias* 16: 283–95
Maguire, H. (1994) "Epigrams, Art, and the 'Macedonian Renaissance'," *DOP* 48: 105–15
Maguire, H. (1995) "Magic and the Christian Image," in *Byzantine Magic*, ed. H. Maguire, Washington, DC, 51–71
Maguire, H. (1999) "The Profane Aesthetic in Byzantine Art and Literature," *DOP* 53: 189–205
Maguire, H. (2004) "Other Icons: The Classical Nude in Byzantine Bone and Ivory Carvings," *Journal of the Walters Art Museum* 62: 9–20
Maguire, H. (2011) "Validation and Disruption: The Binding and Severing of Text and Image in Byzantium," in *Bild und Text im Mittelalter*, eds. K. Krause and B. Schellewald, Vienna, 267–81
Maguire, H. (2012) *Nectar and Illusion: Nature in Byzantine Art and Literature*, Oxford
Maguire, H. (2016) "Where did the waters of Paradise go after Iconoclasm," in *Fountains and Water Culture in Byzantium*, eds. B. Shilling and P. Stephenson, Cambridge, forthcoming.
Maguire, E. Dauterman, H. Maguire, and M. Duncan-Flowers (1989) *Art and Holy Powers in the Early Christian House*, Urbana and Chicago
Maguire, H., and E. D. Maguire (2007) *Other Icons: Art and Power in Byzantine Secular Culture*, Princeton
Majeska, G. (1984) *Russian Travelers to Constantinople in the Fourteenth and Fifteenth Centuries*, Washington, DC
Malkin, I. (2000) "La fondation d'une colonie apolliniènne: Delphes et l'Hymne homérique à Apollon," in *Delphes cent ans après la grande fouille: Essai de bilan*, ed. A. Jacquemin, *BCH supplément* 36, Paris, 69–77
Mango, C. (1950) "Le Diippion: Étude historique et topographique," *REB* 8: 152–61
Mango, C. (1959) Letter to the editor, *AB* 41: 351–6; repr. as "Justinian's Equestrian Statue" in Mango 1993.
Mango, C. (1963) "Antique Statuary and the Byzantine Beholder," *DOP* 17: 53–75
Mango, C. (1965) "Constantinopolitana," *JDAI* 80: 305–36; repr. in Mango 1993
Mango, C. (1972, 1988) *Art of the Byzantine Empire, 312–1453*, Englewood Cliffs; repr. Toronto
Mango, C. (1985) *Le développement urbain de Constantinople (IVe–VIIe siècles)*, Paris
Mango, C. (1990) "Constantine's Mausoleum and the Translation of Relics," *Byzantinische Zeitschrift* 83: 51–61
Mango, C. (1993a) *Studies on Constantinople*, Aldershot
Mango, C. (1993b) "The Columns of Justinian and his successors," in Mango (1993a) X
Mango, C. (1993c) "Constantine's Column," in Mango (1993a) III.
Mango, C. (2010), "A History of the Hippodrome of Constantinople," in Pitarakis (2010) 36–43
Mango, C., and S. Yerasimos (1999) *Melchior Lorichs's Panorama of Constantinople*, Istanbul
Mansel, A. M. (1970) "İstanbul'daki 'Burmalı Sütun,'" *Belleten* 34: 189–209
Marcuse, H. (2010) "Holocaust Memorials: The Emergence of a Genre," *American Historical Review* 115: 53–89

Marinatos, Sp. (1936) "La temple géometrique de Dréros," *BCH* 60: 214–85
Martin, J. R. (1954) *The Illustration of the Heavenly Ladder of John Climacus*, Princeton
Martin, R. (1976) "Bathyclès de Magnésie et le 'trône' d'Apollon à Amyclae," *RA*: 205–18
Mathews, T. (1999) *The Clash of Gods: A Reinterpretation of Early Christian Art*, 2nd ed., Princeton
Mazzi, C. (1901–2) "Sonetti di Felice Feliciano," *La Bibliofilia* 3: 55–68
McDonnell, M. (2006) *Roman Manliness:* Virtus *and the Roman Republic*, Cambridge
Meiggs, R., and D. Lewis (1969) *A Selection of Greek Historical Inscriptions to the End of the Fifth Century B.C.*, Oxford
Meister, R. (1957) "Varia: 1. Zur Inschrift der Schlangensäule; 2. consoles—consol," *Wiener Studien* 70: 232–4
Ménage, V. L. (1964) "The Serpent Column in Ottoman Sources," *Anatolian Studies* 14: 169–73
Milbrath, S. (1999) *Star Gods of the Maya: Astronomy in Art, Folklore, and Calendars*, Austin, TX
Millet, G. (1910) *Monuments byzantins de Mistra: Matériaux pour l'étude de l'architecture et de la peinture en Grèce aux XIVe et XVe siècles*, Paris
Mitchell, C. (1961) "Felice Feliciano *Antiquarius*," *Proceedings of the British Academy* 47: 197–221
Mitten, D. G. (1967) "The Earliest Greek Sculptures in the Museum," *Boston Museum Bulletin* 65: 4–18
Mitten, D. G., and Doeringer, S. F. (1967) *Master Bronzes from the Classical World*, Mainz and Greenwich, CT
Morgan, C. (1990) *Athletes and Oracles: The Transformation of Olympia and Delphi in the Eighth Century BC*, Cambridge
Morris, S. (1992) *Daidalos and the Origins of Greek Art*, Princeton
Moorhead, J. (1985) "Iconoclasm, the Cross and the Imperial Image," *Byzantion* 55: 165–79
Mundell Mango, M. (1986) *Silver from Early Byzantium: The Kaper Koraon and Related Treasures*, Washington, DC
Munro, J. (1926) "The Deliverance of Greece," in *The Cambridge Ancient History*, IV.
Müller-Wiener, W. (1977) *Bildlexikon zur Topographie Istanbuls*, Tübingen
Necipoğlu, G. (1991) *Architecture, Ceremonial, and Power: The Topkapı Palace in the Fifteenth and Sixteenth Centuries*, Cambridge, MA and London
Necipoğlu, N. (2010) "Constantinople on the Eve of the Ottoman Conquest," in *From Byzantion to Istanbul: 8000 Years of a Capital*, ed. K. Durak, Istanbul, 180–7, 253–4
Neils, J. (2013) "Salpinx, Snake, and Salamis: The Political Geography of the Pella Hydria," *Hesperia* 82: 595–613
Nelson, R., ed. (2000) *Visuality before and beyond the Renaissance: Seeing as Others Saw*, Cambridge
Nelson, R. (2003) "Tourists, Terrorists, and Metaphysical Theater at Hagia Sophia," in R. Nelson and M. Olin, eds., *Monuments and Memory, Made and Unmade*, Chicago, 59–81
Nelson, R., and K. Collins, eds. (2006) *Holy Image, Hallowed Ground: Icons from Sinai*, Los Angeles
Nicholson, O. (2000) "Constantine's Vision of the Cross," *Vigiliae Christianae* 54: 309–23
Noegel, S. (2007) "Dismemberment, Creation, and Ritual: Images of Divine Violence in the Ancient Near East," in J. K. Wellman, ed., *Belief and Bloodshed: Religion and Violence across Time and Tradition*, Lanham, MD, 13–27

Noel, W. (1995) *The Harley Psalter*, Cambridge
Ogden, D. (2013) *Drakon: Dragon Myth and Serpent Cult in the Greek and Roman World*, Oxford
Oikonomides, N. (1986) *A Collection of Dated Byzantine Lead Seals*, Washington, DC
Omont, H. (1906) *Psautier illustré (XIIIe siècle)*, Paris
Oppenheim, A. L. (1974) "A Babylonian Diviner's Manual," *JNES* 33: 197–220
Ousterhout, R., and N. Başgelen (1995) *Monuments of Unaging Intellect: Historic Postcards of Byzantine Istanbul*, Istanbul
Ousterhout, R. (2014) "The Life and Afterlife of Constantine's Column," *JRA* 27: 304–26
Pace, V., ed. (2007) *Le Jugement dernier entre Orient et Occident*, Paris
Pancaroğlu, O. (2004) "The Itinerant Dragon-Slayer: Forging Paths of Image and Identity in Medieval Anatolia," *Gesta* 42: 151–64
Pankenier, D. (2013) *Astrology and Cosmology in Early China: Conforming Heaven to Earth*, Cambridge
Panofsky, D. (1943) "The Textual Basis of the Utrecht Psalter Illustrations," *AB* 25: 50–8
Papalexandrou, N. (2010) "Are There Hybrid Visual Cultures? Reflections on the Orientalizing Phenomena in the Mediterranean of the Early First Millennium BCE," *Ars Orientalis* 38: 31–48
Paravicini, W., ed. (1994–2001) *Europäische Reiseberichte des spätens Mittelalters*, 3 vols., Frankfurt am Main
Perdrizet, P. (1896) "Bion de Milet," *BCH* 20: 654–7
Perry, M. (1912, 1913) "On the *psychostasis* in Christian Art," *Burlington Magazine* 116 (November 1912), 94–7, 100–05; *Burlington Magazine* 118 (January 1913), 208–11, 214–18
Petrović, A. (2010) "True Lies of Athenian Public Epigrams," in *Archaic and Classical Greek Epigram*, eds. M. Baumbach, I. Petrovic, and A. Petrovic, Cambridge, 202–15.
Pietsch, E. (2010) *Beseelte Bilder: Epigramme des Manuel Philes auf bildliche Darstellungen*, Vienna
Pitarakis, B., ed. (2010) *Hippodrom/Atmeydanı: A Stage for Istanbul's History*, 2 vols., Istanbul
Pomtow, H. (1924) "Delphoi," in *RE, Supplementband* 4
Porada, E. (1993) "Cylinder Seals," in *Encyclopaedia Iranica*, VI, New York
Pritchett, W. K. (1957) "New Light on Plataia," *AJA* 61: 9–28
Pritchett, W. K. (1979) "Plataiai," *American Journal of Philology* 100: 145–7, 150–2
Pyatnitsky, Y. (2011) "Admirations in Pen and Brush: Russian Sources on Istanbul and the Monuments of the Hippodrome," *Acta Musei Varnaensis* 8: 321–50
Raby, J. (1980) "Cyriacus of Ancona and the Ottoman Sultan Mehmed II," *Journal of the Warburg and Courtauld Institutes* 43: 242–6
Raby, J. (1981) "Mehmed II Fatih and the Fatih Album," *Islamic Art* 1: 42–9
Raby, J. (1982) "A Sultan of Paradox: Mehmed the Conqueror as a Patron of the Arts," *Oxford Art Journal* 5: 3–8
Raby, J. (1987) "Mehmed the Conqueror and the Equestrian Statue of the Augustaion," *Illinois Classical Studies* 12: 305–13
Raby, J. (2000) "Opening Gambits," in *The Sultan's Portrait. Picturing the House of Osman*, ed. S. Kangal, Istanbul, 64–95
Raubitschek, A. (1949) *Dedications from the Athenian Akropolis: A Catalogue of the Inscriptions of the Sixth and Fifth Centuries B.C.*, Cambridge, MA

Reiner, E. (1995) *Astral Magic in Babylonia*, Transactions of the American Philosophical Society 85/iv, Philadelphia

Rhoby, A. (2010) *Byzantinische Epigramme in inschriftlicher Überlieferung*, II. *Byzantinische Epigramme auf Ikonen und Objekten der Kleinkunst*, Vienna

Ricotti, E. S. P. (1987) "The Importance of Water in Roman Garden *Triclinia*," in W. Jashemski, ed., *Ancient Roman Villa Gardens*, Washington, DC, 135–84

Ridgway, B. S. (1977) "The Plataian Tripod and the Serpentine Column," *AJA* 81: 374–79

Ridgway, B. S. (1989) "Laokoon and the Foundation of Rome," *JRA* 2: 171–81

Ridgway, B. S. (1993) *The Archaic Style in Greek Sculpture*, 2nd ed., Chicago

Rizvi, K. (2012) "The Suggestive Portrait of Shah 'Abbas: Prayer and Likeness in a Safavid *Shahnama*," *AB* 94: 226–50

Rizzardi, C. (1970) *I sarcofagi paleocristiani con rappresentazione del passaggio del Mar Rosso*, Faenza

Robinson, B. A. (2011) *Histories of Peirene: A Corinthian Fountain in Three Millennia*, Princeton and Athens

Rochberg-Halton, F. (1991) "The Babylonian Astronomical Diaries," *JAOS* 111: 323–32

Rochberg, F. (1999) "Empiricism in Babylonian Omen Texts and the Classification of Mesopotamian Divination as Science," *JAOS* 119: 559–69

Rodini, E. (2011) "The Sultan's True Face? Gentile Bellini, Mehmet II, and the Values of Versimilitude," in J. Harper, ed., *The Turk and Islam in the Western Eye, 1450–1750: Visual Imagery before Orientalism*, Farnham, 21–40

Roehl, H. (1882) *Inscriptiones Graecae antiquissimae praeter Atticas in Attica repertas*, Berlin

Roehl, H. (1894; 1907) *Imagines Inscriptionum Graecarum antiquissimarum, in usum scholarum*, Berlin

Rolley, C. (1983) *Les bronzes grecs*, Fribourg and Paris

Rolley, C. (1994) *La sculpture grecque, 1: Des origines au milieu du Ve siècle*, Paris

Rupp, W. L. (2007) "Shape of the Beast: The Theriomorphic and Therianthropic Deities and Demons of Ancient Italy," PhD diss., Florida State University, Tallahassee

Rydén, L. (1978) "The Date of the Life of Andreas Salos," *DOP* 32: 129–55

Rydén, L. (1990) "The Date of the Life of St Niphon, *BHG* 1371z," in *Greek and Latin Studies in Memory of Cajus Fabricius*, ed. by S.-T. Teodorsson, Gothenburg, 33–40

Sachs, A., and H. Hungers (eds.) (1988) *Astronomical Diaries and Related Texts from Babylon*, 1: *Diaries from 652 B.C. to 262 B.C.*, Vienna

Sacks, K. (1976) "Herodotus and the Dating of the Battle of Thermopylae," *CQ* 26: 232–48

Säflund, G. (1972) *The Polyphemus and Scylla Groups at Sperlonga*, Stockholm

Salt, A., and E. Boutsikas (2005) "Knowing When to Consult the Oracle at Delphi," *Antiquity* 79: 564–72

Sandler, L. F. (2000) "The Images of Words in English Gothic Psalters," in B. Cassidy and R. Muir Wright, eds., *Studies in the Illustration of the Psalter*, Stamford, UK, 67–86

Saxon, E. (2011) "Art and the Eucharist: Early Christian to ca. 800," in I. Levy, G. Macy, and C. Van Austall, eds., *A Companion to the Eucharist in the Middle Ages*, Leiden, 93–162

Saxon, E. (2011a) "Carolingian, Ottonian, and Romanesque Art and the Eucharist," in I. Levy, G. Macy, and C. Van Austall, eds., *A Companion to the Eucharist in the Middle Ages*, Leiden, 93–162

Schmidt, G. (1995) *The Iconography of the Mouth of Hell: Eighth-Century Britain to the Fifteenth Century*, Selinsgrove and London

Schneider, R. (1986) *Bunte Barbaren: Orientalenstatuen aus farbigen Marmor in der römischen Repräsentationskunst*, Worms

Schoder, R. (1943) "The Artistry of the First Pythian Ode," *CJ* 38: 401–12

Scott, M. (2010) *Delphi and Olympia: The Spatial Politics of Panhellenism in the Archaic and Classical Periods*, Cambridge

Shaw, J. W., et al. (1978) "Excavations at Kommos (Crete) during 1977," *Hesperia* 42: 111–70

Shaw, J. W. (1989) "Phoenicians in Southern Crete," *AJA* 93: 165–83

Shepherd, W. (2012) *Plataea 479 BC: The Most Glorious Victory Ever Seen*, Botley

Shilling, B. and P. Stephenson (2016) *Fountains and Water Culture in Byzantium*, Cambridge

Smith, C. (1987) "Cyriacus of Ancona's Seven Drawings of Hagia Sophia," *AB* 69: 16–32

Smith, G. (2008) "How Thin Is a Demon?" *Journal of Early Christian Studies* 16: 479–512

Snodgrass, A. (1971, 2000) *The Dark Ages of Greece: An Archaeological Survey of the Eleventh to the Eighth Centuries BC*, Edinburgh; 2nd ed. London

Spawforth, A. (2012) *Greece and the Augustan Cultural Revolution*, Cambridge

Spiazzi, A. M. (2004) "116. Calamaio, ora vaso crismale," in *Oreficeria sacra in Veneto: Secoli VI–XC*, ed. A. M. Spiazzi, Venice, 81, 196–200

Spivey, N. (1995) "Bionic Statues," in A. Powell, ed., *The Greek World*, London and New York, 442–59

Spivey, N. (2013) *Greek Sculpture*, Cambridge

Stadter, P. (1978) "The 'Ars Tactica' of Arrian: Tradition and Originality," *CP* 73: 117–28

Steinhart, M. (1997) "Bemerkungen zu Rekonstruktion, Ikonographie und Inschrift des platäischen Weihgeschenkes," *BCH* 121: 33–69

Stewart, A. F. (1977) "To Entertain an Emperor: Sperlonga, Laokoon and Tiberius at the Dinner Table," *JRS* 67: 76–90

Stephenson, P. (2009) *Constantine: Unconquered Emperor, Christian Victor*, London

Stephenson, P. (2010) "Staring at Serpents in Tenth-Century Constantinople," *Bysantinska sällskapet Bulletin* 28: 58–81

Stephenson, P. (2016) "The Serpent Column Fountain," in *Fountains and Water Culture in Byzantium*, eds. B. Shilling and P. Stephenson, Cambridge, forthcoming

Stephenson, P., and B. Shilling (2012) "Nicholas the Monk, Former Soldier," in *Byzantine Religious Culture: Studies in Honor of Alice-Mary Talbot*, eds. E. Fisher, S. Papaioannou, and D. Sullivan, Leiden, 421–38

Stibbe, C. (2000a) *The Sons of Hephaistos: Aspects of the Archaic Greek Bronze Industry*, Rome

Stibbe, C. (2000b) "Gitiadas und der Krater von Vix," *Bulletin Antieke Beschaving* 75: 65–114

Stibbe, C. (2009) "A Silenus and a Maenad: Some Bronze Statuettes from the British Excavations at Sparta Reconsidered," in *Sparta and Laconia from Prehistory to Premodern*, eds. W. G. Cavanagh, C. Gallou, and M. Georgiadis, London, 143–58

Stichel, R. (1997) "Die 'Schlangensäule' im Hippodrom von Istanbul: Zum spät- und nachantiken Schiksal des Delphischen Votivs der Schlacht von Plataiai," *Istanbuler Mitteilungen* 47: 315–48

Stirnemann, P. (1992) "Paris, BN, MS lat. 8846 and the Eadwine Psalter," in Gibson, Heslop, and Pfaff (1992), 186–92

Stout, R. E. (1966) "The Sûr-i-Hümâyun of Murad III: A Study of Ottoman Pageantry and Entertainment," PhD diss., The Ohio State University

Strauss, B. (2004) *The Battle of Salamis: The Naval Encounter that Saved Greece—and Western Civilization*, New York
Strootman, R. (2011) "Hippodroom wordt Paardenplein: De wederopstanding van Constantinopel na 1453," in D. Burgersdijk and W. Waal, eds, *Constantinopel: Een mozaïk van de Byzantijnse metropool*, Leiden, 183–91
Strootman, R. (2014) "The Serpent Column: The Persistent Meanings of a Pagan Relic in Christian and Islamic Constantinople," *Material Religion* 10: 432–51
Stylianou, A., and J. Stylianou (1985) *The Painted Churches of Cyprus*, London
Swetnam-Burland, M. (2010) "*Aegyptus Redacta*: The Egyptian Obelisk in the Augustan Campus Martius," *AB* 92: 135–53
Ševčenko, I. (1992) "Re-reading Constantine Porphyrogenitus," in J. Shepard and S. Franklin, eds., *Byzantine Diplomacy*, Aldershot, 167–85
Ševčenko, N. P. (2009) "Monastic Challenges: Some Manuscripts of the *Heavenly Ladder*," in C. Hourihane, ed., *Byzantine Art: Recent Studies*, Turnhout, 39–62
Tanaseanu-Döbler, I. (2013) *Theurgy in Late Antiquity: The Invention of a Ritual Tradition*, Göttingen
Tanman, M. B., and A. V. Çobanoğlu (2010) "Ottoman Architecture in Atmeydanı and Its Environs," in Pittarakis (2010), II, 232–70
Terzioğlu, D. (1995) "The Imperial Circumcision Festival of 1582: An Interpretation," *Muqarnas* 12: 84–100
Texier, C. (1845) "Phialé, ou fontaine de l'hippodrome à Constantinople," *Revue archéologique* 2: 142–9
Thibault, G., and J.-L. Martinez (2008) "La reconstitution de la colonne des danseuses de Delphes," in R. Vergnieux and C. Delevoie, eds, *Actes du Colloque Virtual Retrospect 2007, Archéovision 3*, Bordeaux, 231–8
Thierry, N., and M. Thierry (1960) "L'église du jugement dernier à Ihlara," *Anatolia* 5: 159–68
Timotin, A. (2006) "Byzantine Visionary Accounts of the Other World: A Reconsideration," in J. Burke, ed., *Byzantine Narrative: Papers in Honour of Roger Scott*, Canberra, 404–20
Tolan, J., H. Laurens, and G. Veinstein (2012) *Europe and the Islamic World: A History*, Princeton
Tselos, D. (1959) "English Manuscript Illustration and the Utrecht Psalter," *AB* 41: 137–49
Tükel, U. (2010) "The Representation of a Festivity in Atmeydanı: The Pictorial Language of Classical Age Ottoman Miniatures," in Pittarakis (2010) 96–110
UNESCO (1985) *Convention concerning the Protection of the World Cultural and Natural Heritage: World Heritage Committee, Ninth Ordinary Session, UNESCO Headquarters, Paris, 2–6 December 1985*: http://whc.unesco.org/en/list/356
Van Buren, E. Douglas (1934) "The God Ningizzida," *Iraq* 1: 60–89
Vasiliev, A. A. (1942–3) "Medieval Ideas of the End of the World, East and West," *Byzantion* 16: 462–502
Vian, F. (1963) *Les origines de Thèbes: Cadmos et les Spartes*, Paris
Vikan, G. (1982) *Byzantine Pilgrimage Art*, Washington, DC
Vikan, G. (1984) "Art, Medicine, and Magic in Early Byzantium," *DOP* 38: 65–86
Vikan, G. (1998) "Byzantine Pilgrim's Art," in L. Safran, ed., *Heaven on Earth: Art and the Church in Byzantium*, University Park, PA, 229–63
Vincent, J.-C. (2003) "Le xoanon chez Pausanias: Littératures et réalités cultuelles," *Dialogues d'histoire ancienne* 29: 31–75

Vlizos, S. (2009) "The Amyklaion Revisited: New Observations on a Laconian Sanctuary of Apollo," in *Athens-Sparta: Contribution to the Research on the History and Archaeology of the Two City-States*, ed. N. Kaltsas, 11–23

Volbach, W. F. (1976) *Elfenbeinarbeiten der Spätantike und des frühen Mittelalters*, 3rd ed., Mainz

Wakeman, M. (1973) *God's Battle with the Monster*, Leiden

Walter, C. (1997) "IC XC NI KA. The Apotropaic Function of the Victorious Cross," *REB* 55: 193–220

Walter, C. (2003) "Saint Theodore and the Dragon," in C. Entwistle, ed., *Through a Glass Darkly*, Oxford, 95–106

Ward-Perkins, J. B. (1952) "The Shrine of St Peter and Its Twelve Spiral Columns," *JRS* 42: 21–33

Ward-Perkins, B. (2012) "Old and New Rome Compared: The Rise of Constantinople," in L. Grig and G. Kelly, eds., *Two Romes: Rome and Constantinople in Late Antiquity*, Oxford, 53–78

Weinryb, I. (2012) "The Bronze Object in the Middle Ages," in D. Ekserdjian, *Bronze*, London, 69–77

Weiss, P. (2003) "The Vision of Constantine," *Journal of Roman Archaeology* 16: 237–59

Weitzmann, K. (1951) *Greek Mythology in Byzantine Art*, Princeton

Weitzmann, K. (1975) "The Study of Byzantine Manuscript Illumination," in K. Weitzmann, et al., *The Place of Book Illumination in Byzantine Art*, Princeton, 1–60

Weitzmann, K. (1979) *The Miniatures of the Sacra Parallela: Parisinus Graecus 923*, Princeton

Weitzmann, K. (1981) "Classical Heritage in the Art of Constantinople," in K. Weitzmann, *Studies in Classical and Byzantine Manuscript Illumination*, ed. H. Kessler, Chicago, 126–50

Weitzmann, K., and G. Galavaris (1990) *The Monastery of Saint Catherine at Mount Sinai: The Illuminated Greek Manuscripts, I: From the Ninth to the Twelfth Century*, Princeton

Westbrook, N., K. Dark, and R. van Meeuwen (2010) "Constructing Melchior Lorichs's Panorama of Constantinople," *Journal of the Society of Architectural Historians* 69: 62–87

White, G. (2007) *Babylonian Star-lore*, London

White, M. (2008) "The Rise of the Dragon in Middle Byzantine Hagiography," *BMGS* 32: 149–67

Wieseler, F. (1864) "Zur sogenannten Schlangensäule in Konstantinopel," in *Jarbücher für classische Philologie* 10: 242–59

Wiggermann, F. (1989) "Tišpak, His Seal, and the Dragon *mušḫuššu*," in O. Haex et al., eds., *To the Euphrates and Beyond: Archaeological Studies in Honour of Maurits N. van Loon*, Rotterdam, 117–33

Wilkinson, K. (2009) "Palladas and the Age of Constantine," *JRS* 99: 36–60

Wilkinson, K. (2010a) "Palladas and the Foundation of Constantinople," *JRS* 100: 179–94

Wilkinson, K. (2010b) "Some Neologisms in the Epigrams of Palladas," *GRBS* 50: 295–308

Wilson Jones, M. (2002) "Tripods, Triglyphs, and the Origins of the Doric Frieze," *AJA* 106: 353–90

Woodhead, C. (2007) "Reading Ottoman *Şehnames*: Official Historiography in the Late Sixteenth Century," *Studia Islamica* 104/105: 67–80

Worthington, M. (2004) "Planets, Livers and Omens in Mesopotamia," *Early Science and Medicine* 9: 136–43
Wortley, J. (1996) *The Spiritually Beneficial Tales of Paul, Bishop of Monemvasia*, Kalamazoo
Wortley, J. (2001) "Death, Judgment, Heaven, and Hell in Byzantine 'Beneficial Tales,'" *DOP* 55: 53–69
Wright, T. (1848) *Early Travels in Palestine*, London
Wright, A. (2005) *The Pollaiuolo Brothers: The Arts of Florence and Rome*, New Haven
Wulff, O. (1898) "Die sieben Wunder von Byzanz und die Apostelkirche nach Konstantinos Rhodios," *Byzantinische Zeitschrift* 7: 317–31
Yenişehirlioğlu, F. (2010) "Ibrahim Paşa and Sculpture as Subversion in Art," in Pitarakis (2010) II, 111–27
Yerasimos, S. (2000) "Recreating a World's Order," in A. Ertug, ed., *An Illustrated Account of Sultan Ahmet III's Festival of 1720*, Istanbul and Bern, 7–13

INDEX

Abdulhamid II, Ottoman sultan, 238
Acanthus Column (Column of the Dancers), 94, 94n129
Actium, Battle of, 95
Acts of St. Marina, 141–2
    dragon in, 171, 177–8, 179
Adam modeled after Herakles, 127, *128*
Aeneid (Virgil), 100
Against Neaira (Demosthenes), 81
Aiginetans' astral mast, 46–7, 48, 90
Aigospotami, Battle of, 47
Aischylos
    on battle between Zeus and Typhon, 50n86
    on darkness of night before battle of Salamis, 47
    Persians, 89
Akathistos Hymn, 166
Alexander of Makedonia, 37, 90n106
    as envoy to the Athenians, 34–5
Alkaios, 87
alphabet, Greek, 54n101
Amandry, Pierre, 18
Amyklaion, 73–4
    bronze tripods at, 75–6
    cult statue at, 74–5
    sculptural tripods, 27
    Typhon and Python, 78
Anastasia, Saint, 143
Anastasios, Roman Emperor, 147
Anastasios of Antioch, 166
Anaxagoras of Aigina, 90
Anderson, B., 124n91
Anderson, Jeffrey, 170
Andreae, Bernard, 106, 125
Andrew of Caesarea, 142
Andrew the Fool, 135, 136–8, 143, 145. *See also Life of St. Andrew the Fool*
Andronikos Komnenos, Eastern Roman emperor, 151
Angiolello, Giovan-Maria
    on Mehmed's preservation of the Serpent Column, 211–13
    on Serpent Column as talisman against snakes, 185
    on statue of Justinian, 186
    on tradition of supernatural arbitration, 157

Anglo-Catalan Psalter. *See* Great Canterbury Psalter
animal statues
    elephant statue as metaphor, 124
    as talisman, 188–91
Annunciation to Mary at the Well, 166
    Serpent Column as fountain in illustrations of, *160*, 160–2, *161*, *162*
Annunciation to St. Anne, 22, 167, *169*, *170*
Anonymous Chronicles, 187
Aphrodite statue with tripod (Amyklaion), 76
Apocalypse (John of Patmos), 142, 174
Apocalypse (Pseudo-Methodios), 142
Apocalypse of Anastasia, 143
Apocalypse of Theotokos, 143
apocalyptic writings, 142–3. *See also Life of St. Andrew the Fool*
    conceptions of Hades and, 142
Apollo
    Constantine and, 102
    Euripides on, 81–2
    slaying of Python, 48, 50
    statues of
        Constantine's interest in, 101
        dedicated after Salamis, 34, 89–90, 91
        Dreros Apollo, 68, 75
Apollodoros
    description of Typhon, 51–2
    story of Kadmos, 55
Apollonius of Tyana, 148
apotropaion, 185, 187. *See also* talismans
    apotropaic animals, 188–91
    apotropaic function of columns, 188, 191, 194
    apotropaic knots, 191, *192*
Aqueduct of Valens (Bozdoğan Kemeri), 24
Aratos, 41
archaeoastronomy, 42
Archäologischer Anzeiger, 11
Archäologischer Zeitung, 11
Archbishop's Chapel mosaic, Ravenna, 174–5, *175*
Arethas of Caesarea, 142
Aristotle, 133–4
Arkadios, 124
    Column of, 125n93
Arrian, 110

263

art. *See also* Christianity, art and writings
  Greek
    celestial phenomena in, 44–5
    historical events in, 92
  Mesopotamian, 58
Artemis
  statue with tripod at Amyklaion, 76
Artemisia of Halikarnassos, 34
Artemision, Battle of, 32
Asklepios
  healing serpents and cult of, 201
  serpentine epiphany, 201
astronomy-astrology, Mesopotamian, 58–9, 58n120
Athena Chalkioikos
  Sparta temple to, 76
Atheneum français: Revue universelle, 11
Athens
  Olympian Zeus, 91
  struggle with Sparta for supremacy, 92
Atlas 408, 17–18, *19*
  as base of Kroton tripod, 18
  imaginary reconstruction, 18, 26
Atlas 509, 17
At meydanı, 216, *217*
  refurbishment, 238
Augustine of Hippo
  devil identified with serpent-tongued men, 196
  on serpent, 195
Augustus
  influence on Constantine, 101
  mythic significance of Persian wars, 95
automata, 159
Ayasofya Mosque, 216

Base G, 18–19
  imaginary reconstruction and, 26
Basil I, Eastern Roman Emperor, 134, 151
Basil II, Byzantine Emperor, 143
  gift of Hellenistic bronze serpent to Arnulfus II, 197–8
Bathykles of Magnesia, 78
battle standards
  Draco standards, 110–11
  labarum, 108, *108*, 109, 110
Baun, Janes, 143
Bayezid II, 213, 215
Bellini, Gentile, 208, 214
Belsius, Johannes, 218
Bertelin, S., 106
Bertoldo di Giovanni, 208
Bertrandon de la Brocquière, 205
Beyan-ı Menazil-i Sefer-i Irakeyn. *See Mecmu-ı Menazil* (Compilation of the halting places)(Süleyman I)

Bible. *See also* Revelation, Book of
  Book of Job, 200
  Book of Matthew, 138
Bibliotheke (Photios), 196
Blau, Otto, 11
Bluebeard, triple-bodied demon, *55*
  Boardman on, 53n98
Boardman, John, 26–7, 53n98, 70n14
Book of Ingenious Devices (Kitáb al- Hiyal) (Banu Musa), 159
Boucher, Guillaume, 158–9
Bouras, Laskarina, 152
Boutsikas, E., 44
Bouvard, Joseph Antoine, 238
bronze
  doors of St. Mary at Aachen, 196
  Gorgon and snakes, 72, *73*
  as material of Serpent Column, 67, 241
  monumental from Sparta, 75
  Near Eastern material in Archaic Greece, 70–1
  powers of, 194, 196
    Byzantine understanding, 133
bronze working, 67–8
  archaic Greek, 68–73
  at Delphi and Olympia, 90n110
  Lakonian, 73–9
    Plataian Tripod and, 80
  serpents as motif, 79
Bryas Palace, 159
Buondelmonti, Cristoforo
  bird's-eye views of the Constantinople, 216
  on Serpent Column, 149, 155, 156, 158
Byzantion. *See also* Constantinople; Istanbul
  chosen as capital by Constantine, 100
  snakes in mythical foundation, 189–90
Byzantium sive Costantineopolis (Vavassore), 216

caduceus, 192, 192n37
  statue of Mercury with, 192, *193*
calendars, Greek, 39, 39n42
Calvert, Frank, 100
Canaanite myth, 45
Canaye, Pierre de, 232
Canning, Stratford, 237
Cappadocian rock churches, 143–4, 144n76
  serpents in paintings, 179–80, 179n88, *181*, 182
Carlier de Pinon, Jean, 158
Cassios Dio, 100
Casson, Stanley
  on hole in base of Serpent Column, 22–3
  on water conduits near Serpent Column, 21
casting
  Carolingian revival of lost-wax casting, 196
  of Serpent Column, 3, 75

cauldrons
  Gitiadas and, 76
  mythic creatures on, 82–3
  on Plataian Tripod, 2
  in reconstructions of Plataian Tripod, 25, 26
Çelebi, Abdülcelil, 231
Çelebi, Evliya, 232
  on talismans protecting Constantinople, 187
Charlemagne, 175
Christ
  militant Christ, 175
  as protection of Christians, 198–9
Christ crucified ivory, *197*
Christianity, art and writings
  Adam modeled after Herakles, 127, *128*
  combat myth and, 56, 56n107
  serpent images
    militant Christ trampling serpent and lion, 174–5
    serpents and dragons, 173–82
    three-headed serpents, 171
Christians, end of persecution of, 103–4
Chrysopolis, Battle of (324), 97
Ciriaco d'Ancona, 216
Clarke, Edward Daniel, 235
Clavijo, Ruy González de
  accurate description of the hippodrome, 157–8
  on Serpent Column, 149
    serpent venom, 184
clay icon of St. Theodore, 179, *180*
Codex Ebnerianus, 168–9, *170*
Coecke van Aelst, Pieter, 122, 217
coins of Constantine, *108*, 108–9
  Christian and non-Christian understanding of battle standard, 110–11
Column of Arkadios, 125n93
columns. *See also* Serpent Column
  apotropaic function, 188, 191, 194
  at entrance of Temple of Solomon, 191
  knotted, 191–2
  spirally fluted, 193–4
combat myth, 110n48
  battle between Yahweh and Leviathan, 56
  Fontenrose on, 48–9
  in the Middle Ages, 56
  in Revelation, 174
  Serpent Column as Greek understanding of primordial, 241
  St. George and the Dragon staged in Istanbul, 226
  variants of, 48, 48n75, 58
Constantine I, Roman emperor, 97
  interest in Apollo, 101, 102
  labarum (battle standard), 108, *108*, 109, 110
  necessity of a new capital, 99–100

Oration to the Saints, 104, 203–4
  as *Sarmaticus Maximus,* 111
Constantine the Rhodian, 135, 148n94
Constantine V, Eastern Roman Emperor, 132–3
Constantine VII, Eastern Roman Emperor, 141, 189
Constantinople, 99. *See also* Byzantion; hippodrome of Constantinople; Istanbul; statues in Constantinople
  dedication, 103–4
  Great Palace mosaic of snake and eagle, 189.*190*
  hydraulics, 159
  in late antiquity, 97–126
  magical powers of animal statues, 189
  in the Middle Ages, 127–50
    millennial fears, 142
  Milion, 131–2
  mythic heroes in art, 105
  serpentine fountains, 151–5, *152, 153*
  serpentine finials, 154
  Tribunal (Delphax), 101
  Triumph of Orthodoxy, 128
  water lines into, 23–4
Constantius, 111n49
consular diptychs, ivory, 117–18
Conticello, Baldassare, 106, 125
Contra Celsum (Origen), 103
Cook, A. B., 45
Copper Horse, 185–8
Corinth
  Poseidon at Isthmia, 91
  treasury, 88
Costanzo da Ferrara, 208
  portrait medallion of Mehmed II, *209*
Crete
  bronze working in, 68, 80
  entwined serpents on helmet, 71–2, *72*
Crispus, 100
cross, serpents and sign of the, 178–9
Crucifixion
  brazen serpent and, 194–8
  as Christian inversion of the combat myth, 195
Curtius, Ernst, 8, 11, 14
Cutler, Anthony, 127, 127n2
Cyprus, 67
  cycle of wall paintings at Moutoullas, 161, 162, *162*
Cyril of Alexandria, 143

Dante, Alighieri, 171
Daphni mosaic on Annunciation to Anne, 167, *168*
Darius, King of Kings, 29
De cerimoniis, 159

Delphi, 67–96
  bronze working at, 90n110
  displays, 85
    of captured booty in creative forms, 93
    Lydian, 85–6
  excavation by the French School in
      Athens, 17–18
  orientalizing bronze works from Crete at, 70
  Plataian Tripod on eastern terrace of Sanctuary
      of Apollo, 67
  Pseudo-Nonnus on, 132
  Siphnos treasury, 203
  spatial politics, 94n128
  statues dedicated after Plataia, 91
  Votive to Apollo after Battle of Salamis, 34,
      89–90, 91
Delphic Tripods in Constantinople, 100
  after Constantine, 111–20
  in hippodrome, 103, 112
  mentioned in *Patria Konstantinoupoleos*, 126
Delphinus, heliacal rising of, 44
demons. *See also* dragons; serpents
  Byzantines and, 199
  defeated by sign of the cross, 178–9
  as serpents, 177, 199
Demosthenes, 81
Den, pharaoh, 207
Denny, Don, 136
Desiderius, Abbot, 144
Dethier, P. A., 11, 237
  reconstruction of Plataian Tripod, 25
  on Serpent Column
    inscription, 8–9, 12, 15
    used as fountain, 20–1, 23
  on stamped lead pipe, 23
Deutsches archäologisches Institut, 11
Devambez, Pierre, 16
*Dialogue on the Shrines and Other Points of
    Interest of Constantinople*, 150
Digenis Akrites, 171–2
Diodoros Sikeliotes
  festival of liberation at Plataia, 38
  on inscription on Plataian Tripod, 81
  on Salamis daughter of Asopos, 57
Dioskouroi (Gemini) as stars, 47
Divine Institutes (Lactantius), 104n19
Domitian, 95
Douce Ivory, 175
Draco
  constellation, 40, 42, 43, 98
    Persians and, 62, 62n143, 147n89
  standards, 110–11, 179
    form of Draco head, 110n45
dragon(s)
  in *Acts of St. Marina*, 171, 177–8, 179

  in illuminations of *Heavenly Ladder*, 139
  maw of Hades as, 141, 179
  as Roman Empire for Mehmed II, 208
  triple-headed, 172
dragon slaying
  in Firdowsi's *Shahnama*, 206
  Persian tradition, 207
Dragon Statue identified as Serpent Column, 124
Dreros Apollo, 68, 75
Dryden Costume Album, 220–1, *221*

Eadwine Psalter, 163, 164, 164n39, *165*
Ecclesiastical History (Eusebios), 108
Edwards, Mark J., 104n19
Egyptian Obelisk. *See* Theodosian Obelisk
Eleusinian Mysteries and night sky, 43
"El Gran Turco," 208, *210*, *211*
end of the world. *See also* apocalyptic writings
  Persian myth, 147n89
Enūma Anu Enlil, 59, 61, 61n132
Enūma Elish, 49, 62, 70, 110n48
Éphémeride archéologique (publication), 11
Ephrem the Syrian, 166
Epic of Baal, 49
Epigrammata Bobiensia, 126
Epigram of the Medes identified as Serpent
    Column, 124
Epigraphik von Byzantion und Constantinopolis
    (Mordtmann and Dethier), 12, 15
Eretria, 30
Eros
  in Byzantine romance, 171
  on silver inkpot, 129, *130*
Ethnika (Stephanos of Byzantion), 55
Eunapios, 114
Euripides
  on Apollo, 81–2
  description of Typhon, 52–3
  on Kadmos slaying Drakon, 54–5
  on stars during the Eleusinian Mysteries, 43
euripos of Constantinople hippodrome. *See*
    hippodrome of Constantinople
Eusebios of Caesarea
  comparing Constantine to Moses, 108–9
  on Constantinople statues, 101–2, 114
  Delphic Tripods in hippodrome, 112
  Lucinius shown as Leviathan, 106–8
  production of Bibles for Constantine, 174
  on Scripture and Greek myths, 103
Eusebius of Alexandria, 171
Eustathios of Thessalonike, 165
extramission, theory of, 133

Fabricius, Ernst
  followers of, 12–13

reconstruction of Plataian Tripod, 25, 26
on Serpent Column inscription, 10, 12
Fatih Album, 208, *210*
Feliciano, Felice, 208–9
  illustration, *212*
festivals, nocturnal aspects of, 43–4
Fontenrose, Joseph, 48–9
Forsyth, Neil, 56n107, 109n43, 195
Forum of Constantine, 101
  illustrations on Column of Arkadios, 125n93
  in *Life of St. Andrew the Fool,* 137–8
  statues in, 135
  water extended to, 24
fountain, Serpent Column used as, 20–1, 23
  illustrations in Annunciation to Mary at the Well, *160*, 160–2, *161*, *162*
  tales of different liquids from, 155–8
fountains, 151–82
  in Daphni mosaic of Annunciation to Anne, 167
  delivering different liquids, 159
  magic fountain of Möngke Khan, 158–9
  serpentine in manuscripts by James, 167
  snakes as in Greco-Roman world, 151
Fourth Crusade and Constantinople's statuary, 148
Fourth Hymn on the Resurrection (Romanos the Melode), 171
Frankenstein, S., 68n9
Frazer, James
  on casting of Serpent Column, 3n6
  commentary on Pausanias, 2, 7
  on location of Plataian Tripod, 17
  on reconstruction of Plataian Tripod, 25
French School in Athens, 17–18
Freshfield Album, 125n93, 216, 219, 219n46
  Hagia Sophia and hippodrome monuments, *219*
  sketches of the Serpent Column, 1, *221*
  sketch of base of Theodosian Obelisk, 116, *118*
Frick, Otto, 237
  on head of serpent, 15
  inscription, 8–9, 11, 12
  on stamped lead pipe, 23
Fu Xi and Nü Wa, 45, *46*

Galerius, Roman emperor, 108
Gauer, Werner, 77
  on inscription on golden bowl, 81n60
  on Plataian Tripod, 67n1
  on script of inscription, 14n42
Gelon of Syracuse, 93
Gemistos Plethon, 134
George, Saint, 180, *181*, 182
  Life of St. George of Amastris, 177
  staging of duel with Dragon, 226

Gigantomachy on Constantinople senate doors, 135
  Andrew the Fool on, 137
Gilles, Pierre, 217
  on Copper Horse, 185–7
  description of menagerie, 220
  lack of access to palace's second courtyard, 214
  on Serpent Column, 1–2, 7, 216
Gitiadas, 76, 76n41
  Pausanias on, 27, 75
Graef, Paul, 12
Great Canterbury Psalter, *163*, 163–4
Greek Anthology, 84, 102–3, 123–4, 214
  on Skylla group on *euripos,* 125
  version of Planoudes, 120
Greek Magical Papyri, 134
Gregory of Nazianzos, 92, 132
  on fresco at Mistra, 154
  manuscript of homilies, 154, *155*, *156*
Greswell, Edward, 39
griffin protome, *83*
Grueber, H. A., 15
Guiliano da Sangallo, 216
Gyges, 85

Hades
  conception of, 141–2
  distinct from hell in Byzantine thought, 145
  maw as dragon, 141, 179
Hanoulth, Nicholas van, 225, 226
Harun ibn Yahya, 123, 189
Heavenly Ladder (John Climacus), 138–41
Hekatompedon, 53
Hellanikos, 55
Hellenes, 91
Hephaistos, 67, 68, 133
Herakles statues
  Adam in posed copied from, 127, *128*
  in hippodrome, 105
  Parastaseis on, 123
Herodian, 100
Herodotos
  on Battle of Marathon, 39
  on Battle of Plataia, 35–8, 39–40
    division of spoils, 80
    list of participants, 9, 37
    Persians before battle, 59–60
  on creation of three great bowls, 26
  on Lydian statues and dedication at Delphi, 85–6
  on Plataian Tripod, 2
    location of, 17, 18
  on Serpent Column, 7
  on serpentine omen, 86n84
  on statue of Apollo dedicated after Salamis, 89–90

Hesiod, 51
Hesychios of Miletos, 189–90
Hetherington, Paul, 161
Hieron of Syracuse, 93
Hinlopen, Gerard, 232
hippodrome of Constantinople, *115*
   in Coecke van Aelst's *Moeurs et fachons de faire de Turcs,* 217
   description by Gilles, 214–15
   early photographs of, 204, 235–6, *236*
   in late antiquity, 115–20
   riots and destruction of, 147
   statues
      of Anastasios on the *euripos,* 147
      crowded *euripos,* 120–1
      Skylla group, 125
      of three Graces and nine Muses, 122–3
   transport of antiquities to New Palace, 213
Historia Turchesa, 212
Hogarth, William, 233, *234*
holy powers and health, 198–202
holy riders
   compared to military saints, 199–200
   iconography, 179, 199
Homer
   on battle between Zeus and Typhon, 49
   on Skylla, 106n33
Homeric Hymn to Apollo, 50–1, 53–4
Homeric Hymn to Asklepios, 201
Homolle, Théophile, 17, 18
Hünername (Book of Skills), 183, *184*, 207, 224, *224*
   New Palace's second courtyard, 214
   Serpent Column in the At meydanı, 223
Hyakinthia festival, 39, 74
Hyakinthos, 74
hydraulics, 23–4, 159
Hygieia, carving of, 104n20, 201, *202*
Hyrtakenos, 154

Ibrahim Pasha, 215, 217, 227, *227*, 232
Ignatius of Smolensk, 149
illuminations. *See also* Serpent Column illustrations
   of dragons in *Heavenly Ladder,* 139
   on Last Judgment, 144
   of tripods, 132–3
images, power of, 128, 133
inkpot of Leon the calligrapher, 129–30, *130*, *131*
Inscriptiones Graecae antiquissimae (Roehl), 12–13
inscription on Serpent Column, 8–15, *10*
   deciphering, 11
   Phokian letters, 13
   photographs by Anne Jeffery, *13, 14*
intromission, theory of, 133

Ioane, 169
Istanbul, 205–39. *See also* Byzantion; Constantinople
   Archaeological Museums, 15, 16
   modern hippodrome, 234–9
   New Palace, 213
   Serpent Column in, *3*, 227
      base, 19–22, *20*
      excavation, 4

Jahrbücher für classische Philologie, 11
Jeffery, Anne, *13, 14*
Jeffery, L. H., 13
Jeremias, Patriarch, 187
Jerome, 24
Job, Book of, 200
John Climacus (Ioannes Klimakos), 138
John of Patmos, 142, 174
John of Plano Carpini, 159n25
John the Paphalgonian, 147
John VIII Palaiologos, 208
   portrait medallion, *209*
Jolivet-Lévy, Catherine, 143–4, 144n76
   on polycephalous snakes in Cappadocia, 179n88
Jónsdóttir, Selma, 144
Journal de Constantinople, 11
Justinian, 147–8
   statue of, 186, *187*, 214
Justinian II, 124, 125

Kadmos, myths of, 54, 55, 55n102, 104–5
Kaldellis, Anthony, 189–90
Kallon of Aigina, 76
   Pausanias on, 27, 75, 76n41
Kanachos, 76n41
Kemal Pashazade, 183
ketos on ivory casket, *108*
Kiev frescoes, 130–1
Kleombrotos, 47n71
Kleterologion, 111
Kluge, Kurt, 3, 16, 26
knots, apotropaic, 191, *192*
Kokkinobaphos' homilies, 170, *170*
Korfiz von Ulfeld, Anton, 235
Kroisos, 85, 86
Kroton, 94
Kugelspiel, 118–19, *121*
Kypselos, 88
Kyros II, Persian king, 86

labarum, 108, *108*, 109, 110
Lactantius, 104n19
Ladder of Divine Ascent. See Heavenly Ladder (John Climacus)

Lafontaine-Dosogne, Jacqueline, 168n48
La Mottraye, Aubrey de, 232–3
  on fall of serpent heads, 233–5
  work illustrated by Hogarth, 233, *234*
Lampadii diptych, 118, *120*
Lampadius, Flavius, 118
Larnaka Tympanum, *160*, 160–1, *161*, 166
Laroche, Didier, 8, 18–19, 26
Last Judgment, 141–7
  ivory plaque, *145*
  monumental depictions, 143–4
  writings about, 142–3
Last Judgment at Autun, France, 136–7, *137*
Lateran Obelisk, 115n65
Leonidas, 32–3
Leviathan
  battle of Yahweh and, 56
  in fourth-century art, 107–8
  Lucinius as, 106–7
Liber Chronicarum (Schedel), 186–7, *187*
  Serpent Column not included in, 217
Liber Pontificalis, 192
Licinius, 97, 106–7
Life of Basil the Younger, 142, 143
  on particular judgment, 136
Life of Constantine (Eusebios), 108
  Constantine as Moses, 108
  on Delphic Tripods, 112
Life of Nicholas of Stoudios, 172
Life of St. Andrew the Fool, 136–8, 142
  influence on *Life of St. Niphon,* 143
  serpentine demons defeated by sign of the cross, 178–9
Life of Stephen the Younger, 132
Life of St. George of Amastris, 177
Life of St. Niphon, 143
Livanos, Christopher, 172
Local Scripts of Archaic Greece (L. H. Jeffery), 13
Logothete's Chronicle, 134
Lokman, Seyyid, 223
Lorichs (Lorck), Melchior, 217
Lubenau, Reinhold, 158
Lucian, 110
Lydians, 85–6
Lysandros, 47
Lysippos, 123–4

mace, iconography of, 207
Madrid Skylitzes, 122
Magdalino, Paul, 142
Maguire, Henry
  on Adam in Herakles' pose, 127, 127n4
  on Gigantomachy on senate doors, 135n29
  on military saints, 179
  on serpent image at Moutoullas, 162

Makremobolites, 154
Malalas, 147
Mamun, Abbasid caliph, 159
Mango, Cyril, 122
Mantiklos, 84
Manuel I Komnenos, emperor, 165
Manuel Philes, 152
manuscripts
  Gregory of Nazianzos's homilies, *155*, *156*
  of *Heavenly Ladder,* 139–41, *140*
  Vatican manuscript, 167–8, *169*
maps
  Constantinople, *99*, 223
  Greece at time of Persian Wars, *31*
  Greek world in archaic and classical periods, *69*
Marathon, Battle of, 30
  painting of, 92
  Spartans waiting for the full moon, 39
Marcellinus, Ammianus, 111n49
Mardonius, 30
  at Battle of Plataia, 38
  sacking of Athens, 35
  wintering with army in Thessalia, 34
Marina. *See also Acts of St. Marina*
  kanon to, 171
Masistios, 35
Masonry Obelisk, 4, 220, 228
  base, 22, *22*
  in Robertson's photograph, 236, *236*
  Wheler on, 232
Master of the Vienna Passion, 208
Matthew, Book of, 138
Maundeville, John, 205
Maurand of Antibes, Jérôme, 218
Mausoleum of Halikarnassos, 237
Maxentius, 100
Mayan murals of plumed serpent, 45–6
Mecmu-ı Menazil (Compilation of the halting places)(Süleyman I), 223
Mehmed, Fındıklılı, 233
Mehmed II, the Conqueror
  construction of the New Palace (Topkapı Palace), 213
  dragon standing for Christian empire, 208
  portrait as El Gran Turco, 208
  preservation of the Serpent Column, 211–12
  private collection of objects of art and devotion, 213–14
  removal of statue of Justinian, 185, 186
  striking off the jaw of a serpent in the hippodrome, 183, 207
Ménage, V. L., 233
Menologion of Basil II, 141
metals. *See also* bronze
  Aristotle on, 133–4

Michael, Archangel, 136
Michael III, Eastern Roman Emperor, 121
Middle Ages. *See also* Constantinople: in the Middle Ages
  apprehension of classical past, 128
  belief in special powers of material, 188
  combat myth, 56
  Constantinople, 127–50
  non-Christian images denied labels, 128
Milky Way, Greek representations of, 45
Miltiades of Athens, 30, 88
Milvian Bridge, Battle of the (312)
  coins minted after, 102
  defeat of Maxentius, 100
  Eusebios on Maxentius as Pharaoh, 108
mitra, 83
model books, 127, 127n1
Moeurs et fachons de faire de Turcs (Coecke van Aelst), *218*
  sketch of Serpent Column in, 217
Monastery of St. Paollo, Egypt, 200
Möngke Khan, magic fountain of, 158–9
Mordtmann, A. D., 12, 15, 25
Moutoullas fresco, 161, 162, *162*
MUL.APIN, 58–9
Murad III, Ottoman sultan, 206, 207
  eulogized in *Shahanshahnama,* 223
Murad IV, Ottoman sultan, 232
myths. *See also* combat myth
  Canaanite, 45
  foundation of Thebes, 105, 105n23
  Greek, as corruption of truths in Scripture, 103
  of Kadmos, 54, 55, 55n102, 104–5
  Persian myth of end of the world, 147n89

Nakkaş Osman, 223
Napier, Lord, 4
Narmer, Egyptian king, 207
Near East, ca. 2200 B.C., *59*
Nenushtan, 194–5
Neoplatonists, 134
New Palace (Topkapı Palace), 213
  capital on grounds of, *215*
  depiction in *Hünername* (Book of Skills), 214
Newton, C. T., 15
  account of 1855 excavation, 20
  on discovery of lead pipe in column, 23
  excavations of the Serpent Column, 4, 236–7
  in favor of Dethier and Mordtmann's reconstruction, 25
  on seeing head of serpent, 15
Nicaea, Second Council of (787), 196
Nicholas the monk, tale of, 172–3
night sky
  above Byzantion before Battle of Chrysopolis, 97–8, *98*
  during campaign season of Battle of Salamis, 47
  Eleusinian Mysteries and, 43
  omens revealed by, 60–1
  over Plataia, 479 B.C., 40–2, *41*, 60–1, *61*
    as cosmic battle of Zeus and Typhon, 48
  similarities between battles of Plataia and of Chrysopolis, 98
Nikandros, 200
Niketas Choniates, 148
  on eagle and serpent sculpture, 189
  on porphyry serpentine fountain, 152
Nikomedia, 99
Nikopolis, 96
Ninĝišzida, 58–9, 62–3
  on cylinder seals, 64–6, *65*
  as god of healing, 201
  libation vase dedicated to, *63*, 63–4
  prayer poem to, 64
Nonnos, 55

Octavian. *See* Augustus
Odysseus, 105–6
Olympia
  bronze working at, 90n110
  colossal statue of Zeus, 44–5
  competitive displays, 85
  Olympian Zeus dedicated after Plataia, 90
  Spartan bronzes at, 75
  Temple of Zeus, 45
omens, 59–60
Öner, A. Tayfun, 25
"On the Brazen Serpent" (Hesychios), 196
"On the Skylla in the circus at Constantinople," 126
Oration to the Saints (Constantine), 104
  on Apollonian Sibyl prophecy of coming of Christ, 203–4
  Edwards on, 104n19
Origen, 195
  on Scripture and Greek myths, 103
Origo Constantini, 97
Orthodox Baptistery of Neon, 175, *176*
Ottoman Empire
  knowledge of Roman Empire, 205
  official court historians, 223
Ousterhout, Robert, 128
Ovid
  on Drakon, 55
  on Skylla, 106

Pala d'Oro (San Marco, Venice), 198, *199*
Palladas, 102–3, 103n15, 126

Panhellenic sanctuaries. *See* Delphi; Olympia
Pankenier, David, 45
Pantokrator as sign of Byzantine influence, 164n40
Papalexandrou, Nassos, 82, 87
Parastaseis Syntomoi Chronikai, 123–4
  Anderson on authors of, 124n91
  expansion by *Patria Konstantinoupoleos,* 126
Paris Psalter. *See* Great Canterbury Psalter
Parthenos Orthia festival, 43–4
Particular Beschreybung, 226
Particular Judgment, 136–8
Passion of St. Perpetua, 141
Patria Konstantinoupoleos, 126, 146
Patrokles, 76n41
Paul, Saint
  epistles on Crucifixion, 195
  and Maltese viper, 175–6
Paulinus of Nola, 175
Paul of Monemvasia, 136
Pausanias, 90
  on chained down statues, 82
  on Chalkioikos, 76
  on colossal statue of Zeus at Olympia, 44–5
  description of Amyklaion, 73, 75, 76, 77–8
  on Kychreus as serpent, 57–8
  on Plataian Tripod
    description of serpent column, 7
    location, 17, 18
    on removal of cauldron, 2
    on stripping of gold, 2
  on sculptural tripods at Amyklaion, 27
  on tripods in Rome, 96
Pausanias (general), 35
  accused of "Medizing," 86
  archegos of the Greeks, 84–8
  list of participants in Battle of Plataia, 9
  as regent of Sparta, 80
  taking credit for Plataian Tripod, 88
Perpetua, Saint, 176
  Passion of St. Perpetua, 141
Persians
  at Battle of Plataia
    arrival, 39
    vision of the night sky, 41–2
    waiting for good omens, 59–60
  Constantine's desire to conquer, 101
  crossing of the Hellespont, 30
  dragon standards, 110
  epic manuscript, 206
Persians (Aischylos), 89
Peter Chrysologus, 171
Philon of Byzantion, 154
Philosophy for Oracles (Porphyry), 134
Phoenicians
  as bronze-workers in Greece, 68
  definition, 68n9
Phoenician Women (Euripides), 53–5
Photios, 55, 196
Pisanello, 208, *209*
Pittakis, Kyriakos, 11
Plataia, Battle of, 35–8. *See also* Persians: at Battle of Plataia
  date, 38, 40, 40n47
  dedications following, 90, 91
  division of spoils, 80
  Greek army at, 35–6
  muster list, 9
  night sky, summer 479 B.C., 40–2, *41*
  topography of battlefield, 35n29, *36*
Plataian Tripod, 2. *See also* reconstruction of Plataian Tripod; Serpent Column
  column of, 2–8, *3*
  epigram on golden bowl, 83–4
  illustrating chaos contained by victory at Plataia, 58
  Pausanias' dedication on, 84–5
  possible bases in Delphi, 17–19
  tripod stolen by Phokians, 94
Plato, 133
Plutarch, 96
  on Battle of Plataia
    cities in, 9
    date, 38
    sanctuary to Athena at Plataia, 92
  on victory of Lysandros, 47
Podromos, Theodore, 197
Pola Casket, 193
Pollaiulo, Antonio del, 208
Pomtow, H., 13, 18
Porphyrios, statue bases of, *122*
Porphyry, 134
portrait medallions, *209*
Prediction or rather prophecy on the coming of the Turk, 208–11
Preparatio Evangelica (Eusebios), 103
Presse d'Orient, 11
Proklos, 23, 115
Prometheus Bound (Aischylos), 50n86
Protevangelion of James, 167, 168n48
protomes
  griffin, *83*
  serpent, 76–7, 94, *95*
Psalm 90, 174, 195–6
Psalm 139 replacing Psalm 90 on Good Friday, 196
Psellos, 134
Pseudo-Methodios, 142
Pseudo-Nonnus, 132, 150
psychostasis, 136

Pyatnitsky, Yuri, 222
Pythian Ode (Pindar), 49–50
   scholion on Hieron's monument, 93
Python, 48, 50–1, 241
   at Amyklaion, 78
   fate compared to that of Typhon, 57

Rausimodus, 111
Realencyclopädie (Pauly-Wissowa), 13
reconstruction of Plataian Tripod, 18, 25–7
Revelation, Book of
   combat of Christ and Satan, 173–4
   commentaries on, 142
   illustration of, 144–5
   impact in Byzantium, 145n82
Rider Painter (Painter of Horsemen), 78, *79*
Ridgway, B. S., 25
Rigveda, 49, 57
Robertson, James D., 204, 235–6
   photograph of the hippodrome, *236*
Roehl, Hermann, 12–13
Romanos the Melode, 171
Roux, G., 90n106
Russian travelers to Constantinople
   on Serpent Column, 149, 158
   on enclosed serpent venom, 184
   Stammbuch and, 222
   on statue of Justinian, 186
Rydén, L., 138

Sacks, K., 47n70
Sacra Parallela, 143
Salamis, Battle of
   Augustus equating Actium with, 95
   date, 47n70, 48n73
   dedications following, 89–90
   participants, 9
   Themistokles' navy at, 33–4
   votive statue in Delphi after, 46–7
Salt, A., 44
Sardis, 30
Sarmatians, 110, 111
Satan
   identified with serpent-tongued men by Augustine, 196
   as serpent or dragon, 176–7
Schedel, Hartmann, 186–7, *187*, 214n26, 217
Schiltberger, Johannes
   on Constantinople hippodrome, 205
   on statue of Justinian, 185–6
Schliemann, Heinrich, 100
Schweigger, Salomon, 218
   on Mehmed II's attack on serpent, 232
şehnamecis (court historians), 223
şehnames (Book of Kings), 223

Selim I, the Stern, Ottoman sultan, 216
Selim II, the Sot, Ottoman sultan, 206, 232
Şemeddin, 186
Septimius Severus, 100
Seraglio Octateuch, 154, 167, 170
Serpent Column, *3*. *See also* inscription on Serpent Column; Plataian Tripod; Serpent Column illustrations
   beheading the serpents, 232–5
   Christian interpretations of, 241
   Constantine's interest in, 101
   in Constantinople
      original location, 103n17
      preservation during Crusades, 149, 155
      unknown date of move, 111, 111n51
   covered by soil from construction, 232
   cracks, *8*
   descriptions, 149–50
   erected as a votive and victory monument, 241
   estimating original height, 7
   as Greek understanding of the primordial combat myth, 241
   holes in, *5*, *6*, *7*
   left in place, 216
   missing lower jaw of one serpent, 183
   number of coils, 7, 8
   as possible inspiration for apocalyptic images of polycephalous serpents, 146
   as possible representation of Milky Way, 45
   represented on Siphnos carved stone plaque, 203
   scratches and cuts, *5*
   similarity to serpent throne, 65, 65n152
   stamped lead fistula, 22–5
   as talisman against serpents, 184, 185, 191, 241
      knowledge of, 202
      in Siphonos plaque, 204
Serpent Column illustrations, *160*, 160–3, *161*, *162*, *163*
   drawing in Freshfield Album, *221*
   in middle Byzantine art, 129–32
   Ottoman miniatures, 223–32
      in *Hünername*, 224, *224*
      in miniature map of *ecmu-ı Menazil*, 223
      in *Shahanshahnama (Şehinşehname)*, 225
   sketches, 216–22
      in Dryden Costume Album, 220–1, *221*
      in Freshfield Album, *219*, 219–20, *221*
      in *Moeurs et façhons de faire de Turcs* (Coecke van Aelst), 217–18, *218*
      in Schweigger's travels, 218
      watercolor in *Stammbuch*, 221
serpent protomes, 76–7
   possibly influenced by Plataian Tripod, 94, *95*

serpents
    in Bible, 138, 173
    brazen serpent as *apotropaion,* 194
    bringing illness and disease, 200
    listed by Nikandros, 200
    slaying from horseback as motif, 179
    tradition of healing, 201
    triple-headed
        in Cappadocia, 179n88
        in *Fourth Hymn on the Resurrection,* 171
serpents, motif of entwined. *See also* Serpent Column
    Asklepios and, 104n20, 201
    on bronze helmet, 71–2, *72*
    in description of Typhon, 52–3
    in dragon at foot of Heavenly Ladder, 139
    in Elamite seal, 65n152
    in finials of fountains, 154
    in ivory carving of Hygieia, 104n20, 201, *202*
    on Mercury's caduceus, 192, *193*
    in myth, 45
    on silver ink pot, *130–1*
    triple-braided snake in *Synaxarion of Constantinople,* 172
    on Vix volute krater, 77
    in wall paintings at Moutoullas, 161, 162, *162,* 166
serpent-trampling, 174–6
Servius, 95
seven, importance of number, 167n44
"Seven against Thebes," 92
Shahanshahnama (Şehinşehname) (King's Book of Kings), 206, 223
    Serpent Column in, 225
Shahnama (Malik Ummi), 206
Shahnama (Shahnameh) (Book of Kings) (Firdowsi), 205–6, 226
    as inspiration for Ottoman court historians, 223
Shatapatha Brahmana, 57
Sikynian treasury, 88
Simonides of Keios, 81, 124
    epigram on Plataian Tripod, 84
Siphnians, 9, 88
Siphnos, 202–4
Siphnos carved stone plaque, 202–4, *203*
Sisinnarios, Saint, 200
Sisinnios, Saint, 200
Siyavuş Pasha, 226
Skylla
    different forms, 106
    fresco at Corvey, 106n34
    Homer on, 106n33
    terracotta from Melos, *107*
Skylla group
    in Constantinople, 148
    drakontaion as, 124–5
    in pool at Castel Gandolfo, 106n35
    in Sperlonga, 105–6
snakes. *See* serpents
Snodgrass, Anthony, 70
Society for the Promotion of Hellenic Studies, 237
Sokrates Scholastikos, 112
Solomon, Saint, 200
Souda, 191
Sozomenos, 112–13
    on Constantine's search for new capital, 100
    tales of St. Arsakios and St. Donatus of Evorea and dragons, 177
Sparta
    kingship, 80, 80n55
    replacement of epigram on Plataian Tripod, 86
    struggle with Athens for supremacy, 92
    war and full moon, 39
Spon, Dr., 232
Stammbuch (Stockheim), 221
statues
    animate, 133–5
    power of, 133
    ritual animation of, 134
statues in Constantinople, 101
    destruction of, 147–8
    different meanings for pagans and Christians, 103
    Parastaseis Syntomoi Chronikai on, 123–5
    removal by Justinian, 147–8
    revealing end of Constantinople, 146
    as source of fear, 135
Stephanos of Byzantion, 55
Stibbe, Conrad, 75, 77
Stichel, Rudolph, 111n51, 112n52, 218
Stockheim, Ludolphus, 221
Stoudios Tetraevangelion, 144
Strabo, 44
strobilion, 153, *153,* 154
Stuttgart Psalter, 175
Suetonius, 96
Süleyman I, the Magnificent, Ottoman sultan, 215, 217, 232
Surname-i hümayun (Book of Imperial Festivals), 225–30, *230, 231*
Surname- i Vehbi, 231
Surname of Murad III. *See Surname-i hümayun* (Book of Imperial Festivals)
Symeon the Stylite, Saint, 201
Synaxarion of Constantinople, 141, 149
    on St. Thomas Dephourkinos, 177
    triple-braided snake, 172

Tafur, Pero
    on apple of Justinian statute, 186
    misinformation given by, 158n17

Tafur, Pero (*Cont.*)
  on Serpent column dispensing wine and milk, 157
Tahmasp I, Safavid ruler, 206
talismans. *See also apotropaion;* columns; Serpent Column: as talisman against serpents
  Copper Horse as, 187–8
  in medieval Mediterranean world, 188
Taras, 93
Temple of Solomon, 191
Tenians, 9
Tertullian, 176
Testament of Solomon, 178, 199, 200
  three-headed dragon demon in, 171
Thebes, 92
  foundation, 54
  two foundations and foundation myths, 105, 105n23
Themistios, 24
Themistokles, 33–4
Theodore, Saint, 179, 180, *181,* 182
Theodore the Stoudite, 143
Theodosian Obelisk, 4, 23, 115–17, *117,* 220
  base in Coecke van Aelst's *Moeurs et fachons de faire de Turcs,* 217
  description by Zosima the Deacon, 149
  drawing of base, *118*
  lower marble base, *116, 117, 119*
  in Robertson's photograph, 236, *236*
Theodosios I, Roman emperor, 23, 115
Theophanes Continuatus
  description of statues in *euripos,* 121
  on monumental depictions of Last Judgment, 143
Theophanes "the Greek," 186
Theophilos, 159
Theriaka (Nikandros), 200
Thermopylai, Battle of, 32–3
Thévenot, Jean de, 232
Thevet, André, 219
Thierry, N., 180
Third Homily on the Passion (Eusebius of Alexandria), 171
Thomas Dephourkinos, Saint, 177
Thrace, 30
Thucydides, 80–1, 87
Tommaso di Tolfo, 215
tourism
  in the hippodrome, 239
  Serpent Column and, 238
Travels and Discoveries in the Levant (Newton), 236–7
triple-headed serpents and dragons
  apocalypse and, 145
  in Cappadocia, 146n86

in *Digenis,* 172
in *Fourth Hymn on the Resurrection,* 171
as talisman in Constantinople, 187–8
Tripod of Kroton, 94, 94n128, 114n63
  Atlas 408 as base of, 18
tripods. *See also* Delphic Tripods in Constantinople; Plataian Tripod; Tripod of Kroton
  erected at Delphi, 93–4
  erected by Augustus, 95–6
  in illuminated manuscripts, 132–3
  as symbol of collective victory, 87
Troy as possible capital for Constantine, 100
Turquie, La (publication), 238
Typhon, 48, 49–50, 51, 241
  at Amyklaion, 78
  description
    by Apollodoros, 51–2
    by Euripides, 52–3
    by Hesiod, 51
  fate compared to that of Python, 57
  visual representations, 52, *53, 54*

'Ulaymī, al-, 188
Ungnad, David, 219n46
upper jaw of serpent's head, 15–17, *16, 17*
Utrecht Psalter, 163–4
  militant Christ in, 175

Vani Gospels, 169, 191
Vatican Job, 200
Vatican manuscript, 167–8, *169*
Vehbi, 231
vexillum, 110
Villard de Honnecourt, 159
Virgil
  Aeneid, 100
  on Skylla, 106
Vision of the Monk Kosmas, 143
Vita Basilii
  on serpentine fountain outside the New Church, 151
  on wine delivered from fountains, 159–60
Vix Krater, 77
volute krater, 76–7, *77*
Vos, Lambert de, 219, 219n46

Wakeman, Mary K., 57
Webbe, Edward, 225
Wheler, George, 232
Wilkinson, Kevin, 103
William of Rubruck, 158

Xanten ivory casket, 127
Xerxes, King of Kings, 30, 34

Yılanlı Kilise (Cappadocia), 145–6

Zeus
　lightning bolt in Greek art, 44–5
　slaying of Typhon, 48, 49–50, 52, *54*
　synonym with Marduk (Melqart), 70

Zosima the Deacon, 149
Zosimos, 114n62
　on battle of Chrysopolis, 97
　on Delphic Tripod, 114, 133, 133n19
Zühlnart, Wolf von, 158